The
Over-the-
Counter
Doctor

The Over-the-Counter Doctor

The Complete Guide to Treating Yourself with Nonprescription Drugs

**Charles B. Inlander,
Sandra Salmans, and
the People's Medical Society**

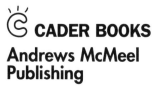

CADER BOOKS

**Andrews McMeel
Publishing**

an Andrews McMeel Universal company

Thank you for buying this Cader Book—we hope you enjoy it. And thanks as well to the store that sold you this, and the hardworking sales rep who sold it to them. It takes a lot of people to make a book. Here are some of the many who were instrumental:

Editorial: Karla Morales, Camille N. Cline, Jake Morrissey, Nora Donaghy, Dorothy O'Brien
Design: Charles Kreloff, Stephen Hughes
Copy Editing/Proofing/Indexing: Saralyn F. Smith, Roland Ottewell, Joan Jackson
Production: Polly Blair, Carol Coe
Legal: Renee Schwartz, Esq.

If you would like to share any thoughts about this book, or are interested in other books by us, please write to:

Cader Books
38 E. 29 Street
New York, New York 10016

Or visit our web site:
http://www.caderbooks.com

Library of Congress Catalog Card Number: 97-16161

Inlander, Charles B.
    The over-the-counter doctor/by Charles B. Inlander.
    — 1st ed.
    p.   cm.

    Includes index.
    ISBN 0-08362-3581-9 (pbk.)
    1. Drugs, Nonprescription.   I. Title.
RM671.A1I64   1997

615'.1—dc21

October 1997
First Edition
10 9 8 7 6 5 4 3 2 1

The People's Medical Society is a nonprofit consumer health organization dedicated to the principles of better, more responsive, and less expensive medical care. For more information, write to the People's Medical Society, 462 Walnut St., Allentown, PA 18102, or call 610-770-1670.

Contents

Preface xi

The Rise of Over-the-Counter Drugs   1

How to Choose a Pharmacist 5
Over-the-Counter Labels 8
Safe Use of Medications 11
Medicine Cabinet Essentials 16
First Aid Supplies 17
Handy Home Remedies 18
Homeopathic Remedies 20
How to Use This Book 21

Conditions   23

Abrasion 24
Acne 24
Allergy 24
Arthritis 24
Asthma 24
Athlete's Foot 25
Atrophy, Vaginal 25
Backache 25
Bad Breath 25
Baldness 25
Bite, Insect 25
Bite, Mosquito 26
Blepharitis 26
Body Odor 26
Breast-feeding 26
Bronchitis 26
Bruise 26
Brush Burn 27
Bunion 27
Burn 27
Calluses 27
Carpal Tunnel Syndrome 27
Chicken Pox 27
Cold 28
Conjunctivitis (Pinkeye) 28
Constipation 28
Contusion 28
Corn 28
Cough 28
Cradle Cap 29

Cramps, Menstrual .29
Cut 29
Cystitis 29
Dandruff 29
Dentures, Slipping .29
Dermatitis, Allergic Contact 30
Dermatitis, Atopic .30
Diarrhea 30
Dysmenorrhea 30
Earache 30
Ear Infection 30
Ear, Swimmer's 31
Earwax 31
Eczema 31
Elbow, Tennis 31
Eyes, Bloodshot 31
Eyes, Dry 31
Eyes, Irritated 32
Eyestrain 32
Fatigue 32
Fever 32
Flatulence 32
Flu 33
Food Poisoning 33
Foot Odor 33
Fracture 33
Gastroenteritis 33
Gingivitis 34
Gout 34
Hair Loss 34
Halitosis 34
Hay Fever 34
Headache 34
Heartburn 35
Hemorrhoid 35
Hives 35
Impetigo 35
Indigestion 35
Infection 36
Infection, Fungal Nail Area 36
Infection, Fungal Skin 36
Infection, Oral 36
Inflammation 36
Influenza 36
Insomnia 37
Jock Itch 37
Knee, Injured 37

Knee, Jumper's 37
Knee, Runner's 37
Laceration 38
Laryngitis 38
Lice 38
Lips, Chapped 38
Miliaria 38
Motion Sickness 38
Mouth, Dry 38
Muscle Cramp 39
Muscle Soreness 39
Nasal Drainage (Runny Nose) 39
Nasal Passages, Congestion of the 39
Nasal Passages, Dry 39
Nausea and Vomiting 39
Nicotine Addition 40
Nipples, Cracked 40
Obesity 40
Otitis Media 40
Pain, Chronic 41
Periodontal Disease 41
Periodontitis 41
Pinkeye 41
Pinworms 41
Plaque, Dental 41
Poison Ivy, Poison Oak, and Poison Sumac ...41
Poisoning 42
Premenstrual Syndrome (PMS) 42
Psoriasis 42
Rash, Diaper 42
Rash, Prickly Heat 43
Rash, Skin 43
Repetitive Motion Injuries 43
Ringworm 43
Scar 43
Scleritis 43
Scrape 43
Seborrhea 43
Shingles 44
Sinusitis 44
Skin, Dry 44
Smoking 44
Sore, Canker 44
Sore, Cold 45
Sprain 45
Sting, Bee 45
Sunburn 45
Tartar 46
Teething 46
Tendinitis 46
Tenosynovitis 46
Throat, Sore 46

Toenail, Ingrown 46
Tooth, Discoloration of 47
Tooth, Sensitivity of 47
Toothache 47
Ulcer, Duodenal 47
Ulcer, Gastric 47
Ulcer, Peptic 48
Urethritis 48
Urinary Tract, Infection of the 48
Vaginitis 48
Vertigo 49
Vomiting 49
Vulvitis 49
Warts 49
Water Retention 49
Wound Infection 49
Wrinkles 50
Yeast Infection 50

Medications   51

**Pain Relievers, Fever Reducers, and
    Anti-inflammatories** **53**
Analgesics (Internal) 56
Counterirritants 58
Antiarthritis Treatments 62
Antipyretics, or Fever Reducers 64
Premenstrual and Menstrual Pain Relievers
    and Menorrhagia Treatments 66

Cold, Cough, and Allergy Remedies **68**
Oral Decongestants 69
Topical Decongestants 70
Nasal Moisturizers 72
Antihistamines 72
Cough Suppressants (Antitussives) 75
Expectorants 76
Lozenges and Mouthwashes/Gargles
    (Sore Throat Relief) 77

Stomach and Intestinal Treatments **80**
Antacids 81
Antiemetics 84
Emetics 86
Oral Rehydration Therapy 87
Antidiarrheal Treatments 88
Antiflatulents 90
Laxatives 91

Skin Treatments **95**
Antipruritics, Anesthetics,
    and Other Therapies 95
Hydrocortisone 96

Local Anesthetics 97
Topical Antihistamines 99
Counterirritants (in brief) 100
Burn/Sunburn Treatments 101
Dermatitis/Dry Skin Preparations 103
Emollients 104
Hemorrhoidal Preparations 106
Insect Bite and Sting Treatments 108
Poison Ivy, Poison Oak, and Poison Sumac
    Treatments 110
Antiacne Preparations 111
Antibiotics 113
Antifungals 114
Antiseptics 116
Astringents 118
Bath Products 119
Bunion Treatments .120
Callus and Corn Removers 120
Chicken Pox Treatments 121
Diaper Rash Protectants 122
Fungal Nail Area Treatments 124
Prickly Heal (Miliaria) Treatments 124
Psoriasis Treatments 125
Skin Protectants 126
Sunscreens 127
Wart Removers 129

Hair and Scalp Treaments **131**
Dandruff, Cradle Cap, and Seborrhea
    Treatments 132
Lice Treatments 135
Hair Growth Stimulant 135

Treatments for the Mouth and Teeth **137**
Toothpastes, Gels, and Powders 138
Tooth Desensitizers .139
Tooth Whiteners 140
OTC Bleaching Kits 140
Denture Adhesives .141
Denture Cleansers 141
Artificial Saliva 142
Mouthwashes and Mouth Rinses
    (for oral health) .142
Oral Debriding Rinses 144
Toothache and Teething Preparations 145
Canker Sore Treatments 147
Cold Sore/Fever Blister Preparations 147

Eye Products and Treatments **149**
Eye-Care Products .150
Ophthalmic Lubricants 151
Ophthalmic Decongestants 153
Eyewashes 154

Eyelid Scrubs 154
Contact Lens Products 155

Contraceptives **161**

Other Medications **164**
Anthelmintics 165
Antiperspirants 165
Appetite Suppressants 167
Bronchodilators 168
Deodorants (for body odor) 170
Deodorants (for foot odor) 170
Diuretics 171
Douches 172
Earwax Removers 173
Ingrown Toenail Treatment 174
Sleep Aids 175
Smoking Cessation Aids 176
Stimulants 177
Swimmer's Ear Preparations 178
Urinary Pain Relievers 178
Vaginal Antifungals 179
Vaginal Antipruritics 180
Vaginal Lubricants .181

Durable Medical Equipment   183

Antisnoring Devices 184
Athletic Bandages 185
Bedpan 185
Braces/Splints/Slings 185
Breast Pumps 186
Canes 186
Cervical Collar 187
Cervical Pillow 187
Cold/Heat Treatment Packs 187
Commodes 188
Compression Shorts 188
Crutches 188
Ear Syringes 188
Enemas 188
Enuretic (Bed-wetting) Alarm 189
Eyeglasses, Ready-to-Wear 189
Humidifiers/Vaporizers 189
Magnifiers 190
Nasal Aspirator 190
Otoscope 190
Perineal Cushion 191
Reachers/Grippers 191
Shower Stools/Chairs/Benches 191
Sitz Bath 191
Toothbrushes, Manual and Electric, and Plaque
    Remover 191

Urinals (Male/Female) 192
Walkers 192

Home Medical Testing   193

Blood Pressure Monitoring 194
Blood Glucose Monitoring 195
Bowel Cancer Test 196
Cholestrol Test 197
Dental Plaque Test 198
Ear Examination 198
HIV/AIDS Test 199
Lung Function Testing 200
Ovulation Prediction Test 200
Pregnancy Test 201
Thermometers 202
Urine Testing 203

Vitamins and Minerals   205

Health and Medical Information   221

Over-the-Counter Drug Manufacturers 221
Poison Control Centers 222
Additional Resources 225
Suggested Reading 226
Pharmaceutical and Medical Terms 228
Appendix............................233

Index   235

Acknowledgments

A book of this size and complexity is not a one-person undertaking. Many people have made substantial contributions to the finished product. We would especially like to thank the following:

KARLA MORALES—People's Medical Society's vice president of editorial services served as both overall editor and as a major contributor. Her attention to detail and concern for accuracy are unparalleled and major factors in making this book as useful and authoritative as it is.

JANET WORSLEY NORWOOD—for creating the Conditions section and her overall input.

In addition, the following PMS staff made major contributions to the book:

MICHAEL DONIO and JENNIFER HAY.

We are also indebted to the fine people at Cader Books for their insight and contribution.

MICHAEL CADER—His intuition and conceptualizing have been major factors in this book becoming a reality.

CAMILLE CLINE—Camille's editorial contribution has been incredible. She deserves our sincere appreciation and gratitude.

We want to especially acknowledge the following individuals and organizations for their input and materials that helped us enhance the information overall and in specific sections:

MEG GRATTAN, Office of Public Affairs, Nonprescription Drug Manufacturers Association

MARTHA OELMAN, Media Liaison, National Center for Homeopathy

ROSE ANN G. SOLOWAY, American Association of Poison Control Centers

KIM KELLER REID, R.Ph., J.D., United States Pharmacopeial Convention

TODD DANKMYER, National Community Pharmacists Association

JEFF WOLDT, Racher Press

At the U. S. Food and Drug Administration:

DON MCLEARN, Office of Public Affairs

LINDA ROBERTS and ROBERT SHERMMER, Division of OTC Drug Evaluation

DAVID LYLE, Division of Clinical Laboratory Devices

KEVIN M. BUDICH, Center for Drug Evaluation and Research

Preface

This is not a pill book! Sure, we cover every over-the-counter product, tell you how it works, when to use it, what to watch out for and more. But it's still not a pill book. And frankly, as a consumer health advocate, I wouldn't suggest that any consumer buy just a pill book. You'd be much better off going to a library when you need to look up a single medication. What makes this book stand out is that *The Over-the-Counter Doctor* is your complete guide to taking care of yourself and your family using over-the-counter products.

This is a health book! And it's like no other book you have ever owned—I challenge you to find any other like it. What makes this a health book rather than just another pill book is that you can approach it from many angles. If you know your ailment, but aren't sure what to take, all you have to do is look up the condition. We direct you to the products. Conversely, if you know a product, but are not sure what conditions it's used to treat, you can look up the product. You are then directed to the appropriate conditions. And, of course, we talk about more than just pills. There's a section on vitamins and minerals and a section on medical tests (like those for blood pressure and pregnancy) that you can do right at home, as well as a section on durable medical equipment (such as canes and walkers). We describe common home remedies and other self-care ideas. Plus, we load you up with helpful and healthful tips on both buying and using OTC products.

Since the founding of the People's Medical Society in 1983, we've averaged more than 1,000 calls and letters a week from health-care consumers. The calls range from complaints about doctors to the growing problem of hospital infections. You name it, we've heard it. But we don't just listen. We answer everyone who contacts us.

And this book is an answer to consumers. Over the years, we have heard from thousands of people who want to know more about over-the-counter health products. Most people are confused about them. Are they safe? Is one ingredient better than another? Are former prescription-only medications better than those that have always been available over the counter? Should your child use them?

But we've also heard other very important questions. One heard most often is just what product should be used for a specific condition. And don't think that question is always easy to answer. There are so many products used to treat a great many conditions that people are often overwhelmed and make the wrong choice or no choice at all.

That's exactly why we wrote this book. Our goal was to end the confusion and give all consumers the knowledge and know-how to take charge of their health through the use of over-the-counter products. As you'll see, this is your one-stop guide to the many products available and is organized to help you make the best choices among them. Use it in good health.

—Charles B. Inlander,
   President, People's Medical Society

The Rise of Over-the-Counter Drugs

Despite the high-tech nature of today's health care, no matter how sophisticated medicine has become, studies show that more than 80 percent of all the medical care we receive is self-care. In other words, most of the time, we're our own doctor. From aches and pains to cuts and bruises, from fever and earaches to rashes and acne, most of us have our own arsenal of favorite, time-tested remedies, elixirs, and treatments to care for our health problems.

The vast majority of the products we use in our self-care are called over-the-counter (OTC) medicines and equipment. And there are between 125,000 and 300,000 OTC products on the market, in a variety of sizes, dosage forms, and strengths. These are products we can buy at drugstores, supermarkets, and department/discount stores, without a doctor's prescription. It's estimated that more than 750,000 stores sell OTC products, compared with 65,000 prescription drug outlets. We wrote this book because we realize how difficult choosing among all the OTC products on the market can be. In the confusion, many people turn to the best-advertised products, which are not necessarily the best products for them.

Over-the-Counter vs. Prescription

As you know, prescription medications can be obtained only from a licensed pharmacy and with a doctor's prescription. Over-the-counter medications and products do not require a doctor's prescription and can be sold just about anywhere. However, just because OTC products do not need a doctor's order does not mean they have not gone through rigorous scrutiny by the U.S. Food and Drug Administration (FDA). In fact, like prescription products, OTCs are very closely regulated by the FDA. But there are differences between prescription and nonprescription products:

Margin of safety

Because OTC products can be purchased without a doctor's prescription, they must have a *higher* standard of safety than prescription products. Since over-the-counter products can be bought and used by anyone, almost anywhere, the federal government requires that they be as safe as possible. This is to assure the consumer that the product can be used safely, following label directions. Because prescription products cannot get into your hands without monitoring from a physician, safety under all circumstances of use is not as high a priority. Thus, OTC products generally consist of ingredients that have a long and established safety record.

Product labeling

Unlike prescription medications, OTC products must carry labels that contain all the information the typical consumer needs for safe and effective use.

Advertising and promotion

Most prescription medications are advertised and promoted to health professionals since they must write the orders for consumers to gain access to the products. Thus, to the prescription drug manufacturer, practitioners are their advertising clients, not consumers. However, OTC products are advertised directly to millions of Americans.

OTC Sales by Category

Category	1996 volume (in millions)
Oral care products	$3,570
Cough/cold remedies	3,450
Internal analgesics	2,910
Feminine needs	2,500
Antacids/laxative	2,250
Adult vitamins*	2,150
Eye/lens care products	1,090
Diet aids/meal replacements	1,060
First aid products	918
Baby care products	745
Foot care products	471
Incontinence products	455
External analgesics/ hydrocortisones	447
Condoms	294
Acne preparations	250
Lice treatments	131

* Includes nutritional supplements, multiple vitamins, mineral supplements, and single-entity vitamins.

Source: *Chain Drug Review*, January 6, 1997.

FDA Categories of Safety and Effectiveness

All new drugs must be shown to be effective for their intended uses, including over-the-counter drugs. In this drug-review process, a Food and Drug Administration advisory panel assigns each over-the-counter product into one of three categories.

Category I: Generally recognized as safe and effective for the therapeutic indication claimed.

Category II: Not generally recognized as safe and effective, or having unacceptable indications.

Category III: Insufficient data to permit final classification.

The Approval Process

Not only are OTC products carefully reviewed by the FDA, they are also subject to the industry's own self-regulation, to assure that OTC products are safe and effective when used properly. And FDA review is not limited to new products proposed for the market. The FDA reviews and, in some cases, removes medications from over-the-counter status if evidence of a significant safety problem with a product or ingredient surfaces. The former OTC product hexachlorophene, an antimicrobial, was put back on prescription status in 1977, as were the antihistamine methapyrilene in 1979 and the laxative danthron in 1987.

In recent years, many former prescription products and ingredients have switched to over-the-counter status. The process can be initiated by the FDA, a pharmaceutical manufacturer, trade associations, or other interested groups. Since 1972, more than fifty ingredients or dosage strengths have made the switch from prescription-only to over-the-counter availability. More than 600 OTC products on the market today use ingredients or dosages available only by prescription twenty years ago. Today, in fact, fourteen of the top twenty-three products switched from prescription to OTC status since 1975 are now the first or second top-selling brands in their respective categories. (See Appendix for potential candidates for Rx-to-OTC switch.)

These switches have been extremely advantageous to us. First, switches have reduced product cost. For example, it is estimated that consumers save $750 million per year as a result of OTC cough-cold medicines that were once available only by prescription. Second, we save the cost of a doctor's fee, lost time from work, and travel costs. When hydrocortisone (0.50 percent) switched from prescription to OTC status in 1979, it was found that consumers saved more than $1 billion in those costs in just the first three years. Third, the switches allow us to take greater control over our own health care. By allowing products that have been proven safe and effective for many years to move from prescription to nonprescription status, we can be more active and involved in maintaining or regaining health.

When to Call a Doctor

It's obvious we use OTC products far more often than we use prescription medication. And we use them for many different medical problems. In fact, for certain ailments we use OTC products the majority of the time. The Nonprescription Drug Manufacturers Association reports that the top ten problems consumers are most likely to treat with OTC medication are the following:

- headache (76 percent of the time)
- athlete's foot (69 percent)
- lip problems (68 percent)
- common cold (63 percent)
- chronic dandruff (59 percent)
- premenstrual symptoms (58 percent)
- menstrual problems (57 percent)
- upset stomach (57 percent)
- painful, dry skin (56 percent)
- sinus problems (54 percent)

But the important question is when should you use an OTC product. How do you decide if your problem is something you can treat or something better left to a medical practitioner? The answer is not always clear. But let's discuss the issue.

Most of us know when a medical problem is serious enough to warrant a visit to an emergency

The Most Recent Switches from Prescription-Only to Nonprescription (1996)

Ingredient	Adult Dosage	Category	Product Examples
minoxidil	2% topical solution	hair grower	Rogaine
nicotine polacrilex	2 mg and 4 mg gum	smoking cessation	Nicorette
nicotine transdermal system	15 mg patch	smoking cessation	Nicotrol
nicotine transdermal patch	21, 14, and 7 mg patch	smoking cessation	Nicoderm
nizatidine	75 mg up to twice daily	acid reducer	AXID AR
micronazole nitrate	2% cream and 200 mg inserts	anticandidal	Monistat 3
clotremazole	1% cream and 200 mg inserts	anticandidal	Gyne Lotrimin 3
bentoquatam	5% lotion	poison ivy protection	Ivy Block

Source: Nonprescription Drug Manufacturers Association.

room or an immediate call to a doctor. Chest pains that intensify and cause shortness of breath are obviously not something to treat with an antacid. Stomach cramps, associated with vomiting and high fever, are symptoms that should be reported to a doctor as soon as possible. Likewise, we usually know when something is not too serious. A mild headache after a particularly stressful day is a prime candidate for an OTC remedy. An upset stomach after a night on the town is probably another one.

The important thing to remember is when in doubt, seek professional medical attention quickly. And if you have been treating the problem yourself, using OTC products, and the condition either worsens or fails to improve, seek professional assistance.

It is also wise to seek a medical practitioner if you're treating an infant or small child. This is especially important if the child is unable to articulate exactly what the symptoms are. And if you are caring for a frail, elderly person or another at-risk person, seek medical advice before using OTC products.

Remember that OTC products cannot do everything. Some conditions, such as bacterial infections or severe cuts, may need stronger products, only available by prescription.

Finally, read the labels and instructions that come with OTC products. All of them contain warnings about when the use of that particular product is inappropriate. Some products should not be used if you are taking another medication. Others should be avoided if you have certain chronic medical conditions. And still others should be used only for a certain time before they become either ineffective or downright dangerous.

Buying Over-the-Counter Products

OTC products are available in a variety of outlets—from supermarkets to mail order, from pharmacies to convenience stores. But there are some tips you should consider before making your OTC purchase.

Look for expiration dates. If the date on the package has already passed, do not buy it. But even if the date has not passed, look for a package with the date the farthest in the future. With many OTC products, you may not intend to use it all immediately or in a short time. Therefore, the longer the product has before its expiration date, the more likely you will be able to use it again with confidence. We discuss this in more detail later.

When in doubt, buy the smallest size. If you are trying an OTC product or a new brand for the first time, buy the smallest size available. By doing so, you will not be wasting your money if you are unsatisfied with the product or suffer side effects.

When you use a specific product often, buy the largest size. Usually, the more you buy the cheaper it is, on a unit-price basis. If you use a product often, this is not only the most economical way to purchase it, but also the more efficient. It means fewer trips to the store, and you will always have a stock at home.

Shop around. Over-the-counter products are plentiful. As a result, there is tremendous competition between manufacturers and retailers. That's particularly beneficial to health-care consumers because it means you can usually purchase OTC products at substantial discounts. Read advertisements in your local paper, look for coupons in the mail, or even call a few stores to find out how much they charge for the products you use. You'll be surprised at just how much you can save if you shop around.

Buy store brands. Store brands are to OTC products what generics are to prescription medication. In other words, they are the same product sold at a lower price than a name brand. The cost is lower because the manufacturer does not need to build in the cost of advertising, display, and a whole host of other nonmanufacturing-related expenses.

Ask a pharmacist. Later in this book we talk about choosing a pharmacist. But here we suggest asking a pharmacist for an OTC recommendation. This is particularly useful when you are buying a type of or specific product for the first time.

Check the packaging. We all recall the horror stories of over-the-counter product tampering. The OTC industry responded well to this crisis by developing many packaging safeguards to protect consumers. Carefully check any package before you purchase it or before you use it at home. If seals are broken or you have any question about the integrity of the package, return it immediately to the store from which you purchased it. And even if you decide not to return it, *do not use it.* Throw it away immediately.

We talk more about this and other issues related to product selection, safety, and appropriateness later.

How to Choose a Pharmacist

The definition of a pharmacist is straightforward enough: *A pharmacist formulates and dispenses drugs or medications and is knowledgeable concerning their properties.* But there's much more to this professional. You see, more than just a pill counter, the community pharmacist is *the most readily accessible health-care professional most of us have.* The pharmacist is an essential link in the chain of health care; however, few people see choosing a pharmacist as important as the choice of a doctor—but it is.

The pharmacist is a highly trained drug expert who probably knows more than your own practitioner about the relative benefits and risks of various drugs, because his or her training specifically focuses on the chemicals and other components that comprise prescription medicines, as well as their uses and effects. And with today's medications more complex and, in some cases, more potent, and with both prescription and nonprescription drug usage on the increase, you need to find a competent and communicative pharmacist.

What Your Pharmacist Can Offer

"Why even worry?" you ask. "We're talking about over-the-counter drugs in this book. Doesn't their availability without a prescription mean that they're safe, and doesn't the FDA oversee the effectiveness of nonprescription remedies as well as prescription drugs?"

As we explain further on page 11, no drug is harmless and completely safe. Each is a chemical designed to alter the body's function in some way—for the better, you hope. Compared with prescription drugs, OTCs are relatively safe. Nonetheless, you must arm yourself with information—which is precisely where this guide and your pharmacist come in—and use any OTC with caution. Indeed, some nonprescription drugs are as strong as the medications your doctor prescribes, and in a growing number of cases *were once only available by prescription.*

As for the FDA's stamp of approval or the agency's ability or willingness to remove a suspect drug from the market, let's just say ineffective and marginally effective drugs do exist.

So what is the pharmacist's role and why is the selection process so critical? As we said before and as we all know, choosing among the many and varied OTC products on the market can be confusing—which is of course why we wrote this book—and in that confusion many people turn to the most visible source of information on an OTC: advertising. While advertisements do keep us abreast of what's on the market and what these products are used for, frankly, broadcast and print ads do not always point us in the most cost-effective direction nor do their claims ensure that we find the safest, most effective drug for our problem or condition.

Another reason for finding a pharmacist who can counsel you wisely is that doctors generally tend to underplay—if not actually dispute—the therapeutic role that OTC medications can play in your health care. The professional right there on the scene, where the OTCs are being sold, is the pharmacist, not the doctor.

The Pharmacist As Communicator

Communicating about medications must become a routine part of any encounter where medications are prescribed, dispensed, or sold. In short, you are shopping for a pharmacist who is comfortable with and adept at his or her role of patient educator.

So the task at hand is to find a pharmacist who will be willing to check your nonprescription drug purchases and point out the OTCs that are appropriate and proven effective for what's ailing you—you can uphold your end of the partnership by sharing the information contained in this book.

Where do you start as you map out this partnership? Perhaps the following most commonly asked questions about OTCs (in descending frequency) can help guide you:

1. What OTC product do you recommend for my specific ailment?

2. What are the side effects of this and other OTC products?

3. What dosage do you recommend, and how long should I continue this therapy?

4. Do you have any information on specific medical conditions?

5. Which one is a better buy?

According to annual surveys, some 98 percent of pharmacists say that their customers usually or always follow their advice on OTC products, including purchasing the products they recommend.

Further, a survey conducted by the National Association of Retail Druggists found that pharmacists, in their day-to-day encounters with consumers, counsel in cases of incorrect dosages, drug-drug interactions, drug allergies and adverse reactions, duplicate therapy, incorrect drugs prescribed, and other contraindications. In 42 percent of OTC cases (and 18 percent of prescription cases), pharmacist interventions, according to the survey, led to the consumer's *not* receiving a medication.

In short, a pharmacist helps select prescription and nonprescription medications to treat your complaint effectively, inexpensively, and safely.

How Qualified Is Your Pharmacist?

To be a pharmacist, a person must train at an accredited school of pharmacy, of which there are seventy-two in the United States and Puerto Rico. Basically, there are two professional degrees awarded in pharmacy: the bachelor of science (B.S. Pharmacy) and the doctor of pharmacy (Pharm.D.). The bachelor's degree—which is as far up the education ladder as most pharmacists go—requires five years of collegiate study in courses covering the fields of physiology, biochemistry, biology, and pharmacology. And as

Top Ten OTC Drug Categories for Which Consumers Seek Pharmacists' Recommendations

(Average number of recommendations per month in surveyed pharmacists.)

Adult cough medications	31.2
Adult cold preparations	28.3
Allergy relief products	28.0
Sinus remedies	25.4
Children's cough medications	24.5
Ibuprofens	22.5
Antacids	16.4
Adult vitamins	15.8
Antidiarrheal preparations	14.5
Stool softeners and other laxatives	13.6

Source: *Drug Topics*, supplement (September 1995).

more pharmacists step from behind the counter and offer more health and drug therapy information, pharmacy schools are shifting their emphasis toward patient care. In addition, depending upon the particular school, the degree requirements may demand some practical experience outside the classroom, through internships in hospital and community pharmacies.

A rarer breed is the pharmacist with a doctor of pharmacy degree. Although the academic requirements are more intensive than with the B.S., enrollment is growing, in large part because of the expanded role of the pharmacist in the health-care system and the chance that the advanced degree will mean more clout in the marketplace.

Does it matter which degree your pharmacist has? Should you go to the trouble of finding one with a doctorate? Probably not. What does matter is whether your pharmacist holds a valid license. In order to receive one, a graduate in pharmacy must pass an examination given by the board of pharmacy in the state where he or she plans to practice. In order to retain the license, many states require the pharmacist to take continuing-education courses. And in the event of misconduct or incompetence, the pharmacist is subject to disciplinary action by the state board.

If you wish to verify that the pharmacist has complied with state licensing requirements, ask him or her to show you the license. It's usually posted on the wall behind the pharmacy counter.

The Consumer-Pharmacist Partnership

In the words of *The Physicians' Desk Reference for Nonprescription Drugs,* "Consumers want and need more information on nonprescription drug therapy." However, the respected resource notes that not everyone can comprehend and apply the manufacturer-supplied product and package labeling information and instructions.

Below are twelve areas in which *The Physicians' Desk Reference for Nonprescription Drugs* sees the pharmacist best able to assist a consumer in his or her self-care with a nonprescription drug.

1. Assist in product selection.

2. Assess patient risk factors.

3. Counsel patients regarding proper use.

4. Maintain a patient drug profile that includes nonprescription drugs.

5. Monitor for drug allergies or hypersensitivities.

6. Monitor for adverse drug reactions.

7. Monitor for drug-drug interactions.

8. Monitor for response to therapy.

9. Monitor for symptoms of drug overuse and dependency.

10. Discourage use of fraudulent and "quack" remedies.

11. Assess the potential of nonprescription drugs to mask symptoms of a more serious problem.

12. Prevent delays in seeking appropriate medical attention.

Source: *The Physicians' Desk Reference for Nonprescription Drugs.* Medical Economics Data Production Company: 1996.

Chain Stores vs. Independents

Speaking of the pharmacy counter—clearly, the pharmacist exists within a setting. When you choose a pharmacist, you "inherit" the culture that's a part of the setting. So let's take a look at what's out there.

While the independently owned community pharmacy is still a visible part of the American scene—the vast majority of retail prescription drugs are dispensed by independent pharmacists, including 75 percent of all Medicaid prescriptions, according to the National Association of Retail Druggists—chain stores owned by large national corporations such as Eckerd's, Revco, and Walgreens are steadily making inroads into the market. Another part of the changing scene is the inclusion of pharmacies in supermarkets and discount stores.

As you shop around for a pharmacist and encounter these settings, you'll probably wonder if there are advantages of one over the other. Frankly, the answer depends upon the individual pharmacy and its policies, as well as the pharmacist and his or her knowledge and communication skills.

However, there are questions you can ask concerning how business is run at a particular pharmacy, whatever the setting:

• What personalized services are offered? Free home delivery? Convenient hours, especially during evenings and weekends? Arrangements for you to receive emergency medications when the pharmacy is closed or the pharmacist is away? Patient medication profiles kept on all consumers? Patient counseling on drug interactions, side effects, and so on? Help with orthopedic and prosthetic devices or other durable medical equipment? Compliance with your preferences, such as non-childproof caps? Capsules instead of tablets?

• Is there an area set aside for you to speak privately with the pharmacist if you wish?

• Are consumer education materials available?

• Does the pharmacy have the refill policies that you want? Phone-in refills? Refills available at other locations? Are the pharmacy personnel willing to contact your physician for you, if necessary?

• Can a rare drug be easily and quickly obtained should your doctor prescribe it for you? Will the pharmacist compound special prescriptions?

• Are the pharmacy's prices competitive with others in your community?

• Does the pharmacy offer a charge account to its customers?

• Does the pharmacy accept your prescription drug insurance?

• Does the pharmacy provide end-of-the-year prescription cost statements for income tax and insurance purposes?

• Does the pharmacy offer a senior citizen discount?

• Is the physical layout convenient? Accessible to the handicapped?

Remember, the partnership you forge with your pharmacist—an important member of your health-care team—and the setting in which he or she practices have a direct bearing on your health and health care. Choose carefully in either case to help prevent allergic reactions to drugs, dangerous interactions, and duplicate medications. Supplement the manufacturer information with the pharmacist's professional experiences and get the inside scoop on how and when to take the medication, what the possible side effects are, and whether there is a potential for dangerous interactions with foods and/or other medications. What other health professional or health setting is as close as the nearest drugstore—and as accessible?

Now let's go on to the responsibility we all, as consumers, assume when we shop for OTC products: How to read the product label.

Over-the-Counter Labels

Next to the medicine itself, the information on nonprescription drug labels is the most important part of self-medication. According to FDA requirements, labeling for an OTC medication, unlike a prescription drug, must provide all the information a consumer needs for safe and effective use. Labels should provide specific details about medicines so that you can properly select and use products without the advice of a health professional. The exact wording, in part, of the FDA requirement is that labeling be "stated in terms that are likely to be read and understood by the average consumer, including those of low comprehension, under customary conditions of purchase and use."

Regardless of the regulation, though, miscommunications and errors in usage do occur. Studies have suggested that some reading comprehension problems may be caused by labels written at a ninth grade—and even higher—reading level, while the average American reads at a lower level, and 20 percent of Americans are functionally illiterate. Even consumers without vision problems or who do not have reading disabilities have found some labels unreadable because of color combinations on the packaging or small or fine print. In 1990, however, the Nonprescription Drug Manufacturers of America (NDMA) issued what it calls an "improved readability program," which consists of guidelines that nonprescription drug manufacturers follow *voluntarily* to make OTC drug labels easier to read and comprehend. These guidelines suggest layout, design, typography, and printing to help make the labels more legible. In the meantime, the NDMA has been working with the FDA to implement a more encompassing proposal, one that *all* OTC manufacturers must follow.

FDA Labeling Standards

In late 1995, the NDMA proposed fundamental changes in OTC medicine labels and recommended that the FDA review and approve these standards for the entire industry. The heart of the relabeling program, if approved and published, would be an FDA-required standard format and headings for presentations of five categories of key user information—active ingredients, actions, uses, directions, and warnings—simplified wording, and assurance that OTC labels would be the same wherever purchased throughout the United States.

These required changes would include uniform headings for key mandatory label information, uniform minimum type size, uniform language for the content of warnings, more reader-friendly paragraph breaks and spacing between paragraphs, and use of approved, more generally understandable language. The intent of the proposed design and format changes and the simpler language is to make OTC labels easier for consumers to read and understand and to reduce the number and complexity of words needed to do that.

In early 1997, the FDA responded by proposing simplified labels on OTC drugs—similar to labels now found on foods—and asking for public comment. Included on every label might be the following, according to the FDA-suggested elements:

• Active ingredient(s)

• Purpose (of the medication)

• Uses (of the product)

• Warnings, worded as "Ask a doctor before use if you have _____ [list of conditions] and if you are _____ [for example, taking certain other medications that might interact in some negative way].

• Special instructions—for example, potential side effects to be aware of; the need to avoid alcohol, tranquilizers, and the like; and the need for caution when driving a car or operating machinery.

• Directions

If the rule becomes final, OTC drug manufacturers would have two years to use up their old packaging and put the labels on all of their products. Accordingly, the changes would take effect no earlier than mid-1999.

How to Read a Label

Critical to safe and effective self-medication is knowing what's on the label (see diagram below). With that in mind, here are some of the FDA-required elements:

• Tamper-resistant feature(s).

• A description of tamper-resistant features to check before you buy the product.

• The product name and statement of identity.

• Ingredients. These are often broken down into a listing of active ingredients (which produce the therapeutic effect) and inactive ingredients (which are the "delivery system" for the active ingredients and also often serve as flavors, colors, binders, lubricants, and preservatives).

• Any recent significant product changes. Manufacturers often make changes in their OTC products to improve safety or increase effectiveness and, further, often introduce—under existing brand names—new products that may contain

What's on the Label

Product information for consumers required by the FDA is shown below. The information in the shaded boxes is often included voluntarily by the manufacturer.

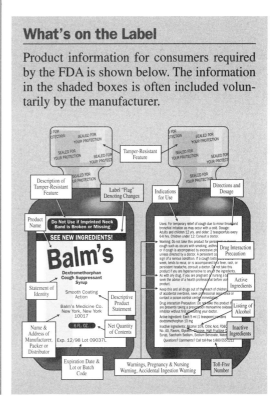

different single ingredients, in order to provide a broader range of available self-care options.

• Indications, which are your symptoms.

• Usual dosage, which are the directions for use: how much to take, when to take it, and for how long.

• Warnings: when to stop taking the medicine, potential side effects (drowsiness, constipation, and so on), when to see a doctor, and whether a product should not be taken by people with certain conditions.

Of course, other information appears—such as the name and address of the manufacturer, packer, or distributor; net quantity of contents; and the expiration date.

Expiration Dates

The FDA requires that drug manufacturers add an expiration date—the date beyond which a product should not be used—to the label of most prescription and nonprescription products. This date is determined by appropriate stability testing. By law, this date is your assurance that a product meets applicable standards of identity, strength, quality, and purity at the time it's sold.

Of course, the potency of all drugs is affected by many factors, including humidity, temperature, light, and in some cases, even exposure to air—the very agents that come into play when you open a product for the first time and subsequently store it. For that reason, obviously, proper storage becomes all-important to the continued quality of the product (see page 12). The truth of the matter, though, is that deterioration begins the moment the drug is made. Sometimes these changes are detectable, a change in odor—such as when aspirin develops a vinegary odor—or in appearance, but more often the changes are unrecognizable.

Besides the important matter of potency, another area of concern is that with time and other factors some medicines actually become harmful as the drug deteriorates. For that reason alone, the safest course is to use all medicines before their expiration dates.

Look for a statement such as "Exp6/98," "Ex-May99" and "Expires 3/98" on the product's la-bel. As with other information on the label, the NDMA's proposed labeling standards call for optimum readability in matters ranging from legibility of type size, location, and placement of the expiration date to wording that is easily understandable by the consumer.

"Flag the Label"

Flag is a term used by the OTC drug industry to designate an attention-getting label signal that alerts consumers to read the label carefully because of significant new information. "Significant" changes include the following: expansion or limitation of indications ("claims"); modification of dosage level; change in active ingredients or in directions for use; and new warnings or new contraindications.

In some cases manufacturers flag the label when these significant changes are made in currently marketed—that is, not new—products or labels.

Look for phrases such as:

• See new directions

• See new label directions

• New information: Read entire label

• See label for new ingredients

• See new warnings

• Read label for current directions and warnings

• See new uses

• See new use

• See new dosage

These flags also should appear on the labels of all *new products* introduced under an existing brand name. Such products are called brand-name, or line, extensions, and the statement in the flag should be accurate representation of the unique/new product feature(s). Look for wording such as:

• *Added new ingredient* or *Added new ingredients* if the brand-name extension is the addition of a second (or third or fourth) ingredient to a single-ingredient brand name.

• *Contains no*—for example, *Contains no antihistamine,* if the brand-name extension is a change in the single ingredient that is (or had been) in the brand-name product.

• *For*—for example, *For constipation* or *For diarrhea,* if the brand-name extension is an extension of a line of products into new pharmacologic categories (e.g., an antacid product now expanded to relief of constipation or diarrhea).

• *New dosage, New timed release formula,* or *New dosage form* if the brand-name extension is a new dosage or dosage form.

A word here about the practice of line extension: As you can imagine, the success of this strategy to introduce new products depends on the trust that consumers develop for the specific brand name. This trust—so the theory goes—leads them to purchase other products with the same brand name.

All flags should appear in conspicuous type size and style on the principal part of the label, be set off by distinctive color or background color from other information, and be carried for at least six months after such a change is made.

Brand-name, or Line, Extensions

Brand-name, or line, extensions are an effective strategy that drug manufacturers use to introduce new over-the-counter products. The practice is so named because an established brand name is extended to an entire line of OTC products. An extra-strength formula of a "regular-strength" product that is marketed under the preexisting product name is an example of a line extension—as is, for example, a no-drowse formula.

Clearly, brand-name extensions are attractive to manufacturers because the trust that you have developed for specific preexisting brand names will in all probability be transferred to other products with the same brand names.

However, critics of the practice—including the FDA—suggest that it can create confusion. On the other hand, the NDMA—admittedly a trade group for drug manufacturers—believes that with safeguards such as clear labeling and explanatory material, brand-name extensions offer you greater choices and ability to "tailor" the OTC product to your specific needs.

Whether or not an OTC product has package inserts is a decision left up to the manufacturer. In short, there is no mandatory requirement on the part of the FDA for such. Further, if the manufacturer does voluntarily enclose package inserts, no standard information is mandated. Whatever the manufacturer decides to include, if anything at all—in addition to the information required for package labeling—varies from manufacturer to manufacturer and may or may not be consistent among even one company's products.

The importance of knowing what should be on an OTC product label and what the information on and all around the packaging means becomes even clearer when you consider your main responsibility besides selecting the right product: ensuring that the medicine is completely safe to use.

Safe Use of Medications

Just as medications bought over the counter and in prescription form are not always foolproof cures or effective treatments for particular medical conditions, neither are they always completely safe to use. Specifically, there are risks involved with taking medications that appear to have been tampered with, stored improperly or not stored in their original containers, and are past their expiration dates. However, you can take steps to protect yourself and your family from any accidental poisonings.

Product Tampering

Because of the publicity surrounding product tampering cases in the 1980s, manufacturers have made extensive changes in the way OTC medications are packaged and labeled. Inner and outer safety seals have been added to virtually every product to make it easier—for everyone, from the store clerk to you—to detect product tampering. In addition, a written warning advises against purchasing or using the product if the safety seal is broken.

Even though manufacturers have added these safety features, it's still your responsibility to examine the package carefully, preferably before purchasing the product but definitely before ingesting it.

Here are a few things to look for when purchasing packaged medications:

• Check to see if the container has been tampered with in any way. If the seal appears to be disturbed, don't purchase the product. Once you open the container after purchase, inspect the inner seals for tampering.

• Outer and inner linings that are open, seals that are disturbed or cracked, or holes could indicate product tampering.

• Products with disturbed caps, cotton plugs, and wrapping should be avoided. The contents of the container should be looked at next.

• Pills, capsules, and tablets should not be discolored, colored differently from one another, crumbly, in different sizes or shapes, deformed, give off an unusual odor, or have smeared or unclear imprints.

• Liquid medications should likewise be checked for uniformity in color, thickness, and texture, any unusual odors, and any foreign particles.

• Creams and ointments should be checked for color and texture. Any sign of discoloration or a sandy feeling could indicate a problem.

If you have any suspicions that something might be wrong, don't purchase the product. If you have already purchased a product, return it to the store where it was purchased or contact the manufacturer. Some manufacturers have toll-free numbers where consumers may report problems with product packaging.

Antitampering Strategies

Manufacturers use any of several different ways of packaging their products to help make them resistant to tampering. These methods, according to Consumer Reports Books' *The Complete Drug Reference*, include:

• Wrapping the form of the medication (tablet, capsule, or whatever) and/or its container in plastic film or bubble pack.

• Sealing each individual tablet, capsule, or whatever in a paper, plastic, or foil pouch or in a blister or strip pack.

• Fitting a shrink seal or band tightly around the cap and container.

• Sealing the bottle opening under the cap or the carton flaps with a paper or foil seal or tape.

• Fitting a breakable metal or plastic cap over the bottle opening.

Proper Storage

You should always store medications in a cool, dry place, in a locked cabinet, and out of reach of children. The glove box of your car may be fine for maps and notepads, but it definitely isn't the place for medications. And storing capsules or tablets in the bathroom, near the kitchen sink, or in any other damp place is not a good idea either. If at all possible, locate your home medicine cabinet elsewhere. Do not store medicines in the refrigerator unless directed to do so.

The best rule of thumb: Protect your medications from heat, freezing, moisture, and direct light. Exposing them to extremes of temperature and moisture could change the chemical makeup of the drugs, thereby defeating their therapeutic purposes. If you ingest medication in this condition, you may also expose yourself to the potential effects of an accidental poisoning.

Store your medications in their original containers, including any outside packaging material, especially if it contains dosage information. The orig-

Shelf Life of Medications

Important to the safe and effective use of prescription and nonprescription drugs is knowing when a drug has gone beyond its expiration date. The shelf life of medications varies, and often it is hard to tell from the look, smell, or flavor of a drug that it is past its prime.

Aside from following the adage "When in doubt, throw it out," don't forget, too, that (1) medications whose labels are lost or unreadable should be discarded; (2) a savvy consumer will record the date that all OTC medications are purchased and first opened; and (3) the pharmacist can be a big help in determining how long to keep medications.

inal containers are designed to protect medication from moisture and exposure to air.

Do not store different medications in the same bottle. This is an accident waiting to happen. And don't think you can tell one pill from the other by color. Some pills and capsules resemble one another, causing you to forget which medications you mixed.

Expiration Dates

Always check the expiration dates on the medications in your home medicine cabinet—even before you buy any medication. Manufacturers put those expiration dates on the products so you won't accidentally take something that is no longer safe and effective and could actually harm you.

Here is the shelf life for some popular nonprescription medications:

Cold tablets	1 to 2 years
Laxatives	2 to 3 years
Minerals	6 years or more
OTC painkiller tablets	1 to 4 years
Travel sickness tablets	2 years
Vitamins	6 years or more

Proper Use of Your Medicines

When all is said and done, a large part of the responsibility for safe use of medicines rests in your hands—literally. How you actually administer the drug—in whatever form: tablet, spray, or other—is critical. In its book *The Complete Drug Reference* (Mount Vernon, N.Y.: Consumer Reports Books, 1996), the United States Pharmacopeial Convention has the following important recommendations:

For Oral (by Mouth) Medicines

• In general, it is best to take oral medicines with a full glass of water. However, follow your health-care professional's directions. Some medicines should be taken with food while others should be taken on an empty stomach.

• When taking most long-acting forms of a medicine, each dose should be swallowed whole. Do not break, crush, or chew before swallowing unless you have been specifically told that it is all right to do so.

• If you are taking liquid medicines, you should consider using a specially marked measuring spoon or other device to measure each dose accurately. Ask your pharmacist about these devices. The average household teaspoon may not hold the right amount of liquid.

• Oral medicine may come in a number of different dosage forms, such as tablets, capsules, and liquids. If you have trouble swallowing the dosage form prescribed for you, check with your health-care professional. Another dosage form that you can swallow more easily may be available.

• Child-resistant caps on medicine containers have decreased greatly the number of accidental poisonings that occur each year. Use of these caps is required by law. However, if you find it hard to open such caps, you may ask your pharmacist for a regular, easier-to-open cap. He or she can provide you with a regular cap if you request it. However, you must make this request each time you get a prescription filled.

For Skin Patches

• Apply the patch to a clean, dry skin area that has little or no hair and is free of scars, cuts, or irritation. Remove the previous patch before applying a new one.

• Apply a new patch if the first one becomes loose or falls off.

• Apply each patch to a different area of skin to prevent skin irritation or other problems.

• Do not try to trim or cut the adhesive patch to adjust the dosage. Check with your health-care professional if you think the medicine is not working as it should.

For Inhalers

• Medicines that come in inhalers usually come with patient directions. *Read the directions carefully before using the medicine.* If you do not understand the directions, or if you are not sure how to use the inhaler, check with your health-care professional.

• Since different types of inhalers may be used in different ways, it is very important to follow carefully the directions given to you.

For Ophthalmic (Eye) Drops

• To prevent contamination, do not let the tip of the eye drop applicator touch any surface (including the eye) and keep the container tightly closed.

• The bottle may not be full; this is to provide proper drop control.

• How to apply: First, wash your hands. Tilt your head back and, with the index finger, pull the lower eyelid away from the eye to form a pouch. Drop the medicine into the pouch and gently close your eyes. Do not blink. Keep eyes closed for one to two minutes.

• If your medicine is for glaucoma or inflammation of the eye: Follow the directions for application that are listed above. However, immediately after placing the drops in your eye, apply pressure to the inside corner of the eye with your middle finger. Continue to apply pressure for one to two minutes after the medicine has been placed in the eye. This will help prevent the medicine from being absorbed into the body and causing side effects.

• After applying the eye drops, wash your hands to remove any medicine.

For Ophthalmic (Eye) Ointments

• To prevent contamination of the eye ointment, do not let the tip of the applicator touch any surface (including the eye). After using, wipe the tip of the ointment tube with a clean tissue and keep the tube tightly closed.

• How to apply: First, wash hands. Pull the lower eyelid away from the eye to form a pouch. Squeeze a thin strip of ointment into the pouch. A 1-cm (approximately ⅓-inch) strip of ointment is usually enough unless otherwise directed. Gently close your eyes and keep them closed for about one to two minutes.

• After applying the eye ointment, wash your hands to remove any medicine.

For Nasal (Nose) Drops

• How to use: Blow your nose gently, without squeezing. Tilt your head back while standing or sitting up, or lie down on your back on a bed and hang your head over the side. Place the drops into each nostril and keep your head tilted back for a few minutes to allow medicine to spread throughout the nose.

• Rinse the dropper with hot water and dry with a clean tissue. Replace the cap right after use. To avoid the spread of infection, do not use the container for more than one person.

For Nasal (Nose) Spray

• How to use: Blow your nose gently, without squeezing. With your head upright, spray the medicine into each nostril. Sniff briskly while squeezing bottle quickly and firmly.

• Rinse the tip of the spray bottle with hot water, taking care not to suck water into the bottle, and dry with a clean tissue. Replace the cap right after cleaning. To avoid the spread of infection, do not use the container for more than one person.

For Otic (Ear) Drops

• To prevent contamination of the ear drops, do not touch the applicator tip to any surface (including the ear).

• The bottle may not be full; this is to provide proper drop control.

• How to apply: Lie down or tilt the head so that the ear that needs treatment faces up. Gently pull the earlobe up and back for adults (down and back for children) to straighten the ear canal. Drop the medicine into the ear canal. Keep ear facing up for about five minutes to allow medicine to run to the bottom of the ear canal. (For young children and other patients who cannot stay still for five minutes, try to keep the ear facing up for at least one or two minutes.)

• Do not rinse the dropper after use. Wipe the tip of the dropper with a clean tissue and keep the container tightly closed.

For Rectal Suppositories

• How to insert suppository: First, wash your hands. Remove the foil wrapper and moisten the suppository with water. Lie down on your side and push the suppository well up into rectum with your finger. If the suppository is too soft to insert, chill it in the refrigerator for 30 minutes or run cold water over it before removing the foil wrapper.

• Wash your hands after you have inserted the suppository.

For Rectal Cream or Ointment

• Clean and dry the rectal area. Apply a small amount of cream or ointment and rub it in gently.

• If your health-care professional wants you to insert the medicine into the rectum: First, attach the plastic applicator tip onto the opened tube. Insert the applicator tip into the rectum and gently squeeze the tube to deliver the cream. Remove the applicator tip from the tube and wash with hot, soapy water. Replace the cap of the tube after use.

• Wash your hands after you have inserted the medicine.

For Vaginal Medicines

• How to insert the medicine: First, wash your hands. Use the special applicator. Follow any special directions that are provided by the manufacturer. However, if you are pregnant, check with your health-care professional before using the applicator to insert the medicine.

• Lie on your back with your knees drawn up. Using the applicator, insert the medicine into the vagina as far as you can without using force or causing discomfort. Release the medicine by pushing on the plunger. Wait several minutes before getting up.

• Wash the applicator and your hands with soap and warm water.

Source: *The Complete Drug Reference.* Copyright 1996. The U. S. P. Convention, Inc. Reprinted with permission.

Remember that you play a large role in the safe use of medications. So look at the label *and at the medicine* every time you take a dose of medication, and follow the directions carefully. Now, let's take a look at the variety of items—both nonprescription medicines and other necessary components of effective and healthy self-care—you might find in the typical home medicine cabinet.

Medicine Cabinet Essentials

These medications and supplies should be kept at home for self-care procedures. Be sure to store them in a convenient dry place, but out of children's reach. Check the expiration dates periodically and discard and replace as needed.

Medications	Use
Acetaminophen	Pain relief, fever reduction
Antacids, liquid or tablets	Stomach upset, heartburn
Antidiarrheal medicine	Diarrhea
Antihistamines	Allergies, cold symptoms relief
Antimotion sickness preparation	Motion sickness
Antiseptic preparation	Abrasions, cuts
Aspirin*	Pain relief, fever reduction, swelling reduction
Cough suppressant without expectorant	Dry cough without mucus
Decongestant (tablets, nose spray)	Stuffy and runny nose, postnasal drip from colds, allergies
Expectorant (with Dextromethorphan)	Cough with mucus
Ibuprofen (adult)	Pain relief, fever reduction, swelling reduction
Laxatives	Constipation

* Do not give aspirin or any medication containing salicylates to anyone twenty-one years of age or younger, unless directed by a physician, owing to its association with Reye's syndrome, a potentially fatal condition.

Source: Don R. Powell, Ph.D. *Self-Care: Your Family Guide to Symptoms and How to Treat Them* (Allentown, Pa.: People's Medical Society, 1996). Reprinted with permission.

Supplies	Use
Activated charcoal (binds certain chemicals when swallowed) Note: Call Poison Control Center first.	Oral poisoning for some poisons
Adhesive bandages	Minor wounds
Adhesive tape, sterile gauze (roll and pads), and scissors	Dressing for minor wounds
Antibiotic cream or ointment	Minor skin infection, wounds
Antifungal preparations	Fungal infections such as athlete's foot
Cotton balls, cotton-tipped applicators	Minor wounds
Ear wax dissolver	Ear wax
Elastic bandages and clips	Minor strains and sprains
Eye drops with artificial tears	Minor eye irritations
Heating pad/hot water bottle	Minor pains, strains, menstrual cramps
Hemorrhoid preparations	Hemorrhoids
Humidifier, vaporizer (cool-mist)	To add moisture to the air
Hydrocortisone cream	Minor skin irritations, itching, and rashes
Ice pack/Heat pack	Minor pain and injuries
Petroleum jelly	Chafing, diaper rash, dry skin
Rubbing alcohol	Topical antiseptic, cleansing of thermometer
Sunscreen (SPF, or sun protection, of 15 or more)	To prevent sunburn, protect against skin cancer
Syrup of ipecac Note: Call Poison Control Center first.	To induce vomiting for some poisons
Thermometer	To measure temperature
Throat antiseptic preparations	Minor sore throat
Tongue depressor, flashlight	To check for redness or infection in throat
Toothache-relief preparation	Toothache, teething
Tweezers	To remove splinters

First-Aid Supplies

First aid is immediate care given to a person who is injured owing to a sudden illness, an accident, or a life-threatening situation. Clearly, though, first aid sometimes consists of ministering to small accidents and everyday incidents such as scrapes, minor burns and cuts, and the like. Many injuries and sudden illnesses can be cared for without immediate or even any medical assistance. And for this reason, it is important to have on hand useful medicines and supplies for such situations— which we have more to say about later—and a comprehensive first aid manual. Two of the more well-known books are *First Aid Handbook,* by the National Safety Council, and *The American Red Cross First Aid and Safety Handbook.*

Your Injury Kit

If there is one essential standby in the home and workplace, or for the athlete, it has to be the injury kit. Stage 1 is our recommended minimum, but the more sports you or your family participate in and the better you are at them, the more you need to be prepared. Add stage 2, then 3.

Stage 1

Home

Box of different-size adhesive bandages

Sterile gauze pads (clean, ironed handkerchief will do), 4 x 4 inches (10 x 10 cm)

Gauze bandages

Box of bandages of various sizes

Plastic bags for ice (or package of frozen peas— ideal shape for applying to injuries) or ice pack kept in freezer

Scissors, for general use

First aid book

Stage 2

Workplace

Safety pins

Sling

Scissors with 2-inch (5-cm) blades, for medical use

Needle

Cotton balls

Antiseptic fluid/wipes

Tweezers

Rubber bands

NSAIDs (nonsteroidal anti-inflammatory drugs) or nonaspirin painkiller

Adhesive tape

Portable razor

Butterfly bandage or adhesive plaster sutures

Eyebath and eyewash

Thermometer

Antacid tablets

Stage 3

Recreation

Strapping tape and/or brace

Underwrap

Tincture of benzoin compound to keep from hurting skin

Aerosol coolant spray

Plastic or "second skin" product for blisters

Fluid replacement drink

Nail clippers

Petroleum jelly

Baby oil/oil of wintergreen/massage cream

Orthopedic felt for padding

Elastic knee/ankle/elbow support

Foot powder

Anti-inflammatory drugs

Source: *What to Do When It Hurts: Self-Diagnosis and Rehabilitation of Common Aches and Pains.* (Allentown, Pa.: People's Medical Society, 1996). Reprinted with permission from Breslich & Foss, Limited.

Handy Home Remedies

Home remedies—using products that are easily obtained and found in many households—are the cornerstone of medical self-care. Frankly, though, no list can ever be complete, given all the thousands of possible remedies (and combinations) and techniques that can be used to soothe or treat everyday health problems. An excellent source on the subject is the book *The Doctors Book of Home Remedies,* Debora Tkac, ed. (Emmaus, Pa.: Rodale, 1990).

Found in probably every household, the following products are basic, useful home remedies. Some of these products are OTC medications—often called home remedies because they are among the most basic of self-care ingredients—while others are common household products. When using household products for medicinal purposes, be sure to read the labels for proper dosing and usage. But remember: In not every case is there one right and effective way to mix, administer, or use the remedy for the relevant condition. For that reason, our directions are as broad or specific (depending upon the remedy) as possible while still ensuring that you know how to use the product effectively and safely. *If there is any doubt as to the proper mixture or application, do not use the product.* Consult a self-care or first aid guide for additional information.

Acetaminophen

A painkiller and fever reducer for people allergic to aspirin and for children. For information on how to use, see page 58.

Alcohol (rubbing)

A mild antiseptic (see page 116). To cool or soothe certain cases of irritated skin and to kill germs on affected areas, apply topically, avoiding delicate areas such as the skin around the eyes.

Ammonia

"Smelling salts," in cases of fainting. Hold an open container under the victim's nose so vapor can be inhaled. Ammonia can also be used as a counterirritant (see page 58) and to neutralize insect bites. In the latter situations, dab ammonia on the sting in order to relieve the pain.

Baking soda

A soothing treatment for sunburn, to reduce its pain, itching, and inflammation. Sprinkle baking soda into tepid, not hot, bath water. Experts also suggest that rather than drying yourself with a towel, you let the solution dry on your skin.

Calamine lotion

A soothing treatment for rashes, sunburn, and minor thermal (heat) burns that do not result in blisters. (See page 118.)

Coffee

A stimulant in shock cases if the victim is conscious. Brew and have victim drink it (but only if he or she is conscious).

Egg white

A demulcent (a substance that soothes or protects irritated mucous membranes) to soothe the stomach and retard absorption of a poison. Before using in suspected cases of poisoning, call your local poison control center, which will instruct you in how—if at all—to administer it.

Epsom salts

A soothing treatment for wounds and to make wet dressings for them. Sprinkle into warm bath water and soak or, depending upon the location of the wound, dissolve 1 tablespoon in 1 quart of warm water and either soak or apply to a dressing to be placed on the wound.

Hydrogen peroxide

A germ killer when in direct contact with bacteria. Follow directions on the product.

Milk

A demulcent (a substance that soothes or protects irritated mucous membranes) to soothe the stomach and retard absorption of a poison. Before using in suspected cases of poisoning, call your local poison control center, which will instruct you in how—if at all—to administer it.

Milk of magnesia

A substitute for magnesium oxide (see *Universal Antidote*). Milk of magnesia is also used in small doses as an antacid (see page 83) for stomach upset and as a laxative (see page 93) for constipation.

Mineral oil

A stool softener (see page 93)—used internally—to promote easier passage.

Oil of cloves

Temporary relief of toothache. Apply a drop or so directly onto the tooth or dab a small amount on a cotton ball and place it next to the ache.

Olive oil

An emollient (see page 104). Rub the oil on dry or rough skin to soften it.

Petrolatum (petroleum jelly)

A skin softener and protective ointment used on wound dressings. Follow directions on the product.

Powdered mustard (dry mustard)

An emetic (to induce vomiting). Dissolve 1 to 3 teaspoons in a glass of warm water and drink. Before using in suspected cases of poisoning, call your local poison control center, which will instruct you in how—if at all—to administer it.

Salt (table salt)

An emetic (to induce vomiting). Dissolve 2 teaspoons in a glass of warm water and drink. Before using in suspected cases of poisoning, call your local poison control center, which will instruct you in how—if at all—to administer it.

Universal Antidote

Recommended as an antidote for poisoning when the poison cannot be identified. The universal antidote is made by mixing ½ ounce activated charcoal, ¼ ounce magnesium chloride, and ¼ ounce tannic acid in a glass of water.

Soapsuds (not detergents)

An emetic (to induce vomiting) and as an antidote for poisoning by certain metal compounds, such as mercuric chloride. Before using in suspected cases of poisoning, call your local poison control center, which will instruct you in how—if at all—to administer it. Soap and clean water can also be used to cleanse wounds.

Starch, cooked

A demulcent (a substance that soothes or protects irritated mucous membranes) to soothe the stomach and retard absorption of a poison. Before using in suspected cases of poisoning, call your local poison control center, which will instruct you in how—if at all—to administer it.

Tea

Made strong, a substitute for tannic acid (see *Universal Antidote*). Tea is also used as a stimulant in shock cases where appropriate (see *Coffee*).

Vinegar (acetic acid)

Recommended treatment for a number of problems, including jellyfish stings, sunburn, and yeast infections. To help neutralize jellyfish stings, splash vinegar over the affected areas. For sunburns, mix 1 cup of white vinegar in a bathtub of cool water and soak. While there are OTC pre-mixed vinegar solutions for yeast infections, the home-mixed concoction for douching is a lukewarm vinegar and water: 4 teaspoons vinegar to 1 pint of water is one of the standard recipes.

Homeopathic Remedies

Long acknowledged as legitimate natural medical remedies and available in Europe, homeopathic remedies are relatively new to the pharmacy shelves in the United States, but they are gaining in popularity. Sales of these products in health food stores and drugstores, according to one source, are rising 25 percent annually. The question is—how do you incorporate them into your OTC home self-care arsenal?

First, let's start with a primer on the beginnings of homeopathy and its guiding principles. Homeopathy is the system of medicine discovered and developed by Dr. Samuel Hahnemann in the late eighteenth and early nineteenth centuries, although the concept dates back to Hippocrates. Through reading, observation, and experimentation, Hahnemann discovered the principle that "like is healed by like"—meaning that the symptoms produced in the body by a substance are similar to the symptoms that the substance is supposed to alleviate, and that medicines that cause symptoms of disease in healthy people will bring about cures in sick people. This principle, called the Law of Similars, is also sometimes used in conventional medicine as with immunotherapy (regular injections for the treatments of allergy).

Homeopathic medicine also believes in the use of a single remedy; thus, practitioners of homeopathy—homeopaths—will administer only one medicine at a time, and if the condition persists, then a second medication is used but never a combination of medications. Finally, because it is concerned with the body's ability to absorb the medication, homeopathic medicine encourages the smallest dose possible in order to prevent outright rejection or reactions from strong doses.

Homeopathic medications are extracted from plant, animal, and other biological sources, and from mineral sources. Preparations include tablets, granules, ointments, liquids, and suppositories. These remedies usually indicate how many times they have been diluted from the original material, although a basic belief of homeopathy is that no matter how many times a solution has been diluted, it will remain effective.

Experts generally agree that homeopathic reme-dies are safe for many symptoms, such as headache, abdominal cramps, cough, and insomnia, and for a wide range of disorders; therefore, they are useful for home treatment. On the other hand, experts say that for more deep-rooted and persistent, or chronic, symptoms and conditions, you should seek out a homeopathic practitioner to go through a more rigorous process of sorting out the symptoms and prescribing treatments or remedies.

For further information, contact:

National Center for Homeopathy
801 N. Fairfax Street, Suite 306
Alexandria, VA 22314
703-548-7790

Below is a list of the most common homeopathic medicines and what symptoms they are used for, as compiled by the National Center for Homeopathy. (See note at the end.) The group explains that such medicines, when used as directed, can be administered safely and effectively at home for simple first aid and acute, self-limiting conditions. But for chronic or recurring acute conditions, you should seek the care of an experienced practitioner. These remedies can be found in health food stores, drugstores, and homeopathic pharmacies:

Aconite
(monkshood)
Earliest stages of a cold; injuries to the eye

Anas barbarae hepatis et cordis
(extract of liver and heart of Barbary duck)
Early stages of the flu (also sold under the trade names Oscillococcinum® and Flu Solution®)

Arnica
(mountain daisy)
Injuries, bruises, falls; shock from injuries; muscle injuries with soreness

Belladonna
(deadly nightshade)
Sore throats, earaches (especially on right side); with sudden onset, high fever, redness, throbbing pain, dilated pupils

Calendula
(marigold—external tincture)
Cuts, abrasions, minor burns, diaper rash

Chamomilla
(chamomile)
Teething, colic, earache, with irritability and

capriciousness (which improves when the child is being carried)

Cocculus
(Indian cockle)
Motion sickness with weakness; dizziness (which worsens in the fresh air, and is better when lying down); aversion to food

Gelsemium
(yellow jasmine)
Flu with aching; drowsiness, fatigue, stage fright

Hypericum
(St. John's wort)
Injuries to nerves, areas rich in nerves, such as fingers, toes, tailbone; after dental drilling

Ledum
(marsh tea)
Punctures; bites from animals and insects; black eye

Nux vomica
(poison nut)
Overindulgence in food or alcohol

Pulsatilla
(windflower)
Cold or earache in child (who is weepy, clingy and wants to be held—but feels better when in the open air)

Rhus tox
(poison ivy)
Sprains and strains (better after warm applications and limbering up)

Symphytum
(comfrey)
Aid in healing of fractures; blows to the eye

For detailed directions on the use of these remedies, including potency and dosage, or for additional guidance, consult a homeopathic practitioner or a self-care book, such as:

Miranda Castro, F.S. Hom., *The Complete Homeopathy Handbook* (New York: St. Martin's, 1991).

Stephen Cummings, M.D., and Dana Ullman, M.P.H., *Everybody's Guide to Homeopathic Medicines* (Los Angeles: Tarcher, 1997).

Maesimund Panos, M.D., and Jane Heimlich, *Homeopathic Medicine at Home* (Los Angeles: Tarcher, 1981).

For serious conditions, you should seek the care of an experienced practitioner.

Note

This list of homeopathic medicines was not designed as a stand-alone, as it does not discuss potency or dosage, and the indications for usage are very brief. Nor does the list discuss the difference between herbal and homeopathic medicines. The medicines listed are intended to be used in homeopathic preparations, and you should consult additional sources for instructions for potency and dosage.

Reprinted with permission of the National Center for Homeopathy.

How to Use This Book

*T*he *Over-the-Counter Doctor* is divided into several easy-to-use and understand sections. It is designed to get you to the information you need as quickly and accurately as possible. And once you are there, our extensive cross-referencing will direct you to other places in the book that are related to the topic or product you are looking up.

We urge you to begin using this book by reading the introductory material. While you may already know a great deal about over-the-counter products, this section of the book will help you gain a better, more knowledgeable understanding of why a product is over-the-counter versus prescription only and how you can better use over-the-counter products in your own self-care. Also, the tips and suggestions we offer in this section will make you a more effective health-care consumer, in much better control over your health.

Once you've reviewed the introductory material, there are several ways to use the book.

Conditions

If you know your condition, but are not sure what products are used to treat it, start in the Conditions section. Here, every condition considered treatable by over-the-counter products is listed alphabetically. Each entry explains the condition (in order to help you be sure this is actually what ails you) and refers you to the over-the-counter products used to treat it. These referrals may send you to medications or other products. We suggest that you look at all of the entries to which you've been referred since the more you know, the more likely you are to find the exact product to suit your needs.

Medications

There is another way to use the book. At times you will know the exact name or type of product. In those instances, go directly to the product or category by referring to the index. We encourage you to read the entire product and category entry. This will give you a better understanding of the product itself, the category, or both. It may also alert you to products that were heretofore unfamiliar to you. One or more of them might be better for your condition than the product you originally came to research.

You will note that for most product entries there is information on the condition(s) it is used to treat. This can come in handy if you have products in your home medicine cabinet that might be useful for treating more than one problem. Before you run out to the store to buy something new, we suggest you look up the products you already have to see if one or more might be helpful for your current condition.

Also, take some time to read both the contents page and to scan the index. These useful sections may alert you to topics, products, or conditions that will help you in your self-care.

There are many other resources to empower you to become a better informed medical consumer. From choosing the best home test to toll-free phone numbers of many major over-the-counter product manufacturers, you'll find a lot of helpful information carefully chosen to give you more control over your health.

Finally, you do not have to do this all alone. As we note later in the book, do not hesitate to consult your pharmacist and your doctor if you have a question about using a specific product or combination of products.

Conditions

Every condition treatable with nonprescription drugs is listed in this section. Conditions included here range from common ailments such as fatigue, indigestion, and headache, to specific diseases and illnesses such as chicken pox, ulcers (duodenal, gastric, and peptic), and carpal tunnel syndrome.

To find the over-the-counter drug that relieves your symptoms, turn first to the condition, listed alphabetically. Make sure that the description matches your symptoms and check other conditions to which you are referred. These cross-references ensure that you are aware of all the conditions with similar symptoms. Then follow the "OTC Treatment" to the proper product in Medications, where everything from toothpastes to antihistamines (oral and topical) can be found.

Abrasion

A shallow wound characterized by a tearing or wearing away of the top layer of skin. Abrasions often occur because of an accident in which the skin is scraped against a rough surface. These surface wounds may hurt more than cuts, but they heal more quickly.

Symptoms:
Topmost layer of skin torn and bleeding.

OTC Treatments:
Antiseptics (page 116); Antibiotics (page 113); Analgesics (Internal) (page 56); Astringents (page 118)

Acne

A skin condition marked by the eruption of pimples. Acne occurs when hair follicles or skin ducts in the skin become clogged with oil or bacteria. It is common in teenagers and can be aggravated by menstrual periods, the use of birth control pills, and stress.

Symptoms:
Blackheads, whiteheads, or pimples on the face, neck, and shoulders.

OTC Treatment:
Antiacne Preparations (page 111)

Allergy

A response by the immune system to a substance the body believes harmful. The immune system response is usually triggered by foreign invaders, such as germs or viruses, but it may react to harmless substances, such as foods, dust, or pollen. The reaction causes the body to produce chemicals known as histamines, which cause allergy symptoms. Different allergies manifest themselves in different ways.

Symptoms:
Sniffling, congestion, wheezing, coughing, difficulty breathing, stomach cramps, diarrhea, unconsciousness.

OTC Treatments:
Antihistamines (page 72); Antipruritics (page 95); Cold, Cough, and Allergy Remedies (page 68); Topical Decongestants (page 70)

See Bite, Insect; Eczema; Hay Fever; Hives; Poison Ivy, Poison Oak, and Poison Sumac; Sting, Bee

Arthritis

Inflammation of a joint or several joints that occurs when the smooth cartilage in a joint breaks down and becomes rough or inflamed. Common types of arthritis include osteoarthritis, rheumatoid arthritis, and gout. Osteoarthritis affects one or two joints at a time and is a result of normal "wear and tear" on a joint. Rheumatoid arthritis, an autoimmune disease, occurs when the immune system triggers inflammation of the membranes lining the joints. It can affect many joints at once. Gout is a form of arthritis that usually occurs in the feet, caused by a buildup of uric acid in the joints.

Symptoms:
Pain, stiffness, and swelling in a joint; pain during movement; a feeling of tenderness or warmth in a joint.

OTC Treatments:
Analgesics (Internal) (page 56); Antiarthritis Treatments (page 62); Counterirritants (page 58); Pain Relievers, Fever Reducers, and Anti-inflammatories (page 53)

Asthma

A condition marked by episodes of wheezing and difficulty breathing. It occurs when the muscles of the airways tighten and the membranes lining the passages swell, restricting breathing. It may be triggered by allergies, exercise, respiratory infection, and certain medications, though sometimes the cause is unknown.

Symptoms:
Tightness in the chest, difficulty breathing, wheezing that is loudest during exhalation, coughing up of mucus.

OTC Treatments:
Bronchodilators (page 168); Cold, Cough, and Allergy Remedies (page 68)

Athlete's Foot

A fungal infection, also called *tinea pedis,* that usually occurs on the feet between the toes (commonly the third and fourth). It may also affect the palms of the hands. Athlete's foot is contagious and is often contracted by walking barefoot on wet surfaces where the fungi thrive, such as those in locker rooms or showers, or by sharing towels. Athlete's foot is often persistent and may recur after treatment.

Symptoms:
Soft, red scales on the feet and between the toes; itching and burning; patches of cracked, peeling skin; small blisters.

OTC Treatment:
Antifungals (page 114)

See Infection, Fungal Skin

Atrophy, Vaginal

Thinning and drying of the lining of the vagina that occurs during menopause because of the decline in the body's production of estrogen. The condition results in less vaginal lubrication during sexual intercourse and an increased susceptibility to infection and irritation, because the lining develops cracks easily. Vaginal atrophy can last indefinitely, while other conditions such as hot flashes usually subside within a few years of menopause.

Symptoms:
Soreness and irritation of vagina, painful intercourse, increase in number of vaginal infections.

OTC Treatment:
Vaginal Lubricants (page 181)

Backache

Pain or stiffness in the back most commonly caused by a muscle strain or sprain, in which the tissues supporting the muscles and bones are torn or stretched. It often occurs after lifting a heavy object, but may happen for seemingly no reason. Back pain can also be caused by arthritis, osteoporosis, urinary tract infection, or a slipped disk or other problem with the spine.

Symptoms:
Pain and stiffness in the back.

OTC Treatments:
Analgesics (Internal) (page 56); Counterirritants (page 58); Pain Relievers, Fever Reducers, and Anti-inflammatories (page 53)

Bad Breath

See Halitosis

Baldness

See Hair Loss

Bite, Insect

An area of redness, swelling, or itching after a bite or sting by a bee, wasp, flea, mosquito, or other insect. Reactions to bites vary according to the insect and the sensitivity of the person bitten. Those severely allergic may experience anaphylaxis (a severe reaction that requires immediate treatment and may cause death) after a bite by a bee, wasp, or yellow jacket. With minor bites, the reaction is temporary and local—meaning that the redness, swelling, and/or itching appear at the site of the bite and then disappear over a period of days.

Symptoms:
Pain, itching, and swelling in area of bite. Anaphylactic reaction includes difficulty breathing, swelling, low blood pressure, unconsciousness.

OTC Treatments:
Insect Bite and Sting Treatments (page 108); Hydrocortisone (page 96); Astringents (page 118); Local Anesthetics (page 97)

See Allergy; Bite, Mosquito; Sting, Bee

Bite, Mosquito

Red, itchy welt that appears shortly after a mosquito bite.

Symptoms:
Red, itchy welt.

OTC Treatments:
Insect Bite and Sting Treatments (page 108); Hydrocortisone (page 96); Astringents (page 118); Local Anesthetics (page 97)

See Bite, Insect

Blepharitis

Inflammation of the edges of the eyelid. This condition is usually caused by seborrhea (a condition in which the skin is greasy and scaling) and a bacterial infection. While blepharitis may cause the eye to become irritated and crusted shut, it rarely interferes with sight.

Symptoms:
Sticky, reddened, crusted eyelids; itching, gritty feeling in the eyes; loss of eyelashes.

OTC Treatment:
Eyelid Scrubs (page 154)

See Seborrhea

Body Odor

Odor produced by bacteria that grow within perspiration, or sweat. Sweat is produced by glands in the skin and cools the body through the process of evaporation. However, if sweat becomes trapped in body hair or within folds of skin, it can attract bacteria that produce odors.

Symptom:
Unpleasant odor.

OTC Treatments:
Antiperspirants (page 165); Deodorants (for body odor) (page 170)

Breast-feeding

See Nipples, Cracked

Bronchitis

Inflammation of the membranes lining the respiratory passages caused by infection (viral or bacterial) or pollution (such as cigarette smoke or chemicals). The membranes become swollen and red and produce mucus, causing the chest to feel tight and sore. It may last from a few days up to two months.

Symptoms:
Coughing, expectoration (coughing up of phlegm), difficulty breathing, chills, fever, fatigue.

OTC Treatments:
Bronchodilators (page 168); Cold, Cough, and Allergy Remedies (page 68)

Bruise

A deep purple, black, or red area that occurs as the result of an injury that breaks blood vessels underneath the skin but not the skin itself. Bruises may be painful to the touch and usually heal quickly. A hard bump or fall may cause a bruise.

Symptoms:
A purple, black, or red area that is painful to the touch; swelling.

OTC Treatment:
Counterirritants (page 58)

Brush Burn

See Abrasion

Bunion

A bony bump on the base of the big toe that occurs when that toe overlaps another. Although a bunion is not particularly painful, it may be complicated by arthritis or bursitis (swelling of the bursa—a sac of fluid that protects a joint). Bunions often have a genetic cause, or they may be the result of poorly fitting shoes.

Symptoms:
Bony lump at base of the big toe, minor foot deformity, pain, restricted movement.

OTC Treatment:
Bunion Treatments (page 120)

Burn

Damage to the skin caused by dry or moist heat, electricity, chemicals, or radiation. A first-degree burn such as sunburn affects only the topmost layer of skin. A second-degree burn, for example, one caused by hot liquid, affects the lower layers of skin as well. The most serious is a third-degree burn, which affects all the layers of skin and possibly underlying tissue and organs. Such burns may be caused by serious fires or electric shock.

Symptoms:
First-degree burns—dry, red, and painful to touch; second-degree burns—painful, swollen, red, and may develop blisters; third-degree burns—black and white in appearance.

OTC Treatments:
Local Anesthetics (page 97); Antibiotics (page 113); Antiseptics (page 116); Burn/Sunburn Treatments (page 101); Astringents (page 118); Skin Protectants (page 126); Hydrocortisone (page 96)

Calluses

Flat areas of dead, thickened skin built up by the body to protect against excess pressure and friction. Calluses commonly occur on feet, knees, and hands. If they occur on areas that bear much body weight, they may become painful. They can be caused by poorly fitting shoes, misaligned toes, or activities that put pressure on hands, knees, and feet.

Symptoms:
Areas of thickened, yellowish-red skin that may or may not be painful.

OTC Treatment:
Callus and Corn Removers (page 120)

Carpal Tunnel Syndrome

A repetitive motion injury that affects the ligaments of the wrist. Small, constant movements cause the tissue surrounding the nerve within the wrist to become inflamed. This puts painful pressure on the nerve. Carpal tunnel is common in people who must do repetitive motions as part of their jobs, for example, operating a computer, cash register, or machine on an assembly line.

Symptoms:
Burning pain in the wrist, a feeling of numbness in the wrist.

OTC Treatment:
Pain Relievers, Fever Reducers, and Anti-inflammatories (page 53)

See Repetitive Motion Injuries

Chicken Pox

A highly contagious viral disease, also called varicella, caused by a herpesvirus and mainly occurring in children five to ten years old. It is marked by a rash of pink spots on the face and abdomen, which blister and dry and cause itching. It is spread through direct contact with the blisters or by droplets spread from the upper respiratory tract of infected persons, usually early in the disease. In adults, the same virus can cause shingles.

Symptoms:
Flat, pink rash on the face and abdomen that develops into blisters; sneezing; coughing; fever; stomachache.

OTC Treatments:
Chicken Pox Treatments (page 121); Bath Products (page 119); Skin Treatments (page 95)

Cold

An infection of the nose and/or throat usually caused by any of more than two hundred different viruses. They can affect normally healthy individuals several times a year. A cold usually lasts seven to ten days. Symptoms typically come on slowly over the course of a few days.

Symptoms:
Sneezing, runny nose, congestion, sore throat, cough, headache, fatigue, fever of 101°F or less.

OTC Treatments:
Cold, Cough, and Allergy Remedies (page 68); Topical Decongestants (page 70); Lozenges and Mouthwashes/Gargles (Sore Throat Relief) (page 77); Antihistamines (page 72)

Conjunctivitis (Pinkeye)

An inflammation of the conjunctiva, the clear membrane that covers the inside of the eyelids and the white of the eye. The condition is also called pinkeye.

Symptoms:
Red, irritated eyes; a yellowish-green discharge from the eye that forms a crust at night; blurred vision.

OTC Treatment:
Ophthalmic Decongestants (page 153)

Constipation

A condition in which bowel movements become too hard to eliminate easily or they become infrequent. Causes include lack of fiber in the diet, lack of exercise, anxiety, overdependence on laxatives, and use of certain drugs. Normal frequency of bowel movements varies from once or twice a day to once a week.

Symptoms:
Difficult bowel movement, abdominal swelling, hard stools, feeling of fullness after a bowel movement.

OTC Treatment:
Laxatives (page 91)

Contusion

See Bruise

Corn

A hard, thickened, sometimes painful area of skin found on or between the toes. Corns are round and yellow and may develop a clear center known as a hen's eye. They are caused by friction and pressure on the feet and may grow larger and more painful with continued friction. Corns may also cause pain by rubbing against a bursa, a sac of fluid that protects a joint.

Symptoms:
A hard, thickened area of skin on or between the toes.

OTC Treatment:
Callus and Corn Removers (page 120)

Cough

The sudden, often loud, forcing of air from the lungs usually done to clear the respiratory passages. A cough can be productive, meaning it brings up phlegm or mucus, or nonproductive, meaning it is dry. A cough can also be a reflex to another problem such as a stomach disorder. A cough may be related to a respiratory condition or may be caused by an irritant such as cigarette smoke.

Symptoms:
Sudden, often loud, forcing of air from the lungs.

OTC Treatments:
Cold, Cough, and Allergy Remedies (page 68); Lozenges and Mouthwashes/Gargles (Sore Throat Relief) (page 77)

Cradle Cap

A rash of dry, flaking skin on the scalp, common in infants between one month and one year old. It develops in patches and may affect the areas around the eyes, nose, and ears. It has no known cause.

Symptoms:
Patches of dry, flaking skin on the scalp; dry patches covered with a yellow crust.

OTC Treatment:
Cradle Cap Treatments (page 132)

Cramps, Menstrual

See Dysmenorrhea

Cut

A wound in which the skin is sliced by a sharp edge. Cuts heal faster when they are closed, and covering a cut also helps prevent infection. If a cut is deep (to the muscle or bone), if it doesn't stop bleeding, or if a lot of blood is lost, seek emergency care.

Symptoms:
Slice in the skin, possibly bleeding (in varying amounts depending upon depth of slice).

OTC Treatments:
Antiseptics (page 116); Antibiotics (page 113); Skin Protectants (page 126)

Cystitis

Inflammation of the bladder usually caused by bacteria that have spread from the rectum to the urethra and bladder. The bacteria then grow within the bladder, causing soreness and pain during urination. Cystitis is a type of urinary tract infection, and diagnosis can be done through a urine test. It is usually not dangerous, though kidney infection may occur if it is left untreated. It is more common in women than in men.

Symptoms:
Frequent urge to urinate; burning urination; blood in the urine; feeling of fullness in the bladder, even after urination; fever, chills, and nausea.

OTC Treatment:
Urinary Pain Relievers (page 178)

See Urinary Tract, Infection of the

Dandruff

Dry, flaking skin that covers the scalp and comes off in small white or gray scales. It is a mild form of a condition known as seborrhea, in which itchy, scaling skin appears around the nose and in the folds of the skin. There is no definite cause of dandruff, though some medical professionals think it may be caused by overproduction of oil by glands in the skin.

Symptoms:
Dry, flaking skin on the scalp; white or gray scales apparent in hair and on clothing.

OTC Treatment:
Dandruff Shampoos (page 132)

See Seborrhea

Dentures, Slipping

Loose or ill-fitting dentures. Loose dentures may cause pain and discomfort, create mouth ulcers, irritate the gums, or slip while talking or eating. Lower dentures are especially susceptible to slipping because when teeth are lost, the bone that supports the dentures tends to shrink.

Symptoms:
Loose dentures, pain in the mouth while using dentures.

OTC Treatment:
Denture Adhesives (page 141)

Dermatitis, Allergic Contact

Inflammation of the skin that is the result of an allergic reaction. Allergens include the sun, dyes, cosmetics, plants (poison ivy, poison oak), clothing, and medications.

Symptoms:
Inflamed, red, itchy rash; blisters.

OTC Treatments:
Antihistamines (page 72); Antipruritics (page 95); Hydrocortisone (page 96)

See Allergy

Dermatitis, Atopic

See Eczema

Diarrhea

Gastrointestinal distress characterized by frequent bowel movements. It is caused by foreign bacteria in the body acquired by ingesting contaminated food or water. The bacteria upset the function of the large intestine and speed the passage of food through the system. Organisms that cause diarrhea include salmonella, shigella, and the bacteria *Campylobacter jejuni* and *Escherichia coli* (the latter also known as E. coli). Generally, diarrhea lasts two to three days in adults. Diarrhea in infants can be serious, and medical attention should be sought at the first sign of it. The risk of contracting *Traveler's diarrhea* is highest in Africa, Asia, Latin America, and the Middle East.

Symptoms:
Frequent bowel movements of unusually loose or liquid stool.

OTC Treatments:
Antidiarrheal Treatments (page 88); Oral Rehydration Therapy (page 87)

Dysmenorrhea

Cramps that occur during a menstrual period, usually within the first few days. They are thought to be the result of abnormally high levels of the hormone prostaglandin in the body, the hormone that causes the uterus to contract. In general, menstrual cramps are mild, although some women experience extremely painful cramps, which may have an underlying cause such as fibroids or endometriosis.

Symptoms:
Pain in the lower abdomen, backache, nausea, diarrhea, fatigue, headaches.

OTC Treatments:
Analgesics (Internal) (page 56); Pain Relievers, Fever Reducers, and Anti-inflammatories (page 53); Premenstrual and Menstrual Pain Relievers and Menorrhagia Treatments (page 66)

Earache

Pain in the ear caused by infection or congestion of the nose, throat, and jaw, or by the blocking of the eustachian tube, which joins the nose-throat cavity and the inner ear. When the eustachian tube is blocked or congested, pressure builds in the middle ear, causing pain. Earache can also be the result of sudden changes in air pressure (such as during ascent or descent in an airplane), ear injuries, earwax, teething in small children, and by the eruption of wisdom teeth in adults.

Symptoms:
Pain or a feeling of fullness in the ear.

OTC Treatment:
Analgesics (Internal) (page 56)

Ear Infection

See Otitis Media

Ear, Swimmer's

Painful inflammation and irritation of the outer ear canal. In swimmer's ear, tears occur in dry or irritated skin in the outer ear. These tears may become infected, possibly by swimming in polluted water. Cleaning the ears improperly or the use of hair spray or other chemicals may also trigger swimmer's ear. It is not serious if treated properly. It can be prevented by keeping ears dry and avoiding hair spray and other chemicals.

Symptoms:
Itching and pain in the ear canal, discharge of pus from the ear, hearing loss.

OTC Treatment:
Swimmer's Ear Preparations (page 178)

Earwax

A buildup of wax, called *cerumen,* within the ear that is a common cause of hearing loss. The wax is produced in the ear canal and helps trap foreign particles before they enter the ear. Usually, the wax falls out of the ear on its own or is loosened by washing. However, an excess of wax can harden, blocking the ear canal. Earwax should not be removed by inserting any objects into the ear, including cotton swabs.

Symptoms:
Earache, hearing loss, feeling of fullness in the ear, ringing in the ears.

OTC Treatment:
Earwax Removers (page 173)

Eczema

A rash characterized by red, blistered, thickened, scaling skin. It is caused by an allergic reaction to various substances, including wool and detergents, and usually occurs on the head and neck and the insides of the elbows, wrists, and knees. It is not contagious, but it may become long-term, or chronic. It often occurs in people with a history of hay fever and asthma.

Symptoms:
Blistered, crusty skin; skin irritation and itching.

OTC Treatments:
Antipruritics (page 95); Bath Products (page 119); Emollients (page 104); Hydrocortisone (page 96)

See Allergy; Dermatitis, Atopic

Elbow, Tennis

Inflammation of the tendons on the outside of the elbow. It is the result of repeated motions of the arm and forearm, especially those used in tennis. The constant rotation and twisting of the muscles and ligaments irritate the tendons and cause them to become inflamed.

Symptom:
Pain near the elbow joint.

OTC Treatments:
Analgesics (Internal) (page 56); Pain Relievers, Fever Reducers, and Anti-inflammatories (page 53)

Eyes, Bloodshot

Condition in which the whites of the eyes become red because the blood vessels are visible. It can be caused by allergies, lack of sleep, and chemical irritation such as from smoke.

Symptoms:
Red, irritated eyes.

OTC Treatment:
Ophthalmic Lubricants (page 151)

Eyes, Dry

Irritation of the eyes caused by a lack of sufficient tears. It can be caused by certain medications (diuretics, antihistamines, sleeping pills, pain relievers, antidepressants); exposure to dust, pollution, or excess wind; and often occurs in women with reduced estrogen production (such as women approaching or going through menopause). It can lead to more serious eye problems if left untreated, and it may prevent the use of contact lenses.

Symptoms:
Irritated, scratchy eyes; burning sensation; blurred vision; feeling that there's something in the eye.

OTC Treatment:
Ophthalmic Lubricants (page 151)

Eyes, Irritated

Irritation can be caused by infection of the eyelids (blepharitis, characterized by reddened and encrusted eyelids), inflammation of the white of the eye (scleritis, marked by redness and inflammation), and corneal infections (characterized by pain, tears, redness, and a scratchy feeling in the eye). It can also be the result of the presence of a foreign object, or a scratch or tear in the eye, as well as dry eye and eyestrain.

Symptoms:
Red, burning eyes; itching; tearing; sensitivity to light.

OTC Treatment:
Eyewashes (page 154)

See Blepharitis, Scleritis

Eyestrain

Weariness and strain of the eyes caused by holding them in the same position for long periods. It can be caused by close work (reading, sewing, working on a computer), poor lighting, and poor posture. It is often accompanied by headaches and neck and back pain. Eyestrain may signal the need for new glasses.

Symptoms:
Pain and stiffness in shoulders, neck, and back.

OTC Treatment:
Analgesics (Internal) (page 56)

Fatigue

A feeling of excessive weariness. It can be caused by lack of sleep, use of certain medications (such as antihistamines and antidepressants), or by another medical condition (for example, chronic fatigue syndrome, Lyme disease, or anemia). Pregnant women also become easily fatigued.

Symptom:
Excessive weariness.

OTC Treatment:
Stimulants (page 177)

Fever

A body temperature that is higher than normal (average temperature is 98.6°F, but normal temperatures can range from 97°F to 100°F). Elevated body temperature is often a sign of infection, but it can also be the result of exercise, weather, and hormonal changes. In general, professional medical treatment is required if temperature goes above 104°F (102°F in the elderly, and around 101°F in children) or if other symptoms such as sore throat, abnormal breathing, or vomiting are also present. However, individual cases may vary—for instance, people in high-risk categories such as those with immune system disorders should seek professional assistance at lower temperature ranges.

Symptom:
Temperature of more than 100°F.

OTC Treatment:
Antipyretics, or Fever Reducers (page 64)

Flatulence

Excessive production of intestinal gas, which may have a foul odor. The gas is usually released as part of a bowel movement, but it may also be expelled throughout the day. It is caused by swallowing air and by gasses produced in the digestive system as foods are broken down. Foods such as peas, beans, wheat, corn, cabbage, and milk often cause flatulence. Flatulence may also be a sign of lactose intolerance, bacterial overgrowth in the intestines (caused by antibiotics), or a problem in the digestive system.

Symptom:
Excessive production of gas that is released throughout the day.

OTC Treatment:
Antiflatulents (page 90)

Flu

See Influenza

Food Poisoning

Common types of food poisoning include gastroenteritis, in which unwashed or contaminated food or water is ingested, and botulism, which results from the ingestion of a toxin often found in improperly canned foods. Gastroenteritis usually occurs within six hours of eating the contaminated food. It usually is not serious and passes in about twelve hours. Botulism, which occurs twelve to thirty-six hours after eating, is very serious and requires medical attention immediately. It can be fatal.

Symptoms:
Gastroenteritis—characterized by stomach cramps, vomiting, and diarrhea; botulism—headache, muscle weakness, nausea, and vomiting.

OTC Treatment:
Emetics (page 86)

See Gastroenteritis

Foot Odor

A foul-smelling foot, usually the result of odor-causing bacteria that grow in sweat trapped in the shoes, socks, and crevices of the foot. Foot odor may also be caused by athlete's foot and other fungal skin or nail infections.

Symptom:
Foul-smelling feet.

OTC Treatment:
Deodorants (for foot odor) (page 170)

See Athlete's Foot; Infection, Fungal Nail Area; Infection, Fungal Skin

Fracture

A broken bone. Fractured bones are common, the result of the bone being exposed to more force than it can withstand. A simple fracture is one in which the bone is broken but does not break through surrounding tissues. In a compound fracture, the bone has gone through the skin. A comminuted fracture involves a bone shattered into pieces. Broken bones may also be classified by the type of break. For example, a greenstick fracture is one in which the bone doesn't break cleanly. A stress fracture is a thin crack only visible through X-ray.

Symptoms:
Swelling, bruising, a twisted or deformed limb, pain that intensifies when the area is touched. Broken bone may show through skin.

OTC Treatments:
Pain Relievers, Fever Reducers, and Anti-inflammatories (page 53); Analgesics (Internal) (page 56)

Gastroenteritis

An inflammation of the digestive tract caused by irritation by a virus or bacterium. It can be the result of food poisoning, a stomach virus, or another stomach disorder. It usually does not last longer than thirty-six hours.

Symptoms:
Stomach cramps, nausea, vomiting, diarrhea, low-grade fever.

OTC Treatments:
Antidiarrheal Treatments (page 88); Oral Rehydration Therapy (page 87)

See Food Poisoning

Gingivitis

A form of periodontal disease caused by dental plaque that makes the gums sore and tender, so that they bleed easily. Plaque, a mucus that contains bacteria and sugar, collects on teeth along the gumline, irritating the gums. It can lead to more serious forms of gum disease, for example, periodontitis and tooth decay.

Symptoms:
Swollen, sore gums that bleed easily; bad breath; receding gumline.

OTC Treatments:
Toothpastes, Gels, and Powders (page 138); Mouthwashes and Mouth Rinses (for oral health) (page 142)

See Periodontitis

Gout

See Arthritis

Hair Loss

In women, hair may thin gradually with age over the entire head, and there may be loss at the crown or the hairline. In men, the hairline gradually recedes with age, and there may be extensive loss, especially at the crown. Hair loss is usually genetic, though it may also be triggered by hormones, especially in women. Sudden hair loss may be caused by a medication, crash diet, sudden hormonal change (such as menopause), or an underlying medical condition.

Symptoms:
Gradual or sudden hair loss, especially at the hairline and the crown of the head.

OTC Treatment:
Hair Growth Stimulant (page 135)

Halitosis

Foul-smelling breath may be caused by the breakdown of food particles in the mouth by bacteria; by gum disease or infection; or by residue of strong-smelling foods such as garlic and onions in your mouth and in your bloodstream. It may also be a sign of lung disease, digestive problems, and a number of other serious disorders.

Symptom:
Bad breath.

OTC Treatments:
Toothpastes, Gels, and Powders (page 138); Mouthwashes and Mouth Rinses (for oral health) (page 142)

Hay Fever

An allergic reaction that occurs in the upper respiratory tract, usually caused by inhalation of pollens of seasonal plants and trees. The reaction causes the body to produce chemicals known as histamines, which irritate the eyes, nose, mouth, and throat. It is not always caused by hay, and there is no fever involved. It usually occurs in spring or fall, but can happen at any time.

Symptoms:
Itchy, watery eyes; runny nose; congestion; bouts of repeated sneezing; coughing.

OTC Treatments:
Antihistamines (page 72); Cold, Cough, and Allergy Remedies (page 68); Topical Decongestants (page 70)

See Allergy

Headache

Pain within the head caused by nerve aggravation (tension headache) or expanded blood vessels (vascular headache). In a tension headache, prolonged contraction of the muscles in the shoulders and neck are thought to cause pain by reducing blood flow to the brain. A vascular headache occurs when expansion or contraction of blood vessels in the head irritates surrounding nerves. A migraine headache is a type of vascular headache. Headaches may last only a few minutes or (in the case of migraines) up to seventy-two hours.

Symptoms:
Tension headaches are marked by constant, moderate pain that does not grow worse with activity; vascular headaches occur on one side of the head more often than the other, with a throbbing, pounding pain. Vascular headaches may be accompanied by nausea, vomiting, and sensitivity to light.

OTC Treatments:
Analgesics (Internal) (page 56); Pain Relievers, Fever Reducers, and Anti-inflammatories (page 53)

Heartburn

A digestive disorder in which stomach acid comes in contact with the sensitive lining of the esophagus, causing a burning pain in the chest. Heartburn often occurs in pregnant women or after meals containing fried or fatty foods or highly acidic foods such as citrus fruits and tomato products. It may also be caused by some medications, smoking, obesity, and stress. It is often mistaken for a heart attack.

Symptom:
Burning pain behind the breastbone.

OTC Treatment:
Antacids (page 81)

Hemorrhoid

The inflammation of a vein in the rectum or around the anus caused by pressure in the region. Hemorrhoids can be internal or external. They are common in people over age fifty and in pregnant women.

Symptoms:
Rectal bleeding, tenderness, and itching; painful bowel movements; feeling of fullness after a bowel movement.

OTC Treatments:
Hemorrhoidal Preparations (page 106); Local Anesthetics (page 97); Astringents (page 118); Hydrocortisone (page 96); Skin Protectants (page 126)

Hives

Itchy, red welts that appear usually on the face or the trunk of the body, less frequently on the scalp, hands, and feet. Hives usually disappear within twenty-four hours, but they often appear and reappear in clusters over several weeks. They are usually the result of an allergic reaction to a substance, but they may appear for many other reasons, such as stress or illness.

Symptoms:
Red, itchy welts on the skin.

OTC Treatments:
Antipruritics (page 95); Antihistamines (page 72); Hydrocortisone (page 96)

See Allergy

Impetigo

A skin infection caused by staphylococci and/or streptococci bacteria. The bacteria usually infect a cut, scrape, or insect bite, causing a red, blistering sore that grows, developing a crust. The fluid within the sore is contagious and can be spread to other parts of the body and to other people. It usually occurs on the face or extremities.

Symptoms:
Red, blistering sore; itching; sore with a yellow or gray crust.

OTC Treatment:
Antibiotics (page 113)

Indigestion

A general term used to describe discomfort in the stomach and abdomen, also called dyspepsia. It can be brought on by smoking and eating too much, or it may be a symptom of a more serious disorder, such as a peptic ulcer or gallbladder disease.

Symptoms:
Discomfort in the abdomen, heartburn, feeling of fullness.

OTC Treatment:
Antacids (page 81)

Infection

The invasion of the body or part of it by disease-causing microorganisms—such as bacteria or viruses—that reproduce and multiply; a disease caused by such an invasion.

Symptoms:
Fever, pain, inflammation, redness.

OTC Treatments:
Pain Relievers, Fever Reducers, and Anti-inflammatories (page 53); Analgesics (Internal) (page 56); Antibiotics (page 113)

Infection, Fungal Nail Area

Infection of the bed of the nail by fungus spores, typically *tinea unguium*. Fungal nail infections can be contracted by a complication of athlete's foot or walking barefoot in well-trafficked places. Nails become thick and discolored. The infection can continue indefinitely, possibly causing the nail to become detached or destroyed.

Symptoms:
Thick, dull fingernails or toenails; discoloration of nails; crumbling nails.

OTC Treatment:
Fungal Nail Area Treatments (page 124)

Infection, Fungal Skin

Common disorder in which fungi called dermatophytes infect dead skin or hair. Types of infection include *tinea corporis* (ringworm), *tinea cruris* (jock itch), and *tinea pedis* (athlete's foot). The fungi thrive in dark, damp areas, and are transmitted through contact with wet surfaces, such as those in a locker room or by a public swimming pool. Fungal infections are usually not serious, though they may recur after treatment. They may also spread to the nails.

Symptoms:
Soft, red, scaling skin; itching; cracking and peeling of skin.

OTC Treatment:
Antifungals (page 114)

See Athlete's Foot; Infection, Fungal Nail Area; Jock Itch; Ringworm

Infection, Oral

Infection of the oral cavity, including the gums and tongue. These often originate as simple lesions, or injuries to the tissue, resulting from dental procedures, orthodontic work and/or apparatus, accidents, and the like; however, given the amount of bacteria ever-present in the mouth, these minor wounds can become infected.

Symptoms:
Red, sore tissue; inflammation.

OTC Treatments:
Oral Debriding Rinses (page 144); Canker Sore Treatments (page 147)

See Wound Infection; Sore, Canker

Inflammation

The response of the body's tissues to irritation or injury.

Symptoms:
Redness, heat, swelling, pain (all at the site), sometimes loss of function.

OTC Treatments:
Pain Relievers, Fever Reducers, and Anti-inflammatories (page 53); Counterirritants (page 58)

Influenza

Infection of the respiratory tract by the influenza, or flu, virus. Influenza is a contagious airborne virus spread by coughs, sneezes, and breathing. It is similar to a cold, but comes on much more rapidly and is more severe. The flu usually lasts ten days, but, if left untreated, it could develop into pneumonia or have other complications.

Symptoms:
Runny nose, fever, sore throat, excessive mucus production, coughing, aching joints, appetite loss.

OTC Treatments:
Cold, Cough, and Allergy Remedies (page 68); Analgesics (Internal) (page 56); Lozenges and Mouthwashes/Gargles (Sore Throat Relief) (page 77); Antipyretics, or Fever Reducers (page 64)

Insomnia

Inability to sleep or stay asleep caused by a variety of factors, including stress, certain medications, and eating and exercise habits. Insomnia can be intermittent and short-term, lasting for three weeks or less, or it may become long-term, lasting for more than six weeks, usually for months or years.

Symptoms:
Inability to sleep or stay asleep.

OTC Treatment:
Sleep Aids (page 175)

Jock Itch

A fungal infection, also called *tinea cruris,* that occurs in the groin and anal area. It is contracted through contact with wet surfaces where the fungi thrive, such as those in locker rooms or showers, or by sharing towels. It may recur after treatment.

Symptoms:
Soft, red scales in the groin area and on the thighs; itching; patches of cracked, peeling skin.

OTC Treatment:
Antifungals (page114)

See Infection, Fungal Skin

Knee, Injured

An injury to the knee joint, a hinge composed of the femur, tibia, and fibula bones and the patella,

or kneecap. Common injuries include *chondromalacia patella,* or runner's knees, in which stress causes inflammation and softens the cartilage under the kneecap; knee sprain, in which the ligaments that hold the joint together are injured; and *patellar tendinitis,* or jumper's knee, in which the tendon connecting the kneecap to the lower leg, or tibia, is overused and becomes painful.

Symptoms:
Pain in the knee, especially during activity; difficulty kneeling.

OTC Treatments:
Counterirritants (page 58); Pain Relievers, Fever Reducers, and Anti-inflammatories (page 53)

Knee, Jumper's

Caused by overuse of the tendon connecting the kneecap to the lower leg, or tibia. It is brought on by frequent jumping up and down, in an activity such as basketball or volleyball. It is also called *patellar tendinitis.*

Symptoms:
Pain below the kneecap when jumping, difficulty kneeling.

OTC Treatments:
Counterirritants (page 58); Pain Relievers, Fever Reducers, and Anti-inflammatories (page 53)

Knee, Runner's

An injury that occurs when repeated stress causes inflammation and softens the cartilage under the kneecap. Causes include a flattened foot, which, when running, causes the lower leg to rotate inward and the kneecap to slide from side to side and rub against the groove of the femur. Prolonged sitting, weak thigh muscles, trauma, muscle imbalance, and neglected injury can also aggravate the cartilage. It is also known as *chondromalacia patella.*

Symptom:
Pain in the knee.

OTC Treatments:
Counterirritants (page 58); Pain Relievers, Fever Reducers, and Anti-inflammatories (page 53)

Laceration

See Cut

Laryngitis

Inflammation of the larynx (voice box) and vocal cords that may be caused by overuse, infection, or irritation from smoke or pollution. The inflammation causes the voice to become hoarse and weak. It may also accompany another illness, such as a cold, the flu, or pneumonia. Viral laryngitis usually disappears on its own within three days. If the laryngitis is caused by overuse or an underlying factor such as smoking, you may need to take steps to stop smoking as well as see a professional for further treatment.

Symptoms:
Hoarseness, tickling feeling in the throat, sore throat, fever, dry cough.

OTC Treatments:
Analgesics (Internal) (page 56); Lozenges and Mouthwashes/Gargles (Sore Throat Relief) (page 77)

Lice

Small parasites that live on the body (body lice), head (head lice), and pubic hair (pubic lice, or crabs). Clusters of the lice eggs, called nits, are often found attached to hair. While lice are not dangerous, they do bite, causing itching and discomfort. They spread rapidly through casual contact. Children often pick up lice at school from contact with other children.

Symptoms:
Itching, small red bites on the skin, nits (which may resemble dandruff or tiny buds) attached to hair.

OTC Treatment:
Lice Treatments (page 135)

Lips, Chapped

Dry, cracked, and reddened lips caused by lack of moisture in the skin. Often wind and cold weather cause lips to chap.

Symptoms:
Dry, cracked, rough lips.

OTC Treatments:
Sunscreens (page 127); Emollients (page 104)

Miliaria

See Rash, Prickly Heat

Motion Sickness

Nausea that occurs as a result of being in motion in a car, airplane, or ship. Motion sickness usually occurs during travel, especially when the ride is rough.

Symptoms:
Nausea, vomiting.

OTC Treatment:
Antiemetics (page 84)

Mouth, Dry

A dryness in the mouth. This is most often a side effect of a drug such as an antidepressant or a therapy such as chemotherapy, a cancer treatment that involves injecting drugs into the system to kill cancer cells. Dry mouth may make eating difficult, resulting in poor nutritional intake.

Symptom:
Dry mouth.

OTC Treatment:
Artificial Saliva (page 142)

Muscle Cramp

A painful spasm that occurs when muscle fibers contract suddenly, usually during exercise. Cramps can last a few seconds or several hours. They generally occur in the legs. Causes include injury; a deficiency in salt and other minerals, especially potassium; slowing of the blood supply to the muscle by repeated muscular contraction; and hyperventilation.

Symptoms:
Sudden pain in a muscle, a lump of contracted muscle that's visible through the skin.

OTC Treatments:
Counterirritants (page 58); Pain Relievers, Fever Reducers, and Anti-inflammatories (page 53)

Muscle Soreness

Stiffness, fatigue, and moderate pain in a muscle, usually caused by working out too hard or too long, or not warming up or cooling down properly before and after a workout. During exercise, the muscles burn lactic acid, which is then removed as a waste product via the bloodstream. Stopping abruptly during exercise, without cooling down, causes the lactic acid to remain in the muscle, which then causes soreness.

Symptoms:
Sore, stiff muscles.

OTC Treatments:
Counterirritants (page 58); Pain Relievers, Fever Reducers, and Anti-inflammatories (page 53)

Nasal Drainage (Runny Nose)

Excessive mucus production, draining from the nostrils. Nasal secretions are usually the result of an upper respiratory infection or allergic reaction. In these instances, a runny nose is the body's method to rid itself of the attacking virus or to eliminate the nasal irritant.

Symptom:
Runny nose.

OTC Treatments:
Antihistamines (page 72); Cold, Cough, and Allergy Remedies (page 68)

Nasal Passages, Congestion of the

Nasal congestion is a symptom of a cold, allergies, or another condition, in which overproduction of mucus by swollen vessels and tissues (triggered by infection) causes the nasal passages to become filled. Nasal congestion may make it difficult or impos-sible to breathe through the nose, and the nose may drip or run. It may lead to other conditions, such as sore throat (because all breathing must be done through the mouth, drying out the membranes there) or earache (because the blocked passages cause a buildup of pressure in the middle ear).

Symptoms:
Difficulty breathing, feeling of fullness in the head.

OTC Treatments:
Cold, Cough, and Allergy Remedies (page 68); Topical Decongestants (page 70)

Nasal Passages, Dry

Condition that occurs when the membranes lining the nasal passages become dry and easily irritated. It may occur during a cold or because of allergies or breathing overly dry or cold air. It may lead to a nosebleed, in which the lining cracks and starts to bleed.

Symptoms:
Irritated, painful nasal passages.

OTC Treatment:
Nasal Moisturizers (page 72)

Nausea and Vomiting

Vomiting is the act of regurgitating the contents of the stomach through the mouth. Nausea is the urge to vomit. Nausea and vomiting accompany a stomach virus, morning sickness in pregnant women, certain medications, food poisoning, and drinking or eating to excess. More serious causes include appendicitis, stomach ulcers, and hepatitis.

Symptoms:
Strong desire to throw up; actual vomiting.

OTC Treatments:
Antiemetics (page 84); Oral Rehydration Therapy (page 87)

Nicotine Addiction

Dependence on the presence of nicotine in the body's system, usually supplied through smoking or chewing tobacco. In one who is addicted, nicotine levels in the blood must remain constant; a drop in nicotine levels produces irritability, insomnia, tremors, and other withdrawal symptoms, which disappear once the urge for nicotine is satisfied. Nicotine addiction is dangerous because of the increased risks of cancer, heart disease, and other serious conditions that come with smoking and chewing tobacco.

Symptoms:
Dependence on having drug in system in order to function; irritability, anxiety, insomnia, tremors, chills when levels of drug drop.

OTC Treatment:
Smoking Cessation Aids (page 176)

Nipples, Cracked

Cracked nipples that occur in some women during breast-feeding. Nipples may become sore, then crack and possibly bleed because of the pressure caused by the infant's sucking and the effects of moisture from the baby's saliva and the breast milk on the skin.

Symptoms:
Cracked, bleeding nipples; painful breast-feeding.

OTC Treatment:
Skin Protectants (page 126)

Obesity

Defined as weighing 20 percent more than the normal, healthy body weight for a person's height and frame. Obesity can contribute to heart disease, high blood pressure, diabetes, arthritis, and certain types of cancer. It may be a result of a high-fat or high-calorie diet, lack of exercise, a slow metabolism, or a medical condition.

Symptoms:
Weight of more than 20 percent above the recommended, healthy weight for your height and frame.

OTC Treatment:
Appetite Suppressants (page 167)

Otitis Media

Condition that occurs when fluid and pressure build up in the middle ear as the result of an infection in the nose, throat, and jaw, or by the blockage of the eustachian tube. Mild forms may involve minor pain caused by a buildup of pressure but no true infection. In more serious cases, the infected middle ear becomes filled with fluid and pus, which may rupture the eardrum and cause permanent hearing loss. Ear infections may accompany upper respiratory infections.

Symptoms:
Sharp, continuous pain in the ear; feeling of fullness in the ear; hearing loss, fever, and chills.

OTC Treatments:
Analgesics (Internal) (page 56); Antipyretics, or Fever Reducers (page 64)

Pain, Chronic

Pain that has lasted longer than six months. Pain can be the result of severe illness such as cancer, angina, or arthritis, or it can affect those who are otherwise healthy and show no signs of illness or injury. Older adults are more likely to suffer chronic pain than younger people. In some, but not all, cases there may be a psychological factor contributing to pain.

Symptom:
Persistent pain that lasts longer than six months.

OTC Treatments:
Analgesics (Internal) (page 56); Pain Relievers, Fever Reducers, and Anti-inflammatories (page 53); Antiarthritis Treatments (page 62)

Periodontal Disease

See Gingivitis; Periodontitis

Periodontitis

A form of periodontal disease in which the gums and the socket of the tooth become inflamed and possibly infected. It is the result of untreated gingivitis and if left untreated may result in loss of the tooth. It is usually painless.

Symptoms:
Swollen, sore gums that bleed easily; bad breath; receding gumline; sensitive teeth; loose teeth.

OTC Treatment:
Mouthwashes and Mouth Rinses (for oral health) (page 142)

Pinkeye

See Conjunctivitis

Pinworms

Parasites that live in the lower intestine. Pinworms lay eggs around the anus at night. The eggs can be spread to other people or can even reinfect the host if they are spread to the mouth via contaminated food, drink, or hands. Swallowed eggs hatch, producing another cycle of pinworms. (Careful handwashing following defecation and avoidance of scratching can help prevent transmission.) Pinworms are not dangerous, only irritating.

Symptoms:
Itching around the anus, insomnia, possible gastrointestinal distress.

OTC Treatment:
Anthelmintics (page 165)

Plaque, Dental

A mucus that contains bacteria and sugar that collects on teeth along the gumline. Plaque causes gingivitis, a condition in which the gums become sore and bleed. It is the predecessor of tartar, a hard, chalky mineral substance that forms on teeth.

Symptoms:
Sore gums that bleed easily, bad breath, receding gumline.

OTC Treatments:
Toothpastes, Gels, and Powders (page 138); Mouthwashes and Mouth Rinses (for oral health) (page 142)

Poison Ivy, Poison Oak, and Poison Sumac

A rash of itchy, oozing blisters that occurs after contact with *urushiol,* a resin that covers the leaves of the poison ivy, poison oak, and poison sumac plants. (The rash is not spread as a result of washing or scratching open rash blisters.) The rash may develop several days after contact and lasts one to two weeks. Some people are more allergic to *urushiol* resin than others; some have no allergic reaction at all.

Symptoms:
Red, oozing blisters; swelling.

OTC Treatments:
Hydrocortisone (page 96); Poison Ivy, Poison Oak, and Poison Sumac Treatments (page 110); Astringents (page 118); Local Anesthetics (page 97)

Poisoning

The condition or physical state produced by the injecting of, ingesting of, inhaling of, or other exposure to a toxic, or poisonous, substance. A poison is any substance that, even when injected, ingested, inhaled, or absorbed into the body in small amounts impairs health or destroys life. While some poisonous substances are familiar—pesticides and household chemicals, for instance, which bear labels to that effect—many substances (including medicines) are poisonous when taken in large quantities. Aspirin and sleep medications are good examples. In general, treatment consists of getting the substance out of the body before it can be absorbed. Treatment varies according to the toxin—ranging from induction of vomiting to administering an antidote to render the substance inert or to prevent its absorption by the body. In all cases, if a qualified medical professional is not available, the nearest poison control center should be contacted immediately.

Symptoms:
Highly variable, depending upon the substance—redness or burning around the mouth; breath that smells like chemicals; difficulty breathing; vomiting, abdominal pain, or other gastrointestinal distress—in general, unusual medical symptoms.

OTC Treatment:
Emetics (in the case of some poisonings and with extreme caution) (page 86)

Premenstrual Syndrome (PMS)

A collection of symptoms that occur in some women each month in the week before menstruation begins. PMS is usually attributed to the hormonal changes of the menstrual cycle, though no one is sure of its exact cause. Stress, diet, and exercise may also affect PMS symptoms.

Symptoms:
Tension, irritability, headaches, water retention, breast soreness, aching, headaches, diarrhea, or constipation.

OTC Treatments:
Premenstrual and Menstrual Pain Relievers and Menorrhagia Treatments (page 66); Diuretics (page 171)

Psoriasis

Scaling of the skin caused by overproduction of skin cells. The scales may have a silverish appearance and can be removed by softening and scrubbing them. The thickening, pitting, or crumbling of fingernails may also be the result of psoriasis. The condition is thought to be the result of a genetic predisposition. It is not contagious and flares up and recedes at intervals.

Symptoms:
Patches of thick, silvery scales on the skin.

OTC Treatments:
Psoriasis Treatments (page 125); Bath Products (page 119); Emollients (page 104)

Rash, Diaper

A rash of tiny pimples that occurs on the buttocks, thighs, and genitals of infants as the result of dampness and contact between bacteria and urine and the skin. It occurs most often in children who wear disposable diapers.

Symptoms:
Patches of small, red pimples; soreness, no itching. Sores may smell of ammonia.

OTC Treatments:
Diaper Rash Protectants (page 122); Astringents (page 118)

Rash, Prickly Heat

A rash of tiny bumps on a patch of red skin, also called *miliaria*. Prickly heat comes on as a result of heavy perspiration; the moisture damages the surface of the skin and prevents the flow of additional perspiration, which becomes trapped under the skin. It commonly occurs on the neck and in the armpit and groin areas.

Symptoms:
Tiny, red bumps; red patches of skin; itching, stinging sensation.

OTC Treatment:
Prickly Heat (Miliaria) Treatments (page 124)

Rash, Skin

See Dermatitis, Allergic Contact; Eczema

Repetitive Motion Injuries

Disorders that include carpal tunnel syndrome, tendinitis, tenosynovitis, and tennis elbow. Repetitive motion injuries are caused by constant, repeated small movements of the fingers, wrists, or other joints, which inflame surrounding tissue and put pressure on nerves. They are common in people who must do repetitive motions as part of their jobs, for example, operating a computer, cash register, or machine on an assembly line.

Symptoms:
Pain in the joint, a feeling of numbness, a burning sensation in the joint.

OTC Treatment:
Pain Relievers, Fever Reducers, and Anti-inflammatories (page 53)

See Carpal Tunnel Syndrome; Tendinitis; Tenosynovitis; Elbow, Tennis

Ringworm

A fungal skin infection, also called *tinea corporis,* characterized by itchy, red rings on the scalp and skin, usually on the torso or back, face, or thighs. As the infection spreads, the rings expand. Ringworm is extremely contagious and may be contracted by using a contaminated comb or hat. It may recur after treatment.

Symptoms:
Slightly raised, irregular red rings.

OTC Treatment:
Antifungals (page 114)

Scar

A mark left in the skin after the healing of an incision or wound.

OTC Treatment:
Emollients (page 104)

Scleritis

Inflammation of the sclera, the tough white outer coat of the eyeball.

Symptoms:
Red, burning eyes (especially the white portion).

OTC Treatment:
Eyewashes (page 154)

See Eyes, Irritated

Scrape

See Abrasion

Seborrhea

A condition characterized by oily, scaling, sometimes reddened skin, also known as seborrheic dermatitis. It usually occurs along the sides of the nostrils, between the eyebrows, above the ears, and within folds of skin. Some people are prone to the condition, which usually persists indefinitely, though it can be kept under control with treatment. Dandruff is a form of seborrhea.

Symptoms:
Oily, scaling skin; reddened skin; persistent dandruff.

OTC Treatments:
Seborrhea Treatments (page 132); Bath Products (page 119); Dandruff Shampoos (page 132); Emollients (page 104)

See Dandruff

Shingles

An infection caused by the herpes zoster virus. Herpes zoster initially causes chicken pox, but it may stay dormant in the system and then recur again years later as shingles. It is characterized by a limited rash of small blisters that is preceded by a tingling sensation. Shingles generally lasts two to three weeks, and it is usually not serious. It is most common in people over age sixty.

Symptoms:
Tingling sensation; limited rash of small, red blisters.

OTC Treatment:
Counterirritants (page 58)

Sinusitis

Infection of the lining of one or more sinus cavities. The infection causes the lining of the sinus to swell, causing breathing difficulty and preventing drainage of mucus. The pressure of the blockage and the swelling causes pain within the head. Sinusitis can be bacterial, fungal, or viral in nature. It usually occurs after a cold. If it is not treated it can become chronic.

Symptoms:
Pain in the eyes and face, breathing difficulty, fever.

OTC Treatments:
Cold, Cough, and Allergy Remedies (page 68); Topical Decongestants (page 70)

Skin, Dry

Dry, cracked, itchy skin that occurs when it loses its natural moisture and oil. It most commonly occurs on the lower legs, arms, and thighs. Cold weather and wind often cause cracked skin because of rapid evaporation of moisture from the skin. Heels may become cracked because of calluses or fungal infection as well.

Symptoms:
Red, dry, cracked skin; bleeding; itching; irritation.

OTC Treatments:
Dermatitis/Dry Skin Preparations (page 103); Bath Products (page 119); Emollients (page 104); Hydrocortisone (page 96)

Smoking

See Nicotine Addiction

Sore, Canker

Red, sore ulcer with a white or yellow center located within the mouth. These usually last one to two weeks, and they often appear at the site of a minor injury in the mouth, such as a bite or cut, or at times of stress and fatigue. They may be the result of an immune system response.

Symptoms:
Painful, red ulcers in the mouth, with a white or yellow center.

OTC Treatments:
Canker Sore Treatments (page 147); Oral Debriding Rinses (page 144)

Sore, Cold

A small, painful blister on an area of red, raised skin caused by the herpes simplex virus. They are most likely to appear on the lips, the outside of the mouth, or on the nose, cheeks, or fingers, and usually last seven to ten days. The virus is transmitted through contact with someone who has the infection. Cold sores may recur during menstruation, fever, or after sun exposure. They are also called fever blisters.

Symptoms:
Small, painful blisters on an area of red, raised skin, especially on the lips and around the mouth.

OTC Treatments:
Cold Sore/Fever Blister Preparations (page 147); Local Anesthetics (page 97)

Sprain

A tearing or overstretching of ligaments, the supporting tissues of muscles and bones, in a joint, resulting in pain and swelling. Sprains occur when a joint is forced beyond its usual range of motion; for example, when it is twisted during athletic activities, or because of a fall or other injury. The ankle—a common site for a sprain—is, like the knee, a hinge joint composed of ligaments, tendons, and connective fibers. Knee sprains are less common in running than in contact sports and skiing, which can subject the hyperextended knee to sideways trauma. Sprains may be mild, moderate, or severe (depending upon the amount of damage to these components).

Symptoms:
Pain, swelling, and restricted movement in the joints.

OTC Treatments:
Counterirritants (page 58); Pain Relievers, Fever Reducers, and Anti-inflammatories (page 53); Analgesics (Internal) (page 56)

Sting, Bee

An area of redness, swelling, or itching after a sting by a bee, wasp, or yellow jacket. Reactions to stings vary according to the insect and the sensitivity of the person. Those severely allergic may experience anaphylaxis, a severe reaction that requires immediate treatment or may cause death. With minor stings, the reaction is temporary and local—meaning that the redness, swelling, and/or itching appear at the site of the sting and then disappear over a period of days.

Symptoms:
Pain, itching, and swelling in area of sting. Anaphylactic reaction includes difficulty breathing, swelling, low blood pressure, and unconsciousness.

OTC Treatments:
Insect Bite and Sting Treatments (page 108); Hydrocortisone (page 96); Astringents (page 118); Anesthetics (page 95); Antipruritics (page 95); Topical Antihistamines (page 99)

See Allergy (although prescription drugs may be required instead if an allergic reaction is triggered)

Sunburn

A burn on the surface of the skin caused by overexposure to ultraviolet rays, usually from the sun. UV rays are not filtered by clouds and can cause sunburn on overcast days and in the winter as well as the summer. Sunburn generally heals in one to two weeks, although recurrent sunburn damage greatly increases the risk of skin cancer. Those with light or red-colored hair, light skin, or blue or green eyes are most likely to burn easily.

Symptoms:
Red, swollen skin that is painful to touch; blisters (in severe cases).

OTC Treatments:
Bath Products (page 119); Burn/Sunburn Treatments (page 101); Emollients (page 104); Topical Antihistamines (page 99); Antipruritics (page 95)

Tartar

A hard, chalky mineral substance that forms on teeth along and below the gumline. It is the result of plaque, a mucus that contains bacteria and sugar that collects on teeth along the gums. The plaque combines with saliva, forming the mineral deposits of tartar. Tartar can cause gum disease, and can result in tooth decay and loss of teeth. It is also called *calculus.*

Symptoms:
Sore gums that bleed easily, bad breath, receding gumline.

OTC Treatments:
Toothpastes, Gels, and Powders (page 138); Mouthwashes and Mouth Rinses (for oral health) (page 142)

Teething

The period when infants' teeth first grow through the gums. Teething may cause pain, crying, and irritability in the baby, though some have no difficulties. Teething does not cause other health problems, such as diarrhea or fever.

Symptoms:
Teeth protruding from gums; increased saliva production; tendency to chew on objects; pain; discomfort.

OTC Treatments:
Toothache and Teething Preparations (page 145); Local Anesthetics (page 97)

Tendinitis

Inflammation of the tissue that attaches the muscles to the bone. It may occur in most joints as the result of repetitive motions, such as those used by people operating computers, cash registers, or machines on assembly lines.

Symptom:
Pain in the joint.

OTC Treatments:
Pain Relievers, Fever Reducers, and Anti-inflammatories (page 53); Counterirritants (page 58)

Tenosynovitis

Inflammation of the membranes that line a joint. Tenosynovitis is a repetitive motion injury, brought on by small, constant movements, such as those used by people operating a computer, cash register, or machine on an assembly line.

Symptom:
Pain in the joint.

OTC Treatments:
Pain Relievers, Fever Reducers, and Anti-inflammatories (page 53); Counterirritants (page 58)

Throat, Sore

Pain or discomfort in the throat that can be caused by inflammation, infection, overuse, or a number of other conditions. A sore throat is often a symptom of another problem, such as a cold, the flu, laryngitis, nasal congestion, or another problem. It may also occur when the throat is irritated by smoke, pollution, heavy alcohol consumption, or excessive talking.

Symptoms:
Pain or discomfort in the throat; difficulty swallowing; hoarseness; dry or tickling feeling in the throat.

OTC Treatment:
Lozenges and Mouthwashes/Gargles (Sore Throat Relief) (page 77)

Toenail, Ingrown

A toenail that has grown into the flesh of the foot. This most often occurs in the big toe. It is caused by curved toenails, shoes that fit poorly, or toenails that are cut improperly. An ingrown toenail may result in an infection in the surrounding tissue.

Symptoms:
A swollen, red, painful toe.

OTC Treatment:
Ingrown Toenail Treatment (page 174)

Tooth, Discoloration of

A tooth that has become discolored or stained. Discoloration can be caused by smoking, drinking dark beverages such as coffee and tea, or a hereditary disposition. A mother's use of the drug tetracycline during pregnancy may also result in discolored teeth in her child.

Symptoms:
Yellowish or brownish discolored teeth.

OTC Treatments:
Tooth Whiteners (page 140); Toothpastes, Gels, and Powders (page 138)

Tooth, Sensitivity of

Pain that occurs when teeth come in contact with hot or cold temperatures or sweet foods. Tooth sensitivity occurs when the enamel of the tooth thins, either as a result of tooth decay or through the normal wear and tear of aging. It often occurs at sites where the gums have receded, revealing unprotected areas of the teeth. Teeth may be bonded or treated with mineral solutions to strengthen enamel.

Symptoms:
Toothache that occurs with exposure to hot or cold temperatures or when eating sweet foods.

OTC Treatment:
Tooth Desensitizers (page 139)

Toothache

Pain that occurs when the pulp at the center of a tooth becomes inflamed or irritated by infection. It is usually caused by tooth decay that has reached the inner layers of the tooth. The soft pulp within the tooth that contains the nerves then becomes infected and swells (called a tooth abscess), causing pressure and pain. The pain disappears if the pulp of the tooth dies; however, the abscess may recur.

Symptom:
Pain within a tooth.

OTC Treatments:
Toothache and Teething Preparations (page 145); Analgesics (Internal) (page 56)

Ulcer, Duodenal

Raw, open sore in the lining of the duodenum (the first part of the small intestine). Duodenal ulcers occur when the balance of stomach acids and juices is disrupted and the stomach acid and pepsin (an enzyme) break through the protective membrane lining of the small intestine, causing pain. The latest research has found that most cases of ulcers are actually related to an infection with a common bacterium, *Helicobacter pylori*. Duodenal ulcers are the most common type of peptic ulcer.

Symptoms:
Gnawing or burning feeling in the upper abdomen or under the breastbone, loss of appetite, bloating, nausea, vomiting, pain within three hours of eating, temporary relief with milk or antacids, black stool (sign of a bleeding ulcer).

OTC Treatment:
Antacids (page 81)

See Ulcer, Gastric; Ulcer, Peptic

Ulcer, Gastric

Raw, open sore in the lining of the stomach. Gastric ulcers occur when the balance of stomach acids and juices is disrupted and the stomach acid and pepsin (an enzyme) break through the protective membrane lining of the stomach, causing pain. They may be caused by a weakness in the protective membrane that lines the stomach, or (less frequently) by overproduction of stomach acids. Gastric ulcers are a type of peptic ulcer. The latest research has found that most cases of ulcers are actually related to an infection with a common bacterium, *Helicobacter pylori*. It may be difficult to distinguish a gastric ulcer from a duodenal ulcer, an ulcer located in the first part of the small intestine.

Symptoms:
Gnawing or burning feeling in the upper abdomen or under the breastbone, loss of appetite, bloating,

nausea, vomiting, pain within three hours of eating, temporary relief with milk or antacids, black stool (sign of a bleeding ulcer).

OTC Treatment:
Antacids (page 81)

See Ulcer, Duodenal; Ulcer, Peptic

Ulcer, Peptic

Raw, open sore in the lining of the stomach or duodenum (the first part of the small intestine). An ulcer can form anywhere exposed to gastric acid and pepsin, a digestive enzyme that helps break down protein—hence the derivation of the broad term "peptic ulcer." Peptic ulcers occur when the balance of stomach acids and juices is disrupted and the stomach acid and pepsin break through the protective membrane lining of the digestive tract, causing pain. The latest research has found that most cases of ulcers are actually related to an infection with a common bacterium, *Helicobacter pylori.* Ulcers in the stomach are called *gastric ulcers,* while ulcers in the duodenum are called *duodenal ulcers.* While many link ulcers with stress, it is more likely that ulcers are hereditary.

Symptoms:
Gnawing or burning feeling in the stomach, loss of appetite, bloating, nausea, vomiting, pain within three hours of eating, temporary relief with milk or antacids.

OTC Treatment:
Antacids (page 81)

See Ulcer, Duodenal; Ulcer, Gastric

Urethritis

Inflammation of the urethra usually caused by bacteria that have spread from the rectum to the urethra. The bacteria then grow there, causing soreness and pain during urination. Urethritis is not dangerous when treated promptly and is more common in women than men. It can be diagnosed through examination of a urine sample.

Symptoms:
Frequent urge to urinate; burning urination; blood in the urine; feeling of fullness in the bladder, even after urination; fever, chills, and nausea.

OTC Treatment:
Urinary Pain Relievers (page 178)

Urinary Tract, Infection of the

Inflammation of the bladder, urethra, or kidney, usually caused by bacteria that have spread from the rectum to the urethra and bladder. Infection of the bladder is known as cystitis; infection of the urethra as urethritis; and infection of the kidney (a more serious condition) as pyelonephritis. Urinary tract infections (UTIs) are more common in women than men. They are diagnosed through examination of a urine sample.

Symptoms:
Frequent urge to urinate; burning urination; blood in the urine; feeling of fullness in the bladder, even after urination; fever, chills, and nausea.

OTC Treatment:
Urinary Pain Relievers (page 178)

See Cystitis; Urethritis

Vaginitis

Inflammation of the vagina. It is usually caused by an infection. Types of vaginitis include trichomoniasis (caused by a parasite), yeast infections (caused by an overgrowth of yeast), and bacterial vaginosis (caused by a number of organisms, including *Gardnerella vaginalis*). Vaginitis may be sexually transmitted. It can be identified through a culture or a microscopic examination of vaginal fluids.

Symptoms:
Discharge from the vagina, itching, irritation, painful intercourse, abdominal pain, vaginal bleeding.

OTC Treatments:
Vaginal Antifungals (page 179); Vaginal Antipruritics (page 180)

See Yeast Infection

Vertigo

A sensation of spinning or whirling motion; a feeling of faintness or an inability to keep normal balance in a standing or sitting position. The term "vertigo" is inaccurately used to describe dizziness or faintness. Vertigo results from a disturbance of inner ear canals or the nerve tracts leading from them. While healthy people can experience vertigo—such as when sailing or when on amusement park rides—the condition may indicate a number of diseases. Often vertigo accompanies an infection such as the flu or otitis media and usually subsides as the infection clears up. Depending upon its cause—a more serious disease, for instance—vertigo may be accompanied by nausea, vomiting, unsteadiness, or tinnitus (ringing in the ears).

Symptom:
Dizziness.

OTC Treatment:
Antiemetics (page 84)

Vomiting

See Nausea and Vomiting

Vulvitis

Inflammation and irritation of the vulva (the outer genitals of a woman). It can be triggered by a medication, a bacterial or fungal infection, an allergy to a detergent or vaginal spray, or poor hygiene. Vulvitis is generally not serious, although it may become chronic. Treatment depends upon a practitioner's specific diagnosis.

Symptoms:
Inflammation and irritation of the vulva; redness; itching; development of thick, whitish skin (if chronic).

OTC Treatments:
Vaginal Antipruritics (page 180); Douches (page 172)

Warts

Small, hard lumps that develop on the skin, usually on the hands or the feet. The common wart—called verruca vulgaris—is a benign tumor caused by a virus that triggers rapid growth of skin cells, creating flesh-colored, pink, or white granulated lumps. They are usually painless unless aggravated (such as by the pressure of standing, in the case of plantar warts on the feet). If left untreated, they may eventually disappear on their own.

Symptoms:
Small, hard lumps usually on the skin of the hands or feet.

OTC Treatment:
Wart Removers (page 129)

Water Retention

Accumulation of water in the body's cells, resulting in bloating and weight gain. Water retention occurs in women during pregnancy and prior to a menstrual period because higher levels of estrogen prompt the body to conserve water.

Symptoms:
Bloating, weight gain, swollen fingers and ankles.

OTC Treatment:
Diuretics (page 171)

Wound Infection

Occurs after bacteria or fungi infects an injury to the skin. There are many types of wound infection that have different symptoms. The area of the wound may become swollen, red, and painful to the touch. A severe infection may result in death of tissue.

Symptoms:
Red, swollen skin around the area of an injury; tenderness; a thin, watery pus.

OTC Treatments:
Antibiotics (page 113); Antifungals (page 114)

Wrinkles

Soft folds of skin that occur naturally with aging. Wrinkles appear when the skin becomes dry, thin, and less elastic as the result of decreased oil production. Skin may also lose some of its color. Wrinkles can be brought on by smoking and overexposure to the sun. In women, wrinkles may appear after menopause.

Symptoms:
Sagging, wrinkling skin.

OTC Treatments:
Emollients (page 104); Bath Products (page 119); Sunscreens (page 127)

Yeast Infection

A form of vaginitis (inflammation of the vagina) caused by an overgrowth of yeast organisms. The infection, also known as *candidiasis* or *moniliasis,* occurs when the balance of bacteria in the vagina changes, prompting the growth of yeast. Yeast infections may be triggered by antibiotics, steroid medications, or hormonal birth control. They should be diagnosed by a practitioner before beginning treatment.

Symptoms:
Thick, white vaginal discharge; a yeastlike odor; itching; irritation.

OTC Treatments:
Vaginal Antifungals (page 179); Vaginal Antipruritics (page 180)

Medications

Many of today's over-the-counter medications were once prescription drugs designed to relieve every type of treatable condition. Most of these medications have changed very little in nonprescription form, but the proliferation of these drugs on the market can cause confusion. This chapter is organized by the way we use medications and where we use them. It includes the brand names found on pharmacy shelves, valuable warnings, and information on formulations and dosages. Where applicable, Medications indicates what type of drug to use when. Every type of medication, from skin treatments such as hydrocortisone to cold, cough, and allergy remedies such as decongestants, can be found here.

Pain Relievers, Fever Reducers, and Anti-inflammatories

Because many of the same medications reduce pain, fever, and inflammation at the same time, they have been combined in this section. Nonsteroidal anti-inflammatory drugs (NSAIDs)—such as aspirin, ibuprofen, and ketoprofen—and acetaminophen are the best defense against pain. All of these over-the-counter drugs have the ability to reduce fever and stop headache or muscle pain, but only NSAIDs can help reduce inflammation. Starting with a general description of NSAIDs and acetaminophen (how they work, various types of formulations, correct dosages, and a general listing of brand names), the section then turns to specific conditions and their remedies, including Antiarthritis Treatments (page 62), Antipyretics, or Fever Reducers (page 64), and Premenstrual and Menstrual Pain Relievers and Menorrhagia Treatments (page 66). Within two of these sections, information on another related drug category, Counterirritants (page 58), is included.

Nonsteroidal anti-inflammatory drugs (NSAIDs), help relieve pain, stiffness, and inflammation associated with a variety of conditions, from routine muscle soreness to rheumatoid arthritis. They are also used to reduce fevers and deaden pain around joints for arthritis sufferers. In addition, NSAIDs are taken to help prevent heart and circulatory problems as well as pain related to premenstrual syndrome and menstruation. They work by blocking the production of prostaglandins at the site of an injury. Prostaglandins are chemicals that are believed to be responsible for producing pain and inflammation. NSAIDs are rapidly absorbed into the bloodstream

and generally relieve symptoms within an hour.

NSAIDs are called nonsteroidal to distinguish them from the corticosteroid drugs, which also have an anti-inflammatory effect but—with the exception of hydrocortisone (see page 96)—require prescriptions. While aspirin, acetaminophen, and ibuprofen have been widely available in generic forms for some time, the most recent addition to the list of NSAIDs available without prescription is ketoprofen; naproxen was switched from prescription-only to OTC a few years ago. As a result, there are now three chemicals (not counting aspirin) approved for over-the-counter sale.

Technically, *aspirin* is a type of NSAID because of its anti-inflammatory action, and it is often referred to as an NSAID. **However, because it also has effects distinct from those produced by the other NSAIDs, such as ibuprofen, it is treated in this book as a separate type of internal analgesic.** Aspirin belongs to a group of drugs called salicylates. Their presence in an OTC drug may be indicated on the package as aspirin, acetylsalicylic acid, sodium salicylate, or magnesium salicylate. In the bloodstream, they are all converted to salicylic acid. Aspirin and other salicylates are often found in combination with other substances in a variety of OTC drugs, including cold medicines. In small doses, aspirin also helps prevent abnormal blood clots and is often recommended for people at risk of stroke or heart attack.

Unlike aspirin and NSAIDs, *acetaminophen* behaves like a narcotic, acting directly on the brain and spinal cord to alter one's perception of pain by reducing the production of prostaglandin *in the brain*. However, it does not affect prostaglandin production in the rest of the body, as aspirin and other NSAIDs do. As a result, while it is effective for pain and fever, it cannot be used to reduce the inflammation from a strained muscle, for example.

Nonsteroidal Anti-inflammatory Drugs (NSAIDs)

Ibuprofen

Brand names:
Addaprin
Advil
Bayer Select Ibuprofen Pain Relief Formula
Cramp Relief Formula Midol IB
Excedrin IB
Ibuprin
Motrin IB
Nuprin
Ultraprin
Valprin

Naproxen

Brand names:
Aleve
Naprosyn

Ketoprofen

Brand names:
Actron
Orudis

NSAIDs and aspirin work by blocking the production of prostaglandins and are used to relieve pain, stiffness, and inflammation associated with a wide variety of conditions, from routine muscle soreness to rheumatoid arthritis. NSAIDs and aspirin also help to relieve menorrhagia, the excessive loss of menstrual blood, by reducing the flow of blood to normal levels. They work by altering the normal balance in the body between vasoconstrictors (natural chemicals that narrow blood vessels, thus reducing blood flow) and vasodilators (natural chemicals that enlarge blood vessels, thus increasing blood flow).

Warning
While the NSAIDs are generally less likely than aspirin to cause stomach irritation or bleeding, gastrointestinal side effects such as stomach upset are fairly common and can increase when NSAIDs are taken with caffeine. Furthermore, if they are taken in larger than recommended doses in combination with alcohol, they can produce stomach or intestinal bleeding severe enough to require hospitalization.

While many people routinely take antacids (see page 81) to block the stomach distress often caused by NSAIDs, one study has found that this may mask the warning signs associated with NSAID-induced ulcers and gastrointestinal bleeding, and that these people are significantly likelier to require hospitalization for gastrointestinal problems.

Do not mix aspirin or other over-the-counter NSAIDs with prescription NSAIDs (such as fenoprofen and flurbiprofen, both used to treat inflammation). It is also important not to use NSAIDs during the last three months of pregnancy unless specifically directed to do so by a doctor, because they may cause cardiovascular problems in the fetus or complications during delivery. If you are pregnant or breast-feeding, consult your doctor before taking an NSAID. Naproxen should not be given to children under the age of twelve, unless directed to do so by a doctor.

Finally, NSAIDs may reduce the effectiveness of a variety of other drugs, including blood-pressure-lowering medication and diuretics. They can also make certain drugs more toxic, including methotrexate (prescribed for certain cancers, severe psoriasis, and rheumatoid arthritis) and lithium (prescribed mainly for bipolar disorder).

Aspirin

Brand names:
Adprin B
Anacin
Anacin Maximum Strength
Ascriptin Regular/Maximum Strength
Aspergum
Bayer Aspirin
Bayer Children's Aspirin
Bufferin
Doan's
Ecotrin Adult Low Strength
Ecotrin Regular Strength
Excedrin Extra Strength (with acetaminophen)
St. Joseph Low-Dose Adult Aspirin
Vanquish (with acetaminophen)

As part of the NSAIDs family, aspirin blocks the production of prostaglandins and also relieves pain, stiffness, and inflammation associated with a wide variety of conditions. The main drawback to aspirin is that it tends to irritate the stomach and even cause ulceration—inflammatory lesions—of the stomach and duodenum, the beginning portion of the small intestine, starting at the lower end of the stomach. In a small percentage of people, aspirin use can produce massive gastrointestinal bleeding. Aspirin should not be taken by people with gastric ulcers. To prevent gastrointestinal problems, it's best to take aspirin on a full stomach. When NSAIDs and corticosteroids are taken with aspirin to improve pain relief, the likelihood of stomach irritation is increased.

To reduce stomach upset, some aspirin is either coated or buffered (but not both in the same product). Buffered aspirin contains drugs such as calcium carbonate that reduce acidity and irritation in the stomach, while coated preparations (called enteric-coated) do not release the aspirin until they are in the small intestine. Aspirin may also be taken in suppository form, but in that case absorption is slow and unreliable. Another means of reducing stomach irritation is to take regular aspirin with an antacid (see page 81) or with a glass of milk.

Warning

Because of its anticoagulant, or blood-thinning, effect, aspirin should never be used in combination with anticoagulants or by people who have an increased risk of abnormal bleeding, such as hemophiliacs. It should also be discontinued at least one week before surgery and should not be used to relieve the pain from surgical procedures.

Do not mix aspirin with prescription NSAIDs (such as fenoprofen and flurbiprofen, both used to treat inflammation). Aspirin sometimes causes allergic reactions, including hives, swelling, or shortness of breath. People with asthma are particularly susceptible to breathing problems from aspirin and should get pain relief from acetaminophen, not from aspirin or NSAIDs. In addition, because of their effect on uric acid secretion and reabsorption, aspirin and all other salicylates should be avoided by people with a history of gout, a form of arthritis that usually strikes a single joint, often the big toe.

The American Academy of Pediatrics has recommended that children through age twenty-one years not receive aspirin if they have chicken pox or influenza (any cold, cough, or sore throat symptoms). The recommendation stems from several studies that have linked aspirin to Reye's syndrome, a rare but potentially fatal brain and liver disorder. Most pediatricians have stopped using aspirin for fevers associated with any illness.

Acetaminophen *best for ache & pain & fever*

Brand names:
Allerest Headache Strength
Allerest Sinus Pain Formula
Anacin Aspirin Free Maximum Strength
Anacin P.M. Aspirin Free
Bayer Select Maximum Strength Headache Pain Relief Formula
Bufferin AF
Excedrin Aspirin Free
Liquiprin Infants'
Midol Menstrual Multisymptom Formula
Panadol Children's
Panadol Maximum Strength
Percogesic Analgesic
St. Joseph Aspirin-Free Tablets for Children
Tempra
Tylenol Extra Strength
Tylenol Junior
Tylenol Children's
Tylenol Regular Strength
Unisom with Pain Relief

Because it does not cause stomach upset or bleeding problems, it is a useful alternative for people who cannot tolerate aspirin or who suffer from gastric ulcers, and is frequently added to cold and cough remedies as an analgesic. (Acetaminophen may be described as "nonaspirin" on the label, but it will be identified as the active ingredient in the fine print.) It can also be safely taken with anticoagulants.

Warning

Acetaminophen has been linked to liver and kidney damage. One study found that taking just one dose of acetaminophen daily for at least a year may double the risk of kidney failure, although it also noted that kidney damage is rare even among people taking acetaminophen a few times a day. Over a long time, large dosages—above the recommended 4 grams or eight tablets per day—may also cause sudden liver failure, particularly in people who regularly drink more than three alcohol-containing drinks daily. (However, it may be safely taken in combination with moderate drinking.) Acetaminophen, even in moderate amounts, has been found to cause liver damage when taken after a fast.

Analgesics (Internal)

NSAIDs, aspirin, and acetaminophen are all used as internal analgesics to help relieve headaches and other types of pain by entering the bloodstream and affecting the entire body. Acetaminophen, though listed below, is less effective than NSAIDs and aspirin in relieving muscle and joint pain. Internal analgesics also work to ease the pain of sprained, strained, and bruised muscles and joints, often in conjunction with counterirritants, medications that are applied to the skin at pain sites to produce a mild local inflammatory reaction, thus distracting from more deep-seated pain. For detailed information about the actions of specific counterirritants, see page 58.

Another group of drugs commonly used to relieve pain are local, or topical, anesthetics (see page 97), many of which are also available without prescription. Unlike internal analgesics, local anesthetics work by blocking the passage of nerve impulses at the site where the medication is administered, deadening all sensation, or feeling, at that site. They are generally applied to the surface of the skin—although they may sometimes be swallowed—and are not systemic; they do not interfere with consciousness.

If NSAIDs and local anesthetics provide inadequate relief, you should consult a physician for diagnosis and to discuss changing to a more powerful prescription drug.

Warning

Some brands of aspirin and acetaminophen, including Anacin (aspirin), Excedrin Extra Strength and Vanquish (both of which combine aspirin and acetaminophen), also contain caffeine. As a stimulant to the central nervous system, caffeine makes most people feel better; it can also be effective in reducing the pain of migraine headaches, by narrowing blood vessels that are dilated. (When blood vessels dilate, the action releases prostaglandins, which produce pain.) However, people who are excessively sensitive to caffeine's side effects or who have been advised to eliminate caffeine from their diets may want to avoid such products despite their analgesic effect.

Nonsteroidal Anti-inflammatory Drugs (NSAIDs)

There are three chemicals currently approved for OTC NSAIDs:

Ibuprofen

The first NSAID to be approved by the FDA for both prescription and OTC use, ibuprofen is similar to aspirin in the way it works and can be used. It has fewer side effects than some of the other NSAIDs, but it is shorter-acting than naproxen (below), for example, and must be taken several times a day to provide relief.

Formulations:
Tablet, caplet, gelcap

Dosage:
Adults take 200 mg every four to six hours while symptoms persist. If pain or fever does not respond, 400 mg may be used, but do not exceed 1,800 mg in twenty-four hours unless directed by a doctor. If you are pregnant or breast-feeding a baby, seek the advice of a health professional first. It is especially important not to use ibuprofen during the last three months of pregnancy unless specifically directed to do so by a doctor, because it may cause problems in the unborn child or complications during delivery. Do not give ibuprofen to children under twelve except under a doctor's supervision.

Naproxen

An advantage naproxen has over other pain relievers is that it provides longer-lasting relief, between eight and twelve hours, compared to four hours for ibuprofen or aspirin.

Formulations:
Tablet, caplet

Dosage:
Adults take 200 mg every eight to twelve hours. For adults over age sixty-five, do not take more than 200 mg every twelve hours unless directed by a doctor. Do not give to children under twelve, except under doctor's supervision. If you are pregnant or breast-feeding a baby, seek the advice of a health professional first. It is especially important

not to use naproxen during the last three months of pregnancy unless specifically directed to do so by a doctor, because it may cause problems in the unborn child or complications during delivery.

Ketoprofen

Recently approved by the FDA, this is the newest NSAID to make the switch to OTC. Like ibuprofen, it is comparatively short-acting and needs to be taken several times a day to provide relief.

Formulations:
Tablet, caplet

Dosage:
Adults take 12.5 to 25 mg every four to six hours, but no more than 75 mg in any twenty-four-hour period. If you are pregnant or breast-feeding a baby, seek the advice of a health professional first. It is especially important not to use ketoprofen during the last three months of pregnancy unless specifically directed to do so by a doctor, because it may cause problems in the unborn child or complications during delivery. Do not give to children under age sixteen unless directed by a physician.

Aspirin

Aspirin is useful for headaches, toothaches, mild rheumatic pain, sore throat, and discomfort caused by feverish illnesses (for more on treating fever, see page 64), as well as for inflammation. However, the manufacturers' recommended dosage for mild to moderate pain management may not always be adequate for pain due to inflammation.

Formulations:
Caplet, tablet, liquid (drops, syrup, or elixir), chewable (tablet or gum), suppository

Dosage:
Adults take 325 to 650 mg every four hours, or 325 to 500 mg every three hours, or 650 to 1,000 mg every six hours, not to exceed 4 g in twenty-four hours. In general, aspirin is not recommended for children, although it may be given under medical supervision and in lower dosages than those for adults. For important precautions concerning the use of aspirin with children with fever, see page 65.

Children can be given 160 mg every four hours up to a maximum of five doses per twenty-four hours; however, dosage increases with child's age and weight. While acetaminophen is generally preferred for children, aspirin may be safely given if the child is not febrile. There are also pediatric formulations of aspirin for children. If you are pregnant or breast-feeding a baby, seek the advice of a health professional first. It is especially important not to use aspirin during the last three months of pregnancy unless specifically directed to do so by a doctor, because it may cause problems in the unborn child or complications during delivery.

For prevention of stroke, the usual dose is 300 to 325 mg four times daily or 600 mg twice a day. For prevention of heart attack, the usual dose is 300 to 325 mg daily.

Warning

The American Academy of Pediatrics has recommended that children through age twenty-one years not receive aspirin if they have chicken pox or influenza (any cold, cough, or sore throat symptoms). The recommendation stems from several studies that have linked aspirin to Reye's syndrome, a rare but potentially fatal brain and liver disorder. Most pediatricians have stopped using aspirin for fevers associated with any illness.

Acetaminophen

Acetaminophen is considered one of the safest of the analgesics for everyday aches and pains and is suitable for children as well as adults. Because it does not cause stomach upset or bleeding problems, it is a useful alternative for people who cannot tolerate aspirin or who suffer from gastric ulcers, and is frequently added to cold and cough remedies as an analgesic. (Acetaminophen may be described as "nonaspirin" on the label, but it will be identified as the active ingredient in the fine print.) It can also be safely taken with anticoagulants.

Formulations:
Caplet, tablet, gelcap, liquid (drops, syrup, or elixir), chewable (tablet or gum), suppository

Dosage:
Adults take 650 to 1,000 mg three or four times daily, not to exceed 4,000 mg in a twenty-four-hour period. Children ages six to twelve take 160 to 325

mg every four to six hours, not to exceed five doses in twenty-four hours. Consult a physician for use by children under six.

What to use when

All internal analgesics described here may be taken to relieve pain and reduce fever. However, only the anti-inflammatory drugs—aspirin, ibuprofen, naproxen, and ketoprofen—are effective in treating inflammation. If you want longer-lasting relief, use naproxen, which can be taken every eight to twelve hours, compared to four to six hours for ibuprofen and ketoprofen. However, ibuprofen is most widely available, especially in generic form. For pregnant women, acetaminophen is the safest analgesic.

Counterirritants

Counterirritants are used primarily to reduce pain from sprained or strained muscles or joints, or arthritic joints, although they may also be used for shingles, insect bites, hemorrhoids, and other causes of pain. They work by stimulating receptors in the skin to create sensations such as cold and warmth. These distract from the deep-seated pain in muscles, joints, and tendons—the main targets of counterirritants.

Because they are applied to the skin rather than taken orally, counterirritants belong to the general category of external analgesics, along with local anesthetics and antipruritics, the difference being that anesthetics and antipruritics act directly on the skin to numb the receptors for pain, burning, and itching (see Skin Treatments, page 95).

Counterirritants have a paradoxical effect: By producing a less severe pain in nearby tissue, they counter a more intense one. There are several theories to explain how they work. One theory is that the stimulation of sensory nerve endings in the skin causes the blood vessels in the muscles to dilate, or expand, thus increasing blood flow to the muscles and, in turn, raising the skin temperature. Yet another theory is that all the pain stimuli are transmitted to the same area of the spinal cord, with the result that the sensation of the pain is wholly or partly obliterated.

The benefits of some counterirritants used to treat musculoskeletal disorders may be due in large measure to the rubbing and massage involved in applying the medication. Massage increases the flow of blood and lymph in the skin and underlying structures. It is also likely that the action of counterirritants in relieving pain has a strong psychological component. In fact, through pleasant fragrances or the sensation of warmth or coolness they produce on the skin, counterirritants may sometimes have a placebo effect—that is, people feel better even though the drug has little or no medical benefit.

Many OTC preparations combine counterirritants from at least two different groups for greater potency. Because the four main counterirritants have a variety of uses, brand names are also provided in other sections—notably insect bites and stings (see page 109), hemorrhoidal preparations (see page 106) and others. Three other counterirritants that are infrequently used are listed here with their brands.

Warning

Counterirritants are not currently approved for treating minor burns because while they reduce pain, they increase blood flow to the area, which causes further swelling; they also further irritate the already sensitized and damaged skin.

If muscle and joint pain persists, counterirritants may also be taken in conjunction with NSAIDs and aspirin.

For muscle and joint pain, counterirritants are often administered as liniments that are rubbed into the affected area. In fact, much of the counterirritant's benefit may come from the rubbing and friction involved in applying the medication, as massage increases the flow of blood and lymph in the skin and underlying structures. Liniments in an alcohol base are useful for a counterirritant effect, because they penetrate deeper into the skin; however, these are more irritating to the skin than non-alcoholic liniments.

Counterirritants may also be administered as ointments or creams which, like liniments, are rubbed into the skin, or as lotions or gels, which are not. The fluidity of lotions allows them to be rapidly and uniformly applied over a wide surface area, and makes them especially suited to hairy body areas. Gels deliver a greater sensation of warmth than lotions or

ointments, and penetrate the skin faster and more extensively. Because this increased penetration may cause an unpleasant burning sensation, users must be careful not to exceed the recommended dosage or rub the gels too vigorously into the skin.

If you're taking anticoagulants, or blood-thinning medication, you should use products that contain salicylates, such as methyl salicylate and trolamine salicylate, only under close monitoring, as salicylates may significantly prolong prothrombin time (a measure of bleeding vulnerability). You should also avoid using drugs containing methyl salicylate or trolamine salicylate in conjunction with a heating pad which, by increasing skin temperature and vasodilation (widening of blood vessels), increases the body's absorption of menthol and methyl salicylate, potentially causing skin and muscle necrosis, or tissue death. For the same reason, do not apply these products after strenuous exercise, especially during hot and humid weather.

Dosage:
Apply liberally to the affected area three to four times a day. Do not use on children under two. To reduce the risk of irritation, redness, and blistering, do not apply any bandage tightly over the affected area.

Oil of Wintergreen

Brand names:
Ben-Gay Extra Strength (30% methyl salicylate, with menthol)
Ben-Gay Greaseless Formula (15% methyl salicylate, with menthol)
Ben-Gay Original Formula (18.3% methyl salicylate, with menthol)
Ben-Gay Ultra Strength (30% methyl salicylate, with menthol, camphor)
Exocaine Medicated Rub, Heet (with camphor and capsicum, in alcohol base)
Mentholatum Deep Heating Rub (with menthol)
Sports Spray Extra Strength (with menthol, camphor)

Belonging to the most potent group of counterirritants and perhaps the most widely used, oil of wintergreen is actually methyl salicylate and is often combined with camphor and menthol for greater effectiveness. Methyl salicylate is an ingredient at very low concentrations in oral preparations (lozenges, page 77; toothpastes, page 138; mouthwashes [for oral health], page 144) for its pleasant flavor and aroma, as well as in higher concentrations (10% to 60%) as an external analgesic. Like other salicylates, it is believed that it acts in part as an anti-inflammatory agent that inhibits prostaglandins, chemicals that are released at the site of an injury and that are believed to be responsible for producing pain. However, in higher concentrations methyl salicylate can cause redness and irritation to the skin.

Because of its high salicylate content, methyl salicylate should be avoided by anyone with an allergy to aspirin, and it should not be used as a topical analgesic on children with fever, due to the risk of Reye's syndrome. By the same token, counterirritants containing methyl salicylate should not be used in conjunction with a heating pad which, by increasing skin temperature and vasodilation, increases the body's absorption of menthol and methyl salicylate, potentially causing muscle and skin tissue death. Users are also cautioned not to apply these products after strenuous exercise, especially during hot and humid weather, as this also increases absorption.

Warning

Individuals who are taking anticoagulants should use methyl salicylate only under close monitoring, as it may allow bleeding to continue for a longer amount of time.

Formulations:
Cream, gel, ointment, lotion, spray

Camphor

Particularly when combined with other counterirritants, camphor stimulates the nerve endings in the skin and masks moderate to severe pain. When applied vigorously—for example, as a muscle rub—it dilates the blood vessels, raising local skin temperature. The recommended concentration for external use of camphor as a counterirritant is 3 to 11 percent, although the highest concentrations are generally not more effective. In lower concentrations, it depresses receptors in the skin and is used as a topical analgesic, anesthetic, and antipruritic for insect bites and stings (see page 109), for example.

Menthol

Brand names:
Absorbine Jr.
Absorbine Jr. Extra Strength
Ben-Gay Daytime Pain Relieving Gel/Vanishing Scent Formula
Eucalyptamint Muscle Pain Relief
Pain Gel Plus
Therapeutic Mineral Ice

Menthol, which is extracted from peppermint oil or prepared synthetically, is often used as a counterirritant. (Peppermint and clove oils are also mild counterirritants, creating a sensation of warmth.) Like methyl salicylate, menthol is widely used in lozenges and toothpastes; it is also used extensively in inhalant preparations for the relief of nasal congestion. Menthol is usually combined with other ingredients with antipruritic or analgesic properties, such as camphor.

In lower concentrations, it acts as an antipruritic (see page 95). Applied topically, in concentrations below 1 percent, it depresses receptors in the skin and has an analgesic, or pain-relieving, effect. In concentrations of 1.25 to 16 percent, it stimulates the same receptors and acts as a counterirritant, producing an initial feeling of coolness by stimulating the nerves that perceive cold while depressing those that perceive pain. This is soon followed by a sensation of warmth.

Warning

One study has found that exposure to menthol caused the heat-sensing threshold to rise significantly—that is, people do not perceive warmth (from another source) as "early" as they would otherwise. This may be because the menthol molecule inhibits or desensitizes warmth receptors. For that reason, menthol should not be used in conjunction with heating pads because of the risk of skin burns.

Formulations:
Cream, ointment, lotion, gel, liquid

Capsicum Preparations

Brand names:
Capzasin-P
Mentholatum Menthacin
Sloan's Liniment
Zostrix
Zostrix-HP

(Capsicum preparations include capsaicin, capsicum, and capsicum oleoresin.) All capsicum preparations contain capsaicin, which is used to relieve pain from arthritis, shingles, and other conditions. It appears to work primarily by depleting substance P, a neurotransmitter, or brain chemical, that is believed to be a factor in the transmission of painful stimuli from the skin to the spinal cord and brain. High concentrations of substance P are present in sensory nerves supplying sites of chronic inflammation.

Capsaicin, the major pungent ingredient of hot pepper, produces a feeling of warmth when applied in concentrations of 0.025 to 0.25 percent. Because it is slow-acting as a counterirritant, it may be combined with fast-acting counterirritants such as menthol and methyl nicotinate.

The more concentrated solutions produce a sensation of burning pain, but even then capsicum preparations do not cause blistering or reddening of the skin because they do not act on capillaries or other blood vessels, and the burning sensation generally stops in several days.

Pain relief usually occurs within 14 days after therapy is begun, but occasionally it will take as long as four to six weeks. Interruption of the therapy will result in reaccumulation of substance P.

Formulations:
Cream, liquid

Mustard Oil

Brand name:
Numol

In this product, mustard oil is combined with methyl salicylate, camphor, menthol, turpentine, and eucalyptus oil (described on page 62).

Also known as allyl isothiocyanate, this agent belongs to the most powerful group of counterirritants (which also includes methyl salicylate), and because of its possible risks it is not widely used as an ingredient in OTC products, although it is FDA-approved.

Warning

In high concentrations, allyl isothiocyanate is absorbed rapidly, and it may cause skin ulcers or lesions if it is not removed soon after it has been applied. Mustard plasters—homemade preparations from powdered mustard, flour, and water—should not remain on the skin for more than a few minutes.

Formulation: Liquid

Dosage:
Adults and children over two should rub into affected area no more than three to four times daily. Do not use with children under two, except under the advice and supervision of a physician.

Turpentine Oil

Brand name:
Sloan's (with capsaicin)

Like mustard oil, this is a powerful counterirritant and FDA-approved but rarely used. Medicinal turpentine oil, also known as spirits of turpentine, is of a higher quality than commercial turpentine oil. While it is considered safe, it tends to dry the skin, causing cracking.

Warning

Turpentine oil can cause severe contact dermatitis —an inflammation of the skin due to an allergic reaction—and other problems, depending on the concentration and dosage.

Formulation: Liniment

Dosage:
Adults and children over two should rub into affected area no more than three to four times daily. Do not use with children under two, except under the advice and supervision of a physician.

Eucalyptus Oil

Like eucalyptol, its main ingredient, eucalyptus oil, has a mild irritant action, causing a sensation of warmth. It is not approved by the FDA as an active ingredient in counterirritants, but has been included as an inactive ingredient in some products sold as external analgesics. As with products listed above, it is usually combined with camphor, phenol, and/or menthol.

Formulations:
Ointment, cream, liquid, gel

Dosage:
Adults and children two and older should gently massage a conservative amount into affected area not more than three to four times daily. For children under two, consult a physician.

Trolamine Salicylate

Brand names:
Aspercreme
Sportscreme

Unlike the other agents listed here, trolamine salicylate is not a counterirritant. Precisely how it works is unknown, but it is believed that it helps relieve pain by acting on the central nervous system—much like aspirin taken orally—and peripherally as an anti-inflammatory agent that inhibits prostaglandins. (Prostaglandins are chemicals believed to be responsible for producing pain and inflammation.) While a 1983 FDA study found trolamine salicylate was no better than a placebo (an inactive substance), subsequent reports have found it may be effective in alleviating pain from sore or bruised muscles or joints, including repetitive motion injuries (see page 43).

Formulations:
Cream, lotion

What to use when

Which counterirritant you choose depends on how you're using the medication and in large part is determined by drug manufacturers. Methyl salicylate may be the most widely used counterirritant, present at very low concentrations in oral preparations such as mouthwashes, as well as in liniments. Often it is combined with other counterirritants, such as menthol or camphor. However, you should avoid methyl salicylate if you are allergic to aspirin; and you should not use it as a topical analgesic on children with fever, due to the risk of Reye's syndrome.

If you want a powerful counterirritant to relieve muscle or joint pain, try capsaicin. Because it is slow-acting, it is often combined in products with one or more of the other counterirritants listed here to increase its speed of delivery.

Antiarthritis Treatments

Antiarthritis products relieve the pain and inflammation caused by many kinds of arthritis, including rheumatoid arthritis (a chronic disease with inflammatory changes occurring throughout the body's connective tissues) and osteoarthritis, or degenerative arthritis, the most common type of arthritis. It is often caused by joint injuries or old age.

The two main categories of OTC drugs used to treat the symptoms of arthritis are internal analgesics and counterirritants, or topical rubs (see page 58). Some products in both of these categories are marketed specifically for people with arthritis. These are listed below.

However, there is nothing magical about their formulations. In 1996, McNeil Consumer Products, a division of Johnson & Johnson, agreed to take its Arthritis Foundation brand off the market. The move followed a deceptive-marketing case brought by nineteen states arguing that the medicines were nothing more than repackaged versions of aspirin, acetaminophen, and ibuprofen.

While some antiarthritis products may contain a higher concentration of the active ingredient, a double dosage of the product that has a lower concentration will be equally effective. The primary OTC analgesics for arthritis are aspirin and other NSAIDs. They fight inflammation by blocking prostaglandins, some of which cause inflammation.

Formulations:
Tablet, caplet

Dosage:
If you have an arthritic condition, you should work with your practitioner to determine how much medication you need to control your symptoms. If you have rheumatoid arthritis, for example, you may need large amounts to control symptoms of joint inflammation; your doctor may recommend taking three or four standard aspirin tablets (a total dosage of 975 to 1,300 mg) four times daily (with meals and a bedtime snack).

On the other hand, if you have mild osteoarthritis—which may involve pain but not inflammation—you may need only a small amount to control the pain, or you may do just as well with acetaminophen, which does not treat inflammation. It may take a few weeks to determine the appropriate dosage to relieve the pain and inflammation from arthritis.

Ibuprofen

Virtually all OTC preparations with ibuprofen contain 200 mg per tablet.

Naproxen

As naproxen is longer-lasting than the other painkillers, standard dosage is one tablet every eight to twelve hours. However, as with other painkillers, dosage may be increased under a doctor's supervision. Naproxen is also used for gout, a form of arthritis that usually strikes a single joint, often the big toe.

Aspirin

Brand names:
Arthritis Pain Formula
Bufferin Arthritis Strength

A standard tablet contains 325 mg of aspirin. An "extra-strength" or "arthritis-strength" tablet usually contains 500 mg.

Warning
The American Academy of Pediatrics has recommended that children through age twenty-one years not receive aspirin if they have chicken pox or influenza (any cold, cough, or sore throat symptoms). The recommendation stems from several studies that have linked aspirin to Reye's syndrome, a rare but potentially fatal brain and liver disorder. Most pediatricians have stopped using aspirin for fevers associated with any illness.

Counterirritants

Counterirritants stimulate receptors in the skin to induce sensations such as cold and warmth, thus distracting from the deep-seated muscle and joint pain characteristic of arthritis. In preparations marketed for arthritis relief, the active ingredient is typically at a higher concentration than in products designed for relief of mild aches and pains.

Formulations:
Cream, gel

Dosage:
Apply generously and gently massage into painful area until cream or gel disappears. Repeat three to four times daily.

Capsaicin

Brand names:
Arthricare Odor Free Pain Relieving Rub
Capzasin-P
Mentholatum Menthacin
Zostrix
Zostrix Hp

Because this is slow-acting, it may be combined (as on page 60) with faster-acting counterirritants such as menthol and methyl nicotinate.

Menthol

Brand names:
Arthritis Hot
Ben-Gay Arthritis Extra Strength Rub
Mentholatum Deep Heating Arthritis Formula Rub

This is often combined with methyl salicylate, as in the products listed above.

What to use when

Because they help relieve pain and inflammation immediately and have few side effects, NSAIDs (not including aspirin) are generally the first-line course of treatment. They may be used in conjunction with counterirritants, which may produce additional relief because they are massaged into the skin. However, you may want to seek professional guidance in applying the counterirritant creams or gels, as massage directly applied to a painful, inflamed joint can be harmful.

Antipyretics, or Fever Reducers

Antipyretics reduce fever, primarily by inhibiting the production and release of prostaglandins at the body's thermoregulatory center, which is located in the brain. The three types of nonprescription drugs that act as antipyretics are internal analgesics: aspirin, acetaminophen, and ibuprofen.

Treating fever is a somewhat contentious issue. Fever is the natural reaction of the body's immune system, usually to disease-causing microorganisms. While many people think it is important to "normalize" their temperatures, there are strong arguments against such treatment. Left untreated, fevers normally run their course and are believed to have possible therapeutic effects by inhibiting the growth of the microorganisms. Accordingly, the main reason to treat fever is to relieve discomfort; it does not help you get better.

Since all nonprescription drugs to treat fever are also analgesics, they serve a twofold purpose: They relieve pain or discomfort while lowering fever. While some OTC products are marketed primarily as treatment for fever in children, they are analgesics, too; examples are Feverall and Tempra, brands of acetaminophen whose names suggest fever control.

Under most circumstances, all three drug types are equally effective: They all require about the same amount of time to reduce fever (thirty to sixty minutes), take about the same amount of time to achieve maximum temperature reduction (two to three hours after dose), and last for approximately the same length of time (four to six hours), although ibuprofen may be effective for six to eight hours against fever, particularly in children. On average, antipyretics achieve a maximum reduction of temperature of only 2 to 3 degrees Fahrenheit, so it is probably futile to try to "normalize" your temperature to precisely 98.6°F—particularly when your normal body temperature can vary by nearly 2 degrees from the "norm" in the course of a day. Some doctors believe a mild fever (up to 102°F) need not be treated at all unless the individual is uncomfortable.

In clinical trials, administering two types of antipyretics—such as aspirin and ibuprofen—concurrently has resulted in greater and longer-lasting temperature reduction. However, the pharmacological community believes that further study is needed before it recommends combined use. It also advises against using the different drugs in an alternating schedule, as that can be confusing and is more likely to result in medication error.

Fevers exceeding 104°F that last more than three days, despite the use of antipyretics, should be evaluated by a physician. An infant with a fever of more than 100°F also requires professional care.

Ibuprofen

Formulations:
Caplet, tablet, gelcap

Dosage:
Adults take 200 to 400 mg every four to six hours, not to exceed 1.2 grams in a twenty-four-hour period. Children with fevers of 102.5°F or higher can take 10 mg per kilogram (a kilogram equals 2.2 pounds) of body weight, not to exceed 40 mg per kilogram in twenty-four hours. Children with fevers below 102.5°F can take 5 mg per kilogram of body weight, not to exceed 40 mg per kilogram in twenty-four hours.

If you are pregnant or breast-feeding a baby, seek the advice of a health professional first. It is especially important not to use ibuprofen during the last three months of pregnancy unless specifically directed to do so by a doctor, because it may cause problems in the unborn child or complications during delivery.

Aspirin

Warning

The American Academy of Pediatrics has recommended that children through age twenty-one years not receive aspirin if they have chicken pox or influenza (any cold, cough, or sore throat symptoms). The recommendation stems from several studies that have linked aspirin to Reye's syndrome, a rare but potentially fatal brain and liver disorder. Most pediatricians have stopped using aspirin for fevers associated with any illness.

Formulations:
Tablet, chewable tablet, gum, caplet

Dosage:
Adults take 650 mg every four to six hours; do not exceed five doses in twenty-four hours. The recommended dose for children ages two to twelve years is 10 to 15 mg per kilogram of total body weight, every four to six hours as needed, up to a maximum daily dose of 65 mg per kilogram for up to five days. If you are using rectal suppositories, use a dosage 25 to 50 percent greater than the recommended oral dosage. For children under two, consult a physician.

If you are pregnant or breast-feeding a baby, seek the advice of a health professional first. It is especially important not to use aspirin during the last three months of pregnancy unless specifically directed to do so by a doctor, because it may cause problems in the unborn child or complications during delivery.

Acetaminophen

Brand names:
Congespirin for Children Aspirin Free
Excedrin Extra Strength (with aspirin)
Feverall Junior Strength
Feverall Children's
Feverall Infants'
Panadol Junior Strength, St. Joseph Aspirin-Free Fever Reducer for Children
Tylenol Infants'
Vanquish (with aspirin)

Formulations:
Caplet, gelcap, tablet, chewable tablet, capsule, suppository, liquid

Dosage:
Adults take 650 mg every four to six hours; do not exceed five doses in twenty-four hours. The recommended dose for children ages two to twelve years is 10 to 15 mg per kilograms of total body weight, every four to six hours as needed, up to a maximum daily dose of 65 mg per kilograms for up to five days. If you are using rectal suppositories, use a dosage 25 to 50 percent greater than the recommended oral dosage. For children under two, consult a physician.

What to use when

Aspirin, acetaminophen, and ibuprofen are all effective antipyretics. Unlike aspirin, however, ibuprofen is approved for treating fever in children. However, acetaminophen is often considered the preferred agent, particularly for children, as it is less likely to cause stomach upset. It is also recommended as a fever-reducing agent in people with blood-coagulation problems, as well as for people who have cancer or are undergoing cancer chemotherapy, and women in the last three months of pregnancy.

Premenstrual and Menstrual Pain Relievers and Menorrhagia Treatments

OTC preparations for premenstrual syndrome (PMS) help relieve pain or reduce water retention, or both. Typically they combine an internal analgesic to relieve pain with a diuretic (see page 171), to reduce water retention. The analgesic most often used is acetaminophen, which acts directly on the brain and spinal cord to alter one's perception of pain by reducing the production of prostaglandins in the brain. However, NSAIDs are also most effective when given for several days premenstrually, and then every six hours throughout the menstrual period.

High levels of prostaglandin make the uterine muscles contract in women who are menstruating. Menstrual pain relief preparations treat difficult or painful menstruation, or dysmenorrhea, by reducing uterine contractions (cramping) and pain. They, too, may include a diuretic, to eliminate retained water.

The diuretic most often used in products for PMS and dysmenorrhea is pamabrom. Some diuretics for general use contain caffeine but because that can increase irritability, these are not recommended for women with PMS. Caffeine may be included in treatments for dysmenorrhea, however.

A number of treatments for PMS and dysmenorrhea also include antihistamines, usually pyrilamine maleate but occasionally diphenhydramine. However, it's not clear that antihistamines provide any benefit. Generic painkillers and diuretics can be taken separately or in combination. Although a number of products are marketed specifically for painful menstruation, as the lists below indicate, it may be possible to achieve the same relief with many other internal analgesics.

NSAIDs and aspirin help to relieve menorrhagia, the excessive loss of menstrual blood, by reducing the flow of blood to normal levels. They work by altering the normal balance in the body between vasoconstrictors (natural chemicals that narrow blood vessels, thus reducing blood flow) and vasodilators (natural chemicals that enlarge blood vessels, thus increasing blood flow). It has also been suggested that NSAIDs may help relieve menorrhagia by increasing the production of leukotrienes, which are powerful vasoconstrictors. Menorrhagia should be evaluated by a physician before being treated with OTC medications, as it can be caused by a number of systemic illnesses and medications or may be most effectively treated with prescription oral contraceptives.

Ibuprofen

Brand names:

Menadol Ibuprofen

Midol IB Cramp Relief Formula

Ibuprofen's pain-blocking action prevents stimulation of the nerve endings at the site of the pain, the uterus.

Dosage:
Take 200 mg every four to six hours for the first forty-eight to seventy-two hours of menstrual flow. If pain does not respond, 400 mg may be used, but do not exceed 1,800 mg in twenty-four hours unless directed by a doctor. If you are breast-feeding a baby, seek the advice of a health professional first.

Acetaminophen

Brand names:
Bayer Select Maximum Strength Menstrual Multi-Symptom (with pamabrom)
Diurex MPR (with pamabrom)
Midol Menstrual Maximum Strength Multisymptom Formula (with caffeine)
Midol Menstrual Regular Strength
Midol Teen (with pamabrom)
Pamprin Maximum Pain Relief (with pamabrom)

Unlike NSAIDs, acetaminophen behaves like a narcotic, acting directly on the brain and spinal cord to alter the person's perception of pain by reducing the production of prostaglandins in the brain rather than at the site of the pain.

Dosage:

Take 650 to 1,000 mg three to four times daily for the first forty-eight to seventy-two hours of menstrual flow; do not take more than 4,000 mg in a twenty-four-hour period.

All of the products listed below contain acetaminophen, pamabrom, and pyrilamine. Products marketed to relieve menstrual pain may also be helpful, as may generic painkillers and diuretics taken separately or in combination.

Brand names:
Diurex PMS
Midol PMS Multisymptom Formula
Premsyn PMS Caplets

Formulations:
Tablet, caplet

Dosage:

Take two tablets/caplets (50 mg pamabrom) every four to six hours as needed, up to a maximum of eight per day.

What to use when

For relief from PMS

Both ibuprofen and acetaminophen are safe and effective. However, if you are breastfeeding, acetaminophen is preferable.

For relief from menstrual pain

Once the menstrual flow begins, treatment should start as soon as pain sets in. To be most effective, the analgesic must be taken on a scheduled basis, not as needed—preferably every four to six hours for the first forty-eight to seventy-two hours of menstrual flow, because that is when prostaglandin release is at its peak. The analgesics in these products are used to prevent cramps as much as to relieve pain. Before judging whether or not your analgesic works—and switching to another, if it does not—you should try it for three to four menstrual cycles.

Cold, Cough, and Allergy Remedies

An enormous variety of OTC medications are available to relieve the symptoms of colds, coughs, and allergic rhinitis—nasal congestion or stuffiness, runny nose, cough, dry or sore throat, fever, and headache. Many combine several different active ingredients to treat multiple symptoms and may be effective and convenient if you have multiple symptoms. These combination products are usually more expensive, however, and may contain unneeded ingredients with adverse effects.

Because this multi-ingredient approach dominates the cold/cough category, this section will include multiple listings for products with two or more of these key ingredients: a decongestant, an antihistamine, a cough suppressant and/or expectorant. In addition, a number of products in this category also include an internal analgesic (see page 56), to treat fever, headache, and other pain often associated with colds and other similar conditions. This is not indicated with the brand names, so check the product's label before you buy. On page 77, the box indicating what to use when for oral decongestants, antihistamines, cough suppressants, and expectorants can be found.

Sore throats may also be treated with lozenges and mouthwashes, gargles, and sprays (see page 77). However, because their ingredients do not reach the larynx (voice box), they probably do not help relieve laryngitis, an inflammation of laryngeal tissue often caused by colds. Water vapor inhalation (see page 189) such as cool mist, several times a day, may be beneficial in acute laryngitis. There is no proof that it helps to add any medications to the steam.

Formulations:

With the exception of preparations with codeine, which are administered only as syrups, most cold/cough and allergy treatments are available in the following formulations: syrup or other liquid, caplet, effervescent tablet, gelcap, capsule, and chewable tablet. Many preparations in liquid or syrup form contain alcohol, with the important exception of pediatric formulations. Formulations for specific types of antihistamines are located in Antihistamines, page 72.

Warning

Cold/cough and allergy preparations that contain alcohol obviously should not be used by people trying to avoid alcohol, such as recovering alcoholics and people with diabetes. Check the labels carefully.

Dosage:

Owing to the great range of cold/cough and allergy treatments, which typically combine two or more ingredients and are widely available in different strengths and formulations, it is not possible here to provide specific dosage information for products. Instead, we list below dosage ranges for the primary ingredients in cold/cough and allergy treatments. See manufacturer's directions regarding dosage for specific brand-name products. You will find dosages for specific types of antihistamines, however.

Oral Decongestants

**Brand names
(many contain analgesics):**
Advil Cold & Sinus (pseudoephedrine)
Allerest No Drowsiness (pseudoephedrine)
Congespirin for Children Aspirin-Free (phenylephrine)
Dimetapp Decongestant
Pediatric (pseudoephedrine)
Dristan Cold Maximum Strength No Drowsiness (pseudoephedrine)
Excedrin Sinus (pseudoephedrine)
Motrin IB Sinus (pseudoephedrine)
Sinarest No-Drowsiness (pseudoephedrine)
Sine-Aid (pseudoephedrine)
Sine-Off Maximum Strength No Drowsiness (pseudoephedrine)
Sinutab (pseudoephedrine)
Sudafed (pseudoephedrine)

Decongestants work by constricting the blood vessels (a process called vasoconstriction), reducing swelling of the mucous membranes that line the nose and sinuses (and thus enlarging the nasal airways) and easing breathing. This action also reduces mucus production.

Decongestants can be oral (taken by mouth) or topical (taken as nose drops or spray). Because topical decongestants are typically limited to a single function and active ingredient, they are listed on page 71.

There are significant differences, in safety and effectiveness, between oral and topical decongestants. Oral decongestants take slightly longer to act than topical decongestants, but may also last longer. Because they cause less intense vasoconstriction, they have not been associated with rebound congestion—the phenomenon in which congestion rapidly returns once medication is discontinued—which is an adverse effect of topical decongestants. On the other hand, because they are not confined to the nose but also affect other areas that contain blood vessels, many oral decongestants can produce other undesirable side effects, such as headache and sleeplessness, and should be avoided at bedtime. An important exception to this rule is pseudoephedrine (see below), which does not stimulate like the other drugs described here.

Warning
Some oral decongestants can raise your blood pressure, putting a strain on the heart and causing palpitations and either wakefulness or drowsiness. If you have hypertension or hyperthyroidism, use these products only on the advice of a physician.

According to the FDA, only three agents have been shown to be effective as oral decongestants.

Pseudoephedrine

By far the most common oral decongestant in cold, cough, and allergy remedies, pseudoephedrine—which means "false" ephedrine—is a close chemical relative of ephedrine (a stimulant drug that opens airway passages). Unlike the other decongestants, it is unlikely to cause anxiety, tremor, and restlessness, or to be a cardiac stimulant.

Pseudoephedrine is most effective about four hours after it is taken. Because it lasts only a few hours, several companies have marketed slow-release formulations to maintain more constant relief from nasal airway obstruction. People whose nasal stuffiness interferes with nighttime sleep may benefit from such a formulation.

Pseudoephedrine is also used to treat middle ear infections (see page 40).

Dosage:
Adults take 60 mg every six hours (maximum dosage 240 mg in twenty-four hours). Children ages six to twelve take 30 mg every six hours (maximum dosage 120 mg in twenty-four hours). Children ages two to six years take 15 mg every six hours (maximum dosage 60 mg in twenty-four hours). Do not give to children under two except under the supervision of a physician.

Phenylpropanolamine (PPA)

PPA is most effective about three hours after it is taken. Compared with other oral decongestants, it has a higher risk of adverse effects: It may raise the heart rate, sharply elevate blood pressure, and cause palpitations, putting a strain on the heart. It is also used to promote weight loss (see page 167) and to relieve stress incontinence.

(see page 167)

Warning

In 1996, the FDA proposed new labeling for all OTC drugs containing phenylpropanolamine. The warnings advise consumers not to take a PPA-containing drug with any other product that contains PPA, ephedrine, phenylephrine, or pseudoephedrine. (The latter two are in numerous products listed in this section.) Some data indicate that PPA in OTC drugs may increase the risk of hemorrhagic stroke, which occurs when vessels in the brain burst and bleed into the brain. Although there is no definite link between such strokes and OTC PPA, the FDA issued this warning pending further study.

Dosage:

Adults take 25 mg every four hours (maximum dosage 150 mg in twenty-four hours). Children ages six to twelve take 12.5 mg every four hours (maximum dosage 75 mg in twenty-four hours). Children ages two to six take 6.25 mg every four hours (maximum dosage 37.5 mg in twenty-four hours). Do not give to children under two except under the supervision of a physician.

Phenylephrine

While oral phenylephrine is generally effective and safe, it is important to use only the recommended dosage because the amount delivered to the bloodstream is difficult to predict. If you are breast-feeding, do not take products containing phenylephrine.

Dosage:

Adults take 10 mg every four hours (maximum dosage 60 mg in twenty-four hours). Children ages six to twelve years take 5 mg every four hours (maximum dosage 30 mg in twenty-four hours). Children ages two to six years take 2.5 mg every four hours (maximum dosage 15 mg in twenty-four hours). Do not give to children under two except under the supervision of a physician.

Topical Decongestants

Topical decongestants help relieve the feeling of stuffiness often caused by colds and allergic rhinitis. Decongestants work by constricting the blood vessels (a process called vasoconstriction), reducing swelling of the mucous membranes that line the nose and sinuses (and thus enlarging the nasal airways), and easing breathing. This action also reduces mucus production.

The same effect may be achieved with oral decongestants. For a discussion of those drugs, see page 69.

see page 69.

Apart from their ingredients, there are significant differences, in safety and efficacy, between the two types of administration. Topical decongestants act faster, starting to relieve congestion within a few minutes. While oral decongestants can affect the entire body, the most common adverse side effect of topical decongestants is irritation of the nasal lining.

There are four agents commonly used in topical decongestants. The main difference among them appears to be how long the effect lasts.

Warning

If used over an extended period and then discontinued, topical decongestants can cause a phenomenon known as rebound congestion. Because blood vessels in the nasal lining are no longer constricted, they may suddenly widen, causing a rapid increase in congestion. To avert this, you should take the minimum effective dose and use decongestants only when absolutely necessary. If you limit your use of decongestants to only three to four days at a time, your risk of rebound congestion is minimal.

Formulations:

Nose drops, spray

Oxymetazoline

Brand names:
Afrin 12-Hour
Dristan 12-Hour
4-Way Long Lasting
Neo-Synephrine 12 Hour
Vicks Sinex 12-Hour

Oxymetazoline lasts longer than other topical decongestants and needs be taken only twice daily. Like another agent, naphazoline (below), it is also used in eye drop preparations to relieve redness (see page 154).

Dosage:
Adults and children over six administer as two to three drops or sprays of 0.05 percent oxymetazoline in the morning and evening. A less concentrated solution can be used in children as young as two, under a physician's supervision.

Phenylephrine

Brand names:
Dristan
4-Way Fast Acting (with naphazoline)
Neo-Synephrine Mild
Neo-Synephrine Pediatric
Vicks Sinex Ultra Fine Mist

This is less powerful than other agents, but may have fewer adverse effects. It can be taken up to four times daily.

Dosage:
Adults apply a 0.25 to .01 percent solution as one to two drops or sprays every four hours. Children over six years should use the 0.25 percent spray or drops. While lower concentrations are available for use in children under six, consult your physician before administering.

Xylometazoline

Brand names:
Otrivin
Otrivin Pediatric

Its effect lasts eight to ten hours, and it can be used only two to three times daily.

Dosage:
Adults and children over twelve administer as two to three drops or sprays of 0.1 percent xylometazoline every eight to ten hours in the morning and evening. A less concentrated solution can be used in children as young as two, under a physician's supervision.

Naphazoline

Brand names:
4-Way Mentholated (with phenylephrine)
Privine

A more potent vasoconstrictor than phenylephrine, it takes effect within 10 minutes, and can be taken up to four times daily. Naphazoline solutions should be not be used in atomizers containing aluminum parts because drug degradation will result. (Sprays are packaged in flexible plastic containers.)

Dosage:
Administer as two drops or sprays every four to six hours. Do not give to children under twelve except under the supervision of a physician.

What to use when

Choose your topical nasal decongestant based on dosing schedule and possible side effects. For example, while naphazoline is more potent than phenylephrine, you may want to avoid it because it has a sedating effect. Because it is long-acting and has relatively few side effects, oxymetazoline is the ingredient used in most of these products.

[handwritten note: pseudoephedrine best in daytime as a stimulant, diphenhydramine at night]

Nasal Moisturizers

Brand names:
Afrin Moisturizing Saline Mist
Ayr
Breath
Free
NaSal
Ocean Mist
Sea Mist

Nasal moisturizers provide soothing moisture to nasal membranes that are dry and inflamed from colds, allergies, low humidity, and other minor irritations. They also loosen and thin mucus secretions to aid the removal of mucus from the nose and sinuses that accumulates as a result of colds and allergic conditions.

There are a number of nasal moisturizers on the market. As they consist primarily of saline (sodium chloride in solution), the primary difference among them is the type of preservative used. Most contain benzalkonium chloride; thimerosal, disodium EDTA, and benzyl alcohol may also be present. Most of these preservatives are also used in eye-care products (see page 151), where they have sometimes caused problems. However, they are unlikely to cause problems in nasal applications.

Formulations:
Spray, drops

Dosage:
Some sprays may be administered on an as-needed basis, others only twice daily; similarly, some may be given to infants, while others are not recommended for children under the age of six years. See manufacturers' directions on dosage for specific brand-name products.

Antihistamines

Brand names
(decongestant plus antihistamine):
Actifed (pseudoephedrine, triprolidine)
Actifed Daytime/Nighttime (pseudoephedrine, diphenhydramine)
Allerest 12-Hour Maximum Strength (PPA, chlorpheniramine)
Benadryl Allergy Decongestant Medication (pseudoephedrine, diphenhydramine)
Chlor-Trimeton 12-Hour Allergy Decongestant (pseudoephedrine, chlorpheniramine)
Contac 12-Hour Cold (PPA, chlorpheniramine)
Dimetapp (PPA, brompheniramine)
Dristan Cold Multi-Symptom (phenylephrine, chlorpheniramine)
Novahistine (phenylephrine, chlorpheniramine)
Sine-Off Maximum Strength Allergy/Sinus (pseudoephedrine, chlorpheniramine)
Sudafed Plus (pseudoephedrine, chlorpheniramine)
Tavist-D Antihistamine/Nasal Decongestant (PPA, clemastine)
Tylenol Children's Cold Multi-Symptom (pseudoephedrine, chlorpheniramine)
Vicks DayQuil Allergy Relief 12-Hour (PPA, brompheniramine)

Most products in this category also contain an antihistamine to help dry up a runny nose and reduce sneezing. However, antihistamines cannot prevent or cut short the common cold, and many health-care professionals believe they should not be included in cold remedies. Various antihistamines are also used in numerous OTC medications to suppress coughing, reduce nausea (see page 84), and relieve itching (see page 99).

The most commonly used antihistamines for colds and coughs are brompheniramine, chlorpheniramine, clemastine, diphenhydramine, and triprolidine. A few preparations contain other antihistamines, notably doxylamine—which has a stronger sedative effect—and pyrilamine; the latter is most often used in products with codeine.

Antihistamines work by countering the effects of histamine, one of the chemicals released in the body when there is an allergic reaction. The release of histamine sets off a local inflammatory response in which the small blood vessels in the nose redden and dilate, swelling, or sneezing ensues.

The antihistamines discussed in this section are targeted for the treatment of allergies and symptomatic relief of colds. Because antihistamines typically produce drowsiness, you may need to avoid driving, operating machinery, or performing other tasks that require physical coordination or mental alertness. However, antihistamines are sometimes combined in cold/cough remedies with a decongestant (see page 72), which has a stimulating effect and tends to counter the sedating effect.

Other common adverse effects of antihistamines include dry mouth, blurred vision, constipation, and difficulty passing urine. These effects usually diminish as you continue to use the antihistamine. If they do not, you can try adjusting the dosage or changing to a different drug. These effects, however, are likely to be amplified if you're taking certain drugs that also have the effect of drying up secretions. These drugs include antispasmodics, antipsychotics, tricyclic antidepressants, and some anti-parkinsonism drugs.

People sometimes find that the type of antihistamine they have been taking regularly over weeks or months becomes less effective. If that happens, they may benefit by switching to an antihistamine from a different chemical class.

Antihistamines are also included in products applied topically for temporary relief of pain and discomfort caused by minor burns (see page 101), itching (see page 99), and insect bites and stings (see page 108). Antihistamines used in these and other types of products are listed under the appropriate treatments.

Warning

People with closed-angle glaucoma—the less common type of glaucoma, in which the canals that drain fluid from the eyes are completely blocked—should consult a physician before taking antihistamines, as antihistamines may nullify the action of other drugs being taken to control the disease. (Antihistamines are not a risk for people with wide-angle glaucoma, the more common type.) Antihistamines should also be used with caution by people with asthma, obstructive disease of the gastrointestinal tract, or benign prostatic hypertrophy (enlarged prostate).

Diphenhydramine Hydrochloride

Brand names:
Actifed Allergy Daytime/Nighttime
Benadryl
Benadryl Cold Nighttime Formula
Benylin
Contac Day & Night
Tylenol Cold NightTime Liquid
Tylenol Flu NightTime Maximum Strength

One of the antihistamines longest in use, this product is used to treat allergic reactions such as itching and hives as well as colds. It acts quickly, but generally produces drowsiness, so it is more often found in products designated for nighttime use. It is also used widely as an antiemetic (see page 85) and a sleep aid (see page 175), although in some individuals—most often children and elderly people—it may actually have stimulant properties.

Formulations:
Caplet, tablet, capsule, liquid, gelcap

Dosage:
Adults take 25 to 50 mg every four to six hours, not to exceed 300 mg in a twenty-four-hour period. Children six to twelve years take half that amount. Children two to six take 6.25 mg every four to six hours, not to exceed 37.5 mg.

Clemastine Fumarate

Brand names:
Contac 12-Hour Allergy
Tavist-1
Tavist-D

In the same class as diphenhydramine hydrochloride, clemastine fumarate is longer acting and can be taken every twelve hours.

Formulation:
Tablet

Dosage:
Adults take 1.34 mg every twelve hours, not to exceed 2.68 mg in twenty-four hours. Because of its greater potency, clemastine fumarate is not recommended for children under the age of twelve.

Chlorpheniramine Maleate

Brand names:
Alka-Selzer Plus Cold Medicine
Alka-Selzer Plus Cold & Cough Medicine
Allerest
Chlor-Trimeton
Comtrex Allergy-Sinus
Contac Maximum Strength 12-Hour
Contac Severe Cold & Flu Non-Drowsy
Dristan Cold and Flu
Novahistine
PediaCare Night Rest Cold-Cough Formula
Sinarest Sinus
Sine-Off Maximum Strength Allergy/Sinus
Sinutab Sinus Allergy Maximum Strength
Teldrin
TheraFlu Maximum Strength NightTime
Triaminicin
Tylenol Allergy Sinus Maximum Strength
Vicks 44M Cough, Cold, and Flu Relief

In the same chemical class as brompheniramine maleate and triprolidine hydrochloride (see below), chlorpheniramine maleate is less likely to produce drowsiness than many other types of antihistamine and, therefore, is widely preferred for daytime use.

Formulations:
Effervescent tablet, chewable tablet, tablet, caplet, powder, liquid

Dosage:
Adults take 4 mg every four to six hours, not to exceed 24 mg in twenty-four hours. Children six to twelve years take half that amount. Children ages two to six take 1 mg every four to six hours, not to exceed 6 mg in twenty-four hours.

Brompheniramine Maleate

Brand names:
Alka-Seltzer Plus Night-Time Cold Medicine
Bromatapp Extended Release
Dimetane
Dimetapp
Dimetapp Allergy
Dimetapp Cold & Allergy
Dristan Allergy
Vicks DayQuil Allergy Relief 4-Hour Tablets
Vicks DayQuil Allergy Relief 12-Hour Extended Release Tablets

Formulations:
Effervescent tablet, chewable tablet, tablet, liquid, caplet

Dosage:
Adults take 4 mg every four to six hours, not to exceed 24 mg in twenty-four hours. Children six to twelve take half that amount. Children ages two to six take 1 mg every four to six hours, not to exceed 6 mg in twenty-four hours.

Triprolidine Hydrochloride

Brand names:
Allerfrim Nasal Decongestant and Antihistamine
Bayer Select Night Time Cold

Formulations:
Tablet, syrup, caplet

Dosage:
Adults take 2.5 mg every four to six hours, not to exceed 15 mg in twenty-four hours. Children six to twelve take half that amount. For children two to six, consult a physician.

Cough Suppressants (Antitussives)

Cough suppressants help reduce coughing by calming the medulla, the part of the brain that governs the coughing reflex. All cough suppressants have a generally sedating effect on the brain and nervous system and commonly cause drowsiness and other side effects.

In general, they should not be used for so-called productive coughs—coughs that produce phlegm, the stringy, thick mucus from your respiratory passages—because they may prolong a chest infection by preventing the normal elimination of the mucus. However, if the productive cough is particularly bothersome or interferes with sleep, an antitussive may be used with caution. For that reason, some products contain both an antitussive and an expectorant (see page 76), which helps in the elimination of phlegm.

Despite the profusion of brands of antitussives on drugstore shelves, there are really only two active ingredients used in cough suppressants.

Dextromethorphan

Brand names
(plus decongestant and/or antihistamine if indicated):
Alka-Seltzer Plus Cold & Cough Medicine (PPA, chlorpheniramine)
Bayer Select Chest Cold
Benylin Adult Cough Formula — best
Comtrex Maximum Strength (pseudoephedrine, chlorpheniramine)
Comtrex Maximum Strength Non-Drowsy (PPA)
Contac Severe Cold & Flu Non-Drowsy (PPA, chlorpheniramine)
Dimetane-DX (pseudoephedrine, brompheniramine)
Dimetapp Cold & Cough Maximum Strength (PPA, brompheniramine)
Drixoral Cough
NyQuil Children's Cold/Cough (pseudoephedrine, chlorpheniramine)

PediaCare Cough-Cold for Ages 6 to 12 (pseudoephedrine, chlorpheniramine)
PediaCare Night Rest Cough-Cold Formula (pseudoephedrine, chlorpheniramine)
Pertussin CS
Robitussin Cough Calmers (lozenge)
Robitussin Maximum Strength Cough & Cold (pseudoephedrine)
Robitussin Pediatric Night Relief (pseudoephedrine, chlorpheniramine)
Robitussin Pediatric Cough
St. Joseph Cough Suppressant for Children
Sucrets 4-Hour Cough Suppressant (lozenge)
Sudafed Severe Cold Formula (pseudoephedrine)
TheraFlu Maximum Strength NightTime (pseudoephedrine, chlorpheniramine)
TheraFlu Maximum Strength Non-Drowsy (pseudoephedrine)
Triaminic-DM (PPA)
Tylenol Children's Cold Multi-Symptom Plus Cough Liquid (pseudoephedrine, chlorpheniramine)
Tylenol Cold and Flu (pseudoephedrine, chlorpheniramine)
Tylenol Cold No Drowsiness (pseudoephedrine)
Tylenol Multi-Symptom Cough
Tylenol Multi-Symptom Cough with Decongestant (pseudoephedrine)
Vicks 44 Cough
Cold & Flu Relief (pseudoephedrine, chlorpheniramine)
Vicks 44 Dry Hacking Cough
Vicks 44 Dry Hacking Cough & Head Congestion (pseudoephedrine)
Vicks NyQuil (pseudoephedrine, doxylamine)

Used in virtually all OTC cough suppressant products, dextromethorphan is effective, does not cause breathing problems, and—unlike codeine, the only other cough suppressant on the market—is not addictive. The most common adverse effects are drowsiness and upset stomach. Because dextromethorphan is sedating, some manufacturers offer day-and-night formulations with dextromethorphan in two different concentrations; other formulations, with lower levels of dextromethorphan and no antihistamine, are often labeled "nondrowsy."

Dosage:
Adults take 10 to 20 mg every four hours, or 30 mg every six to eight hours, maximum dosage not to exceed 120 mg in twenty-four hours. Children

ages six to twelve take half that dosage. Children ages two to six take 2.5 to 5 mg every four hours or 7.5 mg every six to eight hours, total not to exceed 30 mg in twenty-four hours. Do not give to children under two except under the supervision of a physician.

Codeine

**Brand names
(plus other key ingredients if indicated):**
Actifed With Codeine (pseudoephedrine, triprolidine)
Codimal PH (phenylephrine, pyrilamine)
Dimetane-DC Sugar Free (PPA, brompheniramine)
Novahistine DH (pseudoephedrine, chlorpheniramine)
Novahistine Expectorant (pseudoephedrine, guaifenesin)
Robitussin AC (guaifenesin)
Robitussin DAC (pseudoephedrine, guaifenesin)
Tricodene No. 1 (pyrilamine)
Tussar-SF (pseudoephedrine, guaifenesin)

Although a narcotic, codeine is available in OTC products in some states, with stringent controls by pharmacists to prevent abuse and misuse. When it is used in recommended amounts for short periods, it is probably as effective as dextromethorphan and there is no significant danger of psychological or physical dependence. Adverse effects include nausea, drowsiness, lightheadedness, and constipation.

Warning

Because codeine may have a slight drying effect on mucus, it should not be given to people with asthma, emphysema, or bronchitis.

Dosage:
Adults take 10 to 20 mg every four to six hours, maximum dosage not to exceed 120 mg in twenty-four hours. Children ages six to twelve take half that dosage. Children ages two to six take 2.5 to 5 mg every four hours, total not to exceed 30 mg in twenty-four hours. Do not give to children under the age of six except under the supervision of a physician.

Expectorants

**Brand names
(combination of suppressant [dextromethorphan]
and expectorant [guaifenesin], plus decongestant if indicated):**
Bayer Select Head & Chest Cold (pseudoephedrine)
Benylin Expectorant Cough Formula
Dimacol (pseudoephedrine)
Novahistine DMX (pseudoephedrine)
Robitussin CF (PPA)
Robitussin Cold & Cough (pseudoephedrine)
Sudafed Cold & Cough (pseudoephedrine)
Vicks 44e Pediatric Chest Cough & Chest Congestion
Vicks DayQuil Multi-Symptom Cold/Flu Relief (pseudoephedrine)

Brand names (expectorant [guaifenesin], plus decongestant if indicated):
Congestac (with pseudoephedrine)
Primatene Dual Action Formula
Robitussin PE (pseudoephedrine)
Robitussin Severe Congestion (pseudoephedrine)
Scot-Tussin Expectorant
Sinutab Non-Drying (pseudoephedrine)
Triaminic Expectorant (PPA)

Expectorants are the drugs most commonly included in OTC cough remedies for so-called productive coughs—that is, coughs that produce phlegm—when simple home remedies such as steam inhalation have failed to loosen the mucus and make it easier to cough up. In treating dry, or nonproductive, coughs, there is no reason to use an expectorant.

While expectorants are generally believed to make it easier to cough up phlegm, there is no objective data to prove it. As a result, not all health-care practitioners recommend expectorants.

The only expectorant classified by the FDA in Category I (safe and effective) is guaifenesin, although one study concluded, "From a scientific point of view, this drug probably has no rational use in clinical medicine as an expectorant." It is thought to act as an expectorant by stimulating the stomach's gastric juices, forcing up the mucus. (Despite this, the expectorant guaifenesin is seldom associated with upset stomach or nausea.)

Dosage:

Adults take 200 to 400 mg every four hours, total not to exceed 2,400 mg in twenty-four hours. Children ages six to twelve years take 100 to 200 mg every four hours, total not to exceed 1,200 mg in twenty-four hours. Children ages two to six take 50 to 100 mg every four hours, total not to exceed 600 mg in twenty-four hours. However, unless directed by a physician, do not give products containing guaifenesin to children under the age of twelve if they have a persistent or chronic cough, such as occurs with asthma, or if the cough is accompanied by excessive phlegm.

What to use when

Self-treatment of colds, coughs, and allergies is intended to relieve symptoms, not provide cures, so take those products targeted to your specific symptoms. If your primary symptom is a persistent dry cough, for example, use a product whose primary ingredient is dextromethorphan, an antitussive or cough suppressant. While many cold/cough and allergy treatments contain multiple medications, try to minimize your consumption of other medications in order to get the maximum allowable dosage of the ingredient(s) you need and to avoid side effects. Of the specific antihistamines of cold/cough and allergy branded products, your choice should be determined by convenience of dosage schedule, side effects (diphenhydramine is particularly sedating, chlorpheniramine maleate is not), and suitability for various age groups, as indicated above.

Lozenges and Mouthwashes/ Gargles (Sore Throat Relief)

Lozenges, medicated mouthwashes, gargles, and sprays help relieve the discomfort of sore throats. They work through the action of topical, or local, anesthetics (see page 97), which temporarily desensitize, or numb, nerve endings. Some lozenges also help suppress coughs.

Many lozenges also often contain antibacterial agents such as cetylpyridinium chloride or phenol (which, in low levels, is also an anesthetic). However, because sore throats caused by colds are typically the result of viral infections, using antibacterial agents is generally pointless. In fact, a person with a dry or raspy sore throat may obtain just as much relief from sucking a hard candy, which stimulates saliva flow, thus moistening the throat. Internal analgesics (see page 56) such as acetaminophen, aspirin, or ibuprofen may also relieve discomfort from a sore throat.

Furthermore, because the ingredients in lozenges do not reach the larynx (voice box), they probably do not help relieve laryngitis, an inflammation of laryngeal tissue often caused by colds.

A few lozenges also contain a cough suppressant, dextromethorphan (see page 75). If you are already taking a cough suppressant in another medication, combining it with a lozenge containing this ingredient will not make it more powerful or produce adverse side effects. However, the combination may add a few hours to the period for which dextromethorphan is effective.

Lozenges may be taken every two to four hours for temporary relief of sore throat and coughing. There are no statistical data to support one type of lozenge over another, apart from the concentration of anesthetic, and personal experience or word of mouth may be the best guide.

Some mouthwashes that contain antiseptics also claim to treat sore throats by killing germs. However, according to the American Pharmaceutical Association, there is no adequate evidence that individuals benefit substantially from the germicidal activity of mouthwashes; in some cases, in fact, the mouthwashes may actually foster the growth of disease-causing organisms. Furthermore, since most sore throats caused by colds are viral, an antibacterial mouthwash has no effect. If the infection is bacterial, the mouthwash must be held in the mouth long enough to kill the bacteria.

Warning

If your sore throat is not related to environmental factors, an allergy, or a cold, you should consult a medical practitioner. A persistent sore throat—particularly in a child—may indicate a more serious disease, such as strep throat, that demands medical attention. If your child has a sore throat, you should offer lozenges or other OTC medications that provide symptomatic relief *only* until your child's medical practitioner can be seen.

Menthol

Brand names:
Cepacol Menthol-Eucalyptus (cetylpyridinium chloride)
Fisherman's Friend
✓**Halls** Mentho Lyptus Ice Blue Cough Suppressant
N'Ice Cough
Ricola
Robitussin Cough Drops
Vicks Chloraseptic Sore Throat (benzocaine)
Vicks Cough Drops

Menthol, which acts as a counterirritant (see page 60) at higher concentrations, is being used increasingly as an anesthetic in lozenges, often combined with benzocaine (see below). It is also widely claimed to have cough suppressant properties, although that is not established by research.

Dosage:
Dissolve one to two lozenges slowly in mouth, repeating every hour or two as needed. (See manufacturer's directions regarding dosage for specific brand-name product.) For children under six years, consult a physician.

Benzocaine

Brand names:
Cepacol Anesthetic (cetylpyridinium chloride)
Chloraseptic Children's Sore Throat
Cough-X (dextromethorphan)

This is historically the anesthetic most commonly used in medicated lozenges. It is never used in mouthwashes or sprays. While it is generally safe, avoid it if you have a history of allergy to it or any other "caine" anesthetic.

Dosage:
Dissolve lozenge slowly in mouth, repeating every two hours as needed. Children under six years take one lozenge every four hours or consult a physician. (See manufacturer's directions regarding dosage for specific brand-name product.)

Dyclonine

Brand names (for lozenges):
Sucrets Children's
Sucrets Maximum Strength
Sucrets Sore Throat

Brand names (for sprays):
Cepacol Maximum Strength (alcohol)

Like benzocaine, this anesthetic is widely used to treat oral pain. It is used in both lozenges and sprays.

Dosage for lozenges:
Dissolve lozenge slowly in mouth, repeating every two hours as needed. For children under two, consult a physician. A large overdose may cause nervousness, dizziness, hypotension (abnormally low blood pressure), or other adverse effects.

Dosage for sprays:
Spray four times into throat and swallow. Repeat as needed up to four times daily. For children under twelve, consult a physician or dentist.

Phenol

Brand names (for lozenges):
Cepastat
Isodettes Sore Throat

Brand names (for sprays):
Children's Vicks Chloraseptic
Isodettes Spray
Painalay Sore Throat Gargle and Spray
Vicks Chloraseptic Sore Throat Spray/Gargle

Like menthol, phenol is a counterirritant at higher levels, an anesthetic at lower levels, as in lozenges, gargles, and sprays. It also has antibacterial properties and is used as an antiseptic in gargles and sprays.

Dosage for lozenges:
In adults and children twelve years and older, allow the lozenge to dissolve slowly in the mouth. Repeat every two hours, not to exceed eighteen lozenges per day. Children six to twelve may repeat every two hours, not to exceed ten lozenges per day. For children under six, consult a dentist or physician.

Dosage for sprays:
Spray five times directly into throat and swallow, or gargle and spit out. Repeat every two hours. For children under two years, consult a physician or dentist.

Povidone-Iodine

Brand name:
Betadine Mouthwash/Gargle (alcohol)

This agent, which is sold directly as a generic and also added to numerous OTC products such as shampoos and douches, is an antiseptic (see page 117) that may also relieve minor irritation. It is never used in lozenges.

Dosage:
Spray four times into throat and swallow, or gargle and spit out. Repeat as needed up to four times daily. For children under twelve years, consult a physician or dentist.

What to use when

If you are concerned about the possible side effects of dyclonine in lozenges, in the unlikely event of an overdose, use a product containing an alternative ingredient. Otherwise, as no product is clearly superior to another, you should be guided by personal experience or word of mouth.

Stomach and Intestinal Treatments

S tomach and Intestinal Treatments looks at the specific medications designed to relieve stomach ailments such as heartburn, indigestion, poisoning, nausea, and vomiting, as well as intestinal problems such as diarrhea, constipation, and flatulence. Addressing the stomach conditions are the following sections: Antacids, Antiemetics (which abate nausea and vomiting), Emetics (which induce vomiting and are used to re-move most potentially toxic agents from the stomach), and Oral Rehydration Therapy (which restores fluids to a body dehydrated by vomiting or diarrhea). Other treatments for stomach and intestinal conditions include Antidiarrheal Treatments, Antiflatulents (gas-reducing medications), and Laxatives.

Antacids

Antacids help to relieve heartburn, indigestion, pain, ulceration, and inflammatory lesions in the stomach. Until recently, all OTC antacids have worked the same way: As alkalies, they reduce gastric acid by reacting with it to form a salt and water. That means that this original group of antacids takes effect only after excess gastric acid has been produced.

Starting in 1995, however, the FDA approved OTC versions of antacid treatments—Tagamet HB, Zantac 75, Pepcid AC, and Axid AR—that had previously been available only by prescription. This new group of antacids, which were among the most prescribed pharmaceuticals and have become highly popular since their over-the-market introduction, works in an entirely different way: They directly inhibit the secretion of gastric acid rather than neutralizing it once it has been produced. As a result, they can prevent symptoms before they occur—for example, the medication can be taken one hour before eating a meal likely to cause distress.

Gastric acid is normally secreted by the stomach to help digest and absorb food, but excess secretions can cause upper gastrointestinal distress. Because antacids neutralize acid, they help protect the lining of the stomach from irritation, thus preventing pain and ulceration or inflammatory lesions. Contrary to one widely held view, antacids do not actually coat the lining of the stomach.

Another widely used treatment for heartburn and indigestion is Pepto-Bismol, which is not officially an antacid because it does not neutralize the acid in the stomach. Pepto-Bismol contains bismuth subsalicylate, which suppresses the *H. pylori* infection, the bacteria believed responsible for many gastric inflammations. While it contains nonaspirin salicylates, you should not take it if you are allergic to aspirin or give it to children if they have fever (see page 55), as an adverse reaction may occur.

The older types of antacid products contain at least one of the four primary neutralizing ingredients (and most contain at least two). In addition, because they work by producing gas, many also contain simethicone to relieve flatulence (see page 90).

(see page 55)

Warning

Antacids that contain aluminum, calcium, or magnesium can interfere with the body's absorption—sometimes by more than 90 percent—of a number of other drugs. Drugs that may not be properly absorbed include a number of antibiotics (notably tetracycline), some heart and blood pressure medications, thyroid medicine, and some antifungals. Pepto-Bismol can also reduce absorption of certain antibiotics.

Sodium Bicarbonate

Brand names:
Alka-Seltzer
Arm & Hammer (pure baking soda)
Bromo-Seltzer

This is a rapid-acting antacid for short-term relief of indigestion and discomfort from overeating. It reacts with gastric acid to form sodium chloride, water, and carbon dioxide. It is not recommended for long-term use, however, because the sodium can promote water retention and high blood pressure.

Warning

This product should be avoided by people on low-salt diets. One brand, Alka-Seltzer, also contains aspirin (see page 55).

Formulations:
Caplet, chewable tablet, effervescent powder/tablet

Dosage:
With effervescent tablets, dissolve two in 4 ounces of water every six hours, not to exceed eight tablets in twenty-four hours. If you are sixty years of age or older, take no more than four tablets in twenty-four hours. Children may use half of adult dosage. With powders, do not take more than eight level ½ teaspoons, or four level ½ teaspoons if you are sixty years or older, in a twenty-four-hour period. To avoid serious injury, be sure powders are completely dissolved before taking. Adults may take two caplets or tablets every six hours, not to exceed eight in any twenty-four-hour period. For children under twelve, consult a physician.

Calcium Carbonate

Brand names:
Di-Gel (tablet)
Maalox
Mylanta (gelcap)
Mylanta Soothing
Rolaids Extra Strength
Rolaids Sodium Free
Tums
Tums Anti-Gas/Antacid
Tums E-X Extra Strength

Another rapid-acting antacid, this product has the added benefit of providing the body with extra calcium, an essential mineral. Indeed, many people routinely use these products as calcium supplements (see page 216).

Warning
Doses larger than 2 to 2.5 g per day can be harmful. Large amounts of this ingredient can lead to high levels of calcium in the urine and can cause renal stones, which can in turn reduce kidney function. This is a particular danger for people whose kidney function is already impaired.

Formulations:
Tablet, chewable tablet, suspension, caplet, gelcap, lozenge

Dosage:
Chew two to four tablets as symptoms occur; repeat hourly if symptoms return, or as directed by a physician. Allow one lozenge to dissolve in your mouth and, if necessary, follow with a second; do not take more than twelve lozenges in a twenty-four-hour period. Take two to four tablets, gelcaps, or caplets as needed every two to four hours; do not take more than eighteen to twenty-four in a twenty-four-hour period. (As the maximum allowable dosage varies with individual manufacturer's formulation, check the label of each product.) With liquids, do not take more than 16 teaspoons in a twenty-four-hour period. In all cases, do not use the maximum dosage more than every day for two weeks continuously.

Aluminum Salts

Brand names:
Amphojel
ALternaGEL
Basaljel

The most common formulation is aluminum hydroxide, which reacts with gastric acid to form aluminum chloride and water; other aluminum salts used less frequently are aluminum carbonate and aluminum phosphate.

These products can produce constipation. Some manufacturers counteract this tendency by combining these drugs with magnesium or other substances that have a laxative effect (see below).

Warning
Aluminum is known to be toxic to the nervous system. As a rule, it is absorbed in small quantities and eliminated readily in the urine. Long-term use, however, may lead to elevated aluminum concentrations in people with kidney disease, and dialysis is generally ineffective in removing these concentrations. In addition, aluminum reduces the absorption of phosphate, a situation that can lead to anorexia (loss of appetite), muscle weakness, and osteoporosis (loss and thinning of normal bone density). While not a danger for most people, this creates an increased risk for the elderly, alcoholics, and people with chronic diarrhea.

Formulations:
Capsule, tablets, suspension

Dosage:
Take 2 teaspoons six to twelve times daily. One or two capsules or tablets may be taken every two hours, up to six to twelve times daily. (As the maximum allowable dosage varies with individual manufacturer's formulation, check the label of each product.)

Magnesium Salts

Brand name:
Phillips' Milk of Magnesia

Magnesium salts are more potent than aluminum, but less than sodium bicarbonate and calcium carbonate. Typically, magnesium hydroxide reacts with gastric acid to produce magnesium chloride and water; the drug may also be formulated as carbonate or trisilicateoxide. The most common adverse effect is diarrhea.

Warning

As with aluminum, magnesium should be avoided by people with serious kidney disease because of life-threatening toxicity when not rapidly eliminated by the body.

Formulations:
Suspension, chewable tablet

Dosage:
Adults and children twelve and older take 1 to 3 teaspoons with a little water, up to four times a day. Note that this product has a laxative effect when taken in greater amounts and with more water.

Aluminum and Magnesium

Brand names:
Di-Gel (liquid)
Gaviscon
Maalox
Mylanta

This combination reduces the problems of constipation and diarrhea typically associated with the antacids in which aluminum or magnesium is present by itself.

Warning

For the reasons noted separately under aluminum salts and magnesium salts, this combination should be avoided by people with kidney disease.

Formulations:
Chewable tablet, suspension

Dosage:
Chew one to four tablets four times daily or as directed by a physician. (As the maximum allowable dosage varies with individual manufacturer's formulation, check the label of each product.) Take 2 to 4 teaspoons four times daily or as directed by a physician.

New Antacid Products

The neutralizing agents in the new type of antacids work by directly inhibiting the secretion of gastric acid. As a result, they may be able to prevent symptoms altogether before they occur. For example, the medication can be taken an hour before eating a meal likely to cause distress. Of the active ingredients, only cimetidine (see below) has known drug interactions. Cimetidine also makes the claim that it can be taken as little as one-half hour before eating, while the other products must be taken a full hour before. Otherwise, there is minimal difference among the products.

Formulation:
Tablet

Dosage:
One tablet (200 mg) with water as symptoms occur or preventively, up to twice daily. Do not give to children under twelve years old unless directed by a physician. Do not take the maximum daily dosage for more than two weeks continuously except under the supervision of a doctor.

Cimetidine

Brand name:
Tagamet HB

Cimetidine works by inhibiting the secretion of gastric acid and may be able to prevent symptoms altogether before they occur. Of the active ingredients, only cimetidine has known drug interactions. Cimetidine also makes the claim that it can be taken as little as one-half hour before eating, while the other products must be taken a full hour before.

Warning

If you currently take theophylline (an oral asthma medication), warfarin (blood-thinning medicine), or phenytoin (a seizure inhibitor), consult your doctor before taking cimetidine.

Ranitidine

Brand name:
Zantac 75

The neutralizing agents in ranitidine work by directly inhibiting the secretion of gastric acid. As a result, they may be able to prevent symptoms altogether before they occur. For example, the medication can be taken an hour before eating a meal likely to cause distress. It must be taken a full hour before eating a meal.

Famotidine

Brand name:
Pepcid AC

Famotidine works by directly inhibiting the secretion of gastric acid and may be able to prevent symptoms altogether before they occur. It must be taken a full hour before eating a meal.

Nizatidine

Brand name:
Axid AR

The neutralizing agents in the nizatidine work by directly inhibiting the secretion of gastric acid. As a result, they may be able to prevent symptoms altogether before they occur. For example, the medication can be taken an hour before eating a meal likely to cause distress. It must be taken a full hour before eating a meal.

What to use when

For fast relief of symptoms, try the traditional antacids. If they do not provide adequate relief, or if you want to prevent symptoms that you anticipate resulting from a spicy food you expect to consume within an hour, for example, try the new class of antacids.

Antiemetics

Nonprescription antiemetics relieve minor nausea and vomiting-related conditions, specifically motion sickness. In addition to antiemetics, antacids (see page 81) are also widely used to relieve nausea associated with heartburn and acid indigestion from overeating or drinking too much. Nausea and vomiting caused by other conditions, such as medication or pregnancy, should not be treated with these antiemetics.

The primary agents used in OTC antiemetics are certain types of antihistamines (see page 72). They work by having a depressant effect on the labyrinth, or inner ear, which may become overstimulated in some individuals when unusual motion patterns affect the movement of fluid in the ear's three canals.

The antiemetics listed below should be taken thirty to sixty minutes before departure for travel and continued during travel to be effective in preventing motion sickness.

Warning

Like any product containing antihistamine, antiemetics may cause drowsiness. You should not drive or engage in demanding physical or intellectual tasks while using these products. These products should also be used with caution by people with asthma, glaucoma, obstructive disease of the gastrointestinal tract, or benign prostatic hypertrophy (enlarged prostate). Finally, all antiemetics should be used with caution because they may mask symptoms of more severe conditions, including head trauma.

Dimenhydrinate

Brand name:
Dramamine; liquid Dramamine contains 5 percent alcohol
Dimenhydrinate is effective in treating dizziness as well as nausea and vomiting associated with motion sickness.

Formulations:
Tablet, chewable tablet, liquid

Dosage:
Adults take 50 to 100 mg every four to six hours, not to exceed 400 mg in twenty-four hours. Chil-

dren six to twelve years, take 25 to 50 mg every six to eight hours, not to exceed 150 mg in twenty-four hours. Children two to six years, take 12.5 to 25 mg every six to eight hours, not to exceed 75 mg in twenty-four hours.

Diphenhydramine

Brand name:
Benadryl

This antihistamine has a particularly strong sedating effect, although it sometimes has the opposite (stimulating) effect, particularly in children. It is safe for children over 20 pounds.

Formulations:
Tablet, liquid, capsule

Dosage:
Adults take 25 to 50 mg every four to six hours, not to exceed 300 mg in twenty-four hours. Children weighing over 20 pounds take half that amount.

Meclizine

Brand names:
Bonine
Dramamine II

Of the four antihistamines listed here, meclizine is the longest-acting and may be administered only every twenty-four hours. The initial dose should be taken one hour prior to travel, if possible.

Formulations:
Tablet, chewable tablet

Dosage:
Adults take 25 to 50 mg once a day. Meclizine is not recommended for children under twelve.

Cyclizine

Brand name:
Marezine

Cyclizine is not as long-acting as meclizine and therefore requires more frequent dosing, although it belongs to the same group of antihistamine compounds.

Formulation:
Tablet

Dosage:
Adults take 50 mg every four to six hours, not to exceed 200 mg in twenty-four hours. Children ages six to twelve take 25 mg every six to eight hours, not to exceed 75 mg in twenty-four hours. Cyclizine is not recommended for children under six. It should be take approximately one hour prior to travel.

What to use when

As all the antihistamines are similarly effective, your choice should be determined by convenience of dosage schedule, side effects (diphenhydramine is particularly sedating), and suitability for various age groups, as indicated above.

Emetics

OTC emetics induce vomiting and are used to remove most potentially toxic, or poisonous, agents from the stomach. They are used most commonly to treat poisoning. There are two types of emetics, each of which affects the body differently.

Warning

Anyone who has swallowed a caustic substance, such as bleach, should not be given an emetic. Vomiting would reexpose the esophagus and oral cavity to the caustic agent, and more damage could occur. In most cases, the person should be taken immediately to a medical facility.

When poisoning is suspected and before either syrup of ipecac or activated charcoal is administered, the closest poison control center should be called (see page 222). Have that phone number handy at all times.

Syrup of Ipecac

The emetic of choice, syrup of ipecac is prepared from ipecac powder, a natural product that contains two chemicals, emetine and cephaeline. It is thought that syrup of ipecac induces vomiting by irritating the mucous lining of the gastrointestinal tract—the stomach and intestines—and also by stimulating an area in the brain stem called the chemoreceptor trigger zone (CTZ), which signals the stomach to vomit.

When given in doses as directed by the manufacturer, adverse effects are generally mild: diarrhea, slight drowsiness, slowed reflexes, and mild gastrointestinal upset. In larger doses, ipecac can cause repeated vomiting and serious heart problems, including bradycardia (an abnormally slow heartbeat) and fibrillation (in which a chamber of the heart is contracting abnormally).

Syrup of ipecac should be kept in all homes with young children (a 1-ounce bottle for each child under five years of age) and used with the guidance of a poison control center or physician. If your syrup of ipecac is past the expiration date when you need it, don't be alarmed. One study has shown that in all likelihood it can still be used safely and effectively. The ipecac used in the study ranged from one month to sixteen years beyond the expiration date.

Syrup of ipecac is sold only in generic form.

Formulation:
Syrup

Dosage:
For children one year of age and older, the recommended dose is 15 ml (1 tablespoon). This dose can be repeated once if vomiting has not occurred within twenty minutes. Children under one year may be given 5 to 10 ml (1 to 2 teaspoons). For adolescents and adults, the initial dose is 15 to 30 ml; repeat once if necessary.

Because ipecac does not work as well if the stomach is nearly empty, children should be given at least 6 to 8 ounces of clear fluid and adults 12 to 16 ounces immediately after the ipecac dose, to partially distend or expand the stomach. Milk may also be used, but it may lengthen the time needed to induce vomiting and, in any event, may make it harder to find evidence of the poison, such as tablets and capsules, in the vomitus. People suspected of swallowing toxic agents should be encouraged to move around if at all possible, because that seems to help them vomit more quickly. Vomiting should occur within fifteen to twenty minutes of initial dose.

Activated Charcoal

Brand name:
CharcoAid 2000

Usually administered as a water slurry, or slushy drink, an activated charcoal preparation works by binding to toxic substances that have already reached the stomach and intestines. Although it should be given as soon as possible after the toxin has been consumed, in some cases it has been shown to be effective even when used several hours later. It is not effective for all toxic substances, but it can reduce the absorption of many, such as excessively high quantities of analgesics, sedatives, and some antidepressants.

Products in which activated charcoal is premixed with water are commercially available. Even so, it is difficult to administer a therapeutic dosage, especially to children, because of the distasteful nature of the slurry. Although activated charcoal and ipecac are sometimes administered together in hospital emergency rooms, they should not be combined in the home.

Contrary to popular belief, burnt toast is not a substitute for activated charcoal, and is not recommended as an emetic.

Formulation:
Slurry

Dosage:
The dosage for adults is 60 to 100 g of activated charcoal, for children 15 to 30 g, in 250 ml of water. Repeat doses may be given to bind toxins secreted into the gastrointestinal tract. Because activated charcoal is extremely safe, there is no maximum dose limit.

What to use when

Studies have shown that activated charcoal is as effective as induced gastric emptying (by ipecac as well as mechanical means) in hospital-treated patients. In the home, however, activated charcoal is not a viable substitute for syrup of ipecac because children will resist drinking the slurry.

Oral Rehydration Therapy

Brand names:
Kao Lectrolyte
Pedialyte
Rehydralyte
Ricelyte
Resol

Oral rehydration therapy helps restore several of the body's important chemicals lost through vomiting and diarrhea. These products are commonly used in the management of mild to moderate diarrhea, most often in children. (Adults may also use these products but are less likely to need them as their chemical reserves are not depleted so rapidly.) They work mainly by using glucose to increase the body's absorption of sodium and allow for the rapid replacement of extracellular fluid.

The leading OTC oral rehydration products contain, in varying amounts, glucose, sodium, chloride, and potassium. While Gatorade, fruit juices, and carbonated beverages are adequate energy sources and can also be administered, these products are too low in sodium, potassium, and chloride to produce a rapid response in cases of severe dehydration. A product heavy in sodium, such as soup, can create an electrolyte imbalance that can flush more fluid from the body or create a buildup of water in the brain.

If vomiting and diarrhea are severe (resulting in a 5 to 10 percent weight loss), you should seek professional help, as it may be necessary to give fluids intravenously. If a child cannot retain fluid or if watery diarrhea persists, contact the child's medical provider.

Formulations:
Liquid, powder (to mix with water)

Dosage:
As dosage varies with age and weight for very young children (two weeks to six years), see manufacturers' directions for each brand. Children six to ten years should take 960 to 1,920 ml per day; children over ten years and adults should take

1,920 to 2,880 ml per day. However, total daily intake should be adjusted to meet individual needs, based on thirst and response to therapy. The fluid deficit should be replaced as quickly as possible, usually in the first four to six hours after vomiting and/or diarrhea.

Antidiarrheal Treatments

Antidiarrheal drugs relieve nonspecific diarrhea—diarrhea not caused by a significant infection, illness, or medication—through actions that are either antiperistaltic or adsorbent (see definitions below). These drugs are generally taken to provide relief once it is certain that the diarrhea is neither infectious nor toxic. (You should suspect infection if there's a possibility you've eaten improperly cooked poultry or dairy products or ingested contaminated foods or water; the latter is likely if you've been traveling in a developing country. Alternatively, toxicity may be the cause if you've recently started taking a new drug, notably an antibiotic. In such cases, you should not self-treat but instead should consult a physician.)

A third class of antidiarrheal whose action is neither antiperistaltic nor adsorbent is bismuth salicylate. It has been shown to be effective in both preventing and treating symptoms of travelers' diarrhea—caused by exposure to microbes, typically in impure or polluted drinking water, generally on visits to developing countries—because it appears to inhibit intestinal secretions.

Until 1991, paregoric—which contains a narcotic, morphine—was also available as an OTC drug to treat diarrhea. Because of its narcotic content, it was subject to abuse, and for a time sales to any one individual were strictly controlled. Now the FDA requires a prescription for paregoric.

Antiperistaltic drugs inhibit the propulsive activity of the muscles in the small intestine and colon (called peristalsis), so that fecal matter passes more slowly through the bowels. However, if the diarrhea is caused by bacterial infection or antibiotics, antiperistaltic drugs may prolong or enhance the severity of the symptoms because these drugs slow down the motility, or spontaneous movement, of the gut, allowing the substance to remain longer in the body.

Adsorbents, which are the type of drug used most often in OTC antidiarrheal preparations, adsorb, or bind with, the irritants present in the bowel; they also absorb water in the bowel, thus producing larger, firmer, and less frequent bowel movements. Because large doses of adsorbents are necessary for this process, most adsorbent antidiarrheals are formulated as flavored liquid suspensions to make them more palatable. They are generally used to treat mild nonspecific diarrhea and have a gentler effect than the antiperistaltics.

To replace nutrients and fluids lost to the diarrhea, a variety of OTC oral rehydration products (see page 87) are on the market. Such products are an integral part of treatment for persistent diarrhea, particularly in the very young and the frail elderly.

Warning

Diarrhea can be a symptom of a more serious underlying disease. If severe, it should be treated by a physician. If you are self-treating, never combine the two types of antidiarrheals, because a bulky mass could form and obstruct the bowel.

Loperamide

Brand names:
Imodium A-D
Kaopectate 1-D
Maalox Anti-Diarrheal
Pepto Diarrhea Control

A very effective antiperistaltic agent, loperamide is a fast-acting drug that is widely used for both acute (characterized by a sudden onset of loose stools) and recurrent bouts of diarrhea. It reduces the loss of water and salts from the bowel and slows bowel activity, resulting in the passage of firmer bowel movements at less frequent intervals. It is also effective in relieving gastrointestinal cramping. Loperamide has also been shown to be an effective treatment for infectious, or travelers', diarrhea, which is caused by a variety of bacteria.

Formulations:
Caplet, liquid

Dosage:

Adults take 4 teaspoons or two caplets after first loose bowel movement. Take each dose with a glass of water. If needed, take 2 teaspoons or one caplet after each subsequent loose bowel movement. Do not exceed 8 teaspoons or four caplets in any twenty-four-hour period, unless directed by a physician. Children ages six and older should take half that dosage, but children ages nine to eleven should not exceed 6 teaspoons or three caplets a day, and children ages six to eight should not exceed 4 teaspoons or two caplets a day. For children ages two to five, take 1 teaspoon after first loose bowel movement, followed by one after each subsequent loose bowel movement; do not exceed 3 teaspoons a day.

Loperamide and other antiperistaltic drugs should be used for no more than forty-eight hours in acute diarrhea. They may cause constipation if used in excess.

Attapulgite

Brand names:
Diasorb
Donnagel
Kaopectate
Kaopectate Children's
Rheaban

The most widely used adsorbent ingredient in antidiarrheal products, attapulgite is usually taken after each loose bowel movement until the diarrhea is controlled. Alternatively, attapulgite may be used when it is necessary to regulate bowel action over a prolonged period—for example, in people who have had colostomies, a surgical procedure in which the colon is partially removed.

Warning

Adsorption is not selective, and adsorbents such as attapulgite may adsorb, or bind with, nutrients, digestive enzymes, and medication, as well as toxins and bacteria in the gastrointestinal tract. To replace nutrients lost to adsorbents, you may use a variety of OTC oral rehydration products (see page 87).

Formulations:

Chewable tablet, suspension, tablet, liquid, caplet

Dosage:

Adults and children twelve and over take 2 tablespoons or two caplets at first sign of diarrhea, and 2 tablespoons or two caplets after each subsequent bowel movement, not to exceed 12 tablespoons or caplets in twenty-four hours. Take with a glass of water. Children six to twelve years of age, take 1 tablespoon/caplet after the initial bowel movement, and 1 tablespoon/caplet after each subsequent movement, not to exceed 6 tablespoons/caplets in twenty-four hours. Unless directed by a physician do not give caplets to children under six, or liquids to children under three. Products may cause constipation if used in excess.

Bismuth Subsalicylate

Brand names:
Liquid-Bismo
Pepto-Bismol Original/Original Strength

Neither an antiperistaltic nor an adsorbent agent, bismuth subsalicylate has been shown to be effective in both preventing and treating symptoms of travelers' diarrhea. It is believed to work by several mechanisms in the gastrointestinal tract, including normalizing fluid movement by preventing secretions, binding bacterial toxins, and destroying organisms that may be causing diarrhea. A common side effect is black-stained stool, not necessarily caused by the presence of blood in the feces.

Warning

Salicylate may be a problem if you are taking aspirin or other drugs containing salicylates. Do not give these products to children with viral influenza or chicken pox, owing to concern about development of Reye's syndrome (see page 65).

Formulations:

Liquid, chewable caplet

Dosage:

Adults take 2 tablespoons or two caplets every thirty to sixty minutes, if needed, to a maximum of eight doses in a twenty-four-hour period. Drink a glass of water with each dose. Recommended doses for children are by age: ages nine to twelve years, 1 tablespoon or caplet; ages six to nine, 2 teaspoons or $2/3$

caplet; ages three to six, 1 teaspoon or ⅓ caplet. For children under three, consult a physician.

What to use when

If you have mild nonspecific diarrhea—that is, diarrhea not caused by a significant infection, illness, or medication—you should try first the adsorbent drugs (typically containing atta-pulgite). If you have acute diarrhea (character-ized by a sudden onset of loose stools) or recurrent bouts of diarrhea, loperamide and other antiperistaltic drugs are preferable. They are also effective for travelers' diarrhea. To pre-vent travelers' diarrhea, try bismuth salicylate.

Antiflatulents

Antiflatulents reduce the presence of excessive gas in the digestive tract. There are a few products that are specifically antiflatulent; these are listed below. However, many antacids (see page 81) also include an antifoaming agent, usu-ally simethicone, to relieve flatulence.

Simethicone

Brand names:
Gas-X
Mylanta Gas
Mylanta Gas Maximum Strength
Mylicon Gas
Mylicon Infant's
Phazyme-95

Simethicone helps relieve the pain and cramping caused by trapped gas. A mixture of silicon poly-mers, it acts in the stomach and intestines as a de-foaming agent, reducing the surface tension of gas bubbles embedded in mucus in the gastrointestinal tract. As the surface tension changes, the gas bubbles are broken so they can be eliminated more easily by belching or passing gas. It does not actually prevent the gas from forming.

Formulations:
Chewable tablets, drops

Dosage:
Adults chew one to two tablets (about 80 to 160 mg of simethicone) four times a day, after meals and at bedtime. Do not exceed 500 mg of sime-thicone in any twenty-four-hour period. With drops, adults take 1.2 ml four times daily after meals and at bedtime; do not take more than six times per day. Children ages two to twelve take half that amount. Infants under two take 0.3 ml four times daily or as directed by a physician. Drops may also be mixed with liquids for easier administration.

Alpha-galactosidase Enzyme

Brand name:
Beano (classified as a dietary supplement, not a drug)

Derived from a mold, this enzyme breaks down indigestible sugars found in gas-producing veg-etables and legumes, converting them into easily digestible sugars.

Warning

If you are diabetic, be aware that the sugars in these foods increase blood sugar levels more rapidly in this form.

Formulations:
Tablets, liquid

Dosage:
Swallow, chew, or crumble two to three tablets with the first bite of food; place six to eight drops on first bite of food.

What to use when

Simethicone is the antiflatulent for general use. If you experience flatulence only from specific foods, however, you may want to take the alpha-galactosidase enzyme product when you eat those.

Laxatives

Laxatives help relieve constipation. In addition to enemas (see page 188), there are three main types of laxatives: bulk-forming, stimulant, and emollient (lubricant). Other types of laxatives use saline or glycerin—the latter primarily for infants.

In 1996, the FDA told manufacturers of stimulant laxatives to study the long-term safety of five ingredients that are widely used in stimulants, after animal research raised questions of a possible, though unproved, threat of cancer in cases of continual long-term use. The ingredients—present in more than forty laxatives—are phenolphthalein, bisacodyl, senna, aloe, and cascara sagrada. There have been no reports linking stimulant laxatives to cancer in people, and their use for occasional constipation is considered safe. People concerned about this risk, however, can switch to the bulk-forming laxatives or other alternatives.

Once the standard, castor oil—which works as a stimulant—is no longer used routinely for constipation.

Warning
All laxatives can cause diarrhea if they are taken in too great a dosage and lead to constipation if overused. If you're using a laxative for days or weeks (the time varies with the type of laxative, as indicated below), you may develop a dependence on it for normal bowel movement. You should stop using it as soon as normal bowel movements have been reestablished.

Bulk-forming Laxatives

Because they most closely approximate the natural physiological mechanism of elimination of waste products, bulk-forming laxatives are the preferred choice as initial therapy for most forms of constipation. Taken after a meal, this laxative passes through the stomach to the intestines, where it continues to absorb up to twenty-five times its volume in water, softening and increasing the volume of bowel movements.

Bulk-forming laxatives are usually effective in twelve to twenty-four hours, but may take up to three days for some people. It may be necessary to use these laxatives for as long as two weeks to establish improved bowel habits.

When taken properly, these laxatives don't affect the body overall because they are not absorbed. Because they are generally safe and mild, they can be taken for an extended period—months, if need be—and may even be used as antidiarrheal drugs (see page 88).

Warning
Because of the danger of fecal impaction (intestinal obstruction), bulk-forming laxatives should not be taken by anyone with intestinal ulcerations or adhesions. People with abdominal pain should consult their doctors before using. Diarrhea, abdominal discomfort, flatulence, and excessive loss of fluid can also occur.

Formulations:
Tablet, emulsion, wafer, powder (dissolved in water, soft drinks, or juice)—all formulations should be consumed with plenty of such liquids.

Synthetic cellulose derivatives and calcium polycarbophil

Brand names:
Citrucel
Fiberall
FiberCon

Choosing among the different bulk products is a matter of personal preference. The two active ingredients most widely used in bulk laxatives are synthetic cellulose derivatives (methyl cellulose, carboxymethyl cellulose sodium) and calcium polycarbophil. A few of these preparations also include a stimulant laxative (discussed on page 92).

Dosage:
Adults should take 1 rounded tablespoon stirred briskly into at least 8 ounces of cold water, up to three times daily, or two tablets one to four times daily. Children ages six to twelve should take one-half the adult dose in at least 8 ounces of cold water, or one tablet one to three times daily. For children under six, consult a physician. Continued use for twelve to seventy-two hours may be necessary for full benefit.

Psyllium

Brand names:
Effersyllium
Fiberall Natural
Hydrocil
Konsyl
Metamucil
Perdiem (with senna)
Serutan
Swiss Kriss (with senna)

This agent is derived from the plantago seed.

Dosage:
Usual adult dosage is 1 teaspoon to 1 tablespoon, depending on formulation, in 8 ounces of liquid. For children ages six to twelve, use half the adult dose, in 8 ounces of liquid. For children under six, consult a physician. (For other formulations, follow manufacturers' directions for specific brand-name products.) Start by taking one dose per day, gradually increasing to three doses if needed. It may require continued use for two to three days to provide optimal benefit.

Stimulant Laxatives

These laxatives encourage bowel movements by acting on the nerve endings in the wall of the intestines that trigger contraction of the intestinal muscles. This speeds the passage of fecal matter through the large intestine, allowing less time for water to be absorbed. Thus, bowel movements become more frequent and softer. Many stimulant laxatives also contain docusate (see page 93) as a fecal softener.

Since this type of laxative can irritate the stomach, tablets are covered with a protective coating to prevent their breakdown before they reach the intestine. They should be swallowed whole to avoid indigestion or nausea. Taken at bedtime with a snack, they generally stimulate a bowel action in the morning.

Warning
Regular use of stimulant laxatives for more than a week may seriously upset normal bowel action, leading to severe, prolonged diarrhea. This, in turn, may disrupt the balance of potassium in the body and affect nerve and muscle activity, causing weakness and debility. Pregnant women should avoid using stimulant laxatives.

The most commonly used active ingredients in stimulant laxatives are the following:

Bisacodyl

Brand names:
Carter's
Dulcolax
Fleet Bisacodyl

Laxatives with bisacodyl are used mainly before surgery and X-ray exams of the gastrointestinal tract.

Formulations:
Suppository, tablet.

Dosage:
Adults should take one to three tablets (see manufacturers' directions for specific brand-name products) or one suppository once daily. Children six to twelve should take half the adult dosage. For children under six, consult a physician. Do not use for longer than one week unless directed by a doctor.

Phenolphthalein

Brand names:
Ex-Lax Regular Strength
Feen-a-Mint

This product works primarily by stimulating the colon and usually takes effect within six to eight hours. Because part of absorbed phenolphthalein is secreted back into the intestinal tract, it may continue to act for three to four days. It is effective in small doses and is tasteless.

Formulations:
Candy, gum, tablet, chewable tablet

Dosage:
Adults and children twelve years and over should chew/take one to two pieces, preferably at bedtime. Children six to twelve years should chew/take one-half piece. Do not use for longer than one week unless directed by a doctor.

Emollient (Lubricant) Laxatives

Better known as stool softeners, emollient laxatives should be taken for only short periods—less than one week—by people with hard stools. They are of little or no value in treating long-term constipation, and are best suited for preventing the development of constipation when it is desirable to avoid straining at the stool—for example, after labor and delivery or in people with cardiovascular disease. They do not stimulate bowel movements when used alone, but are often combined with bulk-forming or stimulant laxatives. Emollient laxatives are usually effective in one to two days, but for some people they may take as long as three to five days to act. To make these laxatives more effective, also drink plenty of liquids.

The two main agents used in emollient laxatives are the following:

Docusate

Brand names:
Colace
Correctol
Ex-Lax Extra Gentle
Feen-a-Mint (with phenolphthalein)
Phillips' Milk of Magnesia (with phenolphthalein)
Senokot-S (with senna)

Usually combined with sodium, calcium, or potassium, docusate softens the stool by facilitating the mixing of watery and fatty substances in the intestine.

Warning
While docusate itself is not absorbed by the body, it may help transport other substances across cell membranes, so it should not be used by anyone taking prescription drugs or mineral oil.

Formulations:
Capsule, liquid, tablet, gelcap

Dosage:
Adults should take 50 to 200 mg daily. Children between ages six and twelve should take 40 to 120 mg daily. Children between ages three and six should take 20 to 60 mg daily. Infants and children under three should take 10 to 40 mg daily. The higher doses are recommended for initial therapy. See manufacturers' directions regarding dosage for specific brand-name products and formulations.

Mineral oil (liquid petroleum jelly)

Brand names:
Fleet Mineral Oil
Haleys M-O
Kondremul

Mineral oil softens stools by coating them, thus preventing the colon from absorbing water from the stool and leaving it hard. It is less desirable than docusate because it may be readily absorbed by the body and may also reduce the body's ability to absorb certain vitamins; in addition, it can be aspired, or sucked, into the lungs.

Formulation:
Emulsion

Dosage:
Adults should take 14 to 45 ml daily. Children between ages six and twelve should take 10 to 15 ml daily. Mineral oil laxatives should not be given to pregnant women, to the very young or elderly, or at bedtime.

Saline Laxatives

Brand name:
Phillips' Milk of Magnesia

This laxative produces a complex series of reactions in the gastrointestinal tract, drawing water into the gut and increasing intestinal motility (spontaneous movement). The most common of the saline laxatives is magnesium hydroxide, which is also administered as an antacid (see page 83). It generally produces a bowel movement within hours.

Formulations:
Liquid, chewable tablet

Dosage:
Adults and children twelve years and older should take 2 to 4 tablespoons followed by 8 ounces of liquid. Children ages six to eleven should take one-half the adult dosage. Children ages two to five should take 1 to 3 teaspoons followed by 8 ounces of liquid. For children under two, consult a doctor. Do not use for longer than one week.

Glycerin

Brand names:

Fleet Babylax

Fleet Glycerin

Glycerin laxatives usually produce a bowel movement within 30 minutes. They are often recommended for infants.

Formulations:

Suppository, liquid

Dosage:

For infants and children under six years, give suppository of 1 to 1.5 g per kilogram (2.2 pounds) of body weight. For adults and children older than six years, give 3 g as a suppository.

What to use when

Because they are closest to the natural physiological mechanism of eliminating waste products, bulk-forming laxatives are the first choice in treating most forms of constipation. If you need to use a laxative over several weeks or even months, or if you are pregnant, you should use only bulk-forming or emollient laxatives. If you are not pregnant and seek fast relief, you could try a stimulant, saline, or lubricant (mineral oil) laxative. If you are treating a child, a glycerin laxative may be most appropriate.

Some drugs, such as certain antidepressants and aluminum-containing antacids, tend to produce constipation and may require long-term use of laxatives. In such cases, you should use one of the mild bulk-forming laxatives. However, it's recommended that you consult your pharmacist or physician, particularly if the drug causing constipation is a prescription medicine.

Skin Treatments
Antipruritics, Anesthetics, and Other Therapies

Antipruritics and anesthetics comprise several drug groups, including hydrocortisone (see page 96) and antihistamines such as diphenhydramine (see page 100). Antipruritic drugs relieve itching and, depending on the specific drug type, act either by reducing inflammation and therefore irritation of the skin or by numbing the nerve impulses that transmit sensation to the brain. For lists of products to relieve itching caused by specific conditions, see the appropriate treatment sections, such as Burn/Sunburn Treatments (see page 101) and Insect Bite and Sting Treatments (see page 108). For the treatment of itching around the anus, see Hemorrhoidal Preparations (page 106). Itching that is caused by an underlying illness, such as chronic liver failure, cannot be helped by these products and requires treatment for the principal disorder.

Although counterirritants are sometimes used as topical anesthetics and are in some of the creams and lotions listed here, they are used primarily to lessen deep-seated pain. For a full description of counterirritants and the substances that comprise the category, see Pain Relievers, Fever Reducers, and Anti-inflammatories (page 53).

Other skin treatments, such as Antibiotics and Sunscreens, appear alphabetically after Poison Ivy, Poison Oak, and Poison Sumac Treatments (page 110).

What to use when

If you have severe itching caused by dry skin conditions, apply a topical hydrocortisone preparation (see this page) in small amounts to the rash area. In addition, apply an emollient (see page 104), or moisturizer, at least once a day to itchy areas. Emollients lubricate the skin surface and prevent dryness. In treating eczema, you should avoid applying any ointments or petroleum jelly, because these products block the sweat glands, increase the itching, and worsen the rash. In all dry skin conditions, bathing less and using moisturizing bath products (see page 119) more frequently may also be helpful. Emollients can be found with Dermatitis/Dry Skin Preparations (see page 103), and Skin Protectants (see page 126) can be found after subsections relating to burns, canker sores, cold blisters, dermatitis, hemorrhoids, insect bites, and poison ivy, oak, and sumac.

When the itching prevents sleep, you can take an antihistamine (see page 72) at night to promote sleep as well as to relieve itching. Antihistamines are also often included in topical preparations for the relief of skin irritation (see page 99). They relieve the itching, swelling, and redness characteristic of allergic reactions involving the skin. Applied topically, they pass into the underlying tissue and block the effects of histamine on the blood vessels beneath the skin. Taken by mouth, they also pass from the blood into the brain to reduce the perception of irritation. They can act within a few hours. They are more effective when taken before the start of an attack, when itching can be predicted because of exposure to an allergen, for example.

If you have mild itching arising from sunburn, hives, or insect bites, you should try a lotion such as calamine, to which menthol, phenol, or camphor may also have been added. Calamine lotion reduces inflammation and itching by cooling the skin. Local anesthetic creams (see page 97) are sometimes helpful for small areas of irritation, such as insect bites, but are unsuitable for widespread itching.

The following formulations enable you to apply the medication in the most comfortable, effective way. **Ointments** are oil-based preparations that provide a protective film that keeps the skin from drying. In addition to the oil base, they may also contain ingredients with therapeutic claims, such as vitamins A and D and aloe vera. If the skin is broken, however, an ointment may be less appropriate because its impermeability and the presence of moisture may promote the growth of bacteria. To avoid contaminating the ointment, the tip of the container should not touch the skin when the product is applied.

Creams allow some fluid to pass through the film, so they provide less of a medium for bacterial growth and are better for broken skin. Generally, too, creams are a little less messy and less difficult to apply than ointments. To avoid contaminating the cream, the tip of the container should not touch the skin when the product is applied.

Lotions and **gels**, which spread easily, may be more readily applied when the area to be covered is large.

Sprays are generally the most expensive of all the formulations, but they have the advantage of precluding the need to touch the injured area physically, so there is less pain associated with applying the medication. However, because the aerosol is water- or alcohol-based and will evaporate, sprays offer no skin protection.

Hydrocortisone

Brand names:
Bactine Hydrocortisone 1%
CaldeCORT
Cortaid
Cortizone-5
Cortizone-10
Lanacor
Tegrin-HC

Hydrocortisone reduces inflammation and itching. The FDA has stipulated that hydrocortisone may be used for "the temporary relief of minor skin irritations, itching, and rashes due to eczema, dermatitis, insect bites, poison ivy, poison oak, poison sumac, soaps, detergent, cosmetics, and jewelry, and for itching in genital and anal areas."

Applied to the skin's surface, hydrocortisone is absorbed into the underlying tissues and blood vessels, where it prevents the release of histamine, the chemical that causes itching and inflammation. In this way, it allows the blood vessels to return to normal and reduces the swelling.

The soothing effect of hydrocortisone may produce an immediate improvement without the side effects of antihistamines (see page 99). However, it may take a few days for hydrocortisone to reduce itching caused by allergy.

Hydrocortisone is the only steroid anti-inflammatory agent available without prescription. When it was initially switched from prescription to OTC status, the concentrations available were 0.25 percent and 0.5 percent. In 1991, the FDA approved OTC formulations of hydrocortisone in strengths up to 1 percent. Higher concentrations of hydrocortisone are available only by prescription.

In general, hydrocortisone is extremely safe and effective. The FDA has stated that allergic reactions to hydrocortisone at concentrations up to 1 percent are rare. In addition, it found evidence that prolonged administration of 0.5 to 1 percent hydrocortisone did not appear to cause toxic effects through systemic absorption, even when it was applied to large areas of skin that were damaged or scraped.

However, hydrocortisone—even at 0.25 percent strength—is not recommended for use on children under two, except on the advice of a physician. And while older children may safely use 1 percent hydrocortisone, some manufacturers offer a pediatric formulation at 0.5 percent concentration.

Warning

Steroids work largely by suppressing the body's immune system. But because that increases the body's susceptibility to infection, topical steroids, including hydrocortisone, have in some cases been associated with a worsening of bacterial infections. The FDA has stated that short-term topical use of 0.5 to 1 percent hydrocortisone is unlikely to exacerbate skin infections. However, you should avoid applying hydrocortisone in the presence of scabies (a contagious parasitic skin infestation) or bacterial or fungal infections, as it may worsen or mask the underlying condition.

Another problem is the risk of a prompt rebound of certain skin conditions, notably psoriasis (see page 125), when hydrocortisone therapy is discontinued. Long-term use of hydrocortisone can also result in an atrophying, or thinning, of the skin. Finally, if hydrocortisone is used continuously over a long time, it may become less effective.

Formulations:
Creams, ointments, sprays, roll-ons. Ointments are most appropriate to lubricate and soothe dry and scaly skin.

Dosage:
Apply to affected area three to four times daily. For children under two years, consult a physician.

On page 96 there is a brief list of OTC products with hydrocortisone that may be used to treat minor skin conditions. For information about other products with hydrocortisone, see the drug category for each of the conditions mentioned at the beginning of this section.

Local Anesthetics

Local, or topical, anesthetics relieve itching, the pain of minor burns and sunburn (see page 101), cold sores, hemorrhoids, insect bites and stings, poison ivy reactions, teething (see page 145), and many other types of mouth and throat pain (see Treatments for the Mouth and Teeth, page 137, or Lozenges and Mouthwashes/Gargles, page 77). By blocking the passage of nerve impulses at the site, anesthetics deaden all sensation. They do not interfere with consciousness and generally are safe.

The two local anesthetics most often used in nonprescription drugs are benzocaine and lidocaine; benzocaine, one of the first local anesthetics to be approved by the FDA, is generally quite safe and effective, while lidocaine tends to be stronger and may need to be used more cautiously. Other anesthetics found in OTC preparations are dibucaine, butamben, pramoxine, and phenol; sometimes these are used if the person develops a sensitivity to or intolerance for benzocaine or lidocaine. Some of these anesthetics are also discussed in sections on treatments of cold sores, hemorrhoids, and other disorders in which topical anesthetics are applied to reduce pain.

Warning

Frequent use of local anesthetics has been known to lead to skin conditions known collectively as dermatitis (see page 30). They should be applied no more than three or four times daily and should not be used for more than a few days except under medical supervision, since they could mask the symptoms of a more serious disease. They should not be used to treat serious burns, as that may delay the administration of appropriate medical treatment.

Formulations:

All local anesthetics are available as ointments, with additional specific formulations indicated below. The higher concentrations are appropriate when the skin is intact; the lower concentrations are better for skin that has been broken. In addition, ointments may be inappropriate if the skin is broken, as they promote moisture and bacterial growth. Sprays are more expensive but, because they are applied without physically touching the injured area, may sometimes be preferable. The range of approved concentrations for leading anesthetics is indicated in the following discussion.

Dosage:

Ointments for treatment of hemorrhoids, burns and sunburn, and insect bites and stings, and gels for mouth pain, containing one or more of the following active ingredients, may typically be applied three to four times daily for adults; for children under twelve, consult a physician. For teething products for infants, follow recommended dosage on the label and see page 145.

Benzocaine

Brand names:
Dermoplast
Lanacane
Medicone Rectal
Orajel
Solarcaine

Benzocaine is included in preparations for sunburn and burns, mouth pain, hemorrhoids, poison ivy, and insect bites and stings, as well as in throat lozenges (see page 78). Poorly absorbed through the skin and mucous membranes, it rarely causes adverse effects. It typically takes effect within a minute and lasts twenty to thirty minutes. The higher concentrations are appropriate when the skin is intact, or unbroken; the lower concentrations are better for skin that has been broken.

Warning

About 1 percent of people who use it have an allergic skin reaction, with rash and itching.

Formulations:

Cream, ointment, spray, lotion, suppository. It is approved in concentrations of 5 to 20 percent (indicated on the packaging), with the lower concentrations generally for solid dosage forms and the higher for sprays.

Lidocaine

Brand names:
DermaFlex
Neosporin Plus Maximum Strength
Unguentine Plus
Xylocaine
Zilactin-L

This anesthetic, used in preparations for mouth pain, burns and sunburn, poison ivy, and insect bites and stings, is less likely than benzocaine to produce an allergic reaction. It takes effect within two to five minutes and lasts up to one hour.

Warning

Dosages higher than those recommended for therapeutic purposes can lead to central nervous system effects such as agitation, confusion, and drowsiness. Such adverse effects are rare if lidocaine is used on intact skin, on small patches of skin, and for short periods.

Formulations:

Cream, ointment, spray, gel, liquid. More potent than benzocaine, it is approved in concentrations of 0.5 to 4 percent.

Dibucaine

Brand name:
Nupercainal

Dibucaine, which is in the same class as benzocaine, is used in topical anesthetics for insect stings and bites and for anorectal (the area from the anus to the rectum) disorders. It works within minutes.

Warning

Do not apply in large quantities, particularly over raw surfaces or blistered areas, as there is a risk dibucaine will affect internal organs, potentially resulting in convulsions, heart problems, and death.

Formulations:
Cream, ointment, spray; in concentrations of 0.25 to 1 percent

Pramoxine

Brand names:
Caladryl
Itch-X
Ivy Soothe Pain & Itch Derma Spray

Pramoxine is used in preparations for hemorrhoids, burns and sunburn, insect bites and stings, and poison ivy. Adverse effects are rare. The advantage of pramoxine is that because it is in a different chemical family it may be safely used by people who are allergic to benzocaine and related anesthetics. It works within minutes.

Formulations:
Cream, ointment, lotion, gel, spray; in concentrations of 0.5 to 1 percent

Butamben

Brand name:
Butesin Picrate

Used for burns and sunburn. It works within minutes.

Formulation:
Ointment, 1 percent concentration

Phenol

Brand names:
Orabase Lip Cream
Sting-Eze

Phenol is a primary active ingredient in sore throat lozenges (see page 79) and cold sore medications (see page 147), and is also used in some douches (see page 172) and insect bite and sting products (see page 108). While it is sometimes used as an antiseptic (see page 117), it can also work as an anesthetic by depressing the skin's sensory receptors.

Warning

Phenol is caustic when applied in undiluted form to the skin and should never be applied to extensive areas of the body or under compresses or bandages.

Formulations:
Cream, lotion, ointment, gel, liquid. When applied to the skin, it is considered safe in concentrations of 0.5 to 1.5 percent in adults and children two years and older.

What to use when

The topical anesthetics discussed here may generally be used interchangeably. However, if you have an allergic reaction to one of the anesthetics, such as benzocaine, you should try another, such as lidocaine or pramoxine.

Topical Antihistamines

Topical antihistamines work by countering the effects of histamine, one of the chemicals that is released in the body as a reaction to an insect bite or poison ivy, for example. The release of histamine sets off a local inflammatory response, in which the small blood vessels redden and dilate, or swell. Antihistamines compete with histamine and exert a topical anesthetic, or numbing, effect.

Topical antihistamines are considered safe and

effective if used over a limited time. The FDA has recommended that they be used for no longer than seven days except under the advice of a physician. They are generally not absorbed through the skin in sufficient quantities to cause systemic side effects. However, some people develop an allergic reaction, or rash.

Formulations:
Cream, spray, gel

Dosage:
Apply three to four times a day. Do not use for longer than seven days except under the advice of a physician. These products are not recommended for children under two years except under the advice or supervision of a physician.

Diphenhydramine

Brand names:
Benadryl Itch Stopping Cream/Spray/Gel
Calagel Clearly Calamine
Di-Delamine Double Antihistamine (with tripelennamine)
Ivarest 8-Hour
Sting-Eze (with benzocaine)

Virtually all products that contain antihistamine as a topical antipruritic use diphenhydramine, sometimes in combination with tripelennamine or a topical anesthetic. Diphenhydramine is also taken orally as an antiemetic (see page 85).

Tripelennamine

This antihistamine is combined with diphenhydramine in some products.

Pyrilamine

Although available in topical form, pyrilamine is primarily taken orally to relieve colds, coughs, and allergies (see page 72).

Counterirritants (in brief)

Counterirritants are used primarily to reduce pain from sprained or strained muscles or joints or arthritic joints, although they may also be used for shingles, insect bites, hemorrhoids, and other causes of pain. They work by stimulating receptors in the skin to create sensations such as cold and warmth. These distract from the deep-seated pain in muscles, joints, and tendons—the main target of counterirritants. Counterirritants have a paradoxical effect: By producing a less severe pain in nearby tissue, they counter a more intense one.

Many OTC preparations combine counterirritants from at least two different groups for greater potency. Because the four main counterirritants (methyl salicylate, camphor, menthol, and capsicum preparations) have a variety of uses, brand names are provided in other sections—notably muscle/joint pain relief in Pain Relievers, Fever Reducers, and Anti-inflammatories (see page 58), as well as insect bites and stings (see page 109), hemorrhoidal preparations (see page 106), and others. Three other counterirritants (allyl isothiocyanate, turpentine oil, and eucalyptus oil) are listed in Pain Relievers, Fever Reducers, and Anti-inflammatories (see page 58) only.

Warning
Counterirritants are not currently approved for treating minor burns because while they reduce pain, they increase blood flow to the area, which causes further swelling; they also further irritate the already sensitized and damaged skin.

What to use when

Topical antihistamines, hydrocortisone, and anesthetics may be used for many of the same applications, and in fact are often combined in products.

The FDA has stipulated that hydrocortisone may be used for "the temporary relief of minor skin irritations, itching, and rashes due to eczema, dermatitis, insect bites, poison ivy, poison oak, poison sumac, soaps, detergent, cosmetics, and jewelry, and for itching in genital and anal areas." Topical antihistamines are approved by the FDA "for the temporary relief of pain and itching due to minor burns, sunburn, minor cuts, abrasions, insect bites, and minor skin irritations." Local anesthetics relieve itching, the pain of minor burns and sunburn (see this page), and pain and itching from hemorrhoids (see page 106). However, only anesthetics are used to relieve pain from teething (see page 145) and many other types of mouth and throat conditions (see Treatments for the Mouth and Teeth, page 137, and Cold, Cough, and Allergy Remedies, page 68).

If you are concerned about possible side effects of antihistamines and anesthetics, you may want to treat your skin irritation with hydrocortisone only. However, if you want prompt relief from an allergic rash, antihistamine may be more appropriate. If the area you are treating is infected, you should use antihistamine and anesthetic rather than hydrocortisone, which may worsen the condition.

Counterirritants are used primarily to reduce pain from sprained or strained muscles or joints or arthritic joints, although they may also be used for shingles, insect bites, hemorrhoids, and other causes of pain.

Burn/Sunburn Treatments

Products for burns, including sunburn, help relieve pain and inflammation, prevent infection, and allow the skin to heal normally. While most preparations contain two or more ingredients to meet at least two of these objectives, it may be necessary to use more than one type of preparation.

The discussion here is limited to first- and second-degree burns. First-degree burns are superficial, perhaps causing redness, warmth, and slight swelling but usually without blistering. Second-degree burns are deeper, and are characterized by redness, oozing, blisters, and usually more intense pain than first-degree burns. All burns greater than first degree should generally be evaluated by a physician to prevent complications, particularly infections.

Formulations:

This factor is important in selecting the most appropriate product for a burn or sunburn. Ointments are more appropriate for minor burns, in which the skin is intact, or unbroken. Lotions that produce a powdery cover should not be used on a burn, however, because they tend to dry the area, are difficult and possibly painful to remove, and provide a medium for bacterial growth under the caked particles. A full discussion on ointments, creams, lotions, gels, and sprays can be found in the beginning of the Skin Treatments section (see page 96).

Local Anesthetics, Internal Analgesics, and Counterirritants

The primary ingredient in products for burns is a local, or topical, anesthetic (see page 97) such as benzocaine or lidocaine. Internal analgesics (see page 56), in the standard dosages, are also helpful in relieving minor burn pain; aspirin and NSAIDs, because they are anti-inflammatories, may also decrease the swelling and redness in the burned area. Counterirritants (see page 58), which form another group of analgesics, are not currently approved for treating minor burns. The reason is that while they reduce pain, they increase blood flow to the area, which causes further swelling. They also further irritate the already sensitized and damaged skin. When ingredients commonly categorized as counterirritants, such as menthol, are included in products to treat burns, it is in low-level concentrations in which they act as anesthetics.

Because anesthetics are the key ingredients in most products marketed specifically for burns and sunburns, we list treatments here by type of anesthetic. Other useful products, such as hydrocortisone and skin protectants, can be found elsewhere in this book.

Formulations:
Spray, cream, ointment

Benzocaine

Brand names:
Bicozene External Analgesic Creme
Foille Medicated
Medicated First Aid Burn
Solarcaine Medicated First Aid (with alcohol)

Dosage:
Adults and children two years and older, apply liberally to affected area not more than three to four times daily. Children under two, consult a physician.

Lidocaine

Brand names:
Ahhh Sunburn Therapy
Bactine First Aid
Burnamycin
No More Burn
Sunchaser

Dosage:
Adults and children two and older, apply a small amount of product to affected area one to three times daily. For children under two, consult a physician. Dosages higher than those recommended for therapeutic purposes can lead to central nervous system effects such as agitation, confusion, and drowsiness. Such adverse effects are rare if lidocaine is used on intact, or unbroken, skin, on small patches of skin, and for short periods.

Dibucaine

Brand name:
Nupercainal

Dosage:
Adults apply to affected area three to four times daily. Children ages two to twelve years should not use except under the advice and supervision of a physican. Do not use in infants under two or less than 35 pounds in weight. Do not apply in large quantities, particularly over raw surfaces or blistered areas, as there is a risk that dibucaine will affect internal organs, potentially resulting in convulsions, heart problems, and death.

What to use when

Choice of treatment should be determined by both anesthetic and available formulation. While products with lidocaine and dibucaine are more potent, they also carry slightly higher risk of adverse side effects.

Astringents

The inflammations caused by burns may also be reduced by soaking the burned area with an astringent (see page 118) such as Burow's solution, diluted 1:20 to 1:40 in water, for fifteen to thirty minutes, three to six times a day. Soaking is particularly helpful with weeping lesions, because it provides a cooling, soothing treatment that promotes drying and prevents crusting. All soaking solutions should be freshly prepared for each application. If they are kept and exposed to the air, they become concentrated because of evaporation and can cause irritation; they may also serve as a growth medium for bacteria.

Skin Protectants

Once weeping subsides, a skin protectant (see page 126) may be applied to the skin. Protectants make the wound area less painful, protect the burn from mechanical irritation caused by friction and rubbing, prevent dryness, and promote lubrication. The FDA has recognized a number of skin protectants as safe and effective for the temporary protection of minor burns and sunburn. These include products with allantoin, cocoa butter, petroleum jelly, and shark liver oil. The FDA has also recommended that the restriction preventing their use on children under two years be waived for most of these products. (A notable exception is shark liver oil, which remains restricted.) It is important to note that the FDA has not recognized claims by some manufacturers that certain agents, such as allantoin, aloe vera, vitamin E, and shark liver oil, accelerate the healing of minor burns and sunburns.

Boric Acid

Boric acid is widely marketed as a generic product in ointment form for treating burns and sunburns. However, the FDA has proposed that boric acid not be generally recognized as safe and effective as a skin protectant.

Hydrocortisone

Although not approved by the FDA for use specifically in treating minor burns, 1 percent topical hydrocortisone (see page 96), an anti-inflammatory agent, is often used in first-aid treatment of minor burns covering a small area. It should be used with caution if the skin is broken, because it may allow infections to develop.

Antibiotics

Because the burned dead skin may serve as a growth medium for certain bacteria, antibiotic creams (see page 113) may be applied. Antibiotics are probably unnecessary, however, if the skin is unbroken, and should not be routinely applied. Furthermore, many products for burns contain antimicrobial agents to prevent infection.

Dermatitis/ Dry Skin Preparations

Products for the treatment of the various skin conditions with inflammation and reddening of dry skin, which is a form of dermatitis, help moisturize the skin, reduce inflammation and redness, alleviate itching, and dry up areas (if any) that are oozing. Products include emollients, or moisturizers (see page 104), antipruritics (see page 95), including hydrocortisone (page 96) as well as oral and topical antihistamines (see respectively page 72 and page 99).

When the dermatitis is characterized by oozing from lesions or blisters, astringents (see page 118) will dry the skin through evaporation, cause vasoconstriction (narrowing of the blood vessels, thus reducing blood flow), and cleanse the skin of crust and debris. The FDA has identified two astringent solutions as safe and effective: aluminum acetate (Burow's solution) and witch hazel (Hamamelis water), both of which are widely available in generic form.

The precise type of product used depends on the type of dermatitis. In this section, we will refer to product categories that are helpful in treating dry skin, hand dermatitis (better known as "dishpan" hands), and eczema, a genetically predetermined condition that primarily affects the young. Information about specific products for chronic, scaly types of dermatitis—dandruff (see page 132), seborrhea (see page 132), and psoriasis (see page 125)—is contained in the relevant sections. Similarly, for information about treatments for the contact dermatitis caused by poison ivy/poison oak/poison sumac, see page 110.

Dry skin that is not severe may be adequately treated by regularly hydrating, or moisturizing, with a variety of bath products (see page 119) and emollients (see page 104). These leave an oily film on the surface of the skin and promote the retention of water.

Formulations:

Ointments—oil-based preparations that provide a protective film that keeps the skin from drying—with a base of petrolatum (better known as petroleum jelly) are best for keeping the skin moist. Because these tend to be greasy and stain, however, many people prefer creams and lotions, which must be applied more often. Ointments should be avoided in the treatment of eczema, because they block the sweat glands, increase the itching, and worsen the rash. They should also be avoided if the skin is broken, as the presence of moisture may promote the growth of bacteria. Similarly, ointments should not be used in areas such as the armpit or the genital area in any type of dermatitis. If the dermatitis affects a hair-covered area of the body, aerosol sprays, gels, or lotions may be most effective.

Warning

While oil and water are the main active ingredients in products for dermatitis and dry skin, many other substances are added to make them more widely acceptable, as stabilizers and preservatives and for other reasons. Because people with dermatitis are often particularly sensitive to chemicals, it is advisable to review all the ingredients and discuss any concerns with a physician or pharmacist. Many hypoallergenic alternatives—that is, products least likely to provoke an allergic reaction—are on the market.

What to use when

If your skin is dry but not severely dry, you should use bath products and emollients regularly to moisturize your skin. This is also the preferred treatment for most cases of dermatitis (a term for a number of skin conditions with inflammation and reddening, see page 103). However, if you have dermatitis that is wet or oozing from lesions or blisters, do not apply emollients; instead, use astringents. To relieve itching you can use hydrocortisone or antihistamine (oral or topical). Hydrocortisone is particularly effective, as it not only relieves itching, but it also helps alleviate skin rash; however, be certain the area is not infected. If you use topical antihistamine, apply it for no more than seven days; if you use oral antihistamine, be aware that it may have a sedating effect.

Emollients

Emollients moisturize skin that is dry or cracked. They work primarily by leaving an oily film on the surface of the skin. This promotes the retention of water in the skin because the moisture cannot pass readily through the oily barrier. In addition to that clinical action, emollients also have a cosmetic action, making the skin feel soft and smooth by helping to reestablish the integrity of the stratum corneum, the outermost layer.

If you have dry skin, you should apply emollients while your skin is still damp from the bath or shower, and reapply them frequently, preferably when your skin is moist. They are helpful in most cases of dermatitis and dry skin. Dermatitis that is wet or oozing, however, should not be treated with emollients.

Emollients typically consist of an occlusive agent, or moisturizer, which provides the oily film; a humectant, or hydrating agent, whose function is to draw in water from either the dermis (the layer of skin directly below the epidermis, the outer portion of the skin) or the atmosphere, to keep the skin moist; and, in many cases, a keratin-softening agent to soften the skin and improve its appearance by removing scales and crusts. Keratin is a protein produced by cells in the epidermis.

The most commonly used occlusive agents in emollients are (from the most to the least effective): petroleum jelly, mineral oil, lanolin, and dimethicone. A natural product derived from sheep wool, lanolin is likelier than the other occlusives to provoke an allergic reaction such as rash. Lanolin is always used in combination with other medications, and many products contain two or three of these in combination. However, there are many other agents, such as soybean or linseed oil, that are also used in popular emollients.

Two hydrating, or moisturizing, agents are widely used: glycerin and propylene glycol. Glycerin helps decrease water loss by keeping the water in close contact with the skin and accelerating the spread of moisture from the dermis to the epidermal surface. Propylene glycol acts the same way, but can sometimes cause skin irritation.

The main agents used as keratin softeners in emollients are urea (carbamide), alpha-hydroxy acids, and allantoin. While it's probably the most effective, urea may cause stinging and burning. Alpha-hydroxy acids have become increasingly popular ingredients in emollients to treat dry skin conditions. They soften the keratin and also moisturize the skin. The first alpha-hydroxy acid to be widely used was lactic acid. Other alpha-hydroxy acids, found in many fruits, are under study for a number of common skin conditions such as dry skin and fine age wrinkles. These acids include malic acid (extracted from apples), citric acid (oranges and lemons), glycolic and gluconic acid (sugar cane), and tartaric acid (grapes).

Dosage:
Apply as needed, at least once daily.

Petroleum jelly

Brand names:
Aveeno Moisturizing
Chapstick (with lanolin)
Keri Cream (with dimethicone)
Soft Sense Moisturizing Hand & Skin
Softlips
Vaseline Dermatology Formula (with glycerin)
Vaseline Intensive Care Extra Strength (with glycerin)
Vaseline Medicated Anti-Bacterial Petroleum Jelly

The most effective of the moisturizing agents, petroleum jelly has major drawbacks when formulated as an ointment: It tends to be greasy and difficult to spread and remove, and sometimes stains clothing. Ointments should not be applied over infections because they shut off exposure to air and may lead to further inflammation.

Formulations:
Ointment, lotion, cream, stick (for chapped lips)

Mineral oil

Brand names:
Alpha Keri (with lanolin)
Aqua Care (with petroleum jelly)
Eucerin Plus (with urea)
Lubriderm (with petroleum jelly, lanolin)
Nivea Moisturizing Extra Enriched
Nivea Skin Creme Ultra Moisturizing (with petroleum jelly)
Ultra Derm Moisturizer

Products with mineral oil are adsorbed onto—or bind onto—the skin better than those with vegetable oil.

Formulations:
Lotion, cream, spray

Dimethicone

Brand names:
Pacquin Medicated Hand and Body
Silk Solution

Because it acts as a barrier, sealing the skin, this ingredient is also widely used in products to help prevent or treat diaper rash.

Formulations:
Cream, lotion

Vegetable oils

Brand names:
Noxzema Original
Noxzema Plus Cleansing (Both contain linseed and soybean oils)

In general, the vegetable oils—made from linseed, soybean, and sesame, for example—are less effective than mineral oil, but may be more appealing to some consumers.

Formulations:
Cream, lotion

What to use when

If you want the most effective emollient, use one containing petroleum jelly; however, you may want to avoid using it in ointment form, when it tends to be greasy, difficult to spread and remove, and sometimes stains. Alternatively, you can choose an emollient with (from most to the least effective) mineral oil, lanolin, vegetable oil, or dimethicone. However, lanolin is likelier than the other occlusives to provoke an allergic reaction such as rash.

Hemorrhoidal Preparations

Preparations for relief of hemorrhoids shrink swollen hemorrhoidal tissue, relieve pain and itching, and protect the affected area from further irritation. Some preparations also are formulated to prevent infection. To achieve these various objectives, most hemorrhoidal treatments combine a skin protectant (see page 107) with one or more therapeutic ingredients, including vasoconstrictors to shrink the tissue, anesthetics (see page 107) to reduce pain and itching, and astringents (see page 107) to relieve irritation and inflammation. Although most of the products listed below contain multiple ingredients, only primary ingredients appear in parentheses beside the brand names.

Some hemorrhoidal treatments also include hydrocortisone (see page 96) to relieve inflammation and itching or counterirritants (page 58), such as camphor or menthol, to distract from the perception of pain and itching and provide a feeling of warmth or cooling. Some preparations also contain keratolytics, which slough off surface cells and expose the underlying tissue to healing ingredients such as astringents. While a few hemorrhoidal preparations include antiseptics to stop the spread of germs, mild soap and water may be just as effective in preventing anorectal infection—infection of the area from the anus to the rectum.

The choice of therapeutic ingredients depends on whether the hemorrhoids are external (in the region of the anus or the lower anal canal, but not within the rectum) or internal (within the rectum). According to the National Professional Society of Pharmacists, an ideal hemorrhoidal formulation for external use contains a vasoconstrictor, a local anesthetic, and one to four recommended protectants in a single product, like Anusol (ointment) or Hemorid for Women (cream). The protectants, which often double as the base or vehicle for the active ingredients, should total at least 50 percent of the formulation. The product might also contain an analgesic (to relieve pain) and an antipruritic (to reduce itching). Hydrocortisone, counterirritants, and keratolytics are limited to external use only.

For internal use, an effective product would contain an appropriate astringent, a vasoconstrictor, and between one and four skin protectants. Again, the protectants should total at least 50 percent of the formulation.

Warning

Local anesthetics should not be inserted into the rectum because they would be ineffective and could cause systemic problems if absorbed through the mucous membrane lining of the rectum.

Because hemorrhoidal preparations typically contain multiple ingredients, the brand names are listed below according to main therapeutic ingredient.

Because constipation is often a cause of hemorrhoids, you may want to use a laxative (see page 91) while treating the symptoms. Do not mix hemorrhoidal products with a harsh stimulant laxative, as it will only lead to further irritation. A stool softener (see page 93) is preferable.

Formulations:

External hemorrhoidal preparations may be formulated as creams, ointments, suppositories, or towelettes. Internal anorectal products are in ointment form, applied with a finger or an applicator. Suppositories are generally not recommended in treating anorectal problems, because it's difficult to direct the medication to the appropriate area.

Vasoconstrictors

Brand names:
Anusert
Anusol (suppository)
Hemorid for Women
Preparation H (cream, ointment)

These cause constriction of the small arteries, shrinking—although only slightly and temporarily—swollen hemorrhoidal tissue. They also help relieve itching somewhat because they produce a slightly anesthetic effect—how, precisely, is unknown. Four vasoconstrictors are recommended for external use: ephedrine sulfate, epinephrine hydrochloride, phenylephrine hydrochloride solutions, and epinephrine base. Ephedrine sulfate, which is readily absorbed through mucous membranes in the rectum, has a more prolonged effect than the others. When applied topically, it takes effect within a minute, lasts two to three hours, and effectively relieves itching and swelling. Ephedrine sulfate and phenylephrine hydrochloride may be used internally. However, products containing ephedrine sulfate sometimes cause nervousness, tremors, sleeplessness, nausea, and loss of appetite.

Epinephrine hydrochloride and epinephrine base are also effective in relieving itching and swelling. Epinephrine is absorbed through the mucous membranes. However, it is ineffective when used to treat internal hemorrhoids. Phenylephrine hydrochloride is believed to relieve itching caused by histamine release and reduces swollen blood vessels in the entire anorectal area. All brand names listed below contain phenylephrine.

Dosage:

Apply externally to the affected area up to four times daily. For children under twelve, consult a physician.

Local Anesthetics

Brand names:
Americaine Hemorrhoidal (benzocaine)
Anusol (ointment, with pramoxine)
Nupercainal (dibucaine)
Tronolane (paramoxine)

These temporarily relieve pain, burning, itching, discomfort, and irritation by preventing the transmission of nerve impulses to the brain. Anesthetics used in hemorrhoidal preparations may include benzocaine, benzyl alcohol (which is not widely used as an anesthetic), lidocaine, pramoxine, and others.

Dosage:

Apply externally to the affected area up to six times daily. For children under twelve, consult a physician.

Astringents

Brand names:
Fleet Medicated Wipes
Sooth-It
Tucks

Applied to the skin or mucous membranes, astringents work by coagulating the protein in skin cells, resulting in a protective coating under which new tissue may grow. They contribute to drying by reducing the mucus, thus relieving local irritation and inflammation.

The astringents included most often in hemorrhoidal preparations are zinc oxide, calamine, and witch hazel (Hamamelis water). They are typically sold as wipes or pads.

Dosage:

Apply externally to the affected area up to six times daily or after each bowel movement. For children under twelve, consult a physician.

Skin Protectants

Brand names:
Preparation H (shark liver oil, petroleum jelly, lanolin)
Vaseline Pure Petroleum Jelly

Preparation H also contains live yeast cell derivative, a subject of considerable controversy owing to the manufacturer's claim that it promotes the healing of diseased anorectal tissue.

As the name suggests, these protect the affected area, shielding it from irritants such as fecal matter and preventing water loss from tissues, thus leading to a reduction in irritation and itching.

Protectants include aluminum hydroxide gel, petroleum jelly, lanolin, mineral oil, cod liver oil, shark liver oil, and cocoa butter.

Dosage:

Apply externally to the affected area four to six times daily, especially at night, in the morning, or after each bowel movement. For precise dosage for specific brand-name products, see manufacturers' directions. For children under twelve, consult a physician.

Insect Bite and Sting Treatments

OTC preparations for insect bites and stings help alleviate pain and itching, reduce inflammation and redness, protect skin that is irritated or oozing, and prevent and treat secondary infection that may result from scratching.

Most OTC products used for symptomatic relief of insect stings and bites are nonspecific—that is, they are also marketed to relieve sunburn pain, itching, or other minor skin problems. The notable exception is ammonia, which the FDA has recognized specifically for its neutralizing effect when wiped on bites and stings (brand name: After-Bite).

Most products for insect bites and stings contain an external analgesic—an anesthetic (see below), a counterirritant (see page 109), an antihistamine (see below), or a hydrocortisone (see page 109)—to reduce pain and itching. Antibacterial agents (antibiotics, see page 113) are occasionally added to prevent and treat secondary infection that may result from scratching. Skin protectants (see page 126) are often added to these products to soothe and moisturize the skin. (If they are not present in the product, they may be applied separately.) Alternatively, if the skin is oozing, an astringent (see page 118) may be applied to dry up the moisture.

Local Anesthetics

Brand names:
Americaine First Aid (benzocaine)
Aveeno Anti-Itch (pramoxine)
Caladryl (pramoxine)
Chiggerex (benzocaine)
Chiggertox (benzocaine, isopropyl alcohol)
Itch-X (benzyl alcohol, pramoxine)
Nupercainal (dibucaine)
Solarcaine (benzocaine)
Sting Kill (benzocaine)

The main local anesthetics used in insect bite and sting products are benzocaine, dibucaine, and pramoxine. Although generally safe and effective, both benzocaine and dibucaine can cause an allergic skin reaction if used continuously for prolonged periods. In addition, dibucaine carries the warning that it is not to be used in large quantities, particularly over raw surfaces or blistered areas, because of the danger of systemic, or bodywide, toxicity. Other local anesthetics sometimes included in insect bite and sting products are benzyl alcohol and pramoxine hydrochloride.

Formulations:
Ointment, spray, cream, lotion, drops

Dosage:
Adults and children two years of age and older should apply three to four times a day. These products are not recommended for children under two except under the advice or supervision of a physician.

Antihistamines

Brand names:
Benadryl (diphenhydramine)
Caladryl (diphenhydramine)
Di-Delamine Double Antihistamine (diphenhydramine, tripelennamine)
Sting-Eze (diphenhydramine with benzocaine)

Diphenhydramine, tripelennamine, and other antihistamines work by countering the effects of histamine, a chemical that is released in the body in reaction to an insect bite or sting. The release of histamine sets off a local inflammatory response—reddening and swelling of the skin—which these products combat. If you use these products continually over three to four weeks, however, you could develop an allergic rash. In addition, antihistamines over time often lose their ability to relieve itching. Accordingly, it is advisable to use these products for no longer than seven days, except under the advice of a physician.

Formulations:
Drops, spray, gel, cream

Dosage:
Apply three to four times a day. Do not use for longer than seven days except under the advice of a physician. These products are not recommended for children under two years except under the advice or supervision of a physician.

Counterirritants

Brand names:
Aveeno Anti-Itch Cream (camphor)
Rhuli (menthol, camphor)
Sting Kill (menthol)

Camphor, menthol, methyl salicylate, and other counterirritants work by stimulating the skin's sensory receptors to provide a feeling of warmth, coolness, or pain that is milder than the initial pain. In low concentrations, as is the case with products used to treat insect bites or stings, they may depress the sensory receptors in the skin and act as an anesthetic.

Formulations:
Cream, gel, spray, lotion

Dosage:
Adults and children two years and older should apply three to four times a day. These products are not recommended for children under two except under the advice or supervision of a physician.

Hydrocortisone

Brand names:
Maximum Strength Cortaid
Cortaid with Aloe
Kericort HC Cream 1%
Lanacort 10
**Preparation H Hydrocortisone 1% Anti-Itch
  Cream**

An anti-inflammatory agent, topically applied hydrocortisone may be used to relieve pain and itching from insect bites and stings. (For this purpose, it is generally formulated as a cream or lotion, rather than in combination with other active ingredients.) However, hydrocortisone should not be applied when there are scabies (a condition in which mites burrow beneath the skin) or bacterial or fungal infections, as it may worsen or mask the underlying conditions.

Formulations:
Cream, ointment, spray, lotion

Dosage:
Adults and children two years and older should apply three to four times a day. These products are not recommended for children under two except under the advice or supervision of a physician.

What to use when

As all the products listed here are generally safe and effective, your choice may be determined by any special sensitivities or conditions you have. For example, if you have a tendency to develop a skin rash from local anesthetics, especially benzocaine, avoid those products. If you have a bacterial or fungal infection in the area with the insect bite or sting, do not use products containing hydrocortisone.

Poison Ivy, Poison Oak, and Poison Sumac Treatments

OTC products for poison ivy (or poison oak or poison sumac—the treatment described here applies to all) primarily help alleviate the rash's characteristic itching and inflammation. Typically they work through a combination of two or more of the following agents: a local anesthetic (see below), to block the passage of nerve impulses at the site where they're administered, deadening all feeling at that site; an antipruritic (see below), because itching is the most prevalent symptom; an astringent (see page 111), to stop oozing, reduce inflammation, and promote healing; and an antiseptic (see page 111), to prevent secondary bacterial infections.

For individuals who develop poison ivy rash, the choice of products depends on the severity of the condition. People with severe cases should consult a physician and may require prescription steroids. Mild to moderately severe cases, however, can usually be treated with one or more topical OTC products such as those listed below.

Warning

Some ingredients that would normally not affect you can sometimes cause problems if you have a poison ivy rash. Your exposure to *urushiol,* the poison in these plants, may sensitize you to dyes, perfumes, or preservatives, for example. As a result, you could have an allergic response to a cream that would otherwise help soothe the discomfort from the rash. If you do have an allergic response, wash the affected area thoroughly with mild soap and water and discontinue using the product.

Formulations:
Spray, gel, cream, liquid, lotion. While lotions can be effective, if used excessively they tend to cake, and the plasterlike buildup on the skin may be uncomfortable and painful to remove.

Dosage:
Apply to the affected area three to four times a day. See manufacturers' directions regarding precise dosage and age restrictions for specific brand-name products.

Antipruritics

Brand names:
Benadryl 1%
Benadryl 2%
Ivarest 8-Hour
Ivy Dry
No More Itchies

These include antihistamines (see page 72) such as diphenhydramine and tripelennamine; counterirritants (see page 58) such as menthol and camphor, in low concentrations; and 0.5 to 1 percent hydrocortisone (see page 96). Antihistamines may be taken orally as well as applied topically in the combination drugs listed.

Local Anesthetics

Brand names:
Aveeno Anti-Itch
Caladryl
Itch-X
Ivarest
Ivy Dry
Ivy Super Dry
Rhuli

Benzocaine, pramoxine, and benzyl alcohol (not widely used as an anesthetic) are the most common local anesthetics found in OTC products for poison ivy rash. Since they act only at the site where they're applied, these drugs in nonprescription strength are unlikely to produce system toxicity.

Astringents

Brand names:
Aveeno Anti-Itch
Benadryl
Domeboro Astringent Solution
Ivy Dry
Ivy Super Dry

These stop oozing, reduce inflammation, and promote healing. The most commonly used substances—aluminum acetate (Burow's solution), witch hazel (Hamamelis water), alcohol, and zinc oxide/calamine—are widely available in generic form. Some of the products listed above, which combine astringents with other active ingredients, are also listed elsewhere in this section, as they contain anesthetics and/or antipruritics.

Antiseptics

Brand names:
IvyBlock
Ivy Shield
Stokoguard

While antiseptics are sometimes added to products to prevent secondary bacterial infections, it is not clear that they're either needed or effective. Common antiseptics include benzalkonium chloride and alcohol (the latter is already present in many poison ivy products as an astringent).

In addition to products that treat symptoms, a number of OTC products are designed to prevent exposure to *urushiol* by shielding the skin from initial contact with the poison or by removing the poison immediately upon contact. It is unclear how effective these products are. A two-year test of thirty-four such preparations concluded that none could prevent the outbreak of poison ivy rash. However, some researchers have subsequently reported good results with a few products.

Formulations:
Cream, lotion

What to use when

First, to prevent exposure, try the barrier products cited above. If you do develop a rash, you should combine oral antihistamines with application of topical agents, such as anesthetics or astringents, to relieve itching. If you want to avoid drowsiness and other symptoms associated with oral antihistamines, you can apply them—or another antipruritic—topically.

Antiacne Preparations

Topical antiacne products reduce acne either by reducing the production of oil by oil-producing glands or by loosening the dead cells on the skin surface and unblocking the sebaceous glands— those glands that produce and secrete sebum, a mixture of fats and waxes. These products cannot cure acne, only control it enough to improve one's appearance and prevent the development of severe acne that may result in scarring. All OTC antiacne products may take four to six weeks to improve the condition.

Sulfur is the active ingredient used to reduce the production of oil. Keratolytic agents such as benzoyl peroxide or salicylic acid are used to help shed dead skin cells and unblock sebaceous glands. This type of preparation often causes dryness or irritation of the skin, especially at the start of treatment. To prevent this, start with one application daily and gradually increase if needed, or use the product in a lower concentration.

In addition to applying these treatments, you should wash areas affected with acne at least twice a day with warm water and soap. An alternative product, if that schedule is inconvenient, is a cleansing pad that contains alcohol, acetone, and a surfactant—a chemical like a detergent that reduces the surface tension of a liquid to make an object (such as the face) more "wettable." Alcohol, which is desirable for its drying property, is also found in many other antiacne preparations.

Medicated soaps contain salicylic acid and/or sulfur in combination. However, their benefit as ingredients in soaps for the treatment of acne is questionable because little, if any, residue is left on the skin after thorough washing. Soap substitutes containing surfactants are sometimes recommended because they are less drying to the skin. Still, because a mild degree of drying is desirable in the prevention and treatment of acne, ordinary facial soaps that do not contain moisturizing oils are usually satisfactory. There is no conclusive evidence that soaps containing antibacterial agents are effective.

Some cleansing preparations contain pumice or other particles to add abrasive action. Polyester cleansing sponges, for example, help remove the outer layer of dead skin cells by gentle abrasion. Used gently, these abrasive agents may be helpful in treating ordinary acne.

Benzoyl Peroxide

Brand names:
Clear by Design
Clearasil
Fostex 10% BPO
Neutrogena Acne Mask
Noxzema Anti-Acne
On-the-Spot
Oxy-5
Oxy-10

One of the most effective and widely used topical OTC medications for acne, benzoyl peroxide may also promote antibacterial activity against the bacteria that cause acne and reduce inflammation of blocked hair follicles by killing the bacteria that infect them. It is often added to tinted preparations that camouflage as well as treat the condition.

Warning

There is concern that benzoyl peroxide may promote skin tumors and also that it may make users more susceptible to skin cancer from ultraviolet radiation. While safety studies are ongoing, the compound is currently approved but placed in Category III (insufficient available data to make a final determination for OTC first aid use) by the FDA.

Formulations:
Lotion, gel, cream, cleanser, mask, soap. Cleansers and soaps are far less effective than formulations in a drying alcohol base, such as gels. Concentrations range from 2.5 to 10 percent. The lower concentrations are recommended for more sensitive skin, specifically among fair-skinned individuals.

Dosage:
To test for sensitivity, initially apply the product to one or two small areas at the lowest concentration, and wash it off after fifteen minutes. If there's no sensitivity problem, increase the application time in fifteen-minute increments. Once you've established that you can tolerate it for two hours, you can leave it on your skin overnight. Once-a-day applications may be all that are needed; a morning dose may also be used if tolerated. It may take four to six weeks to notice a significant improvement.

Salicylic Acid

Brand names:
BUF-PUF
Clearasil Clearstick Regular/Maximum Strength
Fostex Medicated
Neutrogena Oil-Free Wash
Noxzema 2 in 1 Regular/Maximum Strength
Oxy Clean
Stri-dex Clear

This is the keratolytic agent longest in use. Used properly, it is considered quite safe.

Warning

Used over large areas for prolonged periods of time, salicylic acid may be absorbed through the skin, be metabolized in the liver, and excreted in the urine, having a toxic effect especially for people with impaired liver or kidney function.

Formulations:
Cleansing bar, pad, liquid, lotion, cream; in concentrations of 0.5 to 2 percent. The lower concentrations are recommended for more sensitive skin.

Dosage:
Start with one application daily to the affected area, gradually increasing over the course of a week to two to three times daily. Do not rinse off. Continue using daily to help prevent pimples from forming.

Resorcinol

This compound, which has a keratolytic action, is generally combined with sulfur in antiacne medications.

Warning

Resorcinol may produce a dark brown scale on some darker-skinned people. This reaction is reversible by discontinuing use.

Sulfur

Brand names:
Acnomel (with resorcinol)
Clearasil Adult Care (with resorcinol)
Fostril, Sulray

In treating acne, sulfur works by reducing the production of oil by oil-producing glands. One drawback to products with sulfur is that they have a noticeable color and odor. If this is a problem, use the products after school or at bedtime or in flesh tones.

Warning

Continued use of products with sulfur may tend to produce acne.

Formulations:
Cleansing bar, lotion, cream, mask, stick; in concentrations of 3 to 10 percent; often in combination with resorcinol. Sulfur-resorcinol combination products have the same color and odor characteristic of sulfur-only products.

Dosage:
Apply in a thin film to the affected area once or twice daily. Do not apply to broken skin.

What to use when

Because it is highly effective, benzoyl peroxide is the treatment of choice. If your skin has trouble tolerating it, try one of the other therapeutic agents.

Antibiotics

OTC antibiotics, also known as antibacterials, help kill bacteria when the skin is infected. (Don't confuse them with prescription antibiotics, many of which are taken orally to treat an internal infection.) They may also be used to prevent infection in the case of minor cuts, scrapes, and burns (when the skin is broken). Alternatively, if there appears to be no infection, an antiseptic (see page 116) can be used prophylactically, or as a preventive measure. You should suspect you have a skin infection if the area is red, swollen, and/or tender.

The antibiotics used in topical preparations—that is, applied to the surface of the skin—usually are drugs that are poorly absorbed through the skin. Thus, the drug stays where it is needed to treat the infection: on the surface and in the skin's upper layers.

Often a preparation containing two or more antibiotics is used to ensure that all bacteria are eradicated. For example, one widely used preparation combines bacitracin—an antibacterial that is effective mainly against staphylococcic and streptococcic infections—with polymyxin B sulfate, an antibacterial used to combat other types of bacteria. (A staph infection is sometimes, but not always, indicated by the presence of pus; otherwise, apart from taking a culture, neither you nor a health-care professional can be certain what type of infection is present.) While bacitracin is also marketed by itself, polymyxin B sulfate is sold only in combination with other antibiotics. Some antibiotic preparations also contain an anesthetic (see page 97) to provide fast pain relief, or hydrocortisone (see page 96) to help relieve skin inflammation.

Best bacitracin
or
bacitracin + polymycin
Not -Neosporin or anyother
with Neomycin

Formulations:
Ointment, cream

Dosage:
Apply small amount one to three times daily on the affected area. Do not use longer than one week unless directed by a physician.

Most of the antibiotics on the market contain at least one of the following ingredients:

Bacitracin

Brand names:
Bacitracin
Polysporin (with polymyxin)

This antibiotic should be applied one to three times daily. In commercial products, it is generally combined with polymyxin B sulfate, a complementary antibiotic.

Neomycin

Brand names:
Clomycin
Lanabiotic
Medi-Quick Triple Antibiotic
Mycitracin
Mycitracin Plus (with lidocaine)
Neomixin
Neosporin Ointment
Neosporin Plus Maximum Strength Ointment
Tribiotic Plus

This antibiotic is most frequently used in combination, as part of a triple antibiotic, with bacitracin and polymyxin B sulfate. (The combination helps prevent the development of organisms that are resistant to neomycin.) All brands listed above are triple antibiotics.

What to use when

As a rule, try the combination of bacitracin and polymyxin B sulfate before resorting to a triple antibiotic. Neomycin produces a rash or other allergic skin reaction in 5 to 8 percent of people who use it.

Antifungals

Antifungals relieve athlete's foot and jock itch by destroying fungi or stopping their growth. The reclassification to OTC of two antifungals—clotrimazole and miconazole—that were formerly available only by prescription has resulted in the introduction of a range of more effective products.

Drug treatment is necessary for most fungal infections since they rarely improve on their own. Severe cases, specifically those of the scalp or nails, require prescription oral antibiotics or other treatment. But for the milder cases that typically involve the feet or the groin, a variety of OTC antifungals are available.

A range of compounds is effective against both athlete's foot and jock itch. (For the section on products to treat vaginal fungal infections, see page 179; for a discussion of the cosmetic treatment of toenails infected with fungus, see page 124.) Although the packaging may indicate that a product should be used specifically for either athlete's foot or jock itch, the formulation is often identical. As a rule, the preparation should be applied to athlete's foot infections for up to four weeks and to jock itch infections for up to two weeks.

The choice of chemical agent depends on the type of fungal infection involved. The typical infection, characterized by itching and scaling of the foot or groin, can usually be treated successfully with the fungicides described below. The wet, soggy type of athlete's foot, in which bacteria are involved, should first be treated with an astringent (see page 118) such as aluminum acetate (Burow's solution) to dry the foot and kill bacteria. At that point, the infection can be controlled with one of the standard fungicides.

Formulations:
Most of these products are formulated as creams, sprays, powders, and liquids. However, certain dosage forms, such as liquids and spray liquids, are more appropriate for athlete's foot than for jock itch. Alternatively, while creams and lotions are effective ways of delivering the medication into the skin, they tend to trap fungus-nurturing moisture between the toes. Sprays and powders are generally effective if rubbed well into the entire area. In the case of athlete's foot, the product must go between all toes, the skin around every

toenail, and the entire sole of each foot, even if only one foot appears to be significantly infected.

Dosage:
Apply twice daily (morning and night) for two weeks for jock itch, four weeks for athlete's foot; however, treatment for athlete's foot may require four to six weeks if you have open wounds between your toes or on pressure areas such as the ball of your foot. If there is no improvement by the end of this time, discontinue use and consult a doctor. Do not use on children under two years. To prevent recurrence of athlete's foot, continue to apply once or twice daily.

Tolnaftate

Brand names:
Absorbine Jr. Antifungal Foot
Aftate for Jock Itch
Desenex Antifungal Spray Liquid
Dr. Scholl's Athlete's Foot
Tinactin
Ting

Side effects are rare with this standard topical antifungal medication. Unlike some other antifungal drugs, tolnaftate does not generally cause skin irritation or rash. Occasionally, stinging may occur when it is applied to the skin with an aerosol spray.

Tolnaftate is valuable primarily in the dry, scaly type of athlete's foot. It cools down the infection, reduces itching, and limits the spread of the fungus. Tolnaftate can be used long-term to prevent recurrence of infections in susceptible people.

When medication is applied to pressure areas such as the ball of the foot, where the horny skin layer is thicker than normal, use a keratolytic agent (see page 126) such as a salicylic acid ointment to help shed skin and increase absorption of the drug.

Formulations:
Spray, cream, powder, liquid, solution

Clotrimazole

Brand names:
Lotrimin AF
Lotrimin Jock Itch
Mycelex

Recently reclassified from prescription to OTC, clotrimazole is a synthetic broad-spectrum antifungal agent that kills a wide range of different fungi and yeasts. It works by killing fungus in the multiplying and growing stage of its development.

Formulations:
Cream, solution

Miconazole

Brand names:
Absorbine Jr. Antifungal Foot
Lotrimin AF
Micatin
Zeasorb-AF

Like clotrimazole, miconazole was reclassified from prescription to OTC. Because it also has some antibacterial activity, it is particularly useful in some types of fungal infections complicated by the presence of bacteria—especially the wet, soggy type of athlete's foot, rather than the scaly, dry type.

Formulations:
Spray, cream, powder, ointment

Undecylenate Acid/ Zinc Undecylenate

Brand names:
Cruex
Desenex Antifungal

This combination antifungal agent is widely used to treat various mild superficial, chronic fungal infections such as typical athlete's foot. It is believed that zinc undecylenate releases undecylenic acid, the active antifungal ingredient, on contact with moisture, such as perspiration. In addition, zinc undecylenate has astringent properties that decrease the irritation and inflammation of the infection.

Formulations:
Spray, powder, cream

Clioquinol

Brand names:
Various generics

The antifungal agent clioquinol is generally used in conjunction with hydrocortisone cream for one to two days to relieve itching and redness. Topical hydrocortisone by itself should be avoided because it will encourage the fungi to grow.

Because it contains iodine, clioquinol may interfere with thyroid-function tests. If you're undergoing such tests, you should inform your health care practitioner that you are using clioquinol.

Formulations:
Cream, ointment

What to use when

As all antifungals described in this section are effective in treating athlete's foot and jock itch, your choice may be determined by the availability of the product in a formulation you prefer. However, there are some differences. If you have the wet, soggy type of athlete's foot, try miconazole. If your athlete's foot is dry and scaly, try other antifungals, including tolnaftate, which is also less likely than the others to cause skin irritation or rash.

Antiseptics

By definition, antiseptics prevent the growth of disease-causing microorganisms following a surface wound to the skin, such as a minor burn or abrasion, by cleansing and disinfecting. They are weaker than household disinfectants, which are irritating to the skin.

These products are also known as germicides, skin disinfectants, or first-aid antiseptics. If infection does occur, treatment with an antibiotic preparation (see page 113) may be necessary.

Formulations:
As noted below, antiseptics are in liquid form. With a few exceptions, the leading first aid antiseptics that meet the FDA's criteria for safety and efficacy are sold directly by their chemical names. Accordingly, the following list will not include brand names.

Dosage:
Apply to affected area immediately following burn or abrasion, and again if wound becomes exposed to dirt or other matter.

Hydrogen Peroxide

The most widely used first aid antiseptic, topical hydrogen peroxide works through the enzymatic release of oxygen when the agent comes into contact with blood and tissue fluids. It should not be used on unbroken skin because the release of oxygen is too low. Because the released gas needs to escape, hydrogen peroxide should not be used in abscesses, and bandages should not be applied before the area dries.

Alcohol

Also known as ethanol, this type of alcohol—which is normally denatured (made undrinkable by the addition of a substance such as methanol)—is an effective bactericide. However, it can irritate already damaged tissue and at high concentrations dries out the skin.

Isopropyl Alcohol

Compared with ethanol, isopropyl alcohol—which is not denatured because it is not drinkable anyway—has somewhat stronger bactericidal and astringent, or drying, activity.

Iodine

An iodine solution of 2 percent to 2.5 percent sodium iodine and water may be used as an antiseptic for superficial wounds.

Warning

In general, to avoid tissue irritation you should not bandage after applying iodine. Iodine solutions stain skin, may irritate tissue, and may cause an allergic reaction in some people. If used long-term, they may be absorbed through the skin in amounts sufficient to inhibit thyroid activity.

Povidone-Iodine Complex

Brand names:
Betadine (numerous formulations)
Polydine

This agent is sold directly, used as a preoperative germicide, and also added to numerous OTC products, including shampoos and douches, for its antiseptic effect. It is less likely to irritate, stain, or provoke an allergic reaction than iodine solutions and rarely affects thyroid function.

Formulations:
Solution, cream, spray

Phenol/Camphor

Brand name:
Campho-Phenique

Oily solutions of phenol and camphor are often used as antiseptics in the treatment of minor cuts, insect bites, athlete's foot, fever blisters, and cold sores. Such products contain relatively high concentrations of phenol and must be used with caution, as phenol can be highly irritating. To prevent a caustic concentration of phenol, use only on dry skin.

Merbromin

Better known as mercurochrome (which has 2 percent merbromin), merbromin is less effective for skin wounds than many other antiseptics, but is used in some instances as a preoperative germicide.

Warning

While the other antiseptics in this section are in Category I (safe and effective, according to the FDA classification system), the FDA classifies merbromin in Category III (insufficient available data to make a final determination for OTC first aid use). However, mercurochrome is generally available.

What to use when

As all the antiseptics described here provide good antimicrobial action, with the exception of mercurochrome, you should consider other factors such as whether the antiseptics tend to be irritating (indicated above) and whether they can be combined with bandaging.

Astringents

Astringents help dry skin and mucous membranes that are weeping as a result of abrasions, burns, or other minor injuries. They cool and dry the skin through evaporation, lessen mucus and other secretions, and cause vasoconstriction (narrowing of a blood vessel), thereby reducing local swelling and inflammation. They also help cleanse the skin of crust and debris.

Astringents work by coagulating the protein in skin cells, resulting in a protective coating under which new tissue may grow.

Astringents are sometimes sold alone and applied as dressings or compresses to the affected area. In general, they are combined with other ingredients in a wide variety of preparations, from hemorrhoidal preparations (see page 107) and douches (see page 173) to treatments for insect bites and stings (see page 108) and dermatitis (see page 103).

Aluminum Acetate

Brand names:
Biro-Sol Antiseptic
Domeboro Astringent Solution

This ingredient is also included in treatments for impacted earwax (see page 173) and the wet, soggy type of athlete's foot (see page 114). It is generally sold as Burow's solution, which is about 5 percent aluminum acetate—the package will indicate this—and must be diluted 1:10 to 1:40 with water before use.

Formulations:
Solution, tablet, powder

Dosage:
Apply to affected area as a wet compress for twenty minutes, four to six times daily, for up to one week. Continuous or prolonged use for longer than a week may redden or inflame the skin.

Witch Hazel (Hamamelis Water)

Used for centuries, witch hazel (also known as Hamamelis water, for the tree from which it's extracted) may be applied as often as necessary in treating minor skin irritations caused by poison ivy, insect bites, athlete's foot, or allergic dermatitis. It is sold directly in bottles, without a brand name, and also incorporated in numerous products, including several OTC pads or wipes for hemorrhoidal care. Its effectiveness arises primarily from its 15 percent alcohol content.

Formulation:
Liquid

Dosage:
Apply as needed to treat minor skin irritations. To soak the affected area, apply saturated cloth two to four times daily for fifteen to thirty minutes.

Zinc Oxide/Calamine

Brand names:
Ammens Medicated Powder Original Fragrance
Calamine
Desitin
Dyprotex
Gold Bond Baby
Gold Bond Medicated

Both zinc oxide and calamine—the two are often combined—tend to absorb fluids from weeping rashes. As well as being sold alone, they are primary ingredients in numerous OTC products, including many diaper rash protectants (see page 122). Zinc oxide has mild astringent, protective, and antiseptic actions. Calamine is a mixture of zinc and ferrous oxide; the latter acts only as a color agent and not an active ingredient.

Formulations:
Ointment, paste, powder

Dosage:
Apply three to four times daily as needed.

Bath Products

Bath products help moisturize skin and reduce itching. They may be used in the treatment of dry skin disorders, as well as for other conditions, such as chicken pox (see page 121), in which itching is also a symptom.

There are three types of OTC bath products.

Bath Oils

Brand names:
AlphaKeri
Bath and Body
Calgon
Lubriderm Skin Conditioning
Nutraderm
Sardo

These products usually consist of a mineral or vegetable oil plus a surfactant—a chemical, like a detergent, that reduces the surface tension of a liquid to make an object (such as the face) more "wettable."

Products with mineral oil are adsorbed onto, or bind onto, the skin better than those with vegetable oil. Bath oils work better as you increase the water temperature and the concentration of oil. That aside, according to the National Professional Society of Pharmacists, no one type of bath oil is appreciably better than another.

Bath oils are only minimally effective in improving a dry skin condition because they are greatly diluted by water. The major effect is to give the skin a more lubricated feeling, which may be increased by adding the oil near the end of the

bath and patting the skin dry with a towel after bathing rather than rubbing the oil into the skin.

Warning
Bath oils make the tub and floor slippery, creating a safety hazard, especially for the elderly. People with allergies should also be careful to avoid scented products.

Formulations:
Bath oil, may be packaged as "beads."

Dosage:
Add to bath according to manufacturer's directions. Alternatively, you can apply the bath oils as wet compresses (1 teaspoon of oil in ¼ cup of warm water), which helps moisturize the skin without the drying effects of bathing.

Oatmeal Products

Brand names:
ActiBath Soak Oatmeal Treatment
Aveeno Bath Treatment Soothing Formula
Aveeno Bath Treatment Moisturizing Formula
   (with mineral oil)
Nutra Soothe Oatmeal Bath

Colloidal oatmeal bath products—which are thick suspensions—have a lubricating effect, relieve itching, and soothe irritated skin. The fine-grained oatmeal particles collect surface soils, letting you wash them away while restoring your skin to a healthy pH level. Because they do not contain oil, these products moisturize less than bath oils. A more effective alternative is oiled oatmeal, which combines oatmeal with a bath oil.

Formulations:
Effervescent tablet, powder, bath oil

Dosage:
Add product according to manufacturer's directions to bath under running faucet. To avoid clumping or settling of tablet or powder, stir water thoroughly. Bathe for fifteen to twenty minutes, one to two times daily.

Bath Soaps and Other Cleansers

Brand names:
Alpha Keri (glycerin)
Aveeno for Dry Skin (glycerin with lactic acid and colloidal oatmeal)
Keri Facial Soap (glycerin)
Nivea Shower & Bath (glycerin)
Neutrogena (glycerin)
Oilatum Soap (citric acid)

Most bath soaps remove the lipids, or fats, that keep the skin soft and pliable. People with dry skin should avoid products identified as "soaps" (rather than "cleansing bars") or use only those soaps (such as Dove) to which the manufacturers have added extra oils or cold cream.

The hydrating ingredient added to most moisturizing soaps is glycerin. These soaps have a higher oil content, are closer to a neutral pH—that is, are neither alkaline nor acidic—and are therefore regarded as less drying than conventional soaps, which are alkaline.

A few soaps, as indicated below, also contain alpha-hydroxy acids, such as lactic acid and citric acid, which are being used increasingly in other types of dry-skin products (see Emollients, page 104).

Formulations:
Bar soaps, cleansing bars

Dosage:
Use whenever you would normally use soap.

What to use when

Use bath oils and oatmeal products to add moisture to the skin, special cleansers to reduce the drying effect. Bath oils make cleansing the skin with soaps more difficult. However, because of their inherent cleansing properties, it is often not necessary to use soap when you are using a bath oil or oatmeal product.

Bunion Treatments

Brand name:
Dr. Scholl's Bunion Cushions

A bunion is a bony bump on the base of the big toe that occurs when that toe overlaps another. Although a bunion is not particularly painful, it may be complicated by arthritis or bursitis (swelling of the bursa—a sac of fluid that protects a joint). Nonprescription padding, which is available in any pharmacy, can help decrease the inflammation around the bunion area and minimize any irritation caused by footwear. Bunions cannot be helped by OTC drugs; corrective shoes or surgery may be required. Precut pads are available in two forms: as a "ring" of soft, protective foam that surrounds the bunion, or as a thick felt pad that covers the entire bunion to relieve painful pressure.

Warning
Do not use protective pads on bunions when the skin is broken or blistered.

Dosage:
As needed. In general, constant skin contact with adhesive-backed pads should be avoided.

Callus and Corn Removers

Callus and corn removers help loosen and remove thickened skin, turning the callus or corn white and blister-free so that it can peel off. The only nonprescription drug found by the FDA to be both safe and effective in treating calluses and corns is salicylic acid, which is also found in aspirin.

In their directions to consumers, some manufacturers state that the callus or corn should be soaked in warm water for five minutes before applying salicylic acid, to assist in removal. This was long thought to be the best approach. However, based on findings several years ago that pre-soaking produces no actual benefit, the FDA made this direction optional.

The FDA has also deleted the once-required warning that a film of petroleum jelly be applied to healthy skin near the area under treatment, to protect it from salicylic acid.

Warning

Overusing salicylic acid products for callus and corn removal can potentially burn the skin. These products should not be used on irritated skin or on any area that is infected or reddened. In addition, do not use these products if you have diabetes or poor blood circulation.

Formulations:
Products to remove calluses and corns come in two forms: film and plasters or disks.

Collodion Solution

Brand names:
Dr. Scholl's Liquid Corn/Callus Remover
DuoFilm

This product contains 12 to 17 percent salicylic acid and forms a film on the skin upon application. This more common treatment is also the more effective because the film prevents moisture from evaporating and thus permits the drug to work over a sustained period of time.

Warning

These products are extremely flammable.

Dosage:
Apply once or twice daily as needed for up to twelve days, or until the corn or callus comes off.

Plasters or Disks

Brand names:
Clear Away One Step Corn Remover
Dr. Scholl's Callus Removers
Dr. Scholl's Corn Removers

The plasters are impregnated with 40 percent salicylic acid. This method of delivery is easier to use than the solution.

Dosage:
Apply for at least forty-eight hours at a time, with a maximum of five treatments over a two-week period.

What to use when

The collodion solution is generally preferred because it is less expensive and also more effective. However, disks or plasters may be easier to use with children.

Chicken Pox Treatments

Products for the treatment of chicken pox are designed primarily to relieve the itching that is the main symptom of the disease. The typical product is a topical antipruritic (see page 95) OTC medication, often added to a cool bath every few hours.

If the itching interferes with sleep, an OTC product such as Benadryl, which contains an antihistamine, may be given orally to relieve itching and induce drowsiness; dosage is determined by body weight. The antihistamine works by countering the effects of histamine, one of the chemicals released in the body when there is an allergic reaction or infection. Do not apply hydrocortisone creams; they may cause a bacterial infection on top of the viral infection.

When chicken pox spreads to the inside of the mouth, sores may be relieved with a tablespoon of one of the traditional antacid solutions (see page 81), such as Maalox, after meals. Sores in the genital area may be treated with a local anesthetic (see page 97), applied every two to three hours to relieve the pain.

To prevent the sores from becoming infected, wash your hands frequently with one of the many antibacterial soaps on the market, such as Dial or Safeguard.

Warning

The American Academy of Pediatrics has recommended that children (through age twenty-one) not receive aspirin if they have chicken pox or influenza (any cold, cough, or sore throat symptoms). The recommendation stems from several studies that have linked aspirin to Reye's syndrome, a rare but potentially fatal brain and liver disorder. If your child develops a fever with chicken pox, give him or her acetaminophen to bring it down.

Colloidal Oatmeal

Brand names:
ActiBath Soak
Aveeno Bath Treatment/Moisturizing Cream and Lotion
Nutra Soothe

Colloidal oatmeal bath products contain starch, protein, and a small amount of oil. They have a slight anti-inflammatory effect that is soothing. Because these preparations make the bathtub very slick, you may want to place a nonskid mat in the tub and take other precautions.

Formulations:
Effervescent tablet, powder, cream, lotion

Dosage:
Add product according to manufacturer's directions to bath under running faucet. To avoid clumping or settling of tablet or powder, stir water thoroughly. Bathe for fifteen to twenty minutes, one to two times daily. May also be used for bathing infants, for ten minutes at a time.

Calamine

Brand name:
Aveeno Anti-Itch Cream

A mixture of zinc and iron oxide, calamine is used for its cooling, slightly astringent action; it tends to absorb fluids from weeping rashes. In addition to the brand listed above, it is also widely available in generic form.

Formulation:
Lotion

Dosage:
Place on itchy spots every few hours and/or after a bath.

What to use when

Products can be used in combination or separately.

Diaper Rash Protectants

Diaper rash products reduce and ultimately eliminate the rash, relieve discomfort, and prevent blisters and secondary infection caused by bacteria or yeast. They work primarily by forming a physical barrier to irritants and moisture. In 1992, the FDA declared that OTC antifungals and analgesics that are applied topically, such as local anesthetics, may not make claims as diaper rash treatments, owing to inadequate evidence of safety and efficacy. In addition, the FDA does not currently recognize any OTC antimicrobial ingredient as safe and effective for diaper rash and has encouraged manufacturers to remove such ingredients from all diaper rash products. Some diaper rash products, however, do still include antimicrobials.

The National Professional Society of Pharmacists recommends against treating diaper rash with topical OTC hydrocortisone (see page 96). Steroids applied to skin that is inflamed or scraped, or under dressings such as diapers, are absorbed through the skin and into the bloodstream at higher levels than desired. Also, chronic use of steroids can cause thinning of the skin, with resultant striae—stripes or ridges, similar to stretch marks—and easy bruising.

In many cases, good hygiene—frequent diaper changes, especially after bowel movements, followed by washing the skin with warm tap water—and increased exposure to the air to prevent wetness may be sufficient. However, if the baby's skin is dry and cracked or if the baby has diarrhea, medication should be applied after each diaper change to protect the skin.

Warning
A diaper rash that does not clear up with treatment within a week may indicate the presence of a secondary bacterial or fungal skin infection and should be seen and treated by a physician. It should not be treated with OTC drugs.

Zinc Oxide

Brand names:
A & D Medicated
Caldesene Medicated Ointment
Desitin
Diaparene Diaper Rash Ointment
Dyprotex
Johnson's Baby Diaper Rash Relief

An excellent protectant found in many products to treat diaper rash, zinc oxide is a mild astringent (see page 118) that is also slightly effective against infection. Zinc oxide paste (25 percent zinc oxide, 25 percent cornstarch, and 50 percent white petrolatum) is absorptive because of the powders in its base, and is thus able to take up moisture, keeping the skin dry. All of the above products combine zinc oxide with petroleum jelly.

Formulations:
Ointment (with petroleum jelly), powder

Dosage:
To prevent diaper rash, apply to the diaper area, especially at bedtime when exposure to wet diapers may be prolonged. If diaper rash is present, apply product three to four times daily as needed. If using powder formulation, take precautions described below.

Talc, Magnesium Stearate, Calcium Carbonate, Cornstarch, Kaolin

Brand names:
Ammens Medicated Powder
Baby Magic Baby Powder
Caldesene Medicated Powder
Desitin Cornstarch Baby
Diaparene Baby Powder
Johnson's Baby (powder)
Johnson's Baby Cornstarch

These and other powders—sometimes in combination with zinc oxide—primarily keep the diaper area dry after each diaper change. However, they should never be applied to skin that is acutely inflamed and oozing, because they may promote crusting and infection.

Warning
Powders should be used cautiously because inhaling the dust may harm the infant and could lead to chemical pneumonia. Powder products should be kept away from the child's face and instead should be applied close to the body.

Dosage:
Carefully shake the powder into the diaper or into the hand and apply to diaper area. Apply liberally as often as necessary with each diaper change, especially at bedtime, or any time when exposure to wet diapers may be prolonged.

What to use when

If your baby's skin is dry and cracked, or your baby has diarrhea, apply a zinc oxide–white petroleum jelly ointment to treat and protect the skin. For ordinary rashes, use either the zinc oxide–petroleum jelly product or a medicated powder (containing an antimicrobial agent that kills bacteria). Studies have shown these to be more effective than ordinary soap or unmedicated talcum powder.

Fungal Nail Area Treatments

Fungal nail infection products specifically treat infections *around* and *under* nails. There is no OTC cure for fungal infections of the nail, and anyone with this condition will ultimately require either oral prescription drugs or surgery to remove the area of the fungus. The products listed here contain some of the active ingredients also used to treat athlete's foot (see page 114); they are formulated and packaged differently to facilitate treatment of hard-to-reach areas. Further, one product—Dr. Scholl's Fungal Nail Revitalizer—claims to improve the appearance of infected nails by reducing discoloration and improving smoothness. The effect, however, is purely cosmetic.

Formulations:
Liquid, gel

Dosage:
Apply twice daily (morning and night) for four weeks. If there is no improvement by the end of this period, discontinue use and consult a doctor. Do not use on children under two. To prevent recurrence, continue to apply once or twice daily.

Tolnaftate

Brand name:
ProClearz

This is the standard topical antifungal agent widely used to treat various mild superficial, chronic fungal infections such as athlete's foot (see page 115).

Undecylenate Acid

Brand name:
FungiCure

This is another topical antifungal agent widely used to treat various mild superficial, chronic fungal infections such as athlete's foot.

> ### What to use when
>
> As both antifungals described in this section are safe and effective, your choice may be determined by the availability of the product in a formulation you prefer.

Prickly Heat (Miliaria) Treatments

Brand names:
Ammens Medicated Powder (zinc oxide,talc, cornstarch)
Baby Magic Cornstarch with Baking Soda & Aloe
Caldesene Medicated Powder (talc)
Desitin Cornstarch Baby (zinc oxide, cornstarch)
Johnson's Baby Powder (talc)
Johnson's Baby Cornstarch

Products for prickly heat, which is also known as heat rash or miliaria, generally help protect the skin from irritants while absorbing the sweat that can result in the condition.

Warning
Powders (one of the formulations available) should be used cautiously with newborns, infants, and young children—the age groups in which prickly heat is most common—because inhaling the dust may cause respiratory problems. Powder products should be kept away from the child's face and instead should be applied close to the body. They should never be applied to skin that is acutely inflamed and oozing, because they may promote secondary crusting and infection.

The ingredients most often used in treating prickly heat are talc, cornstarch, zinc oxide—a protectant that is also a mild astringent (see page 118) and antiseptic (see page 116)—and calamine lotion, a product widely available in generic form that combines zinc oxide and calamine. Because many products used for prickly heat contain two or more of these ingredients, the above list includes the leading products with their main ingredients. For more information about these ingredients, see Diaper Rash Protectants, page 122, which may also be treated with these products. However, oils and ointments such as petroleum jelly, which are used routinely for diaper rash, should not be used to treat prickly heat because they can block sweat glands and trap moisture.

Formulations:
Powder, lotion

Dosage:
Smooth on affected areas three to four times daily to treat heat rash, or apply to body creases to prevent rash. Call your child's physician if the rash lasts more than seventy-two hours with treatment.

Psoriasis Treatments

OTC preparations for psoriasis help relieve itching, moisturize dry skin, and remove scales. Because there is no cure for the condition, these products only help control psoriasis.

The choice of treatment depends on the specific area of the body afflicted and the stage of psoriasis. Because dry skin and itching are often the first signs of psoriasis, OTC treatments for the body, arms, and legs include widely used dry skin products such as emollients (see page 104) and oatmeal baths (see page 119). Gentle rubbing with a soft cloth following the bath will help remove the scales characteristic of psoriasis. Shampoos recommended for seborrhea (see page 132), with the exception of hydrocortisone products, may be used to treat scalp psoriasis.

If the condition worsens, stronger OTC products (listed below) designed specifically for psoriasis may be applied to remove scales.

Warning
The FDA recommends that only mild cases of psoriasis be treated with OTC products. If you have a severe case involving large areas of your body, you should be under a physician's care.

Coal Tar

Brand names:
Doak Oil
Lavatar
MG 217
Neutrogena T/Derm
Polytar
Psorigel
PsoriNail
Tegrin

This is obtained from bituminous coal; it is neither pine nor juniper tar, both of which have been banned by the FDA as active ingredients in dermatological treatments because of lack of evidence that they work. Coal tar preparations are the main OTC treatment for psoriasis, but because they are cosmetically unappealing they are often used to relieve psoriasis of the body, arms, and legs only after another agent such as salicylic acid has failed to help.

Coal tar products may be applied at bedtime—sleeping on old sheets is recommended, because of staining—and followed in the morning with a bath to remove the coal tar as well as the psoriatic scale. Sensitive areas, such as armpits, the genitals, and the anus, should not be treated with coal tar as they can become irritated.

To control scalp psoriasis, it may help to paint the lesions, or rash or sores, sparingly with tar oil bath additives, tar gels, or coal tar solutions three to twelve hours before each shampoo.

Warning
In cases of acute psoriatic onset, tar products must be avoided because they may irritate the skin. Emollients should be tried instead.

Formulations:
Bath oil, body oil, cleansing bar, gel, liquid, cream

Dosage:
Apply to affected area one to four times daily. If you've applied at bedtime, in the morning take a

bath to help remove the coal tar as well as the psoriatic scale.

Keratolytic Agents

Brand names:
Panscol
Poslam Psoriasis
Salicylic Acid & Sulfur Soap

In psoriasis treatments, salicylic acid is often combined with sulfur. Keratolytic products may be most appropriate when very thick scales are present over a limited area; application over extensive areas should be avoided because of the potential to be absorbed by the body. Sensitive areas, such as armpits, the genitals, and the anus, should not be treated with salicylic acid because they can become irritated.

Warning

In cases of acute psoriasis, salicylic acid should be avoided in favor of emollients, to avoid irritating the skin. As the psoriasis subsides and the usual thick-scaled plaques appear, keratolytics may be used again.

Formulations:
Cleansing bar, lotion, ointment

Dosage:
Soak the affected area in warm water for ten to twenty minutes before applying the medication. You may apply these products several times a day.

Hydrocortisone

Brand names:
Cortaid Sensitive Skin
Cortizone-5
Cortizone-10
Maximum Strength Cortaid

Hydrocortisone in over-the-counter concentrations is particularly appropriate for sensitive areas such as the armpits, the genitals, and the anus, where coal tar and salicylic acid can irritate. It may also be applied sparingly to lesions on the body, but not to the scalp.

Warning

Prolonged and frequent use of hydrocortisone should be avoided, as it may lead to a prompt rebound, or return of the psoriasis or seborrhea, when the hydrocortisone is discontinued. The psoriasis or seborrhea may even reappear as the more severe pustular form—that is, raised lesions containing pus.

Formulation:
Cream, ointment, roll-on stick, spray

Dosage:
Apply sparingly to affected areas (except the scalp) two to four times daily initially, then intermittently to control flare-ups. Massage thoroughly into the skin. For children under two years, consult a physician.

What to use when

First, try products containing salicylic acid, as they're more cosmetically acceptable. If they're not effective, try the coal tar product next. Use hydrocortisone only when necessary. If problems persist, see a physician.

Skin Protectants

Skin protectants are substances used to protect skin surfaces that have suffered minor injuries by providing a physical barrier to further harm or irritation, preventing dryness or absorbing excess moisture, and making the wound area less painful. In FDA-approved wording, the labeling on many skin protectant products states specifically, "For the temporary protection of minor cuts, scrapes, burns, and sunburns." These products provide protection, not healing.

Zinc oxide and petroleum jelly are the most widely used active ingredients in skin protectants. However, the FDA has recognized a number of agents as safe and effective for the temporary protection of skin damaged by burns and sunburn (see page 101), insect bites and stings (see page 108), diaper rash (see page 122), and anorectal irritation (see page 106). For specific information about those products, see the relevant sections.

In addition to these agents, some OTC products can be applied like bandages to protect minor cuts, abrasions, or burns. These products (brand names: New Skin, Second Skin) dry quickly to form a waterproof, nonsticking covering that allows the skin to breathe and heal. They are formulated as sprays, liquids, and translucent bandages.

Warning

Do not apply a skin protectant over a deep or puncture wound, infection, or laceration. If redness or swelling develops, consult your physician.

Zinc Oxide

Brand names:
A & D Medicated
Caldesene Medicated Ointment
Desitin
Gold Bond Powder

One of the most widely used and clinically accepted skin protectants, zinc oxide is a mild astringent (see page 118) with weak anti-infective properties. It is often combined with petroleum jelly.

Formulations:
Paste, ointment, lotion, powder

Dosage:
Apply liberally as needed or consult your physician.

Petroleum Jelly

Brand names:
A & D Ointment
Vaseline Medicated Anti-Bacterial Petroleum Jelly

While zinc oxide helps seal out moisture, keeping the skin dry, petrolatum (better known as petroleum jelly) may trap moisture beneath it and keep the skin moist. This is appropriate for injuries such as minor burns, but not for skin conditions such as poison ivy (see page 110), where a drying

or astringent action is desirable. Astringents include alcohol, aluminum acetate, witch hazel, zinc oxide, and calamine. For a list of astringent brand names, see page 118.

Formulation:
Ointment

Dosage:
Apply liberally as needed or consult your physician.

What to use when

If you are treating a condition such as poison ivy or anorectal irritation, where a drying or astringent action is desirable, use a skin protectant with zinc oxide rather than petroleum jelly.

Sunscreens

Brand names:
Bain de Soleil All Day Waterproof Sunblock
Banana Boat Tanning Oil (padimate O)
Blistex Lip Balm (padimate O)
Chap Stick Sunblock (padimate O)
Coppertone Moisturizing Sunscreen Lotion
Formula 405 Solar Cream (PABA)
Hawaiian Tropic Sunblock Lotion
Johnson's Baby Sunblock
Neutrogena Sunblock Cream
Nivea Sun Lotion
Oil of Olay Daily UV Protectant
PreSun 15/46 Moisturizing Lotion (PABA)
QT Quick Tanning Suntan Lotion by Coppertone
Shade
Sundown Sunblock
Tropical Blend Dark Tanning Oil (padimate O)
Vaseline Lip Therapy Balm Stick
Water Babies

Sunscreens help protect the skin from damage from sun exposure by absorbing and thus blocking most of the sun's ultraviolet rays. As a result, a smaller proportion of the rays pass through to the epidermis (the outer portion of the skin) to stimulate the activity of melanin, the pigment that gives the skin a tan but can also produce serious long-term damage, including premature aging of the skin and skin cancer.

The SPF (see sidebar) is not the only measure of a sunscreen's efficacy. Another factor is its substantivity—its ability to remain effective during prolonged exercise, sweating, and swimming. Sunscreens in a cream or lotion base appear to stay on, and reduce peeling of skin, better than sunscreens with alcohol bases. Here is a list of the seven groups of agents used in sunscreens:

•*Aminobenzoic acid and derivatives.* For years a primary ingredient of many sunscreens was aminobenzoic acid, or ABA (formerly known as para-aminobenzoic acid, or PABA). While it is a highly effective sunscreen and is also desirable because it does not stain clothing, in alcohol bases it has caused contact dermatitis (skin rash resulting from exposure to either an irritant or to a substance that causes an allergic reaction), photosensitivity (allergic reaction to the sun or light), and stinging or drying of the skin. It may also cause a rash in people who are sensitive to certain drugs, including anesthetics (see page 98) such as benzocaine and lidocaine. If you have this sensitivity, you should not use a sunscreen containing ABA or any of its derivatives, including padimate O (a common ingredient in lip balms).

•*Anthranilates.* The main agent in this group, menthyl anthranilate, is a weak sunscreen. It is usually found in combination with other sunscreen agents.

•*Benzophenones.* Of the three agents in this group, oxybenzone may be the most widely used. They are all good UV absorbers and are often combined with other sunscreens to provide a very broad spectrum of coverage.

•*Cinnamates.* Of the four sunscreens in this group, octocrylene has the greatest absorbance of UVA radiation and is widely used. However, cinnamates do not adhere well to the skin and must be combined with other sunscreens to improve substantivity.

• *Salicylates.* These are weak sunscreens that also do not adhere well to the skin, but are used in combination with many products.

Sunscreens and SPF Ratings

Sunscreens are graded according to the amount of ultraviolet radiation they absorb. The higher the sun protection factor, or SPF, the greater the protection. An SPF of 10, for example, means you can stay out in the sun ten times longer than if you were wearing no sunscreen (assuming the sunscreen is reapplied at the recommended intervals and in adequate amounts) and still get the same degree of redness or sunburn. The FDA has suggested the following guidelines for skin types and sunscreen products:

•SPF 2 to 4: Minimal protection from sunburning, permits suntanning, recommended for people who rarely burn and tan easily and deeply.

• SPF 4 to 6: Moderate protection from sunburning, permits some suntanning, recommended for people who tan well with minimal burning.

• SPF 6 to 8: Extra protection from sunburning, permits limited suntanning, recommended for people who burn moderately and tan gradually.

• SPF 8 to 14: Maximum protection from sunburning, permits little or no suntanning, recommended for people who always burn easily and tan minimally.

• SPF 15 or greater: Ultra protection from sunburn, permits no suntanning, recommended for people who burn easily and never tan.

In theory, as the skin tans, a lower SPF may be adequate to prevent burning. Experts agree, however, that to minimize the danger from sun exposure, people should always wear a sunscreen with an SPF of 15 or higher. Although there are products with SPFs up to 50, the FDA has indicated that there's no incremental benefit when the SPF exceeds 30.

• *Avobenzone.* This agent, which offers extra protection against UVA rays, is currently patented as Parsol 1789. It is available in Shade UVAGuard, in combination with other sunscreens.

• *Miscellaneous.* This group includes agents that work primarily as physical sunscreens, scattering rather than absorbing UV radiation like the chemical agents listed above. The group includes zinc oxide and titanium dioxide; the latter is included in a growing number of sunscreen products.

Sunscreens typically contain two or more active ingredients that provide different benefits. One, for example, may be a strong sunscreen against UVB radiation, which is most closely associated with sunburn, while another may be most effective in shielding the skin from UVA radiation, which penetrates deeper and can cause more serious damage to underlying tissue. Often these are combined to provide broader UV coverage. One of the most common combinations currently is octocrylene, which has good UV absorbance but does not adhere well to the skin, with oxybenzone, which has better substantivity.

Formulations:
Gel, lotion, cream, oil, spray

Dosage:
Apply liberally to all exposed areas. For best results, let dry at least 15 minutes before exposure to the sun. Reapply often, especially after toweling. Do not use on children under six months, as their skin is highly absorptive.

As a cautionary note, the presence of ABA or its derivatives, such as padimate O, is indicated in the list on page 127.

What to use when

If you are sensitive to PABA, avoid sunscreens with that ingredient. Otherwise, your main considerations will be the SPF and the formulation. The FDA has stated that products with an SPF as low as 2 or 3 should not be used on children under two years, as they do not supply adequate protection. Products with a higher SPF, such as 15, should be used.

Wart Removers

Wart-removing OTC products help remove common warts and plantar warts through the application of salicylic acid, which works as a keratolytic agent, sloughing off dead skin. Plantar warts appear on the soles of the feet, while common warts can be recognized by their rough, cauliflowerlike appearance. Common warts are usually located on the hands and fingers.

With self-treatment, small warts will usually disappear in a week or two. Larger or more stubborn warts may take up to twelve weeks to heal completely. If the wart remains after a full course of treatment, a medical practitioner—in the case of plantar warts, this practitioner could be a podiatrist—should be consulted.

In their directions to consumers, some manufacturers state that the wart should be soaked in warm water for five minutes before applying salicylic acid, to assist in removal. This was long thought to be the most effective approach. Evidence submitted to the FDA, however, indicates that presoaking produces no actual benefit, and this direction is now optional.

To avoid the spread of warts, which are contagious, you should wash your hands before and after treating or touching wart tissue.

Warning

Topical salicylic acid preparations for wart removal should not be used on the healthy skin around the wart, on any area that is infected or irritated, if you are diabetic, or if you have poor blood circulation. All wart types other than common and plantar warts should be diagnosed and treated by a physician. Venereal warts occur near the genitalia and anus and cannot be treated with these products.

Formulations:
Products to remove warts come in two forms: a collodion solution and pads impregnated with salicylic acid.

Collodion Solution

Brand names:

Dr. Scholl's Wart Remover Kit
DuoFilm Liquid Wart Remover
DuoPlant Plantar Wart Remover for Feet
Wart-Off

This collodion solution (12 to 17 percent salicylic acid) forms a film over the wart, preventing moisture from evaporating and thus permitting the drug to work over a sustained period.

Dosage:

Apply the solution once or twice daily as needed for up to twelve weeks, or until the wart falls off.

Disks or Pads

Brand names:

Clear Away Plantar Wart Remover
DuoFilm Patch System Wart Remover

Disks or pads are impregnated with 40 percent salicylic acid.

Dosage:

Apply new disk or pad every forty-eight hours, with a maximum treatment period not to exceed twelve weeks.

What to use when

The collodion solution is generally preferred because it is less expensive and also more effective. However, disks or plasters may be easier to use with children. In addition, the solutions are extremely flammable.

Hair and Scalp Treatments

This section addresses conditions ranging in severity from ordinary dandruff and cradle cap to seborrhea. The treatments themselves range from mineral oil to salicylic acid to coal tar. Because these treatments fall into the clear groupings of cytostatic agents (which work by reducing the rate at which the scalp and skin shed their surface cells), coal tar, and keratolytic agents (which work by loosening the scales of dandruff so that they are shed in smaller particles), the brand names, dosages, and formulations can be found under these names. Hydrocortisone is only used for the treatment of seborrhea, so it is listed separately on page 134.

Lice treatments and information about the hair growth stimulant *minoxidil,* which is now available over the counter, are also included in Hair and Scalp Treatments.

Dandruff, Cradle Cap, and Seborrhea Treatments

Dandruff Shampoos

Medicated dandruff shampoos control—but do not cure—dandruff, either by reducing the rate at which the scalp sheds its surface skin cells (shedding is accelerated in people with dandruff), or by facilitating the removal of the skin cells from the scalp in smaller, less conspicuous particles. The precise action depends upon which of the three main types of dandruff shampoos is used.

It may be possible to treat dandruff with a regular, or nonmedicated shampoo, used three or more times weekly. If a medicated, or dandruff, shampoo is necessary, it should remain on the hair for at least five to ten minutes before rinsing in order to be effective. If the condition persists, you may consider trying a prescription product.

Warning

Before buying a dandruff shampoo, examine your scalp closely. There is no inflammation or redness of the scalp with dandruff. If you notice a yellow-reddish color where the flaking occurs, you may actually have seborrhea (see below) or psoriasis (see page 125) and should treat the condition with different OTC products.

Cradle Cap Treatments

There are no specific products for the dry, flaky skin rash that often occurs on infants' scalps. However, depending on the severity of the condition, cradle cap can be self-treated with—from least to most intensive therapy—gentle but thorough washing, a daily antidandruff shampoo, min-

eral oil (see page 105), or, in the more resistant cases and under the advice of a physician, 0.5 percent hydrocortisone cream (see page 96) applied three times a day for four days.

If the scalp is very crusty, mineral oil should be applied to the scalp one hour before washing, to soften the crust. The oil should be entirely washed off or it may worsen the cradle cap.

Untreated, cradle cap often clears up by the time the baby is eight to twelve months old. However, if the condition lasts more than two weeks with treatment or if the rash has spread beyond the scalp, consult a physician.

Seborrhea Treatments

OTC treatments for seborrhea, which tends to occur mainly on the scalp, are primarily medicated shampoos. Like dandruff shampoos, shampoos for seborrhea control—but do not cure—the condition. They work either through reducing the rate at which the scalp sheds its surface skin cells (turnover rate is five to six times faster than normal in people with seborrhea) or by facilitating the removal of the skin cells from the scalp in smaller particles. The precise action depends upon which type of shampoo is used.

Shampoos for seborrhea are similar to those for dandruff, but there are important differences. Some active ingredients used in both, such as pyrithione zinc (see below), may be found at higher levels in shampoos for seborrhea. Another important difference is the use of hydrocortisone (see page 96), which is ill-advised for dandruff but may help in managing seborrhea.

As with dandruff shampoos, the longer the shampoo is on the scalp, the more effective it is. The shampoo should remain on the hair for five to ten minutes before rinsing.

Warning

If the seborrhea worsens or spreads to the ears and areas around the eyes, prescription products may be required and a physician should be consulted.

Formulation:
Shampoo (except where noted)

Cytostatic Agents

**Brand names
(for dandruff shampoos with pyrithione zinc):**
Anti-Dandruff Brylcreem
Head & Shoulders 2-in-1
Head & Shoulders Fine/Oily/Normal to Dry Hair
Head & Shoulders Dry Scalp

**Brand names
(for dandruff shampoos with selenium sulfide):**
Head & Shoulders Intensive Treatment
Selsun Blue
Selsun Gold for Women

Brand names (for seborrhea treatment):
Sebulon
X-Seb Plus
ZNP Bar (cleansing bar)

These chemicals, which work by reducing the rate at which the scalp and skin shed their surface cells, represent the most direct approach to controlling dandruff and are generally the first recommended by pharmacists. The cytostatic agents are either selenium sulfide or pyrithione zinc, at 1 percent concentrations. (Higher concentrations are marketed for seborrhea). Both agents are considered safe and effective. Selenium sulfide is reported to be faster acting, but frequent use tends to leave a residual odor and an oily scalp; it is also more likely than pyrithione zinc to irritate the scalp and adjacent skin areas and to discolor light-colored or dyed hair if not rinsed thoroughly.

For seborrhea, pyrithione zinc may be present at concentrations of 1 to 2 percent. Selenium sulfide may also be tried, but frequent use tends to make the seborrheic scalp oily and may actually worsen the condition.

Dosage for dandruff:
Shampoo into scalp vigorously for at least five minutes; rinse thoroughly. Repeat twice weekly for two weeks, then once weekly as needed.

Dosage for seborrhea:
First, shampoo with a nonmedicated product to remove scalp and hair dirt, oil, and scales. Next, apply the pyrithione zinc shampoo, working it into the scalp vigorously for at least five minutes, followed by thorough rinsing. This treatment should be repeated twice weekly for two weeks, then once weekly as needed. For children under two years, consult a physician.

Coal Tar

Brand names (for dandruff treatment):
Denorex Medicated Shampoo
Tegrin

Brand names (for seborrhea treatment):
Denorex Medicated Shampoo
MG 217
Neutrogena Therapeutic T/Gel Shampoo
Pentrax
Tegrin

Obtained from bituminous coal, coal tar is neither pine nor juniper tar, both of which have been banned by the FDA as active ingredients in dermatological treatments because of lack of evidence that they work. It is not clear how coal tar fights dandruff, but it is believed that regular use retards the rate at which surface skin cells are shed.

Coal tar shampoos may stain the skin and hair—particularly if the hair is light-colored or dyed—as well as clothes, and some formulations may have an unpleasant odor and color. Because these shampoos also contain photosensitizers, which makes a person more likely to sunburn, you should avoid harsh sunlight for up to twenty-four hours after application.

Coal tar products may be applied at bedtime—sleeping on old sheets is recommended, because of staining—and followed in the morning with a bath to remove the coal tar as well as the psoriatic scale. Sensitive areas, such as armpits, the genitals, and the anus, should not be treated with coal tar as they can become irritated.

To control scalp psoriasis, it may help to paint the lesions, or rash or sores, sparingly with tar oil bath additives, tar gels, or coal tar solutions three to twelve hours before each shampoo.

Warning
Coal tar is probably the active ingredient used most often for seborrhea, while it is the third choice for dandruff shampoos. Because the combination of coal tar and ultraviolet radiation is more effective as a treatment for seborrhea, people using these shampoos are often advised to apply them in the evening and spend time in the sunlight on the following day.

Dosage for dandruff:
Rub shampoo liberally into wet hair and scalp. Rinse thoroughly. Briskly massage a second application

of the shampoo in a rich lather, and rinse again. For best results use at least twice a week. If skin becomes irritated, discontinue use.

Dosage for seborrhea:

Wet hair, then massage shampoo into scalp and leave on for several minutes. Rinse thoroughly. Use at least twice a week or as directed by a physician.

Keratolytic Agents

Brand names (for dandruff treatment):
Ionil
Neutrogena Healthy Scalp Anti-Dandruff (salicylic acid, 1.8%)

Brand names (for seborrhea treatment):
Neutrogena Maximum Strength T/Sal
  Therapeutic Shampoo
Scalpicin
Sebucare (lotion)
Sebulex
Sebutone (cream, with coal tar)

These agents, which work by loosening the scales of dandruff so that they are shed in smaller particles, can sometimes irritate the mucous membranes of the nose and eyes, and even damage the hair if used over several months. The agents are either salicylic acid or—less often and always in combination—sulfur. Keratolytic products may be most appropriate when very thick scales are present over a limited area; application over extensive areas should be avoided because of the potential to be absorbed by the body internally. Sensitive areas, such as armpits, the genitals, and the anus, should not be treated with salicylic acid, because they can become irritated.

Dosage for dandruff:

Massage shampoo into wet hair and scalp and leave on for several minutes; rinse thoroughly. Use at least twice a week.

Dosage for seborrhea:

First, shampoo with a nonmedicated product to remove scalp and hair dirt, oil, and scales. Next, apply shampoo, working it into the scalp vigorously for at least five minutes, followed by thorough rinsing. This treatment should be repeated twice weekly for two weeks, then once weekly as needed. For children under two years, consult a physician.

What to use when

For dandruff only: If more frequent shampooing does not control your dandruff, try a cytostatic agent, either pyrithione zinc or selenium sulfide, for several weeks. If they are not effective, try a keratolytic agent. If you still have dandruff, try a shampoo containing coal tar.

Hydrocortisone

Brand name:
Scalp-Cort (lotion)

Hydrocortisone should be used for seborrhea only when all other preparations have failed, and then only on scalp seborrhea when medicated shampoos have failed.

Warning

Prolonged and frequent use of hydrocortisone should be avoided, as it may lead to a prompt rebound, or return of the seborrhea, when the hydrocortisone is discontinued. The seborrhea may even reappear as the more severe pustular form—that is, raised lesions containing pus.

Dosage:

Apply sparingly once a day, working into the scalp thoroughly. You should see an improvement within seven days. For children under two years, consult a physician.

What to use when

For seborrhea only: First, try a shampoo containing salicylic acid or pyrithione zinc. If the condition fails to respond, try a shampoo containing coal tar. Alternatively, apply a coal tar gel sparingly to the lesions (rash or sores) three to eight hours before shampooing. If the condition still persists, try a hydrocortisone lotion.

Lice Treatments

Pediculicides, or anti-louse products, help kill lice and their eggs. The products act on the nerve cell membrane of the louse, causing paralysis and death. No product is completely effective in killing lice and their eggs (nits), however, and often it is necessary to follow up with a second application a week or more after the initial treatment and/or to remove the nits by hand to prevent reinfestation.

Warning

Lice control sprays specifically for bedding, furniture, carpeting, and clothing are also available. These should not be used on humans or animals.

Formulations:
Shampoo, cream rinse

Permethrin

Brand name:
Nix

This is the drug of choice for treating head and pubic (crab) lice and unhatched eggs. The most common adverse reaction is temporary itching or a burning sensation of the scalp. Be careful to keep permethrin out of the eyes, nose, and mouth.

Warning

Permethrin may cause breathing difficulty or an asthmatic episode in people with respiratory problems.

Dosage:
Apply liberally to hair that has been washed and towel dried. Leave on hair for ten minutes but no longer. Rinse with water. If live lice are observed seven days or more after the first application, have a second treatment.

Pyrethrum Extract

Brand names:
A-200
Maximum Strength Rid

This is usually combined with piperonyl butoxide for greater efficacy. It is used to kill head, body, and pubic lice.

Warning

Pyrethrum extract should be used with caution by people who are sensitive to ragweed. Be careful to keep it away from the eyes, nose, and mouth.

Dosage:
Apply to the affected area until all the hair is thoroughly wet with the product. Allow product to remain on the hair for ten minutes but no longer. Rinse thoroughly. A second treatment must be done in seven to ten days to kill any newly hatched lice.

What to use when

Products are equally effective and may be used alternately in applications if lice prove resistant to treatment.

Hair Growth Stimulant

Brand name:
Rogaine Topical Solution

Minoxidil, the only compound currently recognized by the FDA for treating hair loss, helps stimulate hair regrowth in people who have a family history of hair loss. Topical minoxidil, for hair regrowth, was approved by the FDA for OTC sale in 1996. It is sold at the same strength previously available only by prescription.

Precisely how the drug works is not known. Its ability to stimulate hair regrowth was discovered when hair growth was noted in people taking prescription minoxidil orally (swallowed as a pill) for high blood pressure. In fact, minoxidil is one of a handful of drugs prescribed for hypertension that have been found to stimulate hair growth.

Because oral minoxidil has serious adverse effects (primarily a sharp drop in blood pressure, leading to other problems), minoxidil—whether OTC or prescription—is administered only in a topical formulation for hair loss. These adverse effects have not occurred in clinical trials of topical minoxidil. The most common adverse effect is itching of the scalp, reported by about 7 percent of people in the clinical trials of topical minoxidil.

In the clinical trials, men and women reported similar results, with nearly 60 percent reporting some hair regrowth. (However, 40 percent reported hair regrowth with a placebo—an inactive substance.) After four months, 26 percent of men reported "moderate to dense" hair regrowth, compared with 11 percent of men who used a placebo. Nineteen percent of women reported "moderate" hair regrowth after using minoxidil for eight months (compared with 7 percent of women who reported the same improvement after using the placebo). Studies suggest that people who are older, have been balding for a longer time, or have a larger area of baldness may do less well. No one will be able to grow back all of his or her hair.

Of those who respond to treatment, it usually takes at least four months before there is visible evidence of hair growth. In general, new hair is the same color and thickness as the other hair on the scalp. If treatments are stopped, new hair will be shed within a few months, and the progression of baldness will continue as before.

Minoxidil will not prevent or improve hair loss caused by the use of some medications, the presence of certain severe nutritional problems, severely low thyroid states, chemotherapy, or diseases that cause scarring of the scalp. Also, minoxidil will not improve hair loss caused by damage from the use of hair-care products that cause scarring or deep burns of the scalp, or to hair grooming methods, such as cornrowing or ponytails, which require pulling the hair tightly back from the scalp. See your doctor if you're not sure why you're losing hair.

Warning

People taking guanethidine (Esimil or Ismelin) for high blood pressure should not use minoxidil, as there's a theoretical possibility that the drug interaction could result in hypotension (low blood pressure). Furthermore, if you are applying minoxidil to your scalp, you should not apply to the same area as topical hydrocortisone, petroleum jelly, or other agents are applied that are known to increase the absorption of drugs through the skin.

Formulation:
Clear, colorless solution

Dosage:
Apply 1 ml twice daily to a dry scalp with a special "rub-on" applicator enclosed with the product. Do not use more than twice a day. Although packaging is blue for men and pink for women, medication and dosage are the same for men and women.

Treatments for the Mouth and Teeth

Dozens of products are currently on the market that clean and whiten teeth and dentures, relieve tooth and mouth pain and inflammation, and decrease the feeling of dry mouth, but it's often difficult to distinguish which product is most effective. The sections that appear here define and categorize these treatments for clear and easy use: Toothpastes, Gels, and Powders (dentifrices) clean, desensitize, and whiten (OTC bleaching kits are also included here, although they are not technically dentifrices); Denture Adhesives; Denture Cleansers; Artificial Saliva; Mouthwashes and Mouth Rinses (for oral health); Oral Debriding Rinses, for moistening, cleaning, and freshening the mouth, and lessening pain and inflammation; Toothache and Teething Preparations; Canker Sore Treatments; Cold Sore/Fever Blister Preparations.

Toothpastes, Gels, and Powders

Dentifrices—better-known as toothpastes, although they are also formulated as gels and powders—help fight tooth decay and gum disease, reduce mouth odor, and improve personal appearance by reducing debris and discoloring.

Virtually all dentifrices contain abrasives to help remove dental plaque and stains; fluoride to fight cavities; and surfactants—foaming agents that reduce the surface tension of a liquid to make an object more "wettable"—to help remove debris. Other ingredients are added to gels and pastes to prevent them from drying out and to provide resistance to germs. Flavoring and sweetening agents are also added. (The main sweetener is saccharin. No American Dental Association [ADA]–approved toothpaste contains sugar.)

In addition to these common ingredients, many dentifrices also contain chemical agents that purportedly control plaque and help prevent or reduce tartar or calculus (calcified plaque, which, untreated, can promote the progression of periodontal disease, or disease involving the tissues that support the teeth) and gingivitis (an inflammation of the gingiva, the soft tissue surrounding the teeth, and the mildest form of periodontal disease). The ADA does not accept the claim by dentifrice manufacturers that they fight gingivitis. Because toothpastes with fluoride are so common—they are the rule, not the exception—and use identical or similar ingredients, those dentifrices that have fluoride as their only therapeutic ingredient will not be listed here. Most toothpastes with fluoride carry an endorsement by the ADA as decay-preventive dentifrices.

This section discusses dentifrices that purport to provide additional whitening through abrasive action, as well as those that claim to prevent or reduce tartar. For a description of other types of tooth whiteners, see page 140.

Warning

Dentifrices may be only one of many sources of fluoride, along with water and other supplements, that are regularly ingested by children. As a result, some children may exceed optimal daily amounts, particularly if they live in an area where fluoride is already present in the water supply. This places them at risk for mild forms of dental fluorosis, a mottled appearance of surface enamel. This is merely a cosmetic issue if the fluorosis is mild, but more severe cases can result in pitting and surface defects. To prevent this, apply the toothpaste in a pea-sized amount to the child's toothbrush and teach him or her to spit out the toothpaste after brushing

Formulations:
Pastes, gels, powders. Pastes and gels are more effective vehicles than powders for therapeutic agents such as fluoride. Powders, which are generally moistened before use, are more abrasive when used dry.

Whitening Dentifrices

Brand names:
Aim with Baking Soda
Aquafresh Whitening
Arm & Hammer Dental Care
Colgate Platinum
Pearl Drops
Plus+White
Rembrandt Whitening Toothpaste (aluminum oxide, papain)
Ultrabrite
Topol Plus

Abrasives remove stained pellicle—the thin coating that forms on the tooth's enamel, presumably from saliva, and to which plaque adheres. Most whitening toothpastes contain either silica or baking soda as an abrasive.

Unless advised otherwise by your dentist, you should choose the least abrasive dentifrice that is also an effective whitener. The vast majority of whitening dentifrices on the market are low-abrasive, containing a low level of silica or baking soda. Though they are not endorsed by the ADA as tooth whiteners, they are safe to use. They are also as effective in preventing decay as any other fluoride toothpaste. While strong abrasives cannot harm dental enamel, they can damage exposed root surfaces and dentin—that part of the tooth that lies beneath the enamel and makes up the largest part of the tooth structure.

Dosage:

Brush thoroughly, preferably after each meal or at least twice a day, or as directed by a dentist or doctor.

Antiplaque/Antigingivitis Dentifrices

Brand names:

Aquafresh Gum Care
Close-Up Anti-Plaque
Colgate Tartar Control
Cool Mint Listerine
Crest Gum Care
Viadent

No dentifrice is currently accepted by the ADA as effective in this therapeutic category. (Some mouthwashes [see page 143] have received that endorsement from the ADA.) However, the ADA has given numerous products a more qualified endorsement: "[Brand name] has been shown to reduce the formation of tartar above the gumline, but has not been shown to have a therapeutic effect on periodontal diseases." Ingredients most often added to prevent or retard new formation of tartar are zinc chloride, zinc citrate, and soluble pyrophosphates, which inhibit crystal growth. In some cases it is believed they have irritated the gums. If that occurs, you should switch to a non-tartar-control fluoride dentifrice.

Dosage:

Brush thoroughly, preferably after each meal or at least twice a day, or as directed by a dentist or doctor. Plaque found between the teeth can be removed efficiently only with dental floss and other aids.

What to use when

Use either type of toothpaste—whitener or tartar-control—according to your particular need and as advised by your dentist. However, the tartar-control toothpastes may also improve the appearance of your teeth by reducing plaque buildup.

Tooth Desensitizers

Brand names:

Aquafresh Sensitive
Denquel
Oral-B Sensitive Toothpaste
Promise
Sensodyne

Tooth desensitizers are dentifrices that help protect teeth against painful sensitivity to cold, heat, acids, sweets, or contact. They act on the dentin—that part of the tooth that lies beneath the enamel and makes up the largest part of the tooth structure—to block the perception of stimuli. Because the most common cause of tooth sensitivity is exposed dentin, a desensitizing toothpaste must reduce sensitivity while being nonabrasive. Dentin may be exposed by braces, gum recession, trauma, or excessive brushing with an abrasive toothpaste, a hard bristle brush, or an overly aggressive brushing technique.

Tooth desensitizers may take several days to two weeks to take effect. Once the sensitivity subsides, you should then switch to a low-abrasion dentifrice. If your teeth are highly sensitive, avoid any toothpaste that is promoted as a tooth whitener (see page 140), as it is likely to be more abrasive.

The only active ingredient approved by the FDA for Category I (safe and effective) for tooth desensitization is 5 percent potassium nitrate.

Dosage:

Apply at least a 1-inch strip of toothpaste to a soft bristle toothbrush. Brush teeth thoroughly for at least one minute twice a day (morning and evening) or as recommended by a dentist or physician. Make sure to brush all sensitive areas of the teeth. Do not use longer than four weeks unless recommended by a dentist or physician. These products are not recommended for children under twelve.

Tooth Whiteners

Tooth whiteners eliminate stains and whiten teeth, through either an abrasive in the dentifrice, bleaching by an oxidizing agent, or both. Formerly marketed as cosmetics, tooth whiteners containing oxidizing agents are now regulated as OTC drugs by the FDA. These whiteners fall into two main categories.

Warning

No products in either category have been recognized by the American Dental Association as safe and effective tooth-whitening agents.

Whitening Polishes

Brand names:
Arm & Hammer PeroxiCare
Colgate Natural Mint
Mentadent with Baking Soda and Peroxide
Plus+White Plus Peroxide
Rembrandt Peroxide Brushing Gel

Polishes contain a bleaching agent—usually hydrogen peroxide, carbamide peroxide, or perhydrol urea—as well as a strong abrasive. They remove surface stains better than the comparatively milder toothpastes that act only through abrasive action, but they do not penetrate enamel to remove internal discoloration. Furthermore, the high-abrasion agent in polishes may remove enamel and weaken teeth.

Formulations:
Liquid, gel, paste

Dosage:
Brush with product for two minutes, then spit out the excess. For greater effectiveness, do not rinse immediately. Use instead of your regular toothpaste twice a day for four weeks, then as needed.

OTC Bleaching Kits

Brand names:
Plus+White Ultra Teeth Whitener System
Rapid White

Although these are not considered dentifrices because they whiten, but do not clean teeth, we've included them here to round out the category of tooth enhancers. Some of these contain a bleaching solution that is painted on the teeth and left on for a few minutes, but most come with a do-it-yourself mouth guard that you fill with a bleaching gel and wear several hours a day for two weeks. The kits contain more bleach than the whitening toothpastes listed above.

Warning

There are safety concerns that the bleaching agent might leak out during the whitening process. If you have untreated gum disease or cavities, the bleach could cause pain and even irreversible nerve damage. At the minimum, it can irritate the gums and, if swallowed, cause a sore throat or upset stomach. The American Dental Association is also concerned that long-term exposure to oxidizing agents may damage oral tissue and worsen the effect of carcinogens such as cigarettes.

Formulation:
Solution

Dosage:
Depending on specific product, apply for five to ten minutes, one to four times daily, for one to two weeks. (See manufacturers' directions regarding dosage for specific brand-name products.) Do not wear dental braces during applications.

What to use when

Owing to safety concerns with the home bleaching kits, the whitening polishes are preferable.

Denture Adhesives

Brand names:
Effergrip
Firmdent
Orafix Special
Perma-Grip
Rigident Cream
Secure
Super Wernet's
Wernet's

Denture adhesives help hold dentures in place, usually with a type of vegetable or cellulose gum; examples include carboxymethylcellulose and karaya. Adhesives also contain antimicrobials, to prevent infection, and materials that serve as preservatives, fillers, or wetting or flavoring agents.

At most, according to the American Dental Association (ADA), denture adhesives should be used only temporarily—until the dentures can be adjusted—or upon the recommendation of a dentist. Bone resorption over time inevitably affects denture fit, requiring periodic examinations and adjustment of dentures. However, many people use adhesives regularly, even daily. Excessive application of adhesives can actually interfere with correct positioning in relation to supporting bone. "Denture adhesives may be the most overused dental products purchased by patients," according to the National Professional Society of Pharmacists.

Formulations:
Cream, powder, liquid

Because ingredients in denture adhesives are not listed on the packaging, you should consult your dentist or pharmacist or the manufacturer for specific information about individual products, particularly if you have allergies. However, the ADA recommends the above denture adhesives as safe and effective.

Denture Cleansers

Brand names:
Complete
Efferdent Antibacterial
Fresh 'N Brite

Denture cleansers help remove stain, debris, and potentially harmful plaque. Depending on the type, denture cleansers work through either a chemical or an abrasive action. To keep dentures clean, it is advisable both to brush the dentures with a low-abrasion denture paste and to soak them in a cleansing solution to help remove remaining plaque and debris.

Warning
Rinse off all denture cleansers before inserting the denture, or contact may result in serious tissue irritation or chemical burn. Do not use ordinary whitening toothpastes (see page 138) on dentures; such products are too abrasive.

Formulations:
Liquid, paste, tablet, powder

Dosage:
Clean dentures thoroughly at least once daily, following manufacturer's directions.

Because ingredients in denture cleansers and pastes are not listed on the packaging, you should consult your dentist or pharmacist or the manufacturer for specific information about individual products, particularly if you have allergies. The ADA, however, does recommend the denture cleanser products listed above as safe and effective.

Artificial Saliva

Brand names:
Glandosane Synthetic Saliva
Moi-Stir
Saliva Substitute
Salivart (preservative-free)
Xero-Lube

Artificial saliva preparations reduce the sensation of dry mouth by mimicking natural saliva both chemically and physically. (Dry mouth is most often a side effect of a drug such as an antidepressant or chemotherapy.) They do not stimulate natural salivary gland production but instead replace it with a substance to be used as needed. They relieve soft tissue discomfort and are more effective and longer lasting than simple mouth rinses (see below) and lozenges (see page 77).

Warning

Most artificial salivas contain preservatives, which may cause allergic reactions in some individuals.

Formulations:
Spray, swab, liquid

Dosage:
Use as needed.

The artificial salivas above are accepted by the American Dental Association as safe and effective.

Mouthwashes and Mouth Rinses (for oral health)

Mouthwashes and mouth rinses help freshen breath and promote oral health. They act as temporary breath fresheners by rinsing away some debris and providing a pleasant odor that may be either minty (as indicated by the product's green or blue color) or spicy (red). Most mouthwashes and rinses also contain germ-fighting agents. In addition, many contain therapeutic ingredients—specifically fluoride—to prevent cavities.

In recent years there has been a proliferation of mouthwashes that claim to fight plaque and gingivitis—an inflammation of the gingiva, the soft tissue surrounding the teeth, and the mildest form of periodontal disease. Several of these products have received a limited endorsement from the American Dental Association, as effective in combatting plaque and gingivitis. The ADA endorsement notes, however, that the mouthwash's "effect on periodontitis has not been determined." Periodontitis—one of the most common periodontal diseases, along with gingivitis—occurs when part of the ligament attachment and bone support of the tooth have been compromised or lost.

All these mouthwashes, classified according to their primary benefit, are discussed in this section.

In addition to these mouthwashes and rinses, a few oral rinses—more technically known as debriding rinses—are used to cleanse oral sores and wounds and to ease gum inflammation. For a discussion of these, see page 144.

Still other mouthwashes are formulated to relieve sore throat discomfort. These mouthwashes, as well as gargles and sprays, are also addressed in a separate section (see page 77).

Many of the mouthwashes designed to promote breath freshness and/or oral health contain ingredients very similar to those of toothpastes, gels, and powders (see page 138): surfactants (chemicals, like detergents, that reduce the surface tension of a liquid to make the tooth more "wettable" and thus easier to clean), humectants (hydrating agents that provide a vehicle for the other components and offer some resistance to germs), flavoring and coloring, as well as therapeutic ingredients. In fact, a mouthwash may be considered a diluted liquid dentifrice that usually contains alcohol—because it adds freshness, enhances flavor, and contributes to the cleansing action and antibacterial activity—and no abrasive.

Warning

Most mouthwashes contain alcohol. The alcohol content ranges from 8 percent to 27 percent (depending on the brand) and may constitute a danger for young children attracted by bright colors and pleasant flavors. If children drink large quantities, they may suffer acute alcoholic intoxication and even death. These products should be kept out of the reach of children, as well as recovering alcoholics. Some formulations of mouthwash, indicated in this section, are alcohol-free. In addition, mouthwashes should not be used by people with mouth irritation or ulceration, unless advised to do so by a dentist.

Breath Fresheners

Brand names:
Lavoris
Tom's of Maine Natural Mouthwash (alcohol-free)

Products that are intended to eliminate or suppress normal "morning breath" in healthy individuals are considered by the FDA to be cosmetics unless they contain antimicrobial or other therapeutic agents. Because virtually all mouthwashes on the market today—including those listed above—contain some germ-fighting agents, purely cosmetic breath fresheners are limited to a handful of products, such as Binaca breath drops/sprays.

Warning

By concealing bad breath, breath fresheners can disguise problems, such as periodontal disease and respiratory infections, and thus delay treatment. The American Dental Association suggests, "If marked breath odor persists after proper tooth brushing, the cause should be investigated" and not masked with mouthwash.

Dosage:
Use in morning after brushing, or more frequently if desired.

Fluoride Mouthwashes

Brand names:
ACT (alcohol-free)
ACT for Kids (alcohol-free)
Fluorigard (alcohol-free)
Listermint with Fluoride
Oral-B Anti-Cavity Rinse Alcohol Free

The ACT brands also contain some of the therapeutic agents included in the antiplaque/antigingivitis mouthwashes described below.

These provide a therapeutic dose of fluoride—usually included as 0.05 percent sodium fluoride—to prevent cavities. (These mouthwashes have no effect on existing cavities.) Studies of fluoride mouth rinsing show a consistent benefit, especially in children living in areas with nonfluoridated water. People who wear braces may also benefit because they often have difficulty cleaning between their teeth and behind and around their braces.

Dosage:
Use after cleaning teeth and then spit out. Do not eat or drink anything for thirty minutes after use.

Antiplaque/Antigingivitis Mouthwashes

Ingredients added to mouthwashes for plaque control include agents with antimicrobial activity or a detergent system based on sodium benzoate to loosen plaque for easier removal. However, using a mouthwash with plaque- or calculus-control properties should be a supplement, not a substitute, for normal oral hygiene: toothbrushing and flossing.

Dosage:
Use twice daily after brushing. The exception is Plax (see page 144), which should be used prior to brushing.

Antimicrobial and plaque-loosening agents in these mouthwashes include the following:

Aromatic Oils (Thymol, Eucalyptol, Menthol, Methyl Salicylate)

Brand names:
Cool Mint Listerine
Listerine

The American Dental Association has endorsed several products with these ingredients as effective in preventing and reducing "supragingival plaque accumulation and gingivitis." (Supragingival means above the gum line.) The ADA endorsement also notes, however, that the mouthwash's "effect on periodontitis has not been determined."

Cetylpyridinium Chloride

Brand names:
ACT (alcohol-free)
ACT for Kids (alcohol-free)
Cepacol
Oral-B Anti-Plaque Rinse
Scope

Although cetylpyridinium chloride, an antimicrobial, does not penetrate plaque well, some studies have reported that it helps reduce plaque accumulation. It may stain teeth if overused.

Plant Extracts (Sanguinarine)

Brand name:
Viadent

In laboratory experiments, sanguinarine has been found effective against plaque-forming bacteria, but results from clinical trials with people have been mixed, ranging from negligible to significant reduction of plaque and gingivitis.

Sodium Lauryl Sulfate/ Sodium Benzoate

Brand names:
Plax
Scope Original Mint (cetylpyridinium chloride)

Like many of the antimicrobial agents, these agents, which are designed to loosen plaque, also get mixed results in clinical trials.

What to use when

Choose your mouthwash/rinse according to whether you are seeking to prevent cavities, control plaque and gingivitis, or merely freshen your breath. In any case, use the product as an adjunct to proper toothbrushing and flossing.

Oral Debriding Rinses

Oral debriding rinses cleanse sores and wounds inside the mouth and help ease gum inflammation. In addition to treating canker sores (see page 147), they may be used for minor wounds or inflammation resulting from dentures, orthodontic devices, minor dental procedures such as tooth extraction, and accidental injuries such as a bitten or scraped cheek.

Of the four active ingredients accepted by the FDA for oral debriding, three work by releasing oxygen when they come into contact with tissue fluids. The foaming of the liberated oxygen loosens particulate matter and cleanses debris from wounds and may be effective in killing bacteria. After rinsing, all debriding agents should be spat out, never swallowed.

Warning
With prolonged use—more than a week—the oxidizing products can irritate the soft tissue of the mouth and remove calcium from tooth surfaces.

Formulation:
Liquid

Hydrogen Peroxide

Brand names:
Colgate Peroxyl Antiseptic Dental Rinse
Perimed

Dosage:
Rinse mouth with solution, following manufacturer's directions for dosage for specific brand-name product, then spit out. Use up to four times daily after meals and at bedtime, or as directed by a dentist or doctor. For children under two, consult a dentist or doctor.

Carbamide Peroxide

Brand names:
Cankaid Oral Rinse
Gly-Oxide
Orajel Perioseptic

Dosage:
Apply several drops directly to the affected area of the mouth with cotton swab or applicator. Allow the medication to remain in place at least one minute, then spit out. Alternatively, place ten drops on tongue, mix with saliva, swish for several minutes, and spit out. Use up to four times daily after meals and at bedtime, or as directed by a dentist or doctor. For children under two, consult a dentist or doctor.

Sodium Peroxyborate Monohydrate

Brand name:
Oral-B Amosan

Dosage:
Rinse mouth with solution for at least one minute, then spit out. Use up to four times daily after meals and at bedtime, or as directed by a dentist or doctor. For children under two, consult a dentist or doctor.

Sodium Bicarbonate

Sodium bicarbonate rinse is an alternative to the oxidizing products.

Dosage:
Dissolve ½ to 1 teaspoon in 4 ounces of water and swish in mouth over the affected area for at least one minute before spitting out. Use up to four times daily after meals and at bedtime, or as directed by a dentist or doctor. For children under two, consult a dentist or doctor.

What to use when

If you need a debriding rinse for a week or more, or are concerned about possible side effects, use the sodium bicarbonate solution.

Toothache and Teething Preparations

Most toothache products on the OTC market provide temporary relief from pain through the application of benzocaine, an anesthetic (see page 146), to the gum. Some products also include eugenol, a counterirritant (see page 146).

These products should be used only until a dentist can be consulted. There is no product approved by the FDA as safe and effective that may be placed in an open tooth cavity—for example, when the filling has fallen out—to relieve pain.

It is also possible to get short-term pain relief from an internal analgesic (see page 56) such as ibuprofen, aspirin, or acetaminophen. In order to avoid a chemical burn, however, none of these products—particularly aspirin—should ever be placed on the gums or in a cavity.

Products for teething help provide temporary relief of sore gums in infants and children who are at least four months of age. OTC preparations typically include local anesthetics (see page 97).

Nonprescription internal analgesics (see page 56) may also be given in dosages appropriate to the child's age.

Most teething preparations for infants and children have benzocaine as their only active ingredient. The main difference among these products is alcohol content. The American Dental Association accepts a number of teething products that contain benzocaine and are alcohol-free; it does not endorse teething products with alcohol.

Warning

To comfort your teething child, you may want to consider using a teething ring instead of a product with benzocaine, which in rare instances can cause choking owing to numbness in the throat. Use or overuse of benzocaine-containing products has also been associated with certain drug reactions in some infants, including a condition known as methemoglobinemia, in which the infant may turn a blue-brown color. If this occurs, consult your child's medical professional immediately.

Formulations:
Gum, gel, liquid, drops, and lotion for teething preparations

Dosage for children and infants:
Using your fingertip or a cotton applicator, apply a small (pea-size) amount of product to the sore gums not more than four times daily or as directed by a dentist or physician. For infants under four months of age, there is no recommended dosage except under the advice of a dentist or physician.

Benzocaine

Brand names (for toothache pain):
Anbesol Gel/Liquid (alcohol)
Dent's Extra Strength Toothache Gum (eugenol)
Dent's Maxi-Strength Toothache Treatment
  (alcohol, eugenol)
Orajel Gel/Liquid

Brand names (for teething):
Anbesol Baby Gel
Numzit Teething Gel
Numzit Teething Lotion (alcohol)
Orabase Baby Gel
Orajel Baby Nighttime Formula Gel

This standard anesthetic is combined with alcohol in some formulations.

Dosage:
Squeeze a small amount of the gel directly into the cavity and around gum surrounding the teeth. Apply up to four times daily. Do not use for more than seven days. Children under two should not use this product.

Eugenol

Brand name:
Red Cross Toothache Medication Drops

(This is a product of the Mentholatum Company and has no connection with the American National Red Cross.)

Although eugenol has historically been used as an OTC remedy for toothache owing to a cavity until a dentist can be seen, it has fallen out of use as a primary ingredient.

Warning

While eugenol is still used by dentists, the FDA has reclassified it to Category III ("under investigation"), citing the need for controlled clinical investigations that demonstrate its effectiveness in relieving pain. The American Dental Association believes that, used by nonprofessionals, eugenol can cause damage to viable pulp (the soft, spongy tissue found in the pulp chamber of a tooth) and soft tissue.

Dosage:
Moisten cotton pellet with product and place in cavity. Avoid touching tissues other than tooth cavity. Do not apply more than four times daily or as directed by a dentist. Do not swallow. Children under two should not use this product.

What to use when

Due to safety concerns over eugenol, try the benzocaine products first, unless you are allergic to benzocaine.

Canker Sore Treatments

Canker sore treatments help relieve pain and also protect the sore from irritating stimuli so that you can brush your teeth, eat, and drink. None has been shown conclusively to cure the sores or decrease the rate at which they recur. A canker sore is a red, sore ulcer with a white or yellow center located within the mouth. These usually last one to two weeks, and they often appear at the site of a minor injury in the mouth, such as a bite or cut, or at times of stress and fatigue. They may be the result of an immune system response.

The typical canker sore product is a local anesthetic, usually benzocaine, which provides temporary pain relief and coats the sore protectively while it heals. For information about mouth rinses that may be used as cleansing agents after meals to prevent a secondary infection, see Oral Debriding Rinses (page 144).

The FDA has also approved the use of counterirritants (see page 58), such as menthol and camphor, in canker sore products. However, their use is controversial because they can cause tissue irritation. According to the National Professional Society of Pharmacists, counterirritants should be used only in low concentrations for limited time. Further, the American Dental Association does not accept these ingredients as safe and effective in treating canker sores.

Warning

While internal analgesics (see page 56) may provide additional relief from discomfort, no one should hold aspirin in the mouth before swallowing or place it next to a lesion, because of the risk of a chemical burn from salicylic acid.

Benzocaine

Brand names:
Anbesol
Kank-A Professional Strength Liquid
Orabase-B
Orajel Mouth-Aid
Tanac
Zilactin
Zilactin-B

Although other local anesthetics are FDA-approved for canker sore preparations, benzocaine is by far the most commonly used.

Formulations:
Gel, liquid, paste, lotion

Dosage:
Dry the affected area. Apply in a thin coat every four hours for the first three days and then as needed.

Cold Sore/ Fever Blister Preparations

Cold sore and fever blister preparations reduce discomfort, allow healing, and prevent complications, generally by combining a local anesthetic with a skin protectant (see page 148). However, as with canker sores, which may be treated with some of the same preparations, none of these products has been shown conclusively either to cure the condition or to decrease the rate at which it recurs. Cold sores, also called fever blisters, are small, painful blisters on an area of red, raised skin caused by the herpes simplex virus. They are most likely to appear on the lips, the outside of the mouth, or on the nose, cheeks, or fingers, and usually last seven to ten days. The virus is transmitted through contact with someone who has the infection. Cold sores may recur during menstruation, fever, or after sun exposure.

An important factor in treating cold sores, unlike canker sores, is that they be kept moist to prevent drying and cracking, which is painful and increases the possibility of secondary infection. Some preparations also include tints to help conceal the sores. If there is evidence of secondary bacterial infection, such as puffiness, a triple antibiotic (see page 114) should be applied three to four times daily. If exposure to the sun brings on cold sores, a lip sunscreen should be used routinely.

Because cold sores do not respond to steroids, hydrocortisone (see page 96) should not be used. Products that contain astringents (see page 118) should also be avoided.

Camphor/Menthol

Brand names:
Blistex Medicated Lip Ointment
Campho-Phenique Cold Sore Gel
Cold Sore Lotion
Lip Medex Ointment
Vaseline Lip Therapy

The use of such counterirritants (see page 58) as menthol and camphor in cold sores is not recommended as they may cause tissue irritation. However, in lower concentrations (0.1% to 3% camphor, for example) these agents act as anesthetics.

Formulations:
Ointment, gel, lotion

Dosage:
Apply early and often. Use especially before and during sun exposure, after swimming, and again at bedtime.

Skin Protectants

Brand names:
Herpecin-L
Probax

Allantoin, petrolatum, cocoa butter, and padimate O, which is used in some sunscreens, can relieve dryness and keep cold sores soft while they heal. With the ex-

ception of the following products, these are normally combined with camphor, menthol and/or phenol, or an anesthetic. More information on skin protectants (see page 126) can be found in Skin Treatments.

Formulations:
Stick, ointment

Dosage:
Apply early and often. Use especially before and during sun exposure, after swimming, and again at bedtime.

Local Anesthetics

Brand names:
Anbesol Gel
Anbesol Maximum Strength
Orajel Cover Medication (tinted)
Orajel Mouth-Aid
Tanac
SensoGARD

Several local anesthetics, including benzocaine and dyclonine (an anesthetic used primarily in treatments for canker and cold sores), have been approved by the FDA for temporary relief of pain from mouth sores, including canker sores.

Formulations:
Gel, liquid, lotion, stick

Dosage:
Adults and children two and older should apply to cold sores/fever blisters not more than three to four times daily. For children under two, consult a physician.

What to use when

If you have painful cold sores/fever blisters, you may prefer a product containing a local anesthetic. For frequent use, you should use products without anesthetic.

Eye Products and Treatments

Most of the eye-care products included in this section help relieve irritation, clear up bloodshot eyes, and moisten dry eyes, while others act as cleaning and moistening agents for contact lenses. In Eye-Care Products and Ophthalmic Lubricants, various types of artificial tears, or demulcents, are listed, along with the substances that make them work most effectively. Ophthalmic Decongestants, Eye Washes, and Eyelid Scrubs provide similar information on relief from eye discomfort. The final section, Contact Lens Products, details the various types of lenses (hard, rigid gas permeable, and soft) and the cleaning, soaking, conditioning, and rewetting agents that are safest for each.

Eye-Care Products

There are numerous OTC eye preparations for treating dry eye conditions, such as chronic dryness (see page 31), redness (see page 31), and irritation (see page 32), and for facilitating the wearing of contact lenses (see page 155). They provide temporary relief from any feeling of eye discomfort and dryness caused by irritants or exposure to wind or sun. These products alleviate dryness by moisturizing the eye when it is not producing its own tears and increasing the viscosity—the resistance to flow—of the tears the eye does produce, reducing tear evaporation.

In this section, we discuss the two inactive ingredients common to most nonprescription eye care products: drug vehicles and preservatives. These are the most important inactive ingredients in OTC ophthalmic products.

The drug vehicle, or viscosity agent, is the chemical agent that is added to a formulation to increase viscosity, or slowness of flow. Because the eye would normally eliminate substances by tearing, this agent slows drainage of a product's active ingredient from the eye, thus giving it more time to work.

Preservatives are added to destroy or limit multiplication of microorganisms that may be inadvertently introduced into the product while it is being used.

Most eye-care products typically contain one of the two.

Warning

OTC ophthalmic products should be used only in situations in which vision is not threatened. In general, most ophthalmic products should not be used for longer than seventy-two hours without medical referral if the condition being treated persists or worsens. (The obvious exception is contact lens products, which are designed to be used routinely.) If you are already using a prescription ophthalmic product, you should check with your eye-care professional or pharmacist before using a nonprescription eye-care treatment.

Drug Delivery Vehicles

The three most commonly used vehicles are the following:

Polyvinyl alcohol (PVA)

Generally nonirritating to the eye, PVA has actually been found to help the healing of corneal abrasions. It is frequently added to artificial tears (see Ophthalmic Lubricants), ophthalmic decongestants (which reduce eye redness [see page 153]), and some hard contact lens solutions. Although considerably less viscous than methylcellulose, PVA is another commonly used viscosity enhancer.

Warning

While PVA is compatible with many commonly used drugs and preservatives, certain compounds—notably sodium borate, found in some eyewashes (see page 154), and contact lens products (see page 155)—may thicken or gel solutions that contain PVA. Anyone who uses both contact lens solutions and artificial tears should read the ingredients listing on the packaging of the ophthalmic lubricant and make sure that PVA and sodium borate do not both appear on the respective lists.

Methyl cellulose or other cellulose ethers

They stabilize the tear film and prevent tear evaporation without irritating the eye. Some products have higher levels of viscosity to provide extra support for people with severe dry eye syndromes.

Povidone (PVP, or polyvinylpyrrolidone)

Like methyl cellulose, PVP is popular in artificial tear formulations because of its ability to mimic the natural moisture on the surface of the eye. It is used less than the other two drug delivery vehicles described here, and always in combination with one of them, as indicated in the brand names section of Ophthalmic Lubricants.

Preservatives

Preservatives widely used in ophthalmic products fall into two categories: surfactants, which usually kill bacteria, and others—mercury, iodine, and alcohols—which inhibit the growth of bacteria. The most commonly used preservatives are listed below.

Warning

All of the preservatives listed below may potentially cause irritation depending on concentration and individual sensitivity.

Benzalkonium chloride (BAK)

This surfactant is widely used because of its long shelf life and antimicrobial activity. However, it can irritate the eye at high levels of concentration, which may occur if it builds up on contact lenses. While it is included in some formulations for hard contact lenses, it is not used in products for soft contact lenses, which adsorb BAK—that is, collect BAK on the surface of the lens.

Chlorhexidine

Less toxic to the eye than BAK, chlorhexidine may be less effective as a disinfectant in both soft and hard contact lenses. It should not be used in conjunction with eyewashes owing to the risk of thickening or gelling. Solutions containing chlorhexidine that appear greenish should not be used because the color change indicates that the product has decomposed.

Thimerosal

A mercurial preservative, thimerosal has been known to cause allergic reactions of the conjunctiva (the thin tissue covering the white of the eye and the eyelid), and is particularly problematic for wearers of soft lenses, to which it may bind. As a result, thimerosal is disappearing rapidly from use in ophthalmic OTC products.

Sorbic acid/potassium sorbate

Less irritating than thimerosal, sorbic acid and potassium sorbates are the preservative ingredients often included in products labeled "thimerosal-free" or "for sensitive eyes." However, they reportedly may increase age-associated yellowing of some contact lenses.

Ethylenediaminetetraacetic acid (EDTA)

EDTA is used primarily in combination with thimerosal, BAK, and other preservatives. Like them, it can sometimes cause an allergic reaction.

Ophthalmic Lubricants

Brand names:
Bion Tears (preservative-free)
Celluvisc (preservative-free)
Comfort Tears
Moisture Drops (povidone)
Murocel
Refresh Plus CelluFresh (preservative-free)
Tears Naturale
Tears Naturale Free (preservative-free)
Ultra Tears

Ophthalmic lubricants help relieve chronic dry eye conditions. They also provide temporary relief from any feeling of eye discomfort and dryness caused by irritants, exposure to wind or sun, or wearing of contact lenses. There are two types of ophthalmic lubricants: artificial tears, or demulcents, and bland nonmedicated ointments. The key difference among the lubricants is the type of viscosity agent used.

Warning

If you wear soft contact lenses, contact your eye-care practitioner for advice before using any type of ophthalmic lubricant. These products should never be put into the eyes when contact lenses are in place.

Demulcents

Demulcents, or artificial tear solutions, are formulated to match the eye's natural tears closely. Recently, artificial tears have been introduced in preservative-free formulations in small packages for one-time use. These formulations are more expensive and can become easily contaminated during use. In using these tears, you must follow strict hygienic procedures: Wash your hands thoroughly, do not touch the tip of the container to any surface, and promptly discard any unused solution.

Because most demulcents contain preservatives, such as thimerosal or benzalkonium chloride, they may cause irritation. (For information about buffers and preservatives, which vary from one product to another, see Preservatives, page 151.) This risk is increased for people who wear soft contact lenses.

Formulation:
Eye drops

Dosage:
Demulcents are usually administered three to four times daily but may be used as often as hourly if needed.

Polyvinyl alcohol (PVA)

Brand names:
20/20 Tears
Hypotears Drops
Liquifilm
Murine Eye Lubricant
Refresh (preservative-free, with povidone)
Tears Plus (povidone)

Although considerably less viscous than methylcellulose, PVA is another commonly used viscosity enhancer.

Warning
While PVA is compatible with many commonly used drugs and preservatives, certain compounds—notably sodium borate, found in some eyewashes (see page 154) and contact lens products (see page 155)—may thicken or gel solutions that contain PVA. Anyone who uses both contact lens solutions and artificial tears should read the ingredients listing on the packaging of the ophthalmic lubricant and make sure that PVA and sodium borate do not both appear on the respective lists.

Methyl cellulose or other cellulose ethers

This viscosity agent is the most widely used type of viscosity agent in artificial tear solutions.

Bland (Nonmedicated) Ointments

Brand names:
DuoLube
Hypotears
Lacri-Lube
Tears Renewed Ointment

Bland ointments generally consist of petroleum jelly and mineral oil. Their principal advantage is that they have longer contact time with the eye and are longer-lasting.

Formulation:
Ointment. All are preservative-free.

Dosage:
These products may be administered every few hours if needed, or only occasionally. However, because the ointments tend to blur vision, they are best taken at bedtime.

What to use when

Artificial tears are far more popular than the ointments, as they do not blur vision. However, you may prefer ointments if you use them primarily at bedtime—when blurred vision is not a problem—or if you cannot tolerate the artificial tears.

Ophthalmic Decongestants

Ophthalmic decongestants help soothe irritated eyes and eliminate or reduce the redness caused by inflammation or exposure to an irritant such as dust, air pollution, or another environmental factor. However, if the conjunctivitis, or pinkeye—an inflammation or irritation of the conjunctiva, the thin membrane that covers much of the eye—is caused by a virus or bacterium, prescription antibiotics or other medication may be necessary. If the inflammation immediately followed exposure to an environmental irritant, you should assume that was the source of the problem and treat it accordingly. If there was no such exposure and the inflammation doesn't go away within a day or two, you should consult a doctor.

The four chemical agents approved by the FDA for this purpose all work as vasoconstrictors, narrowing the swollen blood vessels of the conjunctiva. Some formulations also contain ophthalmic lubricants (see page 151), to reduce irritation and provide relief from minor pain and dryness.

In differentiating among ophthalmic decongestant products, one major factor is whether they cause the pupils to dilate, or enlarge. Dilation of the pupil can bring on closed-angle glaucoma—a disorder, potentially leading to blindness, in which the canals that drain fluid from the eyes are completely blocked—in people whose eyes are structurally predisposed to that condition.

Warning

Chronic use of some of these products, as indicated below, may lead to rebound congestion, or inflammation, of the conjunctiva, in which the blood vessels become progressively enlarged with continued use of the drug. This phenomenon can create a vicious circle in which the person uses the product for inflammation of the conjunctiva, which becomes progressively more inflamed following each use. Because of the risk of rebound congestion, these products should not be used too frequently or inappropriately—for example, as eyewashes. Never apply these products to the eye when contact lenses are in place. People who have glaucoma are advised not to use any ophthalmic decongestant except under a doctor's supervision.

Formulation:
Drops

Dosage:
Place one to two drops in the affected eye(s) up to four times daily. Before using with children under six, consult your physician.

Phenylephrine

Brand names:
Prefrin Liquifilm
Relief

In prescription strength, phenylephrine is used for short-term dilation for eye examinations. Even at lower OTC concentrations, it is likely to dilate the pupil. Chronic use can lead to rebound congestion.

Naphazoline

Brand names:
Allerest Eye Drops
Bausch & Lomb Allergy Drops
Clear Eyes
OcuHist
Opcon-A

More effective in eliminating conjunctival redness than the other decongestants, naphazoline is also less likely to cause rebound congestion than phenylephrine or oxymetazoline. It does cause pupils to dilate, however, particularly in people with lightly pigmented irises (blue or green eyes).

Tetrahydrozoline

Brand names:
Murine Plus
Optigene 3
Visine
Visine A.C.
Visine Extra

Unlike phenylephrine or naphazoline, tetrahydrozoline does not appear to affect the pupil size. Like naphazoline, it is not associated with rebound congestion. However, some people feel a mild, temporary stinging immediately after applying the drops.

Oxymetazoline

Brand names:
Ocu Clear Drops
Visine L.R.

This agent can induce rebound congestion, but appears otherwise to be free of side effects.

What to use when

To avoid rebound congestion, you should consider using tetrahydrozoline or naphazoline. Naphazoline is also considered the most effective, although dilation may be a problem for some people.

Eyewashes

Brand names:
AquaSite Drops (sodium chloride, sorbic acid)
Bausch & Lomb Eye Wash Liquid (sodium chloride, sorbic acid, EDTA)
Collyrium for Fresh Eyes Solution (water, benzalkonium chloride, sodium borate)
Optigene Eye Wash Solution (sodium chloride, BAK)

Eyewashes clear unwanted materials or debris, such as lint, dust, or a chemical irritant, from the surface of the eye.

Eyewashes are formulated to maintain the moisture and pH (the balance between acidity and alkalinity) of the eye's tissues while cleansing it. They consist primarily of sodium chloride or saline, and typically also contain one or more preservatives (see page 151) as well as ingredients to help maintain the pH of the eye.

Although they may be used to wash out the eyes after contact lenses have been worn, eyewashes have no particular value as contact lens wetting, cleansing, or cushioning solutions (see page 156) and in fact should never be put into the eye when a contact lens is in place.

Warning

You should avoid using eyewashes in conjunction with contact lens wetting solutions or with other eye-care products containing polyvinyl alcohol (PVA), because the washes often contain substances such as sodium borate that react by thickening or gelling the products with PVA. Furthermore, you should try to avoid eyewashes administered with an eyecup because of the potential risk of bacterial, fungal, or viral contamination. Eyedrops are preferable.

Formulation:
Liquid

Dosage:
Apply several drops to the eye, rotating eyeball and blinking repeatedly to ensure thorough washing. Only for short-term use, not for prolonged periods.

Eyelid Scrubs

Brand names:
Eye-Scrub Liquid
Lid Wipes-SPF Pads
Lids & Lashes Hygienic Cleansing Pads
Stye
Stygiene

Eyelid scrubs are liquids used to cleanse eyelids and lashes of the oils, debris, and scaly or peeling skin associated most often with blepharitis, an inflammatory condition of the eyelid. Scrubs help control blepharitis, but do not cure it. They can also be used for hygienic eyelid and eyelash cleansing in people who wear contact lenses.

Eyelid scrubs typically contain a mild detergent cleanser that is compatible with the eye. Some products also contain a gauze pad to provide an abrasive action that complements the cleanser.

Some scrubs have misleading names—such as Stygiene and Stye (see brand names above)—that suggest a treatment for styes (pimples that form on the edge of the eyelids). In fact, the products themselves make no claim to treat styes, which usually go away after a couple of days of treating with hot compresses.

Warning

Eyelid scrubs are designed to be used full strength on eyelid tissues, and must not be instilled directly into the eye. If symptoms fail to improve, you should see a doctor about getting a prescription for an antibacterial agent, as the eyelid may be more seriously infected.

Because of the similarity of these products, we do not differentiate them here by ingredient. The exception is Stye—an ointment consisting of petroleum jelly and mineral oil—which acts as a protectant (see page 127) and emollient (see page 104) rather than as a scrub.

Formulations:
Ointment, liquid, pad

Dosage:
Apply three to four drops of liquid or a small amount of ointment to cotton-tipped applicator or gauze pad. Close the eyes and gently scrub the upper eyelids and eyelashes, using side-to-side strokes; open the eyes and clean lower eyelid and eyelashes. Applications should generally be repeated twice daily.

Contact Lens Products

All contact lens products are designed to facilitate the wearing of lenses—whether hard, rigid gas permeable (RGP), or soft—by keeping them wet, clean of protein deposits, and free of bacterial contamination, and providing cushioning and lubrication between the lens, the surface of the cornea, and the inner surface of the eyelid.

While there are some areas of overlap, each type of contact lens also requires OTC products formulated specifically for that type of lens. It is particularly important that conventional solutions for hard or RGP lenses never be used with soft lenses, as the soft lenses will absorb ingredients and may become

damaged. As a rule, labeling on the OTC product indicates the types of lenses for which the product is approved. If you are in doubt, consult your ophthalmologist, optometrist, or pharmacist.

The main difference among these products involves the preservative and the chemical agent that is added to a formulation to reduce flow, thus slowing drainage of the product from the eye. In the following lists of branded products, only those substances that may be irritating or cause other problems—generally either preservatives or viscosity agents—may appear parenthetically with individual brands. For more information about these preservatives and drug delivery vehicles, which are used in a broad spectrum of OTC products for the eye, see Eye-Care Products, page 150, and Ophthalmic Lubricants, page 151.

Warning

If not handled properly, contact lens solutions can become contaminated by common bacteria that can infect the eye, causing serious damage and even loss of vision. To prevent contamination, never let the tips of lens care product containers touch the eye or any other object. Contact lens solutions should never be reused. They should be discarded if the expiration date has passed or, if the label states, within 90 days after opening. Homemade solutions should never be used, and lenses must never be stored in tap water. The lens case should be cleaned thoroughly at least weekly, with a few drops of lens cleaner and hot water or saline solution.

Hard Contact Lenses

Brand names (combination products):
Clean-N-Soak
Soaclens Liquid (PVA, thimerosal)
Total All-In-One Contact Lens Solution (PVA, BAK, EDTA)

Hard contact lens care requires cleaning, soaking, and wetting. With all three types of lenses, the trend is toward products that combine all three functions. While this is obviously more convenient than buying three separate products, the drawback is that some of the ingredients used perform different and somewhat incompatible functions. For example, high concentrations of the preservative benzalkonium chloride (BAK) are necessary to kill bacteria in soaking solutions. These same concentrations, however, can irritate the eye when applied to a contact lens that is then placed directly in the eye. Similarly, if lenses are stored overnight in a solution containing a high concentration of polymers for cushioning and wetting, the lenses may become gummy and cause discomfort. The degree to which this occurs varies with brands.

Formulation:
Liquid

Cleaning solutions

Brand names:
Blairex Hard Contact Lens Cleaner Liquid
Clens (BAK, EDTA)
Opti-Clean (thimerosal, EDTA)
Titan (potassium sorbate)

Cleaning solutions help eliminate the oils and debris that accumulate on the lens during wear. They typically contain surfactants, foaming agents that reduce the surface tension of a liquid to make an object more "wettable."

Dosage:
Rub lenses carefully on both sides with several drops for twenty seconds before storing.

Soaking solutions

These are used to store hard lenses whenever they are removed from the eyes. In addition to keeping the lens wet so that it does not become brittle, they also help remove protein deposits that accumulate during wear. To maintain sterility and extend the lifetime of the lenses, soaking solutions use essentially the same preservatives as wetting solutions. In fact, soaking solutions are almost invariably combined with wetting solutions in a single product.

Dosage:
Fill lens case to cover lenses. Change solution daily.

Wetting solutions

Brand names:
Adapt (thimerosal)
Clerz 2 Drops (sorbic acid)
Lens Fresh Drops (EDTA, sorbic acid)
Soaclens Liquid (PVA, thimerosal)
Wetting and Soaking Solution (PVA, edetate disodium, BAK)

Wetting solutions provide a cushioning effect between the lens and the eye. Wetting solutions also contain surfactants that help remove debris, preservatives, and chemicals to adjust the pH to that of the eye. The concentration of the cushioning agent affects both eye comfort and the quality of vision immediately following insertion of the lens in the eye. In some individuals, a concentration that is too low causes discomfort after only a short time of wearing the lens. In other wearers, a high concentration results in blurred vision because the solution mixes poorly with tears.

Dosage:
If desired, before inserting lens in eye, apply fresh solution to wet the lens for additional cushioning.

Rigid Gas Permeable Contact Lenses

Brand name (combination product):
Boston Simplicity (PVA)

Care of rigid gas permeable (RGP) contact lenses, like hard lenses, involves solutions for cleaning, soaking, wetting, and rewetting. Those RGP lenses that have a higher silicone content should also receive a once-weekly enzyme cleaning (see Soft Contact Lenses, page 157). As with hard lenses, the trend is for solutions that perform multiple functions, but—presumably because the market for RGP is expanding—there are more product options with this lens type.

Formulation:
Liquid

Cleaning solutions

Brand names:
Bausch & Lomb Concentrated Cleaner
Boston Daily Cleaner
ComfortCare GP Daily Cleaner (potassium sorbate)
Resolve/GP Daily Cleaner

Because of differences among RGP lenses—those with a high silicone content have lower surface wettability—some cleaning solutions designed for hard or RGP lenses may not eliminate all protein deposits. A number of cleaners are specifically formulated to break the adhesive bonds that form between high-silicone lenses and the deposits. These cleaners, however, have also been associated with hairline scratches on the RGP lens. For information on enzymatic cleaners, see RGP and soft contact lens enzymatic cleaners, page 159.

Dosage:
Rub lenses carefully on both sides with several drops for twenty seconds before storing.

Soaking/wetting/conditioning combination solutions

Brand names:
BarnesHind Wetting and Soaking Solution (PVA, povidone, chlorhexidine)
Bausch & Lomb Wetting & Soaking Solution (EDTA, chlorhexidine)
Boston Advance Conditioning Solution (PVA, EDTA)
ComfortCare GP Wetting & Soaking Solution (PVA, povidone, chlorhexidine)

Because high-silicone lenses have lower surface wettability, conditioning solutions are often recommended instead of soaking or wetting solutions to help form the cushioning layer.

Warning

Do not use products containing chlorhexidine, a common preservative, with silicone lenses because it makes the lens surface more difficult to wet and may also cause surface clouding.

Dosage:
Fill lens case to cover lenses. Change solution daily. If desired, before inserting lens in eye, apply fresh solution to wet the lens for additional cushioning.

Reconditioning/rewetting drops

Brand names:
Boston Reconditioning Drops
Wet & Soak Drops

These are formulated to clean and rewet the lens while it is in the eye. While it is healthier for the cornea if the lens is briefly removed, cleaned, and rewetted, it is not dangerous if the lens is not removed.

Dosage:
A few drops, as needed.

Soft Contact Lenses

Brand names (for disposable lenses only):
Opti-Free
ReNu Multi-Purpose Solution

Soft contact lenses require more cleaning and disinfection than the other two lens types because they contain a high percentage of water and thus are most prone to bacterial contamination. Accordingly, the maintenance of soft lenses involves a number of steps.

Soft-lens wearers must clean their lenses daily (or in the case of extended-wear lenses, which may be worn overnight or longer, each time the lens is removed from the eye) to remove lipid, or fatty, deposits. The lenses must also be disinfected by either thermal disinfection (heating in saline solution in a special unit) or chemical disinfection. Either way, the lens must be rinsed with saline or a combination product before it is inserted. In addition, lenses should be soaked weekly in solution with an enzymatic cleaner to remove protein deposits. In the eye, the lenses may be rewetted as needed. They must be stored in a saline or combination solution.

As a result, there are several types of products used in soft-lens care: surface cleaners, disinfectants (chemical and thermal), enzymatic cleaners, and saline solutions.

Many of the products designed for soft contact lenses, including exzymatic cleaners, are also designed for extended-wear lenses, which are intended to be continuously in the eye for days or even weeks at a time. However, because of problems with contamination and infection, extended-wear lenses have mostly been superseded by disposable lenses, which are removed nightly, worn for one to two weeks and then discarded. Because of their short life, the care regimen for disposable lenses is greatly simplified. You should soak disposable lenses overnight in a multi-purpose solution, after which you can place them directly in your eyes.

Warning

While most manufacturers test for compatibility within their own product lines, there is no assurance their products are compatible with those of another manufacturer. Mixing certain types of cleaning solutions, for example, can cause a cloudy precipitate on the lens, while using chemical disinfecting solutions interchangeably can lead to corneal injury known as "mixed solution syndrome." Switching from a chemical disinfecting system containing chlorhexidine to a hydrogen peroxide system may result in fine black deposits on your lenses. So before you mix cleaners or chemical disinfectants, you should talk with your ophthalmologist or optometrist.

Surface cleaners

Brand names:
Bausch & Lomb Sensitive Eyes Daily Cleaner (sorbic acid)
Miraflow Extra Strength (isopropyl alcohol)
Opti-Clean (thimerosal)
Soft Mate Hands Off Daily Cleaner (potassium sorbate)

Some cleaners are more abrasive than others, with pros and cons: They may clean better but are harder to wash off. The addition of isopropyl alcohol to such cleaners as an ingredient is helpful for lens wearers who tend to generate heavy lipid deposits.

Formulation:
Liquid

Dosage:
Place several drops of solution onto the lens surface and gently rub between thumb and forefinger, or place the lens in the palm of the hand and rub gently with a fingertip for twenty seconds.

Chemical disinfectants

Brand names (with antimicrobials):
Bausch & Lomb Disinfecting Solution (thimerosal chlorhexidine)
ReNu Multi-Purpose Solution (EDTA)
Soft Mate Disinfecting (sorbic acid)

Brand names (with hydrogen peroxide):
Aosept
Oxysept 1 Disinfecting/Oxysept 2 Neutralizing
Soft Mate Concept-1 Liquid/Concept-2 Aerosol

Chemical disinfection may be accomplished with either solutions of antimicrobial preservatives or hydrogen peroxide. The antimicrobial solutions contain chlorhexidine, to which some users are allergic, or sorbic acid or other preservatives, which may be less likely to create allergy problems but may also be less effective against infection.

In the hydrogen peroxide method, which is increasingly popular, the lens is placed in solution and disinfected through the liberation of oxygen from peroxide. Household hydrogen peroxide solutions should not be used because contaminants and other chemicals within such solutions may discolor the lens and because the pH may be too low for the eye and thus irritate it. Following disinfection, the peroxide on the lens must be neutralized by diluting the solution with chemicals or saline or by soaking the lens in a different solution; a lens that is still saturated with peroxide will cause great pain and, potentially, injury to the cornea. In some products, a neutralizer is combined with the hydrogen peroxide solution.

Formulations:
Tablet (hydrogen peroxide products only), liquid

Dosage with antimicrobials:
After cleaning each lens, soak the lenses in the disinfecting solution for at least four hours. While the lenses may be stored for longer periods, you should clean and disinfect with fresh solution for at least four hours prior to inserting the lenses.

Dosage with hydrogen peroxide:
Use after cleaning each lens. See manufacturer's directions for specific brand-name product.

Thermal disinfectants

In this method, the cleaned lens is dropped into a storage case filled with saline, and the case is placed in a heating unit or pot of boiling water for at least 10 minutes. Because boiling shortens the life of soft lenses, it has largely been replaced by chemical disinfectants. The advantage to thermal disinfection is that not only does it kill microbes better than any other method, it can be done with a preservative-free solution as the heat prevents bacterial growth. On the other hand, the equipment is expensive and inconvenient to use, and the procedure is hard on lenses.

What to use when

Both disinfecting methods are reliable, but chemical disinfection with hydrogen peroxide has increased in popularity over time. You may switch from thermal to chemical disinfecting methods, but the switch from chemical to thermal may present problems. If lenses that have been chemically disinfected are not completely free from all traces of the chemicals, they can be damaged by heating. To prevent this when you make the switch, soak your lenses for a prolonged period in several changes of saline.

RGP and soft contact lens enzymatic cleaners

Brand names:
Allergan Enzymatic
Extenzyme
Opti-Free Enzymatic
Opti-Zyme Enzymatic
Pro-free/GP
Bausch & Lomb ReNu Thermal
Sensitive Eyes Effervescent Enzymatic
Ultrazyme Enzymatic

For both soft and RGP lenses, enzymatic cleaners help remove protein deposits after the lenses have first been cleaned of other debris. The cleaners use papain or another chemical that breaks down protein.

For soft lenses, the choice of enzymatic cleaner depends on which disinfecting system you use. Some cleaners can be used simultaneously with thermal or chemical disinfection. If you use thermal disinfection, for example, Bausch & Lomb

ReNu Thermal enzymatic cleaner can be combined with it into a single step. If you use a hydrogen peroxide cleaning system, Ultrazyme Enzymatic is a good choice because it can be placed in the peroxide solution, both cleaning and disinfecting at the same time.

If you use an antimicrobial disinfecting system or are cleaning RGP lenses, you can choose among a variety of enzymatic cleaners as long as you are not allergic to a particular ingredient. While some of these products are marketed for different lens types—soft lenses, extended-wear soft lenses, and RGP lenses—they can actually be used interchangeably.

Formulation:
Tablet

Dosage:
Use weekly. Place the tablet in a solution recommended by the manufacturer and soak the lens for as briefly as fifteen minutes (high-water lenses) to as long as overnight (low-water lenses). Before inserting, thoroughly rinse the cleaner from the lens to prevent irritation.

Saline solutions

Brand names:
Alcon Saline (sorbic acid)
Ciba Vision Saline (preservative-free)
Hydrocare (thimerosal)
Lens Plus Sterile Saline (preservative-free)
Opti-Soft (EDTA, polyquaternium)
Bausch & Lomb ReNu Saline (EDTA)
Sensitive Eyes Saline (sorbic acid, EDTA)
Sensitive Eyes Plus
Unisol 4 (preservative-free)

These are the basic solutions for rinsing, thermally disinfecting, and storing soft contact lenses after cleaning. (They may also be used to rinse cleaning solutions and enzymatic cleaners from RGP lenses.) Saline solutions consist of sodium chloride, usually boric acid, and/or sodium borate. The main distinction among saline solutions is what preservatives, if any, are present.

Because thimerosal and chlorhexidine can irritate many users, salines preserved with sorbic acid or polyquaternium are marketed for people with sensitive eyes. In addition, preservative-free saline is available in smaller containers and aerosol sprays. Nonpreserved, nonaerosol saline generally has a shelf life of fifteen days once opened.

Some nonpreserved saline products contain EDTA, which prevents calcium from forming deposits on the surface of the lens. Although not a preservative, EDTA does inhibit the growth of certain bacteria, thus extending the shelf life of the product.

Formulations:
Solution, spray

Rewetting solutions

Brand names:
20/20 (PVA, BAK)
Lens Fresh Drops (EDTA, sorbic acid)
Opti-Free Drops
ReNu Drops
Soft Mate Comfort Drops (potassium sorbate)

These permit rewetting and, in some cases, cleaning of the lens while it is in the eye. They are particularly useful with lenses with a high water content, such as the extended-wear type, which may become dehydrated from exposure to wind and heat.

For more information about rewetting solutions, also known as artificial tears, that may be used by wearers of various types of contact lenses, see Eye-Care Products, page 150, and Ophthalmic Lubricants, page 151.

Formulation:
Drops

Dosage:
Use a few drops, as needed.

Contraceptives

A contraceptive is a device, substance, or method used to prevent pregnancy. Some contraceptives also help to protect against sexually transmitted diseases (STDs).

Several types of contraceptives are available without a prescription: condoms, vaginal pouches, foams, suppositories, creams, and jellies (gels). Over-the-counter contraceptives vary in terms of method of use, effectiveness in preventing pregnancy and STDs, cost, and personal preference. So here's a shopping guide to help you sort through all the options.

Use of condoms and vaginal pouches is called the barrier method of contraception, meaning that such a method utilizes a membrane to block sperm from entering the uterus. Chemical barriers—foams, jellies, films, and suppositories, all of which contain spermicide—utilize chemicals that immobilize sperm and prevent them from joining with an egg.

Condoms

A condom is a sheath of thin latex, plastic, or animal tissue worn over the penis during intercourse. Semen is caught in the tip of the condom before, during, and after ejaculation, preventing it from entering the vagina.

Effectiveness

Protection Against Pregnancy. During the first year of "typical" use—the rate of reliability of a method as it is usually used—of condoms, 12 percent of women become pregnant during the first year. Two percent become pregnant with "perfect" use—the rate of reliability of a method itself when it is *always* used consistently and correctly. Protection is increased when a spermicide is used in addition to the condom.

Protection Against STDs. Condoms help to protect both partners against transmission of many STDs because they block the exchange of body fluids during vaginal, anal, and oral intercourse. Latex condoms offer good protection against trichomoniasis, pelvic inflammatory disease, gonorrhea, chlamydia, syphilis, chancroid, human immunodeficiency virus (HIV), human papilloma virus (HPV), and herpes B virus. In fact, latex condoms are more effective in protecting against STDs than any other contraceptive besides abstinence, according to Planned Parenthood.

Caution should be used, however, with condoms made from animal tissue. These condoms are not recommended for protection against STDs because some bacteria, such as that of hepatitis B and HIV, are very small and may pass through the pores of the condom. Nonetheless, use of any condom protects better against STDs than use of no protection at all.

Proper Use

A water-based lubricant, such as K-Y Jelly, should be used inside and outside the condom to prevent rips and tears and to increase sensitivity. Many condoms are available prelubricated. Oil-based lubricants, such as petroleum jelly, cold cream, or mineral and vegetable oils, should not be used with latex condoms because they damage latex, causing the condom to become ineffective. Care, too, should be used in unwrapping the condom to prevent breaks or tears.

A condom may be used until the expiration date or five years after the date of manufacture. If a condom is stiff, sticky, or brittle, it should not be used. Condoms should be stored in a cool, dry place and not stashed continually in a wallet or glove compartment. A fresh condom should be used for each act of intercourse.

Options

Condoms are available in packages of three or a dozen and in many varieties, including transparent, opaque, tinted, nipple-ended, rippled, powdered, or lubricated, with spermicide or without.

Vaginal Pouches

A vaginal pouch (or "female condom") is a plastic sheath with a flexible ring at each end. When the pouch is inserted into the vagina, the ring at the closed end holds it in the vagina, while the ring at the open end stays outside the vaginal opening. Like a condom, the pouch collects semen before, during, and after ejaculation and keeps sperm from entering the vagina.

Effectiveness

Protection Against Pregnancy. With typical use, 25 percent of women become pregnant during the first year of use. With perfect use, this rate drops to between 5 and 10 percent.

Protection Against STDs. The pouch provides protection against many STDs, including HIV.

Proper Use

Do not use a condom with the pouch, as friction between them could cause either one to break. A new pouch should be used for each act of intercourse, even if intercourse occurs more than once during the same session.

Foams

Brand names:
Delfen
Emko Foam

Vaginal contraceptive foam, which contains spermicide, is applied to the inside of the vagina up to the cervix. The bubbles help the spermicide cover the cervix and spread evenly throughout the vagina.

Effectiveness

Protection Against Pregnancy. With typical use, foam prevents pregnancy in 20 percent of women during the first year of use. With perfect use, this prevention rate is increased, and when used in conjunction with a condom the rate is even higher.

Protection Against STDs. Foam does not protect either partner against STDs.

Proper Use

The container should be shaken before use. The more you shake it, the bubblier the foam becomes, making for a better barrier throughout the vagina. More than one application of the foam may be necessary; check the instructions for proper use. Fill the applicator, which works the same way a tampon applicator does, according to the instructions enclosed in the package. To increase effectiveness, foam should be inserted very shortly before each episode of intercourse; when the foam dries it becomes ineffective. After intercourse, a woman may want to lie down for a while until the foam has sufficiently covered the cervix. Foam should be stored at room temperature.

Suppositories

Brand names:
Conceptrol
Encare
Semicid Inserts

Suppositories are capsules, tablets, or films containing spermicide that melt into a liquid after being placed in the vagina. Effervescing suppositories, which create bubbles, help to provide a barrier to sperm.

Effectiveness

Protection Against Pregnancy. With typical use, 20 percent of women will become pregnant after the first year. With perfect use, this rate is decreased. When used with a condom, effectiveness is increased.

Protection Against STDs. Suppositories do not protect either partner against STDs.

Options

Suppositories are available in packs of twelve, twenty, or thirty-six.

Creams and Gels

Brand names:
Gynol II
Koromex
Ortho-Gynol

(The latter two contain octoxynol and should be used with a barrier contraceptive.)

Contraceptive creams and gels contain spermicide. Some are designed to be used with a cervical cap or diaphragm, two barrier methods of contraception that must be prescribed by a health practitioner. Some creams and gels, however, may be used alone, without another form of contraceptive, but it is recommended that a condom also be used to optimize protection. Allergic reaction such as skin irritation, although rare, may be experienced by either partner.

Effectiveness

Protection Against Pregnancy. With typical use, 20 percent of women who use contraceptive creams or gels become pregnant during the first year. With perfect use, effectiveness is increased. Creams and gels are most effective when used in conjunction with a condom.

Protection Against STDs. Neither creams nor gels protect either partner against STDs.

Proper Use

Follow instructions on the package for correct insertion, as many creams and gels are inserted a bit differently. Most are inserted in the same way a tampon is. Make sure that the gel or cream is inserted evenly throughout the vagina. Creams and gels should be stored at room temperature.

Options

Creams and gels are available with disposable, prefilled applicators. Some are packaged with a reusable applicator.

Other Medications

There are many drugs that do not fit into broader categories such as Cold, Cough, and Allergy Remedies. These drugs cover everything from taming your appetite (see Appetite Suppressants, page 167) to helping you sleep (see Sleep Aids, page 175). Other Medications supplies treatments and preparations for every condition treatable with over-the-counter drugs.

In this section, you will find Antiperspirants and Deodorants, Swimmer's Ear Preparations and Ear Wax Removers, and Vaginal Antipruritics and Vaginal Antifungals. You'll even find relief for an ingrown toenail (see Ingrown Toenail Treatment, page 174).

Anthelmintics

Anthelmintics are used to treat worm (helminthic) infections. The only nonprescription anthelmintic presently on the market, *pyrantel pamoate,* is approved only for pinworms. The drug acts by paralyzing pinworms, causing them to lose their grip on the intestinal wall. The pinworms are then eliminated from the body in the stool.

When one individual in a household has pinworms, the entire household should be treated at the same time.

Pyrantel Pamoate

Brand names:
Antiminth Suspension
Pin-X
Reese's Pinworm

This compound was first used in veterinary practice but became available for use in humans because it is not toxic and rarely causes side effects.

Formulations:
Suspension, liquid, caplet

Dosage:
For adults and children two years and older, oral dosage is a single dose of 5 mg of pyrantel base per pound, or 11 mg per kilogram, of body weight, not to exceed 1 gram. For example, a 150-pound person would take 1 tablespoon of liquid. A dosage schedule by weight is included with the product. Standard treatment tables recommend retreatment two weeks after the initial dose, even if symptoms have not recurred.

Antiperspirants

Antiperspirants reduce the amount of perspiration secreted by the underarm eccrine glands and thus the likelihood of body odor, which is produced by bacteria that grow in the sweat. Precisely how antiperspirants stop sweat isn't clear. One theory is that they make sweat ducts more permeable, causing the sweat to be reabsorbed. Another theory is that the antiperspirant forms a plug that extends down the length of the ducts, physically obstructing them until they are replaced by normal cell renewal in several days. As a result, antiperspirants have prolonged action. Sweating resumes within a week after the antiperspirant is discontinued. Several years ago, some research suggested a link between aluminum and Alzheimer's disease. However, there's no evidence that the body's uptake of aluminum from antiperspirants has any effect.

The FDA regulates antiperspirants as drugs because they influence the body's physiological process. Deodorants (see page 170), which primarily mask odor with fragrance and do not affect physiological processes, are labeled cosmetics and are not regulated in the same way. However, deodorizing fragrances are often included in antiperspirants.

Antiperspirants are not effective the first time they are applied; repeated applications over time are needed to achieve the maximum effect. However, response to antiperspirants varies markedly from person to person and from product to product. Some people actually perspire more after some applications. If one product does not perform satisfactorily, try others.

No nonprescription product stops underarm wetness completely. As a rule, you can expect a sweat reduction of only 20 to 40 percent. Antiperspirants rarely reduce wetness enough to cause a significant decrease in body odor—hence their combination with deodorants. However, antiperspirants generally include antiseptics (see page 116) or antibacterials (see page 113), such as triclosan, to prevent the growth of microorganisms that cause odor.

The most common adverse effect of OTC antiperspirants is skin irritation—tingling, stinging, or burning—which is caused by the formation of hydrochloric acid, a normal occurrence. Some antiperspirants are buffered with a chemical to prevent irritation. Normally, however, irritation can be reduced by decreasing the frequency or amount of antiperspirant used. Antiperspirants should not be applied to skin that is broken, freshly shaved, or wet—the latter because moisture increases the production of hydrochloric acid.

The contents of all antiperspirants are fully labeled, so if you're sensitive to a specific ingredient you can choose a different formulation. If you are allergic to all formulations, you could try a deodorant (see page 170).

Warning

Nonprescription antiperspirants cannot relieve hyperhidrosis, a condition characterized by excessive perspiration. (Normal underarm moisture is called hidrosis.) If you think you suffer from hyperhidrosis, consult a physician.

Formulations:
To work effectively, antiperspirant ingredients must be in liquid form. If the product is in powder form, it is generally a deodorant that absorbs moisture, not an antiperspirant.

Dosage:
Apply daily, or after each washing.

Aluminum Zirconium

Brand names:
Almay
Arm & Hammer
Arrid
Ban
Degree
Dry Idea
5 Day
Irish Spring
Mitchums
Secret
Speed Stick
Sure

This aluminum salt is by far the most common ingredient in nonaerosol antiperspirants. It has been banned from aerosol products because it may cause nodules in the lungs if inhaled.

Formulations:
Roll-on (gel or powder)

Aluminum Chlorohydrate

Brand names:
Arrid XX
Dry Idea
Mitchums
Mum
Right Guard Sport
Secret
Soft & Dri
Suave Regular

Generally nonirritating, this is the only aluminum salt with sufficient safety data to be used in aerosol form. Aluminum chlorohydrate is also available as propylene glycol, which is a common ingredient (alone or in combination with aluminum zirconium) in numerous antiperspirants.

Warning

As the contents of aerosol products are under pressure, follow manufacturer's warnings regarding use and storage.

Formulations:
With the exception of Mitchums, all products listed above are sprays.

What to use when

If spray formulation is not a problem, choice of antiperspirant is a matter of personal preference.

Appetite Suppressants

Appetite suppressants help curb hunger and are used to achieve weight loss. Although they have been on the market for decades, appetite suppressants remain highly controversial. Some studies have shown placebos (inactive substances given as though they are real drugs) to be equally effective.

Efforts to lose weight with these products should be limited to three months, as that should be enough time to establish new eating habits as well as a routine of physical activity.

Formulations:
Capsules, caplets, tablets

Phenylpropanolamine (PPA)

Brand names:
Acutrim
Dexatrim
Dietac
Dieutrim (with benzocaine)
Protrim (with benzocaine)
Protrim S.R.

This is the active ingredient in most OTC appetite suppressants. Precisely how it works is not known, but it is thought that PPA suppresses the appetite center in the brain. Chemically related to the stimulants ephedrine and amphetamine—the latter is sometimes prescribed by physicians to treat obesity—PPA is also found in many cold and sinus preparations as a decongestant (see page 69), although at a much lower dosage.

Side effects can include hypertension (high blood pressure), nervousness, restlessness, insomnia, dizziness, tinnitus (ringing in the ears), headache, and nausea. It has been suggested that hypertension is more likely to occur when PPA is in the immediate release form. Accordingly, many appetite suppressants contain PPA in timed-release tablets or caplets.

Warning
Diet aids with phenylpropanolamine should not be used in combination with any nasal decongestant that also contains PPA, as overdoses can result in life-threatening elevation of blood pressure. It is also important to avoid caffeine or other stimulants.

Recently the FDA mandated that weight control products containing PPA be restricted to use by adults eighteen and above.

Dosage:
Adults take one capsule/caplet/tablet at midmorning with a full glass of water. Swallow each pill; do not divide, crush, chew, or dissolve it. Do not take more than one pill per day. Exceeding the recommended dose has not been shown to result in greater weight loss. Persons between twelve and eighteen or over sixty should consult their physician before using the product.

Benzocaine

Brand names:
Dieutrim (with PPA)
Protrim Caplets (with PPA)

The only other OTC compound rated safe and effective by the FDA for short-term weight control, benzocaine is traditionally used as a local anesthetic (see page 98). It is assumed that it may have a slight numbing effect in the oral cavity, reducing taste and thus the desire to eat, though scientists are not certain how it works.

Appetite suppressants that use benzocaine generally combine it with PPA. However, a study found that not only did benzocaine produce less weight loss than PPA alone, appetite suppressants containing PPA did not become more effective when benzocaine was added.

Dosage:
Adults take one tablet just prior to snacks and meals.

What to use when

Appetite suppressants with PPA are likelier to produce weight loss but also carry more risk.

Bronchodilators

Bronchodilators are used by people with mild asthma to relax the muscles surrounding the bronchioles—the narrow tubes through which air passes in and out of the lungs—and to improve breathing or prevent an asthmatic attack.

Until recently, there were three active ingredients in OTC bronchodilators: epinephrine, ephedrine, and theophylline. In 1995, the FDA banned the sale of OTC bronchodilators that combined theophylline with other compounds, because of concerns about dangerous drug interaction. These combination products had been on the market for decades. Now only epinephrine and ephedrine are in general use. However, also in 1995, the FDA proposed banning OTC bronchodilators containing ephedrine. The U.S. Drug Enforcement Administration claims that ephedrine is being used to make illegal drugs, and the FDA has found that some drug manufacturers promote ephedrine for unapproved uses, such as weight control. Pending federal action, several states have switched or are considering switching some ephedrine products to prescription-only status to prevent drug abuse. Ask your pharmacist if OTC ephedrine is available in your state.

The bronchodilators approved for OTC use are sympathomimetic drugs—that is, they interfere with nerve signals passed to the muscles through the autonomic nervous system, the involuntary nervous system that governs the actions of the muscles of organs and glands. Sympathomimetic drugs also stimulate the production of an enzyme that helps relax smooth muscles in the airways and reduce swelling of the mucous membrane.

Bronchodilators are typically delivered through inhalers, whose pros and cons—and delivery system—are discussed at length below.

Warning

All bronchodilators must be used with caution by people with heart problems, high blood pressure, thyroid disease, diabetes, difficulty urinating because of an enlarged prostate gland, or who are taking a monoamine oxidase inhibitor (MAOI), an antidepressant. You should use a bronchodilator only if your doctor has made a diagnosis of asthma and you're not taking any other medications for asthma unless directed to do so by your doctor.

Epinephrine

Brand names:
Adrenalin Chloride
Asthma Nefrin
Bronitin Mist
Bronkaid Mist
Primatene Mist

Epinephrine is a hormone produced naturally in the center of the adrenal glands and is better known as adrenaline—the substance that provides the "rush" the body feels when it is preparing for a physical challenge. It can be used to treat both periodic and acute severe bronchospasm. Although the various products containing epinephrine differ slightly in the dose delivered, there is no significant difference between prescription and nonprescription epinephrine for inhalation.

Warning

Excessive use of epinephrine may cause nervousness, rapid heartbeat, and possible adverse effects on the heart. It may increase certain symptoms of Parkinson's disease, such as tremor and rigidity.

Because it is the only compound delivered by inhalation—the favored means of delivery—epinephrine is the primary OTC bronchodilator. The advantage of inhalers, particularly for children, is that they produce comparatively few adverse reactions. These occur mostly when the user gets no relief and overuses the product.

Inhaled bronchodilation does have drawbacks. Recent research has found that regular use of inhalers may actually worsen chronic asthma and lung function unless it is accompanied with anti-inflammatory drug therapy—probably corticosteroids, which are available only by prescription. (Asthma is primarily an inflammatory disease of the airways, and the main nonprescription bronchodilators provide little anti-inflammatory activity.) However, there are concerns about long-term use of corticosteroids, particularly by children.

Especially with low-dose inhalation, far less drug gets into circulation. Most people do not use inhalers correctly, and even when they're correctly used, inhalers deposit less than 10 percent of their medication into the lungs. Here are the steps for correct inhaler use:

1. Remove duster cap.

2. Shake canister. This distributes the drug particles evenly throughout the suspension.

3. Position mouthpiece to bottom.

4. Tilt head back.

5. Breathe out to functional volume.

6. Close lips on inhaler or hold inhaler 1 to 2 inches from open mouth. This decreases the amount of drug adhering to the back of the throat.

7. Actuate while inhaling slowly and deeply. The slower the breath, the greater the likelihood that the drug will reach the smaller airways.

8. Hold breath five to ten seconds or as long as possible.

9. Breathe out slowly. Steps 8 and 9 increase the amount of drug retained in the airways.

10. Wait one to ten minutes before second inhalation. This allows the epinephrine to work and may increase delivery of drug to the airways with subsequent inhalations.

Formulation:
Inhaler. Most asthma products with epinephrine are sold as metered-dose inhalers (the inhaler contains a specific number of sprays). However, some are packaged in solution form, to be administered via nebulizer—a device for delivering vaporized drugs. Generally, children under the age of five require a nebulizer.

Dosage:
For adults and children four years or older, the dosage recommended is one inhalation, followed by a second inhalation if symptoms have not been relieved after at least one minute; it should not then be repeated for at least three hours. (For children under four, a physician should be consulted.) The peak effect occurs within five to ten minutes after use, and the drug is effective for one to three hours. If symptoms are not relieved within twenty minutes or become worse, medical help should be sought.

Ephedrine

Brand names:
Bronkaid (with guaifenesin)
Bronkolixir (with guaifenesin and phenobarbital)
Primatene

Used in treating only mild forms of seasonal or chronic asthma, ephedrine is usually combined with phenobarbital, which has a sedating effect, and/or guaifenesin, an expectorant (see page 76).

Warning

The principal adverse effects of ephedrine are nervousness, tremor, sleeplessness, nausea, loss of appetite, tachycardia (rapid heartbeat), and urinary retention. To prevent insomnia from ephedrine, the drug should not be taken less than a few hours before bedtime. While the phenobarbital is generally sedating, occasionally it has the opposite effect, mainly in children. Ephedrine should not be taken with alcohol or other medications affecting the central nervous system. It may also reduce the effectiveness of oral contraceptives, requiring additional precautions.

Formulations:
Capsule, tablet, syrup

Dosage:
Adults and children twelve years and over, take one tablet (or syrup equivalent: follow manufacturer's directions) initially and then one every four hours, as needed, not to exceed six doses in twenty-four hours. The peak effect of ephedrine in dilating the airways occurs in one hour and lasts three to five hours. If symptoms are not relieved within an hour or if they become worse, medical help should be sought. Consult a doctor for use of ephedrine in children under twelve years.

What to use when

Epinephrine is the first-line treatment, partly because it is available in inhaler form, partly because of the many problems associated with ephedrine. Apart from safety issues, ephedrine has other limitations. It is beneficial for only mild forms of seasonal or chronic asthma.

Deodorants (for body odor)

Deodorants work by masking body odor with perfume or through germicides such as triclosan—which is found in many deodorant soaps—that inhibit the growth of bacteria whose decomposition in perspiration produces body odor.

No product labeled exclusively as a deodorant can make antiperspirant (see page 165) claims. Many commercial products, however, are combinations of antiperspirants and deodorants.

Because they do not affect physiologic processes, deodorants are considered cosmetics, not drugs, by the FDA. Because these products are very similar, we do not include a list of ingredients or brand names.

In addition to topical deodorants, two compounds taken as tablets have been reported by some people to have deodorant properties. While there is no objective evidence that they reduce the usual body odors, the FDA has found chlorophyllin copper complex (available in the OTC product Pals) and bismuth subgallate (Devrom, also available OTC) to be safe and effective in reducing odor from a colostomy (in which the colon is partially removed) or an ileostomy (in which the entire colon and possibly part of the small intestine are removed).

Warning

Chlorophyllin copper complex may cause some cramping or diarrhea.

Formulations:
Gel, powder. Deodorants in powder form also work by absorbing moisture.

Dosage:
Apply daily, or after washing.

Formulation:
Tablet

Dosage:
Use four times daily.

Deodorants (for foot odor)

Brand names:
Desenex Foot & Sneaker Deodorant Spray
Dr. Scholl's Odor Destroyer Deodorant Spray
Odor-Eaters Foot Powder

Foot deodorants absorb moisture and prevent the growth of bacteria that can cause odors. While some also contain antifungal ingredients, the main ingredient is generally talc, baking soda, or cornstarch, or a combination of two or three of these.

Formulations:
Powder; spray that turns to powder on the foot. A few manufacturers also offer odor-controlling insoles to be inserted in shoes. These contain activated charcoal as well as absorbent powders such as baking soda.

Dosage:
Apply powder or spray to soles of feet and between toes each morning. If using spray, also apply over entire area of shoes or sneakers. If using shoe inserts, change every few months.

What to use when

While all deodorant products are similarly helpful in absorbing perspiration, spray formulation may provide greatest comfort and cooling sensation. Alternatively, the insoles provide some support and cushioning for the feet.

Diuretics

Diuretics help relieve water retention, weight gain, bloating, swelling, and a full feeling, which may be caused by premenstrual syndrome (see page 42) or other causes, such as certain medications. Diuretics work by reducing the amount of sodium and water that the kidneys take back into the bloodstream, thus increasing the volume of urine produced. In this way, the water content of the blood is reduced and excess water is drawn out of the tissues for elimination as urine.

Warning

If you take diuretics regularly for minor fluid retention, it can activate salt- and water-retaining hormones. When the diuretics are discontinued, the high hormone levels cause significant sodium and water retention. This condition is known as rebound edema. Take only as needed, and try to reduce water retention through other means such as lowering salt in your diet.

Ammonium Chloride

Brand names:
Aqua-Ban
Aqua-Ban Plus (both also contain caffeine)

Unlike the two other active ingredients listed here, ammonium chloride is sold primarily as a diuretic, not as a component of a product for premenstrual syndrome.

Formulation:
Tablet

Dosage:
Take three times daily, not to exceed 3 g per day, for no more than six consecutive days. Larger than recommended doses can produce significant gastrointestinal or central nervous system problems.

Pamabrom

Brand names:
Bayer Select Menstrual Multi-Symptom Formula
Diurex-2 Water Pills
Diurex Water
PMS Multi-Symptom Formula Midol
Teen Multi-Symptom Formula Midol

Pamabrom is included in numerous products designed primarily for the relief of menstrual discomfort and premenstrual syndrome (see page 42), but also in products that are specifically diuretic.

Formulations:
Tablet, caplet

Dosage:
Adults take doses of 50 mg four times daily, up to 200 mg per day. For children under age twelve, consult a doctor.

Caffeine

Brand names:
Femcaps
**Midol Menstrual Maximum Strength
   Multisymptom Formula**

Caffeine, which acts as a diuretic by inhibiting the kidney's reabsorption of sodium and water, is sometimes added to products for the relief of premenstrual syndrome (see page 42) or is combined with other diuretics such as ammonium chloride (see above). If you are consuming caffeine-containing beverages, foods, or medications at the same time that you are taking caffeine for diuresis, you may develop anxiety, gastrointestinal irritation, insomnia, irritability, or other side effects associated with caffeine consumption.

Formulations:
Caplet, gelcap

Dosage:
Adults take doses of 100 to 200 mg every three to four hours. For children under twelve, consult a doctor.

What to use when

If you are treating water retention related to premenstrual or menstrual discomfort (see page 42), take one of the products designed specifically for that purpose. For water retention unrelated to menstruation, take one of the ammonium chloride or pamabrom products designed specifically for diuresis.

Douches

Douches irrigate the vagina, thus clearing away mucus and other accumulated debris. Because they do not influence any body process, they are considered cosmetic—nondrug—cleansing agents for the vagina. Washing the vagina by hand with a mild soap and water is arguably as effective. In fact, there is growing belief in the health-care community that douching, which can irritate the vagina, can do more harm than good.

Some douches contain nothing more than vinegar or sodium bicarbonate (baking soda), to change the vagina's pH. Others may include an antimicrobial agent (to fight infection), external analgesics such as counterirritants (see page 58), and astringents (see page 118). Because douches are cosmetic products, manufacturers are not required to list concentrations of ingredients, so it is often impossible to assess the efficacy of ingredients such as antimicrobial agents.

Warning

Douching has been associated with pelvic inflammatory disease (PID), a serious infection of the reproductive system that requires immediate medical attention. It has also been associated with a higher incidence of ectopic pregnancy, in which the fetus grows outside the uterus, often in a fallopian tube.

Formulations:
Powders, liquids, liquid concentrates

Guidelines for Douching

Do not douche if you are pregnant.

Do not douche as a means of birth control or for self-treatment of any sexually transmitted diseases, pelvic inflammatory disease (PID), or a vaginal infection of any kind. If you suspect you have one of these infections or PID, stop douching and see your doctor immediately.

Discontinue douching if irritation develops.

Keep all douche equipment clean and dry.

Use all products strictly according to manufacturers' instructions. Some manufacturers recommend douching no more often than twice a week.

Use lukewarm water to dilute products.

Do not douche until at least eight hours after intercourse if you've used a diaphragm, cervical cap, contraceptive jelly, cream, or foam.

Do not douche twenty-four to forty-eight hours before any gynecologic examination.

Antimicrobial Agents

Brand names:
Betadine Medicated Douche (povidone-iodine)
Massengill Medicated (povidone-iodine)
Massengill Vinegar & Water Extra Cleansing (cetylpyridinium chloride)
Summers Eve Medicated (povidone-iodine)
Summers Eve Vinegar & Water Disposable Douche (benzoic acid)

Those used most often are cetylpyridinium chloride, benzoic acid, povidone-iodine, and boric acid. Usually these are present in concentrations that preserve the douching solution from infection but have no therapeutic value. Antimicrobial agents kill microbes. They do not perform the same function as astringents or counterirritants. Some may cause local irritation and an allergic skin reaction.

Warning
Repeated douching with a povidone-iodine solution by pregnant women may result in goiter (an enlargement of the thyroid gland) and hypothyroidism in the fetus.

Counterirritants

Brand names:
Massengill Unscented Douche Powder
PMC Disposable Douche

The greatest contribution of these ingredients—methyl salicylate, eucalyptus oil, menthol, and other agents—may be in masking odors. Although they are sometimes included for their anesthetic or antipruritic (anti-itching) effect, there is no proof they work.

Astringents

Brand names:
Massengill Unscented Douche Powder
PMC Disposable Douche

Substances such as ammonium salts may be added to some douches to reduce local swelling, inflammation, and oozing. Note dilution directions carefully. The concentration is important because they are ineffective if diluted too much but may be irritating in moderate or high concentrations.

Substances Affecting pH

Brand names:
Feminique (sorbic acid, lactic acid)
Massengill Baking Soda (sodium bicarbonate)
Massengill Douche Country Flowers (lactic acid)
Massengill Douche Spring Rain (lactic acid)
Summers Eve Hint of Musk (citric acid)

Most douches contain substances that give them an acidic or alkaline effect. Sodium perborate and sodium bicarbonate (baking soda) provide alkalinity, and lactic acid and citric acid provide acidity. While even daily use of douches will not significantly alter vaginal pH, the douche solution itself may render the vagina's pH alkaline for a short time.

What to use when

Because the therapeutic value of douches generally is not established and they are even suspected of causing problems, the main criteria in choosing a douche are that it does no harm and provides good vaginal hygiene. If you have a vaginal infection, use a vaginal antifungal (see page 179) or consult a physician.

Earwax Removers

Earwax removers help remove cerumen, or earwax, that is excessive or impacted (wedged so tightly inside the ear canal that it cannot be readily removed). They consist of carbamide peroxide in a lubricant base—usually an oil such as mineral oil. The lubricant penetrates and softens the wax, while the release of oxygen from carbamide peroxide provides a bubbling action that helps break up the softened wax accumulation. It is usually necessary to remove the loosened wax by gently flushing the ear with warm water.

Alternatively, earwax can normally be dislodged with body-temperature water, squirted into the ear with a rubber ear syringe (available at most pharmacies). If the wax refuses to budge, it may be softened with a few drops of mineral oil, olive oil, or glycerin that have been warmed to body temperature, or with a dropper of diluted hydrogen peroxide solution. Put in three drops twice a day for three days. When the wax is soft, irrigate it out with a syringe or Water Pik at the lowest settings. Use water at body temperature. Irrigate several times until the ear canal seems open when you look into the ear with a light.

To prevent cerumen buildup, to which some individuals are particularly prone, you can irrigate the ear canal every few days with warm water, normal saline, a mixture of alcohol and water, carbamide peroxide, or aluminum acetate (Burow's solution), an astringent (see page 118). Ask your pharmacist for the correct ratios of ingredients in these solutions.

In addition to the standard earwax removers, another OTC preparation that softens impacted wax is Colace (docusate sodium), a stool softener that is available in liquid form (see page 93).

Formulation:
Drops

Warning

Drops should never be put in the ear if there is any chance the eardrum has a hole in it or after ear surgery, unless directed by a doctor. If fluid is draining from the ear, you should suspect that the eardrum is punctured.

Carbamide Peroxide

Brand names:
Debrox Drops
Ear Wax Removal System
Murine Ear Wax Removal System/Ear Drops

This is in a lubricant base, usually an oil such as mineral oil. The lubricant penetrates and softens the wax, while the release of oxygen from carbamide peroxide provides a bubbling action that helps break up the softened wax accumulation. In addition to removing cerumen, carbamide peroxide helps kill bacteria through the release of oxygen.

Dosage:
Put five to ten drops in the ear and allow to remain at least fifteen minutes, by either tilting the head (affected ear up) or inserting a small amount of cotton into the canal opening. Do not allow the tip of applicator to enter ear canal. Use twice daily for up to four days if needed. Any wax remaining after treatment may be removed by gently flushing the ear with warm water, using a soft bulb ear syringe. For children under twelve, consult a physician.

Ingrown Toenail Treatment

Brand names:
Outgro Pain Relieving
Dr. Scholl's Ingrown Toenail Reliever

The OTC treatment for ingrown toenails is applied to the soft tissue surrounding the nail, in which the nail has become embedded. The product hardens the nail groove and shrinks the soft tissue, providing enough room for the nail to resume its normal position adjacent to soft tissue. To protect the toe temporarily while the ingrown nail is being treated, you may use a soft foam toe cap. However, continual use of a toe cap without removing the source of the problem merely delays treatment.

The active ingredient in OTC products for ingrown toenails is tannic acid. The products listed above also contain isopropyl alcohol as an antiseptic, to prevent infection that can occur where the tissue is irritated by the embedded nail.

Formulation:
Liquid

Dosage:
Place a small piece of cotton in the nail groove (the side of the nail where the pain is) and wet the cotton thoroughly with the solution. Repeat several times daily until discomfort is relieved, but do not use more than seven days. Do not apply to open sores or if there is discharge around the nail. If you have diabetes or circulatory disease, don't use these products without consulting a physician.

Sleep Aids

OTC sleep aids help produce drowsiness and sedation. They work through the use of antihistamines, which block the actions of chemicals such as histamines. However, it is unclear precisely what antihistamines do to induce sleep.

Antihistamines are effective in treating short-term insomnia, particularly if the sleep problem is related primarily to difficulty falling asleep, as opposed to other sleep problems such as difficulty in staying asleep for a desired number of hours. However, the drowsiness is typically short-lived and sometimes very mild, and some people are not helped at all. Sleep problems that persist beyond seven to ten nights may require medical or other professional care.

It should be noted that normal sleep involves a cycle from rapid eye movement (REM) sleep through four progressively deeper phases followed by a return to REM sleep. Most sleep aids reduce REM sleep. Therefore, even if the amount of sleep gained from sleep aids is adequate (seven to nine hours for most people), insufficient REM sleep may leave the user with a lingering sense of fatigue.

Because pain is often a factor in insomnia, a number of sleep aid products contain both an antihistamine—either diphenhydramine or doxylamine—and an analgesic (see page 56), usually acetaminophen. This combination is typically indicated in the name, such as Unisom Pain Relief or Tranquil Plus. In addition, some cold remedies have specific formulations for nighttime because they contain ingredients—notably antihistamines—that block cold symptoms but also cause drowsiness (see page 72).

In theory, you could also obtain the equivalent amount of antihistamine from products in other categories, notably treatments for itching caused by allergies and insect bites or stings (see page 108). By taking these products, however, you are ingesting ingredients not required to treat sleeplessness. As a rule, it is preferable to take products with as few active ingredients as possible, partly to reduce the risk of side effects.

Warning

Overdosing with a sleep aid product may lead to a range of symptoms, from sedation and slowed responses to stimulation, particularly in children; in more severe cases, coma or seizures may occur.

More common adverse effects of antihistamines, such as dry mouth, constipation, and blurred vision, may occur. Do not take these products if you have asthma, glaucoma, cardiovascular disease, or enlargement of the prostate, except under the advice and supervision of a physician. Alcohol and other drugs that depress the central nervous system will heighten the sedating effect of sleep aids and should not be taken in combination.

Diphenhydramine

Brand names:
Compōz
Nytol Quick Caps
Sleep Rite
Sleep-eze 3
Sominex
Tranquil
Tranquil Plus
Unisom Maximum Strength Sleepgels
Unisom Pain Relief

The FDA has declared diphenhydramine to be the only agent, based upon clinical trials, that is safe and effective for nonprescription use, and it is present in the vast majority of sleep aid products. Diphenhydramine attains peak concentration within one to four hours, and sedates for three to six hours. Studies have found, however, that an individual's race may have a marked impact on the drug's effectiveness, with Asians requiring nearly twice as much diphenhydramine as Caucasians.

Formulations:
Caplet, tablet, gelcap

Dosage:
Take one to two pills (50 mg) at bedtime if needed, or as directed by a doctor. If sleeplessness persists continuously for more than two weeks, consult your physician. Do not take this product if pregnant or breast-feeding, and do not give to children under twelve, except on the advice of a physician.

Doxylamine

Brand names:
Maximum Strength Nytol
Unisom Nighttime Sleep Aid

Although the safety and effectiveness of doxylamine have not been fully established to the satisfaction of the FDA, it has been allowed to remain on the market, pending further studies. In one clinical study, it was found to work faster than other antihistamines in causing sleep.

Formulations:
Tablet, caplet

Dosage:
Take one pill (25 mg) thirty minutes before going to bed. Take once daily or as directed by a physician. If sleepless persists continuously for more than two weeks, consult your physician. Do not take this product if pregnant or breast-feeding, and do not give to children under twelve, except on the advice of a physician.

What to take when

Before it is rated safer by the FDA and is more widely available, diphenhydramine is your first choice. If it does not help, try doxylamine.

Smoking Cessation Aids

Brand names:
NicoDerm CQ (patch)
Nicorette (gum)
Nicotrol (patch)

Smoking cessation aids help people who wish to quit smoking by reducing their physical addiction to nicotine through gradual withdrawal. They provide nicotine—the only active ingredient in these products—to the user's bloodstream at a lower level than that provided by cigarettes.

In smoking cessation aids, nicotine is absorbed into the bloodstream through the lining of the mouth (if the product is formulated as chewing gum) or through the skin (if a transdermal patch is used). The blood level of nicotine obtained with the gum depends upon the vigor and duration of chewing, while the patch delivers a consistent amount over a twenty-four-hour period.

Because they do not contain the tar and carbon monoxide of cigarette smoke, smoking cessation aids do not have the same health dangers as tobacco. But they can also be addictive: People who have developed a physical dependence on nicotine in cigarettes occasionally transfer that dependence to the nicotine in these products. Furthermore, it is possible to overdose, either by consuming too much of the product or continuing to smoke while using the product.

Those most likely to benefit from these products are smokers who have a strong physical dependence on nicotine—experiencing withdrawal symptoms such as headache when they try to quit, for example—and who smoke more than fifteen cigarettes a day. However, some of the products come in different dose levels, with less nicotine for lighter smokers.

Warning
These products are to be used as an adjunct to a smoking cessation program. (The products are generally packaged with such programs.) They are not intended to be used for more than three months, and there is no evidence that they are effective unless the person also participates in a behavioral modification program to quit smoking.

Formulations:
Transdermal patch, chewing gum

Dosage:
Apply patch daily or chew one piece of gum every one to eight hours, as needed. See manufacturers' directions regarding dosage for specific brand-name products. The FDA has approved the use of these products only for people at least eighteen years old.

What to use when

If you like to feel that you're in control of your dosing regimen, you may prefer the gum; alternatively, if you like automatic dosing, you may prefer the patch.

Stimulants

Brand names:
Caffedrine
Nō-dōz
Vivarin

Stimulants help increase alertness and decrease fatigue and drowsiness. They should never be used as a substitute for adequate sleep and rest, and they do not reverse alcohol impairment.

Caffeine, the only FDA-approved stimulant for nonprescription use, works by stimulating the central nervous system. As well as being a common ingredient in coffee, tea, soft drinks, and chocolate products, it is also present in many headache and cold remedies, menstrual pain relief products, and diet aids. In the latter two categories, it also functions as a diuretic (see page 171), relieving bloating by turning excess body water into urine.

Caffeine concentrations vary among these types of products. In general, preparations that are designed specifically as stimulants—as opposed to some cold remedies (see page 72), for example—contain the highest concentrations of caffeine. To get an idea of the likely effect of a stimulant, keep in mind when you read the label that a 5-ounce cup of coffee has 40 to 180 mg of caffeine.

While its effect on sleep varies greatly among individuals, caffeine may be associated with insomnia and increased awakenings. At higher doses, it may produce tremors, nervousness, headache, irritability, diarrhea, and palpitations (irregular, rapid heartbeat). Gastrointestinal distress increases when NSAIDs (including aspirin—see page 55), corticosteroids, or alcohol are taken with caffeine. Also included in products for premenstrual syndrome (PMS), caffeine has been associated with worsening in the behavioral symptoms of PMS, such as irritability.

Warning

Several reports have suggested that heavy caffeine consumption is associated with coronary heart disease. While its effect on cardiac rate and rhythm is unclear, in very high concentrations it may cause tachycardia (excessively rapid heartbeat) and arrhythmia (heartbeat irregularity). Stimulants should be discontinued if rapid pulse, dizziness, or heart palpitations occur.

Some studies also suggest links between caffeine consumption and increased cholesterol levels, and caffeine consumption and decreased fertility. There are also indications that caffeine consumption by women with fibrocystic breasts (a condition characterized by the formation of noncancerous cysts in one or both breasts) may lead to benign breast nodules, tenderness, pain, and nipple discharge.

Finally, physical dependence may result from prolonged caffeine consumption. When people abruptly stop consuming caffeine, they may experience withdrawal symptoms, notably fatigue and headache, even when they are normally well rested.

Formulations:
Caplet, tablet, chewable tablet, timed-release capsule

Dosage:
Adults take 100 to 200 mg (200 to 250 mg in timed-release products) to restore mental alertness or wakefulness—and not more often than every three to four hours. If you use a timed-release preparation, do not take it fewer than six hours before bedtime. Use these products only occasionally, and do not give them to children under twelve. Use these products cautiously if you have or have had peptic ulcer disease, cardiac arrhythmias, or a history of mental illness.

Swimmer's Ear Preparations

OTC medications for swimmer's ear help dry the external ear canal, inhibit bacterial and fungal growth, and maintain the canal's normal acid mantle following swimming, showering, bathing, or hair washing. Accordingly, most products contain an astringent (see page 118) and often an anti-infective, as described below. As an alternative to brand name products, some people use acetic acid solution in the form of household vinegar, or aluminum acetate solution (Burow's solution), a widely available astringent.

Warning

Do not use these products in your ear if the tympanic membrane (eardrum) is perforated or punctured. While a hole is not always self-evident, you should consult a doctor if fluid is draining from the ear.

Formulation:
Drops

Dosage:
Put a few drops of solution in each ear, for one to two minutes, before and after swimming or bathing, or as directed by a physician.

Isopropyl Alcohol

Brand names:
Auro-Dri
Swim-Ear

A mild astringent and antiseptic, isopropyl alcohol helps dry and toughen—thus preventing infection—the skin lining the external ear canal.

Boric Acid

Brand names:
Dri-Ear Drops
Ear-Dry Drops

A weak, nonirritating local anti-infective, boric acid (see page 103) is added to isopropyl alcohol in some swimmer's ear products, such as those previously listed. However, do not use boric acid alone.

What to use when

The solutions that combine alcohol with boric acid are more effective in preventing infection than alcohol alone.

Urinary Pain Relievers

Brand names:
Azo-Standard
Prodium
Uristat

OTC products for urinary pain provide temporary relief from the pain of urination caused by urinary tract infections. The only OTC agent approved by the FDA for urinary pain relief is phenazopyridine hydrochloride, which acts specifically on the mucosa of the urinary tract to provide prompt relief from pain and burning. Until recently, phenazopyridine was available only by prescription. It is now available in a lower concentration in the OTC formulation.

Phenazopyridine hydrochloride, however, does not actually treat the urinary infection, which requires antibacterial medication available only by prescription. Users are advised to take phenazopyridine for no more than two days, unless recommended otherwise by a physician.

You should be aware that the orange-red dye present in this medication will color your urine as long as phenazopyridine hydrochloride is in your system. It may also stain fabric.

Warning

If you have impaired kidney function, you should use phenazopyridine hydrochloride with caution. If you cannot eliminate the drug from your body sufficiently in your urine, you could develop liver and other problems.

Formulation:
Tablet

Dosage:
Take two tablets with water after meals, as needed, up to three times a day. Do not take for more than two days. Do not give to children under twelve without the supervision of a physician.

Vaginal Antifungals

Vaginal antifungals kill the organisms that cause candidal vaginitis, better known as candidiasis or a yeast infection. If the candidal infection recurs, which is the case for nearly half of all women who develop this infection, it may need to be treated with longer courses of therapy or with prescription medication. Some physicians also recommend using the antifungal agents preventively—or at least during courses of antibiotic treatment, one of the risk factors for candidiasis. In addition, if you are taking oral contraceptives and have recurring vaginal candidiasis, you may want to ask your physician about alternative methods of birth control.

In recent years, three active ingredients previously available only by prescription have been made available as over-the-counter remedies for candidiasis. (Two of these are the same compounds also reclassified for OTC treatment of athlete's foot and jock itch. See Antifungals, page 114.) Studies rate their effectiveness at 90 percent, without major side effects.

Before these antifungals became available without prescription, the only OTC treatments for candidiasis were creams that provided symptomatic relief only. Although their use has decreased now that antifungals are readily available, the creams may still be used to provide relief from vaginal itching.

Warning

Pregnant women have an increased risk of candidal vaginitis and are also less likely to be helped by these products. If you are pregnant, you should consult your physician before using a vaginal antifungal. Vaginal antifungals should not be used by girls under the age of twelve. Do not use these products if you have abdominal pain, fever, or foul-smelling discharge, which could indicate a systemic, or bodywide, and more severe infection. Do not use tampons while using these medications.

Formulations:
Cream, suppository, tablet

Butoconazole Nitrate

Brand names:
Femstat 3

This is the newest of the vaginal antifungals to be switched to OTC, and the first to offer a cure in three days, not the usual seven. Another advantage is that it is less likely to leak after it has been inserted in the vagina.

Dosage:
Insert one applicatorful of cream into the vagina, preferably at bedtime. Repeat this procedure daily for three consecutive days. If the infection does not clear up easily with proper treatment or if symptoms return within two months, consult your physician.

Clotrimazole

Brand names:
Gyne-Lotrimin
Mycelex-3
Mycelex-7

Also used to treat athlete's foot and jock itch, clotrimazole kills a wide range of fungi and yeasts. Candidiasis should improve in three days, and be cured in seven, with this agent.

Dosage:
Insert one tablet or applicatorful of cream into the vagina, preferably at bedtime. Repeat this procedure daily for three or seven consecutive days, depending on the product. If the infection does not clear up easily with proper treatment, or if symptoms return within two months, consult your physician.

Miconazole

Brand names:
Monistat-3
Monistat-7

Like clotrimazole, miconazole is used for a variety of fungal infections, with similar success. Like butoconazole nitrate, there is now a formulation for a three-day treatment.

Dosage:
Insert one tablet or applicatorful of cream into the vagina, preferably at bedtime. Repeat this procedure daily for three or seven consecutive days, depending on the product. If the infection does not clear up easily with proper treatment, or if symptoms return within two months, consult your physician.

What to use when

Try preparations with either butoconazole nitrate or miconazole first, as they may clear up infection in only three days.

Vaginal Antipruritics

Antipruritics for vaginitis help relieve the characteristic itching and pain or irritation involving the external female genitalia—not the vagina itself—associated with vaginitis. They typically contain an antipruritic (see page 95) such as hydrocortisone and/or a local anesthetic (see page 97), usually benzocaine. Some treatments also contain agents to prevent bacterial infections.

While these products are easy to apply and provide prompt symptomatic relief, they do not treat vaginal infections, either bacterial or candidal (yeast). If symptoms, such as discharge, indicate some type of infectious vaginitis, a vaginal antipruritic may simply mask the underlying cause of symptoms and delay an accurate diagnosis and treatment.

Formulation:
Cream

Dosage:
Apply three to four times daily to the external area around the vagina, for no more than seven days. Do not insert in the vagina itself.

Benzocaine

Brand names:
Vagisil
Yeast-Gard

Although it is one of the most widely used local anesthetics in OTC drugs, it sometimes leads to rash and itching. Both products named above also contain anti-infectives.

Hydrocortisone

Brand names:
Cortef Feminine Itch Cream
Gynecort
Vaginex

While hydrocortisone reduces itching and inflammation, it should only be used externally and not within the vagina, to prevent its being absorbed generally by the body. The products listed below are similar to other hydrocortisone-based products, and may in fact be used to treat itching and inflammation caused by insect bites, for example. However, before using other hydrocortisone-based products to treat vaginal itching, consult your pharmacist or physician.

What to use when

If the primary symptom is itching, try a product with hydrocortisone. If you have pain, you may find a product with benzocaine more helpful.

Vaginal Lubricants

Brand names:
Astroglide Lubricant Gel
Gyne-Moistrin Moisturizing Gel
H-R Lubricating Jelly
K-Y Jelly
Lubrin Vaginal Inserts Suppositories
Moist Again Gel
Replens Gel

Vaginal lubricants provide moisture to vaginas that have become dry, to facilitate sexual intercourse. There are a number of nonhormonal lubricants that are water-soluble, unscented, colorless, odorless, and tasteless. (Non-water-soluble lubricants do not wash off easily, with the result that the vagina is more likely to become infected.) The key ingredient in most of these products is glycerin, which keeps the vaginal tissue continually moist as long as the lubricant is in place.

In addition to the products marketed specifically for vaginal dryness, many water-soluble moisturizers (see page 104), such as Lubriderm and Keri Cream, also work as vaginal lubricants. Oil-based products like petroleum jelly or other homemade recipes, which can irritate, should be avoided. It is also advisable to avoid douching, which has a drying effect.

Warning
Vaginal dryness that is severe or leads to bleeding or intense itching could indicate a more serious problem for which you should see your medical practitioner.

Formulations:
Gel, suppository

Dosage:
Use as needed, following manufacturers' directions regarding dosage for specific brand-name products. Some products provide lubrication that lasts for days, while others are effective only for several hours.

What to use when

As vaginal lubricants contain the same active ingredient, you should make your choice based on your experience with the product and its dosage schedule.

Durable Medical Equipment

Electric toothbrushes, crutches, and vaporizers are all durable medical equipment—the technical term for products we use every day. They aren't pills or testing devices, but they are equipment and other items that may help keep us healthy, heal us, make us comfortable, or help us stay on the move. You can use home health equipment, such as breathing aids and other respiratory equipment and monitors, treatment-oriented equipment (dialysis, pain control), functional aids (ostomy products, feeding mechanisms), and daily living and ambulatory aids (beds, lifts, wheelchairs, walkers) almost anywhere, anytime.

So what exactly is it? Durable medical equipment is equipment that can stand repeated use, is primarily and customarily used to serve a medical purpose, generally is not useful to you in the absence of illness or injury, and is appropriate for use at home.

Clearly, though, in no drugstore or drug section of even a large supermarket or mass merchandiser will you find every item of durable medical equipment available. But in most cases, if the pharmacist has an equipment distributor, you can order any product, or you can contact a local medical and surgical supply house and request a catalog or a listing of the house's in-stock product. This is why such equipment is included in a book about over-the-counter products. On the other hand, the reimbursement issue—whether or not your insurance plan will cover all or even part of the costs for such equipment—is a cloudy one.

Reimbursement

While it is true that in theory anyone can order and purchase any piece of equipment without a physician's prescription or order, before any insurance plan—be it Medicare, Blue Cross, or any of the commercial insurance companies—will pay or reimburse for the item, two general rules apply:

1. The piece of equipment or item must be covered by the medical plan—that is, specified in the schedule of benefits.

2. It must be deemed "medically necessary" as defined by the benefits plan as per a doctor's order.

Medicare

Because Medicare remains such an important source of payment for most durable medical equipment and home-care products, let's look closely at its general policies and what it covers.

Medicare Part B (medical insurance) helps pay for durable medical equipment that your doctor prescribes for you for use in your home. A hospital or facility that primarily provides skilled nursing or rehabilitation services cannot be considered your home. So to repeat the most important factor here: In order for Medicare to consider anything durable medical equipment, the equipment must be able to withstand repeated use, primarily serve a medical purpose, and be appropriate for use in your home.

Medicare Part B will pay 80 percent of the Medicare-approved amount for the product after a $100 yearly deductible has been met—as long as the equipment meets the Medicare program's criteria for appropriateness and reimbursement.

According to the Medicare handbook, issued by the Health Care Financing Administration (the agency that administers the Medicare program), only your doctor should prescribe medical equipment. An equipment supplier *should not:*

1. contact you first and offer to get your doctor or the Medicare program to approve an item. (It is okay, however, for the supplier to contact you in response to calls from your doctor or other health-care professionals.);

2. say he or she works for or represents Medicare;

3. deliver equipment to your home that neither you nor your doctor ordered;

4. send you used items, while billing Medicare for new ones.

Indeed, some of these actions may be against the law. File a complaint with your Medicare carrier if you believe a supplier has taken any of these actions and you know that your doctor has not ordered the item. (By the way, Medicare regulations make it illegal, too, for a supplier to offer you items or equipment at no cost to you or to offer to pay the Medicare coinsurance—the 20 percent you're responsible for under Part B.)

Further, Medicare pays for different kinds of durable medical equipment in different ways. Some equipment must be rented; other equipment must be purchased. And some equipment may be either rented or purchased.

Finally, before Medicare will pay your claim, suppliers of medical equipment and home-care products must be approved by Medicare and have a Medicare supplier number.

All of these items are available over the counter in pharmacies or through medical equipment supply houses or home health-care agencies. Not by a long shot is this a complete list of the thousands of products available. Instead this list represents items you may reasonably expect to be stocked in a moderate-size drugstore, large supermarket, or mass merchandiser.

Finally, it's important to remember that many, if not most, medical supply houses and possibly even pharmacies offer the option to rent this equipment. *So be sure to ask what options for purchase, payment, and/or rental they offer.* Depending upon the length of time you need the item—for example, a hospital bed for a convalescing but not totally debilitated person—you may save money in the long run.

Antisnoring Devices

Snoring usually occurs when the air squeezing through your airways causes surrounding tissues to vibrate—a problem that typically increases as people age and their throats get fleshier and looser, narrowing their air passages. It may also result from nasal allergies, deviated septums, or other conditions that cause congestion or obstruct nasal breathing.

There are several types of antisnoring devices available over the counter:

Nasal dilators

These devices, which open the nostrils to let in more air, come in a few forms. One that has been on the market for a while employs a pair of stainless steel coils that may be inserted into each nostril. One drawback is that the coils tend to fall out during the night.

Perhaps the most widely known snore fighter is the Breathe Right adhesive strip, which was originally designed for people with nasal congestion who wanted to let in more air and was given clearance by the FDA in 1995 for marketing for snoring prevention. It is a simple Band-Aid-like nasal strip that, properly placed over the bridge of the nose, flares open the nostrils to let in more air. While it is often helpful, it may take a week of consecutive use for sleepers to relearn to breathe through their noses and close their mouths when asleep.

Jaw-positioning devices

These are often plastic molds that users may boil in water and then bite to form an impression. The mold fits over the teeth to thrust the lower jaw forward so that the relaxed tongue does not slip into the throat, blocking airways. Jaw positioners are most effective when they move from side to side and also force the jaw forward in small increments according to need. While they are generally effective, they can cause drooling and may fall out during the night. More serious risks are jaw stiffness and joint pain, loose teeth, and muscle spasms.

Tongue retainers

These devices hold the tongue in place with suction or force it to protrude between the teeth, thus preventing it from slipping into the throat and blocking air passages.

Athletic Bandages

Athletic bandages—also known as elastic bandages—are something of a misnomer. While they are often used for extra support during strenuous activity, they may also be worn to provide temporary support and compression for individuals who have suffered a slight sprain or strained muscle.

Athletic bandages may be self-adhering or may fasten with clips. Either way, they can be washed and reused.

Bedpan

A bedpan may be used by anyone for whom a trip to the bathroom is inconvenient or impossible. While in theory any large basin will do, a proper bedpan will be appropriately contoured to the shape of the body and will be smooth around the edges to avoid scratching or bruising the user. Some models feature pontoonlike sides to add stability and balance and to help prevent tipping and spillage. Bedpans should be made of materials that are easily sanitized with disinfectant.

Braces/Splints/Slings

Braces and splints are designed to provide support for weakened muscles, tendons, and ligaments and to help reduce the chance of injury recurrence during activity. They are contoured to the natural shape of the joint being protected, to minimize slipping, provide even compression, and ensure comfort.

Braces and splints provide more support than athletic bandages (see above) and are worn for more severe injuries. Like athletic bandages, however, they permit a full range of movement.

Braces are available for the ankle, elbow, knee, and hand/wrist. They are sold in a range of sizes. Two specific types of braces need further explanation:

Knee braces

These devices often consist of an open knee design that surrounds the kneecap and flexible metal side stabilizers that provide medial/lateral support and stability. They simulate the action of natural knee ligaments without restricting normal knee movement. The metal stabilizers also prevent rolling at the top of the knee brace.

Hand/Wrist braces

The use of braces or splints for repetitive stress injury is highly contentious. Some doctors and physical therapists recommend that they be worn only at work. However, according to Emil Pascarelli, M.D., author of *Repetitive Strain Injury,* splints worn for carpal tunnel syndrome should be worn only at night (to prevent you from flexing your wrists in your sleep), unless your practitioner tells you otherwise.

Slings

Slings are used to immobilize and support the arm or shoulder and are generally available in two styles:

1. *Pouch.* This style uses straps around the wrist and shoulder;

2. *Envelope.* This style allows the weight of the arm to be carried by the shoulder. As the name implies, the envelope sling opens and closes easily by using snaps and Velcro closures.

Breast Pumps

Breast pumps are used mainly if breast-feeding is inconvenient—when the mother returns to work outside the home, on other occasions when the mother is regularly separated from the baby, but also for circumstances such as the infant being too weak to nurse.

Pumps are available in a remarkable variety of styles. The most basic type of pump—a hand pump—is adequate for occasional or short-term pumping; however, if the baby is unable to nurse for more than two weeks, according to experts, an electric pump is more reliable.

The following are the primary types of pumps:

Hand, or manual, pumps

• *Battery-operated pumps.* Relatively new to the market, this type requires only one hand for operation, which is an advantage.

• *Cylindrical pumps.* Using two tubes, fitted inside each other, the pump draws milk when a vacuum is created by pulling the outer tube away from the breast. An advantage is that the pump converts into a feeding bottle.

• *Horn or bicycle pumps.* This type has a rubber bulb, a plastic "horn," and a depression in the horn where the milk is collected. Most experts caution that the bulb cannot be sterilized.

• *Modified bulb pumps.* This type has a plastic flange and rubber bulb attached to a collection bottle. Again, experts caution that the bulb cannot be sterilized.

• *Trigger pumps.* This type has a glass flange attached to a collection bottle or jar and a tube that leads from the jar to a trigger. The trigger is squeezed to create a vacuum.

Electric pumps

Traditionally, electric breast pumps were rather large, but nonetheless considered portable. Because of better nipple stimulation, they are more efficient than hand pumps in emptying the breasts and maintaining milk production, according to most reports. A drawback, however, has been their cost; consequently, most women rent them.

Relatively recently, a personal-size, handheld model came on the market, at greater convenience and less cost.

Electric pumps have either automatic or semiautomatic suction. In the former, all the woman has to do is place the flange over her nipple, then the pump does all the work. In semiautomatic suction pumps, the woman creates and controls the suction. As you can imagine, the automatic models are acknowledged to be more effective.

Canes

While there appears to be a wide variety of canes, the main variation comes in material—wood or aluminum—and platform. Regarding the latter variation, in addition to the standard cane, there is also a "quad cane" which has four feet for extra stability. The quad cane, as well as other canes that are shaped in different ways to provide extra support, are all-aluminum.

Also available are folding canes, which fold to less than 12 inches in length.

Aluminum canes are generally lighter in weight than wooden canes. Both types of canes have rubber tips that absorb shock.

The length of a cane is critical to how well it functions. When fitting a cane, you should stand as naturally upright as possible on a firm, flat surface and wear the same shoes you will be wearing when you are using the cane. In most cases, the top curve, or handhold, of the cane should be even with the hip joint.

If you have a wooden cane, remove the rubber tip, mark the correct length, and cut off the excess with a saw, allowing approximately ¼ inch for the thickness of the bottom of the rubber tip. If it is necessary to shorten an aluminum cane more than the height adjustment allows, a tubing cutter should be used, not a hacksaw. The tubing cutter will make a clean, square cut.

Cane tips, which should be skid-resistant, will need to be replaced from time to time. They can be purchased in the cane-and-crutch section of most drugstores. Make sure the tip of your cane corresponds to the size shown on the box. Tips that are too loose should not be used.

To use the cane, ask your doctor or physical therapist to show you the proper walking gait.

Wooden canes should always be stored in cool, dry places. Avoid long storage exposure to direct sunlight or proximity to heat outlets. Neither wood nor aluminum canes are recommended for people weighing more than 250 pounds.

Cervical Collar

A cervical collar—a usually soft collar that wraps around the neck—has been worn most often by people who have suffered whiplash, usually as a result of a car collision. (*Cervical* refers to the neck or upper portion of the back.) However, a collar may also be worn effectively by anyone whose neck muscles are sprained or strained. They may be used day or night.

Cervical collars are available in a range of sizes and may have an adjustable closure to facilitate fit and comfort. They are also available in firm or medium-density foam.

Cervical Pillow

A cervical pillow fits around the neck. To prevent a sore neck, it may be used to keep the neck from rolling from side to side during sleep or long-distance travel. The pillow keeps the neck properly aligned and supported, thus neck muscles are relaxed and free from stress. The pillow can be particularly useful for traveling in cars and planes, when one is sleeping in an upright position.

Cold/Heat Treatment Packs

Cold and heat are believed to work as counterstimulants, or counterirritants. They work on the nervous system to block pain signals temporarily, typically from sprains or strains. They are helpful in reducing swelling, slowing inflammation, and relieving soreness, particularly when applied in the first 48 hours after the injury or after the pain flares up.

Cold also acts as an anesthetic by numbing sore tissues. Essentially, the cold contracts the veins, reducing circulation. This may be useful for treating insect bites, bumps and bruises, toothaches, and simple headaches, as well as the more common sprains and strains.

Once the cold application is withdrawn from the injured area, the veins overcompensate and dilate, or expand, allowing blood to rush to the sore area. This blood, along with the oxygen it carries, begins healing the damaged tissue. The process is accelerated if cold treatment is followed with heat, which promotes healing by increasing circulation and relaxing muscle spasm.

The wide variety of cold and heat treatments includes cold packs and compresses and heating pads with dry or moist heat. Cold compresses are available in many forms, including a soft, pliable fabric that stays dry and contours to the body's injured area: Cold packs are available for the throat, neck, hand/wrist, knee/thigh, ankle/foot, shoulder/scapula, eye, and so on. Cold packs should be placed in the refrigerator or freezer for a period of time—which is usually specified in the manufacturer's directions—before applying to injured area.

Heating pads can cause skin burns, particularly if used in conjunction with certain medications, such as some counterirritants (see page 58). One study, for example, found that exposure to menthol caused the threshold for warmth to rise significantly, possibly because the menthol molecule inhibits or desensitizes warmth receptors; as a result, users may be unaware that they are applying excess heat.

Furthermore, counterirritants containing methyl salicylate should not be used in conjunction with a heating pad, which, by increasing skin temperature and vasodilation (dilation, or widening, of blood vessels), increases the body's absorption of menthol and methyl salicylate, potentially causing skin and muscle tissue death.

Also, ice or cold packs should be wrapped in a cloth or towel to avoid overexposure of cold to skin tissue.

Commodes

Commodes may be used by people at home who have difficulty using a conventional toilet because of either its structure or its distance from the bed and bedroom.

There are a variety of commodes. The simplest form of commode is the raised toilet seat. This is placed on top of the standard toilet and raises it some five inches to facilitate sitting and standing. This may be useful for anyone who has difficulty lowering himself or herself to the standard toilet seat and/or difficulty in getting up from that position. In most cases the raised toilet seat may have design features such as contouring, a wider seating area, and an extra deep "lip" for stability.

A more elaborate form is the bedside commode, a freestanding commode with a safety frame that eliminates the need for the person to walk to a bathroom. In most cases the seat height adjusts. Variations in this theme include a commode chair sized for obese people weighing up to 650 pounds, a drop-arm commode chair for people who must transfer between commode and bed or wheelchair, and even an adaptive commode/shower chair.

Compression Shorts

Compression shorts, which look like exercise shorts—and, in fact, may be constructed with Lycra spandex—are worn to provide support for groin, thigh, and hamstring muscles. Compression increases blood flow to muscles, keeping them loose and pliable, helping to reduce muscle fatigue and susceptibility to injury.

Compression shorts, which are sold in a range of sizes, may be worn by men or women. In a drugstore, they are generally sold in the same area as athletic bandages and braces.

Crutches

Crutches are used primarily to provide support and stability in walking for people who have badly sprained knees or ankles, or broken knees, ankles, or legs. Available in different sizes and heights—youth, adult, and tall adult; or small, medium, large, and extra-long—crutches come in basically two designs: the forearm crutch and the standard crutch.

Forearm crutch

This is designed to place the person's weight directly over the tip for the greatest stability. Usually this crutch has independently adjustable leg and forearm sections.

Standard (axillary, or underarm) crutch

Even here, there is some variation. The standard design may incorporate what's sometimes called a *prebent bow design,* which is supposed to provide added strength at the crutch's stress points.

In addition to the crutch, you will also need to purchase handgrips, which provide a soft, sturdy grip and help prevent blistered hands. Other essential accessories are underarm pads. These should fit snugly under arm and resist sliding. Safety crutch tips, which are skid resistant and should provide maximum contact with the floor, are also essential. Other optional accessories include crutch cushions that fit on top of the crutch.

Ear Syringes

Rubber ear syringes may be used to irrigate the ear to flush out packed earwax. To prevent dizziness, make sure that the water is at body temperature.

Warning
Never put water in your child's ear if there is any chance the eardrum has a hole in it or if your child has ventilation tubes (sometimes surgically implanted in cases of chronic ear infection).

Enemas

Enemas may be used to relieve acute constipation. There are two basic types: enemas with mineral oil or another lubricant, which work by softening hard stools and lubricating their passage through the bowel; and plain saline enemas, which work by increasing water in the intestine.

Enemas with lubricant are typically used when the feces are impacted. This type of enema should be followed with a cleansing enema, such as a saline enema, to remove the stool and other residue. Saline enemas can also be used alone, for relatively minor constipation. In either case, they usually work within two to fifteen minutes.

Warning

As with laxatives, do not use enemas when nausea, vomiting, or abdominal pain are present, unless you are directed to do so by a physician. If you notice a sudden change in bowel habits over a period of two weeks, consult a physician first. Rectal bleeding or failure to have a bowel movement after use of an enema may indicate a serious condition. Discontinue and consult physician. Do not use enemas for longer than one week, if you are on a low-salt diet, or if you have kidney disease, unless directed by a physician.

Enuretic (Bed-wetting) Alarm

Moisture-sensitive devices that set off an alarm can be used to teach children to awaken when they need to urinate during the night. These alarms, which run on batteries, are small, lightweight, sensitive to a few drops of urine, and easy for a child to set up by himself.

Because bed-wetting is generally a developmental problem that most children outgrow, it is advisable to wait until the child is six before using a nighttime alarm. Furthermore, although these alarms are effective in the short run, the relapse rate is high. Your child's practitioner may want to include an alarm as part of a treatment program, along with reduced fluid consumption prior to bedtime and a system of rewards or incentives.

Eyeglasses, Ready-to-Wear

Many drugstores, mass merchandisers, and even supermarkets now offer ready-to-wear nonprescription (eye professionals refer to them as "self-prescribed") eyeglasses. Consumers can select a pair by testing their vision with a reading chart on the kiosk where the glasses are sold. The test allows people to determine what strength they need, based on their diopter—the unit of curvature and of the power of lenses. Generally, the diopter strength is a measure of the eye's ability to bend, or refract, light and focus it on the retina. The more nearsighted (or farsighted—see below) a person is, the higher the power (of lenses) needed for correction.

For some time now in most pharmacies, ready-to-wear reading glasses have been available in a range of diopter strengths: +1 for the person having slight difficulty in reading or seeing close-up to +4.0 (or even higher) for someone having greater difficulty.

Warning

Ready-to-wear nonprescription eyeglasses are not intended to replace prescribed corrective lenses or examination by an eye-care professional. Periodic eye checkups are necessary to determine eye health and for proper correction of vision problems.

Humidifiers/Vaporizers

Humidifiers help prevent colds or croup by moistening dry mucous membranes, which may be more susceptible to infections. They also help loosen up coughs (which are worsened by dry air), treat congestion, and are helpful in treating sinusitis and allergy conditions. Humidifiers are also effective in moisturizing dry skin and throats, in dry climates, or in areas with cold winters where heat dries the air.

Vaporizers, which work by boiling water to produce steam, are also helpful in treating colds, coughs, congestion, and sinusitis as well as allergy symptoms. The steam helps loosen mucus that is thick or difficult to cough up.

The vaporizer generally has lost much of its market to the humidifier, however, for reasons of both safety and efficacy. Vaporizers do not deliver humidity at as fast a rate as humidifiers do. One item, however, that is still competitive is the personal steam inhaler. Rather than being sized for an entire room, the personal steam inhaler is for use by one person, in very close contact with the device and the steam. A user puts his or her face into a hood directly over the source of the steam. An adjustable steam control allows cool air to mix with the steam, to enhance comfort and prevent burns.

Depending on the model of vaporizer, various features are available. Water capacity, or reservoir size, varies, and some include a medicine cup to add medicine or aromatic oils to the water. Some have automatic shutoff when the reservoir is empty.

For your health, be sure to heed the manufacturer's directions for regular cleaning, owing to the buildup of mineral deposits and possibly bacteria in the reservoir.

The most popular humidifier is the cool mist, or ultrasonic, variety. It is not only quieter than its predecessor, but it also kills molds and most bacteria that might be in the water. However, distilled water is preferred over tap water. Some experts believe that even these humidifiers should be cleaned weekly, with a solution of bleach or malt vinegar. Depending upon the model, various features are available: dust-trap filters, directional spout, and large capacity reservoir, just to name a few.

Warning

Vaporizers can cause severe burns if they overturn or if the user's face is too close to the point where the steam is coming out.

Contrary to some manufacturers' recommendations, do not add medicine, such as camphor or menthol oils, to the water in the humidifier, because it irritates some people's coughs.

Magnifiers

People who have trouble seeing close objects, and whose vision cannot be corrected with ordinary glasses or lenses, may use simple magnifiers for such tasks as reading fine print, sewing, or doing hobbies. These are available in a variety of shapes—magnifiers on stands for people who have difficulty holding the printed material or who are doing close work for long stretches of time, lighted magnifiers, magnifiers with neck straps, even a magnifier device for a reader confined to bed and lying flat on his or her back.

Another option is magnifying spectacles—high-powered magnifying lenses that can be worn for reading, writing, and other close work.

Magnifiers come in various powers, designated as the amount of magnification—for example, *2X power* refers to magnification that is two times larger than normal.

Nasal Aspirator

Also known as a nasal suction bulb, a nasal aspirator is most often used to help young babies and children with breathing difficulties owing to sticky or dried nasal secretions. (Most children are developmentally unable to blow their noses until the age of four.)

Some suction bulbs on the market have a small, clear plastic tip which traps the mucus and can be removed from the rubber suction bulb for cleaning. Alternatively, the bulb tip can be cleaned by squirting the secretions into a tissue.

To remove secretions from the back of the nose, you will need to seal off both nostrils completely, using the tip of the suction bulb on one side and your finger on the other.

Warning

Do not insert the tip of the suction bulb too deeply, or a nosebleed may result.

Otoscope

The home otoscope is a simple, handheld lighted instrument, with a magnifying lens and a viewing cone, that is used to monitor the health of the ear canal and the eardrum, and specifically to look for middle ear infections, or *otitis media* (see page 40). Experts generally agree, however, that while helpful, the home otoscope is not as good as the otoscope used by medical practitioners. For one, the optics and the lighting of physician otoscopes are far superior (also far more expensive).

In addition, the home otoscope, unlike the professional model, features no way to assess eardrum mobility, often a critical part of an ear exam. Even with much practice, some kinds of ear infections will be impossible to see. Medical professionals caution that it is dangerous to rely on home otoscopes in lieu of follow-up ear checks.

The common condition of prolonged clear fluid, which can reduce hearing, is almost impossible to detect with a home otoscope. Still, with a home model, a person can expect to eventually become fairly proficient at identifying eardrums when acutely infected. Home otoscopes usually come with a few pictures to help give you a general idea of what to look for when examining a person's ear—specifically how to distinguish between a normal and an infected ear.

Perineal Cushion

A perineal cushion is most often used for people with discomfort in the perineum (area between the scrotum and anus in men, and the section of fibrous tissue between the anus and vagina in women), typically owing to hemorrhoids or postchildbirth pain and/or injury. The perineal cushion is designed to prevent pressure on the painful or uncomfortable area. Generally molded of soft, durable urethane foam, the cushion has a cut-out design—hence the popular name, *doughnut,* for such a product—to relieve rectal and/or perineal discomfort. Some cushions are inflatable for ease in storage and travel.

Reachers/Grippers

Reachers may be used by people with limited mobility who need to reach objects beyond their immediate range and/or people with little hand or finger strength. Reachers, which may be made of aluminum or wood, often have a metal "jaw" at one end that is activated by a hand-operated trigger. Some reachers also have a short metal pole at the end, which may be used as a dressing aid, while others may also have a magnet on the jaw to help pick up metal objects.

Gripping tongs are used to grab round or flat objects. Generally, grippers have a pivoting gripping claw that can be operated with very little pressure. They come in a few lengths and have a pistol grip handle to fit the hand.

Shower Stools/Chairs/ Benches

Shower stools, chairs, and benches are designed specifically for added security in the shower or bath, for the elderly, infirm, or convalescent. Whether a stool, chair, or bench, it should have a sturdy, textured plastic seat—with no sharp edges—that does not become slippery when wet. In some cases, the device may have a perforated top that allows the water to run through. It should have large handholds for extra safety. Similarly, the legs of the stool should be made of a material that resists corrosion from moisture, and should have slip-resistant, nonscratching, rust-resistant feet for extra stability.

Sitz Bath

A sitz bath, which is a molded plastic tub or portable unit that fits over the toilet seat, facilitates constant cleansing of irritated areas. Typically it is used as treatment for hemorrhoids, anal tears, and rectal itching. Warm (not hot) water relaxes the anal sphincter muscle so that it is less likely to squeeze tender protrusions. It also cleans the area of any fecal soil which may be causing itching.

The standard sitz bath kit is a portable unit that may come with a control handle, approximately eight feet of plastic tubing, a rubber faucet attachment with a faucet adapter, and a spray wand. Or a sitz bath may come with a vinyl water bag and tubing.

Toothbrushes, Manual and Electric, and Plaque Remover

There is great diversity in low-tech and high-tech toothbrushes. Traditional manual toothbrushes are available in a variety of styles. Some have a mixture of long and short bristles designed to fit between the peaks and valleys of the teeth, to better scrub all surfaces. Still others have narrow heads and shorter bristles to reach the back teeth, and others have angled handles, supposedly to reach hard-to-reach places in the mouth. Some have longer outside bristles that massage the gums while the inner bristles scrub the surfaces of the teeth. They may also have a rubber tip on the handle that is used to massage the gums. And these are just a few of the broad variations.

High-tech (electric) versions generally have bristles that automatically rotate, go back and forth, and/or move up and down. These models are merely held against the surfaces of the teeth and guided by the user. Some models claim great success in combating the formation of plaque. Plaque is a thin, bacteria-filled film that continuously forms on all tooth surfaces and that, unless removed, will attack gum tissues, eventually leading to gum disease, or gingivitis.

The consensus is that these automatic models are more effective for improved dental hygiene, given the constant movement and speed of the bristles and the ability to gently massage the gums and reach all tooth surfaces. They're easy to use and require a minimum of pressure to hold the bristles in contact with the teeth; in fact, some models have an automatic slowdown or shut-off feature when too firm a contact is made between bristles and teeth. In this way, damaging overbrushing is less likely to occur.

Indeed, a disadvantage of manual toothbrushes is that it's very easy to apply too much pressure—thereby wearing down the surface of your teeth—or use inappropriate brushing techniques that result in poor dental hygiene.

Many electric toothbrushes also double as plaque removers. The brush head uses an oscillating motion to simultaneously remove plaque from tooth surfaces, between the teeth, and below the gum line.

Clearly, though, the manual toothbrush is more convenient to use, and its maintenance and replacement costs are less than those of electric toothbrushes.

Urinals (Male/Female)

Portable plastic urinals may be used by people who need to urinate and/or who have difficulty in getting to the bathroom—either because they are bedridden or because of the frequency of urination, as well as by anyone who needs to measure the amount they urinate, for medical purposes. For that reason, many urinals are calibrated in ounces and cubic centimeters (cc).

The female urinal should have a specially contoured opening that conforms to the curvature of the female anatomy and allows the user to achieve a secure seal during use.

All urinals should have caps that close tightly to prevent spillage and confine odors. They should also be stain- and chemical-resistant and easily sanitized.

Walkers

Walkers, four-legged frames made of lightweight, sturdy aluminum, are used to provide support and stability to people who have difficulty walking unassisted. The front legs are sometimes on wheels for increased mobility. Some models feature a folding side to allow the person to negotiate narrow hallways or bathrooms, and oversize tips with angled foot pieces to provide maximum floor contact for safety.

For convenience, most walkers can be folded, sometimes by pressing an open palm on the access release mechanism located below each handgrip. In addition, the cross braces may be positioned to allow the walker to be placed over the toilet. Many accessories for walkers are available, including brakes, carrying baskets, trays, and foam handgrips.

Walkers come in many shapes and sizes—adult, junior, child, and toddler—and can usually be adjusted for height.

Home Medical Testing

The availability of sophisticated and reliable equipment has added a whole new emphasis on home medical tests. It's easy to forget that just less than a decade ago, home testing was much more limited. In a relatively short time, we have gone from thermometers and blood pressure monitoring devices to a home kit that lets you take your own blood sample and test for the human immunodeficiency virus (HIV), which causes AIDS—the latest home testing kit to be made available to the public.

Nowadays, home testing devices are used to monitor blood pressure *and* blood sugar. Mechanical equipment can be used to examine an eardrum for infection. Other chemically based tests use specially treated paper, in the form of dipsticks, to test blood and urine.

Home testing is not designed to replace professional medical care; however, it can help you determine when you need professional care. When used properly, home medical tests enable you to determine, monitor, and screen for various illnesses and conditions—and, armed with that information, get the most out of your partnership with your health-care provider. In some cases, you may be asked to take the identical test—this time, administered by a medical professional—to allow for your practitioner to confirm the results. But think of what you have gained by seizing control and self-testing early on—at the very least, time to mull over your options, become better informed, and perhaps even provide the impetus to seek a professional opinion.

Home testing, however, is not foolproof. Like testing that takes place in medical laboratories, the outcome of the test is largely dependent on human factors such as proper testing protocol and timing of the test. With that in mind—especially since *you* are in the driver's seat with home testing—certain precautions are worth noting.

Here are some consumer tips issued by the Food and Drug Administration. Keep these suggestions in mind when using all self-care test products.

• Before you buy, note the expiration date for kits that contain chemicals. Don't buy a test if the expiration date is past.

• Follow storage instructions. Keep containers tightly capped. Avoid moisture, light, and extremes of heat and cold. Keep out of reach of children.

• Read and study the package insert. Make sure you understand the test and how to use it. Follow instructions exactly. Do not skip steps. If the test is timed, use a clock or a watch to be precise.

• Note special precautions such as avoiding certain foods, drugs, or vitamins before testing. Take the test at the recommended time, if any is specified.

• Some tests use colors to indicate results. If you are color-blind, have someone who can discern color help you interpret test results.

• Some tests require collecting urine. Always collect urine in a clean, dry container. Soap or other residue can cause faulty test results.

• Know what to do if test results are positive, negative, or unclear.

• If you have questions about a test, consult a pharmacist or other health-care professional. Also check the package insert for a telephone number you can call.

As you will see, a large range of tests for a number of conditions is available to you—some simpler and easier to conduct and compute than others. Some of these tests require special equipment, while others do not. We'll describe the test, tell you how it's conducted, and suggest where it might be available. Let's get started.

Blood Pressure Monitoring

High blood pressure is called the silent killer because unlike other diseases it often remains hidden. You don't get a rash or a sore spot, so you may have it but not know it. However, you can learn to monitor your blood pressure—and should do so regularly. Discuss this routine with your practitioner.

The standard apparatus used to measure blood pressure is the sphygmomanometer (pronounced sfig-mo-muh-NOM-ih-tur), better known as a blood pressure cuff. The way it works is this: A wide band, or cuff, is wrapped around your upper arm. The cuff is then inflated by air pressure. At the same time, the air pressure pushes a column of liquid mercury (*Hg* is the chemical abbreviation for mercury) up along a numbered scale measured in millimeters (usually abbreviated as *mm*).

It's difficult to say whether you will be able to manage any of the following devices on your own, without a friend's or family member's help. All are designed for use by one person, but then again, not everyone is physically capable of such. Our best advice is to experiment.

Before we discuss the devices, let's review some critical terms. *Blood pressure* is the force of your blood's trip from your heart to and through the rest of your arterial and vascular system. When your heart beats—when that portion of your heart called the left ventricle contracts—oxygenated blood is literally shot into your arteries. *Systolic* is the measurement of blood pressure when the left ventricle contracts and the blood's force against the vessel walls is at its greatest strength.

Diastolic is the measurement of blood pressure when the heart is in its resting or relaxation phase, just before the next heartbeat.

How to Use

Now to the devices themselves. With the standard sphygmomanometer, you place a stethoscope against your brachial artery (the artery running down the length of the arm), at the crook of your arm. When the cuff has been inflated enough to cut off circulation to the lower part of the brachial artery, you will hear no sound. As you slowly release the pressure, the cuff loosens, the blood begins to flow again into the lower artery, and the column of mercury falls. At the point when the stethoscope can pick up the tapping of the heartbeat in the artery, the millimeter level of mercury indicates a figure approximately equal to the systolic pressure. (That's the first, or higher, number in a blood pressure reading.) Soon, as the pressure in the cuff is further released, the beating sound disappears. The number on the millimeter scale at that point is approximately that of your diastolic pressure (the second, or lower, number in a blood pressure reading).

So if your blood pressure is 120/80, or 120 mm Hg/80 mm Hg, or 120 over 80, your systolic pressure was detected and measured when the column of mercury was at a height of 120 millimeters, and your diastolic pressure was detected and measured when the column of mercury was at a height of 80 millimeters.

There are a great variety of blood pressure measuring devices for self-testing. Here are the different types:

• Devices that use mercury that rises and falls within a glass tube and require a stethoscope to listen for the pulse sounds. This is the most accurate and durable type of blood pressure monitor, but it's also the most complicated to use. For example, some people have difficulty pumping the cuff tight enough and, as a result, get blood pressure readings that are too low.

• Aneroid devices that convert mm Hg into figures on a gauge or circular dial face (similar to a thermometer). Some of these require a stethoscope, but others use a built-in microphone instead.

• Digital devices that directly display the diastolic and systolic pressures.

• Automatic devices that inflate the cuff to the proper level and then release the air at the proper time. These provide a digital display of your blood pressure and sometimes your pulse rate. Some of these even produce a printed readout of your blood pressure and pulse. These devices are the easiest to use because they do the pumping for you. However, automatic devices are more expensive than manual sphygmomanometers.

• Devices that measure blood pressure via cuffs wrapped around a finger or a wrist. Often these inflate automatically.

• Devices that fit over a finger. While this sounds like the most convenient, it may also be the least accurate. One study found that finger monitors produced blood pressure measurements that fell within 4 mm Hg of traditional sphygmomanometer readings in less than 25 percent of cases.

One final note: If you're like most people, there's a good chance that your drugstore or supermarket has a blood pressure monitoring booth. Thanks to the relative ease and adaptability of blood pressure monitoring, self-testing booths have proliferated nationwide.

Typically, you place your arm in a device that at the press of a button automatically inflates and calculates your blood pressure readings as the cuff deflates. Then the readings are posted digitally—all for a small fee, usually a quarter.

Accuracy

How accurate are these and should you place your trust in these readings? Some studies have found that the blood-pressure-cuff computers found in many stores are incorrect more than sixty percent of the time, compared with readings taken with a sphygmomanometer. Clearly, the wise consumer will not rely solely on one reading in determining whether he or she has—or doesn't have—high blood pressure.

Availability

Blood pressure home monitoring kits are available at most pharmacies, health and beauty stores, and through mail-order companies.

Warning

Before buying any blood pressure home test, try it out in the pharmacy to make sure you can use it easily and properly. You should also try out two or three of the same model, as well as a few different

brands, to see whether the readings are nearly identical. After you buy a device, it is also a good idea to take your sphygmomanometer to your practitioner's office and compare the readings of the two devices.

Blood Pressure: What's Normal?

Category*	Systolic BP(mm Hg)	Diastolic BP(mm Hg)
Optimal	< 120	< 80
Normal	120–129	80–84
High normal	130–139	85–89
Hypertension		
Stage 1	140–159	90–99
Stage 2	160–179	100–109
Stage 3	180–209	110–119
Stage 4	210	120

* Based on an average of two or more readings on two or more occasions in individuals not taking antihypertensive medications and not acutely ill. When average falls in different categories of systolic and diastolic blood pressure, the higher category applies. Table based on recommendations of the Fifth Joint National Committee on Detection, Evaluation and Treatment of High Blood Pressure, National Heart, Lung and Blood Institute, National Institutes of Health.

Blood Glucose Monitoring

If you have diabetes, naturally you have the most pressing need for blood glucose monitoring, which tracks the level of glucose in the blood. Diabetes is characterized by an abnormally high and persistent concentration of glucose, or sugar, in the bloodstream. (Glucose, a simple sugar found in certain foods, is the product of carbohydrate metabolism—indeed, diabetes is often called a metabolic disorder. Glucose is the chief source of energy in living organisms.) Home glucose monitoring enables you to take control of your life and take precautions against secondary illnesses, such as kidney disease, blindness, nerve damage, and heart disease.

However, even if you do not have diabetes, you may want to consider home blood glucose monitoring. That's especially true if there's any evidence of diabetes in your family.

The glucose monitors of today are very sophisticated and quite accurate, a far cry from the early chemical dipsticks that many diabetic people used.

Blood Glucose: What's Normal?

Blood glucose, or blood sugar, levels vary during the course of the day. In normal adults, blood glucose levels range from 60 to 100 milligrams per deciliter (designated mg/dl) of blood plasma when a person is fasting. By fasting, the medical profession means that the person hasn't eaten for three or more hours (before breakfast, for example). Blood glucose numbers are slightly higher for children.

When fasting blood sugar is between 115 and 140 mg/dl, doctors become mildly concerned. If your doctor runs multiple fasting tests on your blood and the results are over 140 mg/dl, you are considered to have diabetes. In short, your blood sugar levels are too high.

How to Use

Two popular methods for monitoring glucose are reagent pads and glucose meters. In either case, you begin by pricking your finger with a lancet. Then you place a drop of blood either on a test strip or on a specially treated sensor pad on a glucose meter (a device about the size of a hand calculator). Some test strips change color depending upon the amount of glucose in the blood, and you compare the color to a master chart. Other strips are inserted into the glucose meter, which indicates just how many milligrams of glucose are present in a deciliter of blood. The reading appears on the meter's digital display panel in numbers. The whole test is done within forty-five seconds to two minutes.

There's an even more sophisticated—and expensive—version of the glucose meter with 250-test memory and automatic fourteen-day and 30-day test averages. It can "flag" test results with activities that affect blood glucose levels, such as meals and exercise, and record insulin types and dosages to keep track of medication adjustments.

If you have diabetes and use insulin, you use blood glucose monitoring to determine how much insulin to take, so you may average four checks a day—before each meal and late in the evening. Some people also like to take an occasional reading after a meal because that's the time when blood sugar shoots up, and the test can help them gauge how high sugar goes after eating.

Accuracy

No reliable information or statistics on accuracy are available.

Availability

Both types of blood glucose monitors are sold in pharmacies.

Bowel Cancer Test

While colorectal cancer is a common fatal cancer for both men and women, if detected early it is highly treatable. (Colorectal cancer, or cancer of the large intestine, is marked by dark, sticky stools containing blood, and a change in bowel habits.) The home screening test is designed to detect the presence of occult (hidden and in small quantities) blood in the stool, caused by bleeding from cancerous lesions.

The American Cancer Society has recommended that people age fifty and older should have a fecal occult blood test performed each year. High-risk groups—individuals with a family history of cancer, for example—should begin testing sooner. According to the American Gastroenterological Association guidelines—which are endorsed by the American Cancer Society and other medical groups—taking this simple test every year after age fifty could cut colorectal cancer deaths by one-third.

The guidelines do offer options, however, including testing once every ten years via an endoscopic examination (in which a fiberoptic tube is snaked into the colon). This test looks for precancerous growths that could be removed to help prevent cancer from ever forming. In contrast, the simpler stool test detects cancer early enough to cure.

How to Use

The fecal occult blood test available for home use is known as the bowl test. It does not require handling the stool, only dropping a test pad in the toilet after a bowel movement. If occult blood is present, the hemoglobin oxidizes the reagent in the layers of the test pad to produce a noticeable color change.

Because cancerous lesions may bleed intermittently, they may fail to be detected with a single test. Test kits contain material to test three consecutive bowel movements.

Accuracy

The reagents may be affected by toilet bowl cleaners, deodorants, and disinfectants. Accordingly, you should remove any cleaner from the tank, flush three times before testing, and refrain from throwing toilet paper into the bowl before the test is complete.

The reagents in some of the tests may also be affected by dietary sources of peroxidase or hemoglobin, such as red meats, broccoli, horseradish, turnips, cucumbers, grapefruit, and cauliflower. These foods should be avoided for at least two days before and during the testing period for fecal occult blood. Use of rectal ointments and medications should also be avoided during the same period.

False-positive results may occur if you have recently taken medications such as aspirin, potassium products, and products with iron, all of which can irritate the gastrointestinal tract and cause bleeding. (A false-positive result indicates that a disease or condition is present when in fact no disease is actually present.) To prevent this, avoid these medications for at least two to three days before performing the first test and during the testing period.

Availability

Home screening tests for colorectal cancer are available from pharmacies, health and beauty stores, and through mail-order companies.

Warning

It is important to note that a positive result does not indicate the presence of cancer, only the presence of blood within the gastrointestinal (GI) tract. Blood found on the surface of the stool is most likely from a source in the lower gastrointestinal tract, while blood found within the stool is mostly likely from the upper GI tract, such as a bleeding peptic ulcer.

Do not perform the test if you are menstruating, constipated, or have bleeding hemorrhoids.

Cholesterol Test

Cholesterol is a white, waxy substance found naturally throughout the body, including the blood, and is essential for good health. Like any wax or fat, cholesterol does not dissolve in water. So in the blood, cholesterol is carried around in an envelope of protein. This cholesterol-protein package, called a lipoprotein, stays soluble in the watery serum portion of the blood.

That's why when doctors measure cholesterol, they often do it in two ways: First, they measure total cholesterol—all the cholesterol in your blood. Then they measure each of the different lipoproteins in your blood that, together, make up your total cholesterol: High-density lipoproteins (HDL) are the so-called good cholesterol that help to escort cholesterol from the body. High levels are linked with *reduced* risk for heart disease. Low-density lipoproteins (LDL) are the so-called bad cholesterol. (Actually, LDL cholesterol is measured indirectly, by subtracting other components from your total cholesterol.) High levels of LDL have been linked with *increased* risk for heart disease.

Triglycerides are other fatty compounds found in the blood. High triglyceride levels frequently go hand in hand with low levels of HDL, the good cholesterol, and one important study found that people with high blood triglyceride levels alone—no other risk factors—had about a 50 percent increased risk for coronary-artery disease, compared with people with normal levels. All of these amounts are measured as milligrams per deciliter (mg/dl).

In short, high levels of cholesterol may put you at increased risk for heart disease or stroke.

Of course, the big question is who should be tested? According to the National Cholesterol Education Program (NCEP), a group that includes medical organizations such as the American Medical Association and the American College of Cardiology, anyone age twenty or older should have his or her total cholesterol and HDL cholesterol measured at least once every five years.

Pediatricians don't normally check a child's cholesterol until at least age two. After that age, NCEP recommends testing only in children with a family history of premature heart disease (heart attack before age fifty-five) or other apparent risk factors, such as severe obesity.

Guidelines vary about when you should have your cholesterol rechecked. It depends on your levels of different lipoproteins, the number of risk factors you have for heart disease, and how aggressively you're trying to lower your cholesterol.

How to Use

Cholesterol levels can be monitored with a simple apparatus that takes the drop of blood you get when you prick your finger, separates it into its components, reads it, and displays the total cholesterol level. The apparatus is basically the same test widely used by doctors and provides results within fifteen minutes—although be prepared: Your medical practitioner may wish to retest under what he or she considers more "controlled" circumstances.

High Cholesterol: What's Normal?

The National Cholesterol Education Program Cholesterol Classification Guidelines for adults are:

Total Cholesterol*

Desirable:	Less than 200 mg/dl
Borderline high:	200–239 mg/dl
High:	240 mg/dl or higher

HDL Cholesterol

Desirable:	50–75 mg/dl or higher
Borderline low:	35–49 mg/dl
Low:	Less than 35 mg/dl

LDL Cholesterol

Desirable:	Less than 130 mg/dl
Borderline high:	130–159 mg/dl
High:	160 mg/dl or higher

Triglycerides

Safe:	200 mg/dl or less
Borderline:	200–400 mg/dl
High:	400–1,000 mg/dl
Very high:	1,000 mg/dl or above

* At this time, results of self-testing of cholesterol are confined to total cholesterol (the sum of HDL and LDL cholesterol levels) and do not differentiate between HDL and LDL cholesterol levels. (The manufacturer, ChemTrak, Inc., of Sunnyvale, California, is researching the possibility of producing a home test that would screen for HDL.) The palm-sized cassette-type, called Choles-Trak is highly accurate, according to its manufacturer. But many experts maintain that a test's accuracy is difficult to determine reliably.

Accuracy

As a matter of fact, the best advice of experts is not to rely on any one test, including home testing, as your only source of information about your cholesterol. Any one cholesterol reading is never final because cholesterol can change from day to day and in response to several factors, such as weight loss, illness, or stress. For best results, it is recommended that you establish a baseline cholesterol reading by repeating the test several times. Talk with your medical practitioner about this.

Availability

You can purchase Choles-Trak (see box) through your pharmacist or call the manufacturer's help line at 800-927-7776.

Dental Plaque Test

Dental plaque, a major cause of tooth decay and gum disease, is a thin film on teeth made up of material found in saliva and often filled with bacteria. The best way to get rid of plaque is through proper daily brushing and flossing of the teeth. However, since plaque is virtually invisible, you need help in finding it. Such help comes in the form of special plaque-disclosing tablets, such as Red-Kote or X-pose.

How to Use

After your regular brushing and flossing, chew one of the tablets; make sure you thoroughly mix it with your saliva. As the tablet dissolves, it leaves behind a red stain that adheres to the plaque. You may need a small light and dental mirror to complete your examination. The darkest areas are those with the most plaque and other debris.

Regular use of plaque-disclosing tablets will help you in your battle against tooth decay and gum disease.

Accuracy

No reliable information or statistics on accuracy are available.

Availability

Dental disclosing tablets and other dental self-care tools are available from dentists and pharmacies.

Ear Examination

Young children often have more than their share of earaches and other ear problems and often seem to have the problems when the doctor is out, typically in the middle of the night or on the weekend. In many instances, parents can diagnose the problem and monitor the general health of the ear canal and the eardrum with an otoscope (see page 190), a handheld lighted instrument with a magnifying lens and a viewing cone.

Let's first take a look at ear infections, though: Infections can be caused by a variety of bacteria and viruses—from staphylococcus to herpes. These organisms, which make their way into the ear from outside or inside the body, settle in areas where the environment is conducive to their growth.

Infections can occur anywhere throughout the ear and are usually referred to according to their location. However, when people talk about ear infections, particularly children's ear infections, they're usually referring to bacterial infections of the middle ear, called *otitis media*. Otitis media is the most common cause of conductive hearing loss and the most common cause of temporary hearing loss in young children.

Anything that causes the eustachian tube to swell or be blocked, so that it provides inadequate ventilation into the middle ear, can cause an infection. And allergies and colds and other upper-respiratory infections can travel into the ears via the eustachian tubes.

The pain associated with middle-ear infections is caused either by infected fluid in the middle ear pressing against the eardrum or by negative air pressure in the middle ear causing the eardrum to be sucked into the middle ear as if by a vacuum.

How to Use

As medical equipment goes, the otoscope is relatively simple. To use it properly, however, you'll need to learn to identify the basic structure of the ear and eardrum, as well as the symptoms of ear infections. This includes identifying the normal color and shape of the eardrum, the location of the bones of the middle ear, and the signs of pressure behind the eardrum. (A bulging eardrum will cause earache.) Work with your child's health-care practitioner in this learning process.

Of course, if the problem is a middle-ear infection, you'll still need to get a prescription for an antibiotic.

Availability

Otoscopes can be purchased at most pharmacies and through mail-order companies.

HIV/AIDS Test

The newest group of home tests is for human immunodeficiency virus (HIV), which causes AIDS (acquired immune deficiency syndrome). After a decade of being rebuffed by the Food and Drug Administration, HIV/AIDS home tests became available in mid-1996. They are Confide, marketed by Direct Access Diagnostics (a division of Johnson & Johnson), and Home Access Express and Home Access, both marketed by Home Access Health Corporation. Persuaded by intensive lobbying by manufacturers and mounting evidence, the FDA reversed its earlier position. The FDA now says that the tests' benefits outweigh the risks.

How to Use

None of the tests is true home testing because they require the use of a laboratory run by the company. Here's how they work: You use a lancet in the kit to prick your finger and place a few drops of blood on a test card with an identification number. You mail the card to the laboratory for HIV testing. To get results, call a week later and punch your identification number into the phone.

If your test results are positive or inconclusive, you will be connected to a counselor who will explain the results, urge medical treatment, and, if necessary, make a referral to a local doctor or health clinic. If your results are negative, you will be connected to a recording that advises you of that fact, although it also cautions that it's possible to be infected with HIV and still test negative, if the antibodies to HIV haven't yet developed. A counselor will be available for anyone who tests negative and wants to discuss results.

Confide and Home Access offer results in seven business days. With Home Access Express, which costs $10 more, results are available in three business days. While the tests may cost more than a visit to a clinic, secrecy outweighs prices for many people.

The main difference between the two tests is that with the Home Access kits, there's the opportunity for counseling before the test. Individuals who buy one of the kits can call a toll-free number, respond to a series of questions to determine their risk of HIV infection, and listen to educational messages about transmission and testing. (The Confide kit does include pretest counseling and informational material.) Callers can also speak with a professional counselor at any time during the call.

However, neither test offers face-to-face counseling. For that reason, the tests have been criticized by some AIDS activists, who believe that such emotional and medical support is important at the time of diagnosis.

Accuracy

The FDA says the kits are as reliable as tests conducted in doctors' offices and clinics.

Availability

Both tests are sold in pharmacies and other national retail outlets, and may also be available at public health clinics and on some college campuses. You can also purchase the tests by phone. To order Confide, call 800-THE-TEST. To order the Home Access kits, call 800-HIV-TEST.

Lung Function Testing

The amount of air you can take into your lungs with a deep breath and how quickly you can expel it can be important in evaluating different kinds of breathing problems. Home testing may be particularly useful if you have chronic lung diseases, such as asthma, emphysema, or chronic bronchitis. Two home testing devices allow you to test your lung function: a peak flow meter and a spirometer.

How to Use

The peak flow meter measures your peak expiratory flow rate, or the maximum amount of air you are capable of exhaling. Take a deep breath and blow into the mouthpiece of the peak flow meter, which registers in liters the volume of air leaving your lungs. Repeat this test three times to establish a baseline. If the volume of air you exhale decreases over time, that could indicate a potential problem and should be closely monitored.

The spirometer measures the amount of air entering and leaving your lungs. There are three tests you can perform with a spirometer:

1. Forced Vital Capacity (FVC). Take a deep breath and blow into the mouthpiece of the spirometer as long and hard and fast as you can. This measures how much air you can expel from your lungs after a deep breath.

2. Forced Expiratory Volume (FEV) in one second. Some spirometers will also calculate your forced expiratory volume in one second. This is a measure of how much of your normal lung capacity you can expel in one second. If your measure is less than 75 percent, it could indicate the need for further testing.

3. Maximum Voluntary Ventilation (MVV). The purpose of this test is to measure the maximum volume of air that you can inhale and exhale in one minute. For this test, you need a spirometer and the FVC reading from your earlier test. Holding the spirometer in your hand, inhale and exhale as fast as you can for fifteen seconds. Note the reading on the spirometer and multiply it by four. That gives you your MVV for one minute. You should repeat this process at least three times in order to determine your average MVV.

The amount of air you are able to inhale and exhale depends on your age, body size, lung capacity, and general state of health. Your MVV should be about fifteen to twenty times greater than your FVC reading. If your MVV falls short of this range, it could indicate that you need a complete pulmonary workup.

Availability

Peak flow monitors and spirometers may be purchased at pharmacies and through mail-order companies.

Ovulation Prediction Test

Ovulation testing enables women to track their periods of maximum fertility and use that information to control their reproductive activities (whether it's to conceive or not to conceive). One of the principal methods to determine the time of ovulation is to take basal body temperature (see page 202), which rises at ovulation and stays up until menstruation. In addition, a home testing kit measures the sudden monthly surge in luteinizing hormone (LH), which peaks shortly before ovulation—when an egg is released from the ovary—and is excreted in the urine.

Small amounts of LH are present during most of the menstrual cycle, but the level of LH normally rises sharply about twenty-four to thirty-six hours before ovulation. The LH surge can usually be detected in the urine eight to twelve hours after it occurs in the blood. Sperm can fertilize an egg for many hours after sexual intercourse. So if sexual intercourse occurs during the two to three days after the test indicates an LH surge, the chances of becoming pregnant are maximized.

How to Use

All ovulation tests use dipsticks that are treated with monoclonal antibodies specific for LH, as well as with a chemical to elicit a color change proportional to the level of LH in the urine. (Dipsticks are specially treated papers or coated sticks that contain chemicals that react to the various components of urine.)

Accuracy

Commonly used nonprescription drug products should not interfere with the results. However, medications used to promote ovulation, such as menotropins (brand name: Pergonal), may interfere and give a false-positive result because LH levels are artificially elevated. (In this context, a false-positive result indicates that you are ovulating when in fact you are not.) Medical conditions associated with high levels of LH, such as menopause and polycystic ovary syndrome, may also cause false-positive results. A false-positive result may also be obtained if the test user is already pregnant.

There is some variation among the kits. Some require first morning urine, in which LH is most highly concentrated, while other tests accept a sample taken at any time during the day (as long as it's at the same time each day). Some allow for five days of testing, some for as much as ten days. Theoretically, the earlier testing begins in a cycle and the more consecutive days tested, the greater the likelihood of predicting ovulation. However, the shorter range is generally sufficient for women who have a reasonable idea of the approximate time of the month that they ovulate.

Ovulation testing is predicated on a reasonably normal menstrual cycle. If your time between menstrual periods fluctuates considerably or if ovulation is delayed because you have recently discontinued using oral contraceptives, the test may not be a satisfactory guide to ovulation.

Availability

Home tests for ovulation are available in most pharmacies, health and beauty stores, and even some supermarkets.

Pregnancy Test

Within days of conception, a fertilized egg implants in the wall of the uterus and tissue starts to develop between the egg and the uterine lining. This newly formed tissue begins to secrete a hormone, human chorionic gonadotropin (HCG), into the bloodstream, with some excreted in the urine. Like ovulation testing, pregnancy testing is also hormonally based. It looks for this hormone, HCG, in urine.

How to Use

Pregnancy tests use an immunoassay to produce a color change to indicate a positive result in urine. (An immunoassay is a method for determining the quantity of chemical substances that utilizes highly specific binding between an antigen and antibodies.) If HCG is present in the urine, it is trapped in the antibody, and a color change or line shows up on a specially treated dipstick. (Dipsticks are specially treated papers or coated sticks that contain chemicals that react to the various components of urine.)

Accuracy

In general, the test is highly reliable and easy to use. One of the main reasons for a false-negative result is if the test is performed too soon after conception. (In this context, a false-negative result indicates that you are not pregnant when in fact you are.) While some HCG is produced as early as seven days after conception, the hormone reaches its maximum level at six weeks after conception. Pregnancy tests typically detect HCG in urine as early as the first day of a missed menstrual period.

Certain drugs that contain HCG or that are used in combination with HCG (such as Pregnyl, Profasi, and Pergonal, which are taken in cases of infertility to stimulate ovulation) and rare medical conditions may give a false-positive result. The test may also give a false-positive result if the woman has recently had a miscarriage or given birth. This is because the test may detect HCG still in her system from the previous pregnancy.

If a second test still gives a negative result and the woman has not menstruated, she should see her health-care practitioner.

Availability

Pregnancy tests are available in most pharmacies, health and beauty stores, and supermarkets.

Thermometers

Monitoring the body's temperature is probably the easiest home test there is, and one you've most likely done hundreds of times.

How to Use

The most common types of thermometers are the following:

Glass bulbs

The most popular type of thermometer, generally known as a fever thermometer, these are found in virtually every home. They are usually filled with mercury or some other chemical that expands quickly in the presence of heat. The mercury-filled thermometer appears to have a silver streak in the center, while the other chemicals usually appear red.

There are several types of glass bulb thermometers:

• *Oral.* This is the basic thermometer. Because the bulbs on oral thermometers are more fragile, they should not be used in the rectal method. Oral temperature can be affected by hot and cold foods, routine breathing, and smoking. Most experts agree that the thermometer must be left in the mouth, under the tongue and enclosed tightly by the lips, for a full three minutes. They believe that if left in for only two minutes, there is a one in three chance that the temperature reading will be in error by at least half a degree.

Oral thermometers can also be placed under the armpit with the arm pressed against the body for a full five minutes before reading. This is called the axillary method. The axillary temperature is typically 0.5° to 1° lower than the oral temperature. Axillary temperature measurements are the least accurate. Because the glass is more fragile, oral thermometers should not be used in the axillary method for children or convulsing adults.

• *Rectal.* This is generally intended for infants and very young children who are too young to tolerate holding a thermometer in their mouths or under their arms. The rectum is considered the most accurate location to measure internal body temperature. The normal rectal temperature is typically 0.5° to 1° higher than the oral temperature. A rectal thermometer has a shorter, rounder bulb to fa-

cilitate entry into the rectum, and because it is in close contact with the rectum, the mercury will rise within seconds.

Though rectal thermometers are less likely to break than oral thermometers when used in the axillary method, use caution, particularly with children and convulsing adults. The thermometer should be placed under the armpit with the arm pressed against the body for a full five minutes before reading. The axillary temperature is typically 0.5° to 1° lower than the oral temperature. Axillary temperature measurements are the least accurate.

• *Basal.* This thermometer is used by women who are monitoring their daily basal body temperature as a way of predicting their ovulation, as a means either of birth control or of improving their chances of conceiving. (Basal body temperature is the lowest temperature of a normal healthy person during waking hours.) The woman takes her temperature immediately upon waking—before rising, eating, and so on. The thermometer remains inserted for a set period—usually around four minutes—and always in the same place for measurement each time (either in the mouth, the rectum, or the vagina).

The basal body temperature is usually below normal during the first part of the female reproductive cycle; after ovulation, it rises to a level closer to the norm. While an ordinary glass bulb or electronic thermometer may be used instead, these special thermometers are easier to read; they are specially marked in tenths of degrees and thus offer a shorter temperature range. Sometimes they are sold with graph paper for recording daily readings. Experts generally agree that records kept over a period of six to eight months usually give a good indication of the pattern of ovulation.

Electronic, or digital, thermometer

A heat-sensitive metal tip is placed in the mouth (or rectum or under the arm) and a computer chip electronically reads and displays the temperature in digital form. An electronic thermometer beeps when the temperature reaches the maximum point and shuts off automatically to save batteries. To keep it as clean as possible, disposable probe covers may be purchased for use with this thermometer. The main advantage is speed: Electronic thermometers can give a readout in fifteen seconds. This is probably the most expensive type of thermometer, and it is used primarily in doctors' offices. There are also more affordable plastic thermometers that give digital readouts, although they may take sixty seconds to produce a reading. While these thermometers are easier to read than the ordinary glass-bulb variety, they are no more accurate.

Aural thermometer

Placed at the opening of the ear, this reads body temperature from the eardrum within seconds. According to manufacturers, this thermometer, if used properly, is 97 percent accurate and directly comparable to an oral reading.

Plastic strip thermometer

A plastic strip is placed against the forehead to read the temperature. Some of these temperature strips may be left on the forehead to continually monitor the presence of a fever. These strips may display the temperature or change color to indicate a fever. They are inexpensive, retailing for about $2. However, the color strips aren't particularly sensitive, mostly indicating changes of a couple of degrees. There are also mouth strips, which are more reliable.

Warning

When using plastic fever strips or other skin-surface types of thermometer, be sure that no lamp or even direct sunlight shines on the thermometer's surface, as it will elevate the reading.

Infant pacifier with temperature indicator

This changes color when the baby's temperature rises. It has three temperature levels—slight, moderate, and high—as well as normal. If you suspect your child has a fever, allow him or her to use a fever pacifier for about five minutes. To determine actual temperature, however, use a more precise thermometer.

Availability

Pharmacies, health and beauty stores, and supermarkets carry thermometers.

Body Temperature: What's Normal?

You may be surprised to learn that researchers are revising the common wisdom about what constitutes so-called normal body temperature.

The 98.6°F (37°C) is a standard that was based on a German study of more than 1 million people in 1868. According to a study published in the *Journal of the American Medical Association* in 1992, in which today's more accurate thermometers were used, 98.9° overall should now be regarded as the upper limit of the normal oral range in healthy adults age 40 and younger.

However, healthy body temperatures vary from person to person, from season to season, and from hour to hour. (Temperature, for instance, tends to be lower in the morning and higher toward evening and also tends to rise by a degree or more if you exercise on a hot day.) "Normal" body temperature can range from 96.5°F to 99.0°F or higher.

Urine Testing

Simple-to-use home urinalysis products make it easy to test for the presence of urinary tract infections (UTIs), diseases that affect the kidneys, ureters, bladder, and urethra, and which, left untreated, can lead to serious kidney disease. Urine can also be tested for the presence of glucose or ketones (composed primarily of two different acids and acetone), which may indicate diabetes; however, the blood glucose test is far more reliable.

How to Use

Clinical urinalysis is performed with dipsticks, specially treated papers, or coated sticks that contain chemicals that react to the various components of urine. There are multiple-test dipsticks that make it possible to perform a series of tests with one urine sample.

Some multiple-test dipsticks include the tests for two common UTIs (and can also be used to monitor the effectiveness of antibiotic therapy for UTIs):

Leukocytes

A leukocyte is a white blood cell. An increase in white blood cells indicates that the body is fighting an infection, so an increase in leukocytes in the urine usually indicates an infection somewhere in the urinary tract.

Nitrite

A certain type of bacteria converts the nitrates in our diet to nitrites. If nitrites are in the urine, then an infection may also be present. Because not all types of bacteria affect urine in the same way, this test is not definitive. However, if a UTI is suspected, the test can help provide confirmation.

Availability

Urine dipstick tests are available from pharmacies and through mail-order companies.

Vitamins and Minerals

Vitamin and mineral supplementation is big business, as is evident from the well-stocked shelves of drugstores, grocery stores, and discount stores. In 1995, annual sales of vitamin and mineral supplements in the United States amounted to approximately $4 billion, and, according to the journal *Drug Topics* (October 21, 1996), drugstores' share of such sales amounted to slightly more than $1 billion. Although it is true that in recent years vitamin sales have been growing faster in food stores and other mass merchandisers than in drugstores, vitamins rank number three in dollar sales among all the categories of products sold by drugstores, according to the trade journal.

A note of caution, though: While vitamin and mineral supplements can help a person obtain adequate or optimum amounts of important nutrients, there can be too much of a good thing. Some vitamins and minerals can be dangerous in doses that exceed the recommended dietary allowance, or RDA (see page 209). Fat-soluble vitamins tend to stay in the body longer than water-soluble vitamins, so they can build up to unhealthy or toxic levels more easily. (We talk more about this later.) Be alert to the levels at which a vitamin or mineral becomes toxic (see "possible toxicity problems" discussed with every vitamin and mineral).

Do You Need Special Formulations?

Not only do over-the-counter vitamin supplements come in various forms (tablet, capsule, gelcap, powder, sublingual, lozenge, and liquid), combinations, and amounts, but they are also formulated for what advertisers call "special needs." For men. For women. For pregnant women. For post-menopausal women. For older people. For dieters. For the stressed-out. You name it. So the question is, should you select one such special formulation?

The quick answer is that, without a doubt, vitamin supplements are almost routinely prescribed and indicated for certain subgroups—pregnant women being the most obvious. It is also true, however, that pregnant women should not take any supplement without discussing the matter with their practitioners. The same holds true in the case of supplementation for children and infants. Many experts, too, have raised red flags about the creative and flavorful way that children's vitamins are often formulated—their argument being that the supplements' candylike appearance (and taste) is too attractive and holds great potential for overuse.

Thanks to these special formulations, the selection process is simpler, yet most experts agree that the formulations are not necessarily the way to go. They do not take the place of a well balanced multivitamin and mineral supplement. Indeed, most contain only two or three nutrients, sometimes in high doses. A premenstrual formula, for instance, may offer many times the RDA of vitamin B$_6$, but contain very little of other B vitamins. An osteoporosis formula may contain calcium but not much of other minerals important for bones. And many agree that the stress formulations seldom include nutrients that research shows to be promising in this context—for example, vitamin E, tyrosine, and magnesium.

Among other experts, Dr. Sheldon Saul Hendler, author of *The Doctors' Vitamin and Mineral Encyclopedia* (New York: Simon and Schuster, 1990), believes that nutrient needs are broadly similar for all

Natural Vitamins Versus Synthetic—What's the Difference?

Natural vitamins are derived from foods. Natural vitamin E, for instance, is isolated from soybean oil. Natural beta-carotene can be derived from carrots or algae. Natural vitamin C can be taken from citrus fruits.

Synthetic vitamins, on the other hand, are constructed from organic molecules found in an array of substances, such as petroleum oil and corn oil. Synthetic vitamins, too, are much less expensive to make than natural vitamins.

According to Sheldon Saul Hendler, M.D., Ph.D., a noted authority and author of *The Doctors' Vitamin and Mineral Encyclopedia* (New York: Simon and Schuster, 1990), many of the products touted as natural actually contain only a small amount of key substances derived from natural sources, and "natural" products go through most of the same processing procedures that the synthetic ones do. He sums up his position on the question of natural versus synthetic by saying: "*The fact is, in any event, that natural and synthetic versions of the same substance are necessarily chemically identical.* There is absolutely no reason, therefore, to expect that the action of the two versions will be different in any respect."

Vitamin E, however, is a bit more confusing where this philosophy is concerned. It is true that the synthetic version of vitamin E, dl-alpha tocopherol, is different from the natural form, d-alpha tocopherol. According to the experts, the natural form has slightly more biological activity in the body. What this means is that a person has to take slightly more synthetic vitamin E to match the effects of the natural version.

Finally, minerals are derived only from natural sources—either made from materials mined from the ground or otherwise found in nature. Calcium, for instance, is derived from limestone, oyster, or egg shells or from naturally occurring beds of calcium carbonate. Then there's the matter of *chelated* mineral supplements. What are they, and do such minerals make a difference in the performance of the mineral? Chelation is a process that attaches amino acids to minerals. According to Mary Dan Eades, M.D., in *The Doctor's Complete Guide to Vitamins and Minerals* (New York: Dell, 1994), "Chelation allows for better absorption [into the intestinal lining] without the risk of competition causing deficiencies in other minerals." Chelated minerals also are better tolerated by the body. With chelated minerals, you'll have less stomach upset; furthermore, she says, "The less obvious benefit is that you absorb what you spent your hard-earned dollars to buy, and therefore, get the health benefit you see from taking less of it."

Tangential to the issue of natural versus synthetic is the question of additives—artificial preservatives, dyes, fillers, and other ingredients used to form the tablet, capsule, or whatever. Cornstarch, for example, is often used as a filler or binder, and vanilla as a flavoring agent. And it's not unusual for supplements—whether or not they're labeled "natural"—to include artificial colorings, preservatives, sugar, and starch, just to name a few. Clearly, if you have demonstrated allergies to or intolerances of any such substances, you should stay away from the products that contain them. Aside from that, there is no consensus among experts about whether these additives are especially harmful or beneficial, although many speculate that additives may cause health problems in people taking megadoses—i.e., doses greatly in excess of the amounts usually prescribed or recommended—of supplements containing them.

healthy adults, regardless of age, though he suggests a few nutrient intake changes for postmenopausal women (notably, supplementary calcium, boron, and vitamin K to help in the prevention of osteoporosis). In his book, he outlines various micronutrient formulas designed for people "in different life situations"—ranging from formulas for athletes and pregnant and postmenstrual women to people interested in weight loss, cancer, and cardiovascular protection. Like many others in the field—for example, James F. Balch, M.D., and Phyllis A. Balch in *Prescription for Natural Healing* (Garden City Park, N.Y.: Avery, 1997)—he pegs his prescribed intakes for healthy adults to the high sides of the recommended allowances.

So if you should generally steer away from special formulations—without first carefully reading a product's label to see if it matches your needs—do you resolve yourself to taking a whole handful of vitamin supplements every day? Part of the temptation to buy these special formulations blindly is the desire *not* to depend upon five, six, or more bottles of supplements to meet your needs. But frankly, the answer to the above question varies depending upon whom you ask. Some doctors say that a person who uses a large number of single-nutrient vitamin and mineral supplements is simply wasting her money. Others recommend individual supplements of at least some nutrients, especially minerals (calcium, magnesium, selenium, and chromium, just to name a few), because they might be supplied in a form that people with absorption problems can more readily utilize or because the individual nutrients are available in higher doses than a multiple offers.

Other Issues That You Should Know About

According to experts, you should be concerned about whether the supplements you are buying will dissolve properly and be absorbed. They say that vitamin manufacturers have addressed the problem of dissolvability but still have a ways to go.

One assurance that the vitamins you are buying will dissolve properly is to look for the letters "U.S.P." on the label. This means that the supplement meets manufacturing standards set by the U.S. Pharmacopoeia, an independent, not-for-profit organization that sets standards for strength, quality, purity, packaging, and labeling for medical products used in the United States.

The first standard states that water-soluble vitamins (C and B vitamins) should disintegrate in an environment that stimulates the digestive tract within 30 minutes if they're uncoated or 45 minutes if coated. Timed-release and chewable supplements aren't covered by these standards, and currently there are no dissolvability standards for fat-soluble vitamins.

One helpful hint here about dissolvability and absorption: Usually, you can help your body absorb nutrients in a supplement by taking it at the end of a meal. The digestive juices stimulated by food help the supplement break down and be absorbed. (Some experts disagree with this, however, recommending instead that fat-soluble vitamins be taken before meals and water-soluble vitamins after meals, unless the directions specify otherwise.) Here are other tips for buying and maintaining the highest quality of supplements:

1. Shop prices carefully—expensive is not necessarily better. Some large retailers, such as Wal-Mart and K-mart, sell store brands that are similar in formulation to expensive brand-name vitamins but cost much less.

2. Realize that cost is more than price. You must analyze the price in terms of how many tablets or capsules are in the bottle. Further, weigh the price with the amount of nutrients in each tablet or capsule. Bottles of the same supplement, manufactured by different companies, may be the same size and contain the same number of tablets or capsules, but if the products contain significantly different amounts of nutrients, this is a noteworthy distinction. (See the recommended levels for all vitamins and essential minerals on pages 210–219.)

3. Check labels carefully and be prepared to ask questions. At the very least, this strategy helps assure that you are getting the best for the least amount of money. If the manufacturer's label, for example, claims that the product is more absorbable or better balanced, you may want to contact the manufacturer and ask for research that backs up such marketing claims and any others.

4. Don't be concerned if the labels don't carry expiration dates—such labeling is not required. Of course, if the product includes an expiration date, don't buy beyond the date. And when buying in large quantities, don't buy too close to the expiration date. For these reasons, bargain-table products may not be the best value, as these products may have been on the shelf for too long.

5. Make sure the products do not contain more than you bargain for, such as unwanted additives like yeast and dyes.

6. Check the packaging, especially the seals, both outer and inner. Obviously, you want a product that is tightly capped and sealed to maintain freshness.

7. Buy supplements in containers dark enough to properly shield the contents. (Or transfer the contents into an opaque, preferably glass container.)

8. Keep the lids tightened when the products are not in use, and try to minimize exposure to air (such as when you open the container).

9. Store supplements in cool, dry, dark places—not in the bathroom medicine cabinet (too much moisture) and not in the refrigerator (unless the instructions on the label specifically say to do so). Sunlight and other forms of direct light can decrease the potency of most vitamins.

10. Discard vitamins that have undergone changes in color, taste, smell, and appearance. Minerals, on the other hand, are more stable and can usually be used indefinitely.

What Are Vitamins and Minerals?

Vitamins and minerals are nutrients—food components obtained from our diets—that have been found to be essential in small quantities for human life.

Vitamins are a group of chemically unrelated organic substances. Organic substances are compounds containing the chemical element carbon, and they come only from living materials—plants, animals, or substances that were once living materials, such as petroleum oil or coal. Minerals, on the other hand, are nonorganic compounds. This means that they do not contain carbon and do not

How Many Vitamins Are There?

There are thirteen known vitamins. Four are fat-soluble—A, D, E, and K; and nine are water-soluble—the B vitamins and vitamin C. Fat-soluble vitamins need a bit of fat in the diet to be absorbed, and when supplements of these vitamins are taken, it is best to take them with a meal that contains some fat. Further, fat-soluble vitamins tend to stay in the body longer than most water-soluble vitamins, so some of the fat-soluble vitamins can build up to unhealthy levels more easily than most water-soluble ones can. These toxic levels are likely to be reached only by taking supplements or by eating foods exceptionally rich in particular nutrients.

The B vitamins essential for human health are B_1, or thiamin; B_2, or riboflavin; niacin; B_6; B_{12}, or cobalamin; folic acid; pantothenic acid; and biotin.

Other substances—sometimes called quasi-vitamins—are occasionally considered to be essential vitamins. Their vitamin status, however, has not been established. These substances include choline, bioflavonoids, paraaminobenzoic acid (PABA), and a few others.

Beta-carotene, which has been getting a lot of public attention of late, is a precursor to vitamin A. In other words, it's a substance from which vitamin A can be made. Even though in itself beta-carotene is not considered a vitamin, it does seem to have activity in the body independent of its conversion to vitamin A, and much of the activity seems to revolve around cancer prevention and protection against heart disease. However, early studies—which continue to be debate—have shown that beta-carotene supplementation may be harmful to smokers.

originate from living organisms. Both vitamins and minerals are found in the foods we eat; minerals are also found in the water we drink.

Vitamins and minerals perform countless different functions in the body, and individual vitamins and minerals have special functions. As a group, for instance, almost all vitamins share in certain functions, such as promoting growth, promoting the ability to produce healthy offspring, and maintaining health. They must be present for the body to be able to utilize other essential nutrients, such as minerals, fatty acids, amino acids (compounds that form the chief constituents of protein), and energy sources (for example, carbohydrates and sugar). Without adequate amounts of vitamins and minerals, the body would not function properly.

The Food and Nutrition Board, a committee of nutrition experts at the private, nonprofit National Academy of Sciences, has established Recommended Dietary Allowances (RDAs), levels of intake that on the basis of scientific knowledge are judged to be "adequate to meet the known nutrient needs of practically all healthy persons."

A person who takes in the RDAs of all essential nutrients is expected to receive adequate nourishment. He may not, however, be obtaining the optimum amounts of these nutrients. Newer thinking on the subject holds that RDAs do not account for the amounts needed to maintain maximum health, rather than borderline health. In recent years, studies have found that higher amounts of certain vitamins and minerals not only prevent deficiency diseases (such as scurvy, which is a vitamin C deficiency–related disease) but also help protect against chronic diseases, such as cancer, heart disease, and diabetes. Consequently, more and more experts in the field are speaking in terms of *optimum daily allowances,* or ODAs, which they define as the amounts of nutrients believed to be needed for "vibrant good health," in the words of James F. Balch, M.D., and Phyllis A. Balch.

Vitamin and Mineral Supplements

While it is possible to obtain an adequate amount of every nutrient through food, it's not easy. And it is extremely difficult—if not impossible—to attain optimum amounts of certain nutrients through diet alone. As a result, many people choose to take vitamin and mineral supplements.

There are hundreds of different formulations for multivitamin and mineral supplements, and even single-nutrient supplements, such as vitamins C

How Many Minerals Are There?

Currently, fifteen minerals are considered essential for humans:

calcium	iron	potassium
copper	magnesium	selenium
chlorine	manganese	sodium
chromium	molybdenum	sulfur
iodine	phosphorus	zinc

There are other possibly essential minerals besides the ones mentioned. These are fluorine, tin, boron, vanadium, silicon, nickel, arsenic, cadmium, and lead. But what role, if any, these elements play in human nutrition has yet to be determined. Trace minerals—minerals that we need only in traces, or very small amounts—exist in foods in such small amounts that the equipment and procedures needed to detect them are fairly sophisticated and expensive.

or E, come in a variety of dosages and types. Ideally, before you shop, you should have a pretty good idea of what nutrients you are looking for and in what amounts.

In shopping for the right supplement, it's helpful to be acquainted with the measurement standards for vitamins and minerals. Here are a few facts to keep in mind:

• A milligram (abbreviated mg) is 1/1,000th of a gram; there are 1,000 milligrams in a gram.

• A microgram (abbreviated mcg) is 1/1,000 of a milligram; there are 1,000,000 micrograms in a gram.

• There are 28.35 grams (abbreviated g) in 1 ounce. (This should give you an idea of how small a gram is.)

• An international unit (abbreviated I.U.) is an arbitrary unit of measure that has been used for vitamins A and E.

• A retinol equivalent (abbreviated RE) is a unit of measure used for vitamin A and its various forms.

• A tocopherol equivalent (abbreviated TE) is a unit of measure used for vitamin E and its various forms.

Misconceptions About Supplementation

We are always looking for the magic bullet, the certain cure for whatever ill we have, and playing right along with this natural human motivation are the oft-touted claims that a certain vitamin or mineral can "cure whatever ails you."

Nowhere is this misconception more obvious than with vitamin C, the subject of the first controlled clinical experiment in recorded medical history. A lot of claims have been made regarding this vitamin. And true, vitamin C has a variety of roles, all indispensable to good health (see page 214). Indeed, Nobel Laureate Dr. Linus Pauling, probably the most well-known of *all* proponents of *any* vitamin, spent much of his life and work claiming vitamin C's effectiveness in preventing and alleviating colds and in treating cancer.

Many of the claims, according to most experts, including Hendler, cannot be fully supported by the best available evidence. Not to take *anything* away, however, from the evidence touting the good that vitamin C can do. Studies have found, for instance, that the vitamin can help to prevent—not cure—cancer, boost immunity against colds and other infections (and possibly even shorten the duration of a cold), combat heart disease, speed wound healing, and help prevent bedsores. Vitamin C, according to the best evidence, can be of benefit in managing asthma and does offer some protection against heart disease.

Along these same lines is the mineral zinc. Recent claims have been made concerning its role in preventing and shortening colds and in preventing cancer. While it is true that studies have suggested that one form of zinc, called zinc glutonate, can help to reduce the symptoms of the common cold, more definitive research is needed before such claims can be fully substantiated. In the matter of cancer prevention, even, research findings have been contradictory.

Your best guide, therefore, is caution—in the sense that not every claim, not even every definitive association between a vitamin or a mineral and a health benefit has been firmly established.

Below we list the essential vitamins and minerals, the roles they play in the body, RDAs, signs of deficiency, and signs of toxicity. Keep this list handy as you navigate through the array of vitamin and mineral products that your drug-, grocery-, or health-food store stocks. But remember: The labels on supplements cannot tell you exactly how much to take; instead, they tell you that one tablet (or more, depending upon the nutrient) provides such and such a percentage of the daily requirement. Nobody but you knows what your health status and dietary regimen are, as well as your lifestyle. So go to those shelves armed with this intimate knowledge, as well as information about the role of specific vitamins and minerals and recommended allowances for each.

Vitamins

Vitamin A and Beta-carotene

What it is:
Vitamin A is a clear yellow oil that is fat-soluble; this means that it is absorbed and transported through the body in a manner similar to that of fats. Beta-carotene is a carotenoid, a substance that the body can convert to vitamin A.

What it does:
Vitamin A is required for the maturation of epithelial cells, cells that cover the internal and external surfaces of the body. If these cells fail to mature because of a vitamin A deficiency, an alteration in skin and mucous membranes that resembles a precancerous condition can result. Given the proper conditions, this condition can lead to cancer. Vitamin A deficiency can also lead to night blindness; a lack of normal mucus secretion, including dry eyes and mouth; susceptibility to infection; *xerophthalmia,* an eye condition characterized by swollen lids and sticky discharge from the eyes; and a condition called *follicular hyperkeratosis,* in which the skin feels like coarse sandpaper.

In addition to converting to vitamin A, beta-carotene appears to play some independent roles in the body. Research indicates that beta-carotene may provide some protection against heart disease. Observational studies have also indicated that beta-carotene may provide some protection against cancer. However, other studies indicate that beta-carotene may be harmful to smokers.

RDA:
For men, 5,000 I.U. (1,000 RE); for women, 4,000 I.U. (800 RE)

Signs of deficiency:
Night blindness; dry eyes and mouth; susceptibility to infection; swollen eyelids and sticky discharge from the eyes; coarse, rough skin

Possible toxicity problems:
A single large dose of 250,000 to 300,000 I.U. or smaller amounts of 50,000 I.U. for long periods of time can cause symptoms of toxicity, such as bone and joint pain, hair loss, skin dryness, itching and flaking, weakness, headache, and vision problems.

Vitamin B_6

What it is:
Vitamin B_6 is a water-soluble B-complex vitamin that comes in three chemically related forms; the most common of these forms, pyridoxine, is what is used in vitamin supplements and food fortification.

What it does:
Vitamin B_6 is essential for the release of energy from food, a process known as metabolism. It helps convert the calories we take in as carbohydrates into usable energy. It is required for the proper functioning of more than sixty enzymes and is essential for the body's manufacture of nucleic acid, the genetic building block for all cells. This vitamin plays a role in cell multiplication, including the red blood cells and the cells of the immune system and, as such, may play a role in preventing cancer and fighting infection. It also influences the nervous system through its effects on neurotransmitters, the messengers of the central nervous system, and it has been used to treat a variety of mental symptoms, including depression.

RDA:
For men, 2 mg; for women, 1.6 mg

Signs of deficiency:
Deficiency rarely occurs alone and is most commonly seen in people who are deficient in several B-complex vitamins. Signs of deficiency include weakness; sleeplessness; nerve problems in hands and feet; inflamed lips, tongue, and mouth; and reduced resistance to infection.

Possible toxicity problems:
Taken in large amounts for a long period of time, vitamin B_6 can cause difficulty in walking and a loss of sensation in the feet and hands. Toxicity has been observed, although rarely, with doses of 100 to 200 mg. Most problems, however, have occurred at doses higher than 500 mg a day.

Vitamin B_{12}

What it is:
Vitamin B_{12} is a water-soluble B-complex vitamin. It has the most complex structure of any of the B vitamins and is a bright red color. At its core is a molecule of cobalt, which explains its official name, cobalamin.

What it does:
Vitamin B_{12} is important in manufacturing chemical compounds that support the growth and normal function of nerves and the spinal cord. It is also essential for the normal functioning of all body cells, particularly those of the bone marrow (which produces red blood cells), the nervous system, and the gastrointestinal tract. Vitamin B_{12} is also needed for the body to make nucleic acid, the genetic material found in all cells.

RDA:
For men and women, 2 mcg

Signs of deficiency:
Symmetrical tingling or loss of sensation or weakness in hands or feet, diminished sensitivity to vibration and position sense, difficulty in walking, memory loss, fatigue (often initially without anemia), changes in personality or mood, hallucinations

Possible toxicity problems:
Vitamin B_{12} has no known toxicity. Dietary levels of at least several hundred times the nutritional requirements are considered safe.

Folic Acid (Folate)

What it is:
Folic acid, or folate, is a bright yellow powder that is one of the water-soluble B-complex vitamins.

What it does:
Folic acid is essential for normal growth and reproduction, for the prevention of blood disorders, and for important biomechanical mechanisms within each cell. Folic acid is involved in the synthesis of nucleic acid, the genetic building block for all cells. As a result, deficiencies are associated with neural-tube birth defects, anemia, and increased risks for some types of cancer.

RDA:
For men, 200 mcg; for women, 180 mcg

Signs of deficiency:
Fatigue, loss of appetite, anemia, inflamed tongue, gastrointestinal problems, diarrhea

Possible toxicity problems:
Toxicity is considered rare, and not all studies have produced signs of toxicity, even at very high doses. In one study, doses of 15 grams a day caused gastrointestinal problems and sleep disturbances. Doses of 8 grams or more may cause neurological injury when given to people with undiagnosed pernicious anemia. Folic acid can interfere with the effectiveness of antiseizure drugs. And people taking drugs that interfere with the body's ability to use folic acid—drugs used to treat cancer, arthritis, or other conditions—should take folic acid only with their doctor's approval.

Niacin (B$_3$)

What it is:
Niacin, also known as vitamin B$_3$, is one of the B vitamins. A water-soluble white powder, niacin comes in two forms: nicotinic acid and nicotinamide.

What it does:
Niacin is crucial for the body's manufacture of enzymes that provide the body with energy and the building blocks for cell reproduction and repair. It is known to be involved in more than two hundred enzymatic reactions in the body related to the metabolism of carbohydrates, fats, and proteins. In addition, niacin has been identified as part of the chromium-containing glucose tolerance factor in brewer's yeast, which enhances the body's response to insulin (a hormone that helps transport glucose, or blood sugar, into cells and to store it in the liver and muscles). Niacin has been used to help lower blood cholesterol and triglyceride levels as well as to treat depression, dilate blood vessels, stimulate tooth eruption, increase the flow of gastric juices, and increase intestinal motility (movement). Research shows that it may play a part in protecting the body against cancer.

RDA:
For men, 19 mg; for women, 15 mg

Signs of deficiency:
Irritability; anxiety; depression; sore mouth and tongue; inflamed membranes in the intestinal tract (with bloody diarrhea in the later stages); reddish skin rash, especially on the hands and feet when they are exposed to sunlight, which later makes the skin rough and dark

Possible toxicity problems:
Doses of several hundred milligrams of nicotinic acid can cause flushing of the skin and intense itching. Doses of 1,500 to 3,000 mg can cause jaundice and have the potential to cause liver damage. About one-third of people on high-dose therapy show abnormal results in one or more tests of liver function. In most cases, liver function returns to normal once nicotinic acid is stopped. Severe heartburn, nausea, and vomiting may also occur at high doses.

Thiamin (B$_1$)

What it is:
Thiamin, formerly known as thiamine, is a B-complex vitamin.

What it does:
Thiamin works in the release of energy from food. It helps our bodies convert the calories we take in as carbohydrates into usable energy, through complex chemical reactions that involve oxygen. Thiamin is essential for nearly every cellular reaction in the body—for normal development, growth, reproduction, maximum physi-

cal fitness, and good health. It is needed for normal skin and hair, brain and nerve function, blood production, and normal defense against infections and disease. Thiamin deficiency causes the disease known as *beriberi,* which is characterized by numbness and tingling in the toes and feet, stiffness of the ankles, cramping pains in the legs, difficulty in walking, and finally, paralysis of the legs with wasting of leg muscles. Deficiency can also contribute to heart disease.

RDA:
For men, 1.5 mg; for women, 1.1 mg

Signs of deficiency:
Numbness or tingling in toes and feet, stiffness, cramping pains in the legs, difficulty in walking, digestive problems, lack of appetite, fatigue, depression, irritability

Possible toxicity problems:
Long-term toxicity can produce symptoms of hyperthyroidism (headache, irritability, trembling, rapid pulse, and insomnia). Five milligrams daily is the lowest oral dose known to cause side effects, but most people apparently tolerate much higher amounts with no ill effects. Reports of side effects are rare.

Biotin

What it is:
Biotin is a water-soluble B-complex vitamin that is produced in our intestines as well as obtained from foods.

What it does:
Like other B vitamins, biotin is essential for the body's metabolism of carbohydrates and fats and for making protein. It plays a crucial part in the production of nucleic acid, the substance from which a cell's genetic material is formed.

RDA:
No RDA, but an Estimated Safe and Adequate Daily Dietary Intake of 30 to 100 mcg is recommended for men and women.

Signs of deficiency:
In adults, loss of hair; a scaly red rash around the nose, mouth, and other body orifices; intense depression; hallucinations; sleeplessness; muscle

pain. In infants, signs also include profound development delay and a lack of muscle tone.

Possible toxicity problems:
No evidence of toxicity.

Pantothenic Acid

What it is:
Pantothenic acid is a water-soluble B vitamin that is present in all foods.

What it does:
Pantothenic acid is involved in proper skin growth and nerve function and in maintaining the health of the adrenal glands (the pair of endocrine glands located on top of each kidney that produce a number of different hormones). Pantothenic acid is known to be involved in the production of cortisone and two other related hormones produced by the adrenal glands. These hormones play an important role in metabolism and in the body's reaction to stress, including inflammation. It also plays a vital role in energy metabolism.

RDA:
No RDA, but an Estimated Safe and Adequate Daily Dietary Intake of 4 to 7 mg is recommended for men and women.

Signs of deficiency:
Fatigue, headache, sleep disturbances, personality changes, nausea, abdominal distress, numbness and tingling of the hands and feet, burning sensations in the feet, muscle cramps, impaired coordination, immune problems

Possible toxicity problems:
Most experts consider the risk of toxicity to be extremely low. Dosages considered very large—10 to 20 grams a day—have not produced reactions more severe than mild diarrhea and fluid retention.

Riboflavin (B$_2$)

What it is:
Riboflavin is a yellow-orange, water-soluble B-complex vitamin.

What it does:
Like other B-complex vitamins, riboflavin is needed for the conversion of food to energy. It is carried through the blood to all cells in the body, where it is used to make enzymes important for energy metabolism. Riboflavin-containing compounds are essential for the metabolism of carbohydrates, amino acids, and fats. They are also crucial for the proper development and maintenance of nerves and blood cells, for iron metabolism, for adrenal gland function, for the formation of connective tissues, and for proper immune function. In studies, riboflavin deficiency has been associated with an increase in throat cancers and with the development of cataracts.

RDA:
For men, 1.7 mg; for women, 1.3 mg

Signs of deficiency:
Skin problems, including a greasy, scaly condition on the face; red, swollen, cracked lips, especially at the corners of the mouth; sore, red tongue; loss of appetite; weakness; fatigue; depression; anemia; dimness of vision; burning of the eyes; decreased sensitivity to touch, temperature, vibration, and position in the hands and feet

Possible toxicity problems:
Risk of toxicity is very low. Probably because high doses are not well absorbed, high oral doses of riboflavin are essentially nontoxic.

Vitamin C

What it is:
Vitamin C, or ascorbic acid, is a white powder that dissolves easily in water.

What it does:
Vitamin C is needed for the body to make connective tissue, which is found throughout the body and helps maintain the structure of tissues, including skin, muscles, gums, blood vessels, and bone. Vitamin C also acts as an antioxidant. This means that it helps to neutralize potentially harmful reactions in the body—reactions that can lead to cell damage associated with cancer, heart disease, and an array of other health problems. Studies have found that it can help prevent cancer, boost immunity against colds and other infections, combat heart disease, speed wound healing, and help prevent bedsores. A vitamin C deficiency can lead to scurvy, a disease in which small blood vessels break open, skin and gums redden and bleed, and teeth loosen. Scurvy can lead to general weakness and, ultimately, death.

RDA:
For men and women, 60 mg; for smokers, 100 mg

Signs of deficiency:
Easy bruising, bleeding gums, muscular weakness, swollen or painful joints, nosebleeds, frequent infections, slow healing of wounds

Possible toxicity problems:
Vitamin C is considered quite safe, even in large amounts, since any vitamin C that the body cannot use is eliminated by the body. Doses as low as 500 mg can cause diarrhea in some people, but many people can take much larger doses with no problems. People prone to gout or kidney stones or people with kidney diseases should take large amounts only with medical supervision.

Vitamin D

What it is:
Vitamin D is a fat-soluble vitamin that is unique in two ways: It can be synthesized in the skin from sunlight, and it is the only vitamin whose biologically active form is a hormone—calcitriol. Vitamin D is converted into this hormone in the kidneys before it performs its role in the body.

What it does:
Vitamin D regulates two minerals, calcium and phosphorus, which are important for normal growth and development, especially the hardening of bone. Vitamin D stimulates the absorption of calcium from the gut. Without it, calcium cannot be absorbed. It also helps harden bones and stimulates the kidneys to reabsorb some calcium, thus saving the body from excreting calcium. A vitamin D deficiency increases the body's production

of a hormone that removes calcium from bones. In children, this results in rickets, a condition characterized by bones so soft that they develop curves. In adults, vitamin D deficiency results in osteomalacia, which is also characterized by soft bones.

RDA:
For men and for women ages eleven to twenty-four, 400 I.U.; for women ages twenty-five and older, 200 I.U.

Signs of deficiency:
In children, bones so soft they develop curves when subjected to the body's weight; in adults, bone pain and tenderness; muscle weakness

Possible toxicity problems:
High doses of vitamin D may cause too high levels of calcium in the blood and calcium deposits in soft tissues. Symptoms include loss of appetite, nausea, vomiting, constipation, and fatigue. Doses less than 1,000 I.U. daily are unlikely to cause adverse effects.

Vitamin E

What it is:
Vitamin E is a fat-soluble vitamin. It is a light yellow oil that comes in a variety of forms, both natural and synthetic. The most common naturally occurring forms are alpha-tocopherol and d-alpha-tocopherol. The most common synthetic forms are dl-alpha-tocopherol acetate and dl-alpha-tocopherol.

What it does:
Vitamin E acts as an antioxidant in the body. This means it helps neutralize potentially harmful oxidative reactions that can lead to cell damage associated with cancer, heart disease, and other problems. Vitamin E works in concert with other antioxidants, especially vitamin C and the trace mineral selenium, to provide antioxidant protection throughout the body. Research suggests that it can reduce the risk of heart disease and, perhaps, reduce the risk of cancer. Vitamin E also plays a crucial role in normal nerve function; a deficiency can contribute to nerve damage and some neurological disorders.

RDA:
For men, 15 I.U. (10 mg TE); for women, 12 I.U. (8 mg TE)

Signs of deficiency:
In infants, irritability; fluid retention; and anemia. In adults, lethargy; apathy; inability to concentrate; loss of balance; staggering gait; and anemia.

Possible toxicity problems:
Toxicity is considered low. The Food and Nutrition Board conceded that there is little evidence of harm at doses of less than 1,000 I.U. per day.

Vitamin K

What it is:
Vitamin K is a fat-soluble vitamin.

What it does:
Vitamin K is used in the liver to manufacture at least four different proteins important in blood clotting. Without this nutrient, a simple cut or scrape could cause excessive blood loss. Vitamin K is also involved in the production of two other proteins—one related to bone metabolism, the other to kidney function.

RDA:
For men, 80 mcg; for women, 65 mcg

Signs of deficiency:
Prolonged clotting time, easy bleeding and bruising, frequent nosebleeds

Possible toxicity problems:
Large amounts from foods or supplements can interfere with the action of blood-thinning drugs.

Minerals

Calcium

What it is:
Calcium is a silvery white metallic element found in such common substances as chalk, granite, eggshell, seashells, hard water, bone, and limestone. It is the most abundant mineral in the body.

What it does:
Calcium is essential for building bones and teeth and keeping them hard. It is also essential for nerve conduction, muscle contraction, heartbeat, blood clotting, the production of energy, and the maintenances of immune function. Research shows that getting enough calcium early in life, up to age thirty, can help prevent osteoporosis—a weakening of the bones that causes them to fracture easily.

RDA:
For men and women, 800 mg (The National In stitutes of Health has made these special recommendations: premenopausal women, 1,000 mg; postmenopausal women not taking estrogen replacement, 1,500 mg; postmenopausal women taking estrogen, 1,000 mg.)

Signs of deficiency:
Abnormal heartbeat; muscle pains and cramps; numbness, stiffness, and tingling of the hands and feet; dementia

Possible toxicity problems:
Doses up to 2,500 mg a day are considered safe. Gastrointestinal complaints such as nausea, gas, and constipation can be avoided by taking divided doses with meals or sticking with calcium gluconate or calcium lactate, the two most soluble forms. Early signs of high blood calcium—vomiting, nausea, loss of appetite—occur only in people who have taken doses of 25,000 mg or more. High blood levels of calcium rarely happen as a result of calcium intake alone.

Chromium

What it is:
Chromium is an essential trace mineral—the same metal that was once used to make the shiny chrome-plated bumpers on cars.

What it does:
Chromium aids the body in burning sugar for energy, a process called glucose metabolism. Chromium becomes part of an enzyme called glucose tolerance factor. This compound enhances the body's response to insulin, helping to move glucose into cells where it can be burned for energy. People with hypoglycemia (low blood sugar) or with a condition called insulin resistance show improved glucose metabolism when given 250 mcg of chromium. This helps to keep blood-sugar levels stable and so prevents damage to blood vessels and organs.

RDA:
No RDA, but an Estimated Safe and Adequate Daily Intake is 50 to 200 mcg for both men and women.

Signs of deficiency:
Glucose intolerance, weight loss, diabetes-like symptoms, nerve degeneration

Possible toxicity problems:
Little is known about the possible toxic effects of chromium, including how much is too much. While people with diabetes may benefit from chromium supplementation, their insulin requirements may change as a result; thus, their use of supplements should be monitored by a doctor.

Copper

What it is:
Copper is an essential trace mineral. It is the brownish metal that was once used to make pennies.

What it does:
In the body, copper combines with proteins or with other metals, such as iron or zinc, to make chemical compounds that have biological activity. Copper is necessary for the formation of red blood cells and helps to carry and store iron. It is neces-

sary for the formation of collagen, the connective tissue used to form bone, cartilage, skin, and tendons. It helps produce melanin, a pigment that gives color to skin and hair.

RDA:
No RDA, but an Estimated Safe and Adequate Daily Intake of copper for adults is 1.5 to 3 mg.

Signs of deficiency:
Anemia, paleness, bone and connective-tissue disorders, disorders of blood-fat metabolism, hair that feels like steel wool, internal hemorrhaging, problems with temperature regulation, convulsions, impaired glucose tolerance, increased blood pressure, heartbeat problems

Possible toxicity problems:
Experts say that occasional intake of up to 10 mg a day is safe, but that copper intake over extended periods of time should be in the range of 2 to 3 mg a day. People with Wilson's disease, a genetic condition marked by overaccumulation of copper, should not take copper supplements.

Iodine

What it is:
Iodine is a nonmetallic, blackish gray element. When isolated under laboratory conditions, iodine is a gas. However, in nature it is found only as a compound and as a liquid or solid.

What it does:
Iodine is necessary for the formation of two hormones produced in the thyroid gland, the largest of the endocrine glands. The thyroid gland produces hormones that are vital for growth, reproduction, nerve formation and mental health, bone formation, the manufacture of proteins, and a cell's oxidative processes. These hormones serve as the major regulators of energy metabolism in the body.

RDA:
For men and women, 150 mcg

Signs of deficiency:
Chronic fatigue, apathy, dry skin, intolerance to cold, weight gain, enlargement of the thyroid (goiter)

Possible toxicity problems:
Elemental iodine—the kind that's used as an antiseptic—can be deadly even in amounts as small as 2 grams. Several milligrams of daily iodine compounds have been linked with thyroid problems or inflammation of the salivary glands. High doses may aggravate or precipitate acne in adults in mild cases of sensitivity.

Iron

What it is:
Iron is the major metal on earth, making up 35 percent of the earth's interior.

What it does:
Iron carries oxygen throughout the body. Since oxygen is required in every cell to produce energy, iron is the backbone of energy production. Iron is a part of hemoglobin, a protein that carries oxygen in red blood cells. It is also part of oxygen-carrying proteins in the muscles. Iron is involved in the production of thyroid hormones, in the production of connective tissues, in the maintenance of the immune system, and in the production and regulation of several brain neurotransmitters.

RDA:
For men and for women ages 50 and older, 10 mg; for women ages 11 to 50, 15 mg

Signs of deficiency:
Anemia, fatigue, rapid heartbeat, breathlessness, inability to concentrate, disturbed sleep, severe menstrual pain and bleeding, hair loss

Possible toxicity problems:
Constipation is the most common side effect associated with iron supplements. Children who take many tablets of iron-containing supplements may end up in a hospital emergency room, since large doses are poisonous to them. High body levels of iron may be associated with an increased risk for heart disease and, possibly, cancer. The risk of getting too much iron from foods is considered to be quite low. However, the risks of long-term use of moderate-to-high doses of iron, 25 to 75 mg a day, are unknown.

Magnesium

What it is:
Magnesium is a silvery white metallic element related to calcium and zinc.

What it does:
Magnesium is necessary for every major biologic process in the body, including the production of energy from sugar and the manufacture of genetic material. It is important for muscle contraction, nerve conduction, and blood-vessel tone. Magnesium interacts with calcium to regulate how much calcium enters cells to control such vital functions as heartbeat. Low intakes of magnesium have been associated with high blood pressure and heart disease.

RDA:
For men, 350 mg; for women, 250 mg

Signs of deficiency:
Loss of appetite, nausea, vomiting, diarrhea, confusion, tremors, loss of coordination, muscle cramps, dizziness, apathy, depression, irregular heartbeat

Possible toxicity problems:
Magnesium has a good safety record. Symptoms of overdose have been seen with abuse of magnesium-containing antacids. They include low blood pressure, lethargy, weakness, slight slurring of speech, unsteadiness, fluid retention, nausea, and vomiting. The lowest level on record causing harm to an individual with healthy kidneys is 1,700 mg a day. People with kidney problems should take supplemental magnesium only with medical supervision. Experts consider a safe dose for such people to be about 600 mg a day.

Potassium

What it is:
Potassium is a soft, silvery white metal found in nature only in compounds called potassium salts. It is one of the most abundant minerals in the body. Potassium is located almost entirely within cells. It is concentrated chiefly in muscles, but it is also found in skin and other tissues.

What it does:
Potassium plays a major role in many important functions, including muscle contraction, nerve conduction, regulation of heartbeat, energy production, and the manufacture of genetic material and protein.

RDA:
None. The National Research Council estimates the minimum requirement to be 1,600 to 2,000 mg daily.

Signs of deficiency:
Fatigue, weakness, muscle pains, abnormal heartbeat, drowsiness, irrational behavior

Possible toxicity problems:
High doses of several grams—the result of misuse of supplements or salt substitutes—can result in heart failure. Other symptoms of toxicity include muscle weakness; mental confusion; numbness and tingling of the extremities; and cold, pale skin. Potassium supplements containing more than 99 mg per tablet are available only by prescription and should be used only with medical supervision. Diabetics, people with kidney problems, people taking a potassium-sparing diuretic called spironolactone, and people taking Angiotensin-converting enzyme (ACE) inhibitors may all retain potassium. Their use of potassium supplements should be medically supervised.

Selenium

What it is:
Selenium is one of the trace minerals essential for human health. It is closely related chemically to sulfur.

What it does:
Selenium acts as an antioxidant. It is essential for the formation of an enzyme, glutathione peroxidase, that is known to have powerful antioxidant properties. This means that it helps neutralize potentially harmful oxidative reactions in the body—reactions that can lead to cell damage associated with cancer, heart disease, and other problems. In studies, selenium appears to help prevent some types of cancer and heart disease, to boost the body's infection-fighting abilities, to detoxify potential cancer-causing heavy metals, and to dampen inflammation.

RDA:
For men, 70 mcg; for women, 55 mcg

Signs of deficiency:
Muscle pain and wasting, heart problems

Possible toxicity problems:
The level of dietary selenium that causes chronic poisoning is not known with certainty. However, 5 mg a day from foods results in fingernail changes and hair loss. The early signs of selenium toxicity include fatigue, irritability, and dry hair. Mining and foundry operations may expose workers in those occupations to high amounts of selenium, causing them to develop garlic breath, dry skin and hair, brittle nails, nausea, vomiting, and nervous-system problems such as unusual or diminished sensation or paralysis.

Zinc

What it is:
Zinc is a silvery blue metal used to galvanize iron and as a component in flashlight batteries.

What it does:
Zinc is involved in the structure and function of cell membranes and in the production of more than 200 enzymes, including those involved in the production of nucleic acid, a cell's genetic material. It is essential for proper wound healing and healthy skin; for a strong immune system; for normal taste, smell, and sexual function; for bone metabolism; and for vision.

RDA:
For men, 15 mg; for women, 12 mg

Signs of deficiency:
Growth retardation; poor appetite; underfunctioning sex glands; mental lethargy; delayed wound healing; abnormalities of taste, smell, and vision; skin changes; increased susceptibility to infection

Possible toxicity problems:
Zinc competes with copper for intestinal absorption; some researchers believe that people taking amounts of zinc as low as 15 mg should also be getting about 2 mg of copper. In a recent study, high doses of zinc depressed immune function; even 25 mg, considered a fairly low dose, led to poorer immune function after six months of supplementation.

Health and Medical Information

Over-the-Counter Drug Manufacturers

American Lifeline
103 S. Second Street
Madison, WI 53704
800-257-5433
800-836-3477

AML Laboratories
1753 Cloverfield Boulevard
Santa Monica, CA 90404
800-800-1200

Astra USA
50 Otis Street
Westborough, MA 01581-4500
800-262-0460 (for medical emergencies)

Bausch & Lomb
Personal Products Division
1400 N. Goodman Street
P.O. Box 450
Rochester, NY 14692-0450
800-553-5340
800-572-2931 (for medical emergencies)

Bayer Corporation
Consumer Care Division
36 Columbia Road
Morristown, NJ 07960-4518
800-331-4536

Blaine Company
1465 Jamike Lane
Erlanger, KY 41018
800-633-9353

Blairex Laboratories
3240 N. Indianapolis Road
P.O. Box 2127
Columbus, IN 47202-2127
800-252-4739

Boiron
6 Campus Boulevard, Building A
Newtown Square, PA 19073
800-258-8823

Bristol-Myers Products
345 Park Avenue
New York, NY 10154
800-468-7746 (for medical emergencies)

Care-Tech Laboratories
3224 South Kingshighway Boulevard
St. Louis, MO 63139
800-325-9681 (for medical emergencies)

Church & Dwight Company
469 N. Harrison Street
Princeton, NJ 08543-5297
800-228-5635, ext. 7

Effcon Laboratories
P.O. Box 7499
Marietta, GA 30065-1499
800-722-2428

Iyata Pharmaceutical
735 N. Water Street, Suite 612
Milwaukee, WI 53202
800-809-7918 (for medical emergencies)

Johnson & Johnson
1 Johnson & Johnson Plaza
New Brunswick, NJ 08933
800-526-3967

Kyolic Ltd.
23501 Madero
Mission Viejo, CA 92691
800-421-2998

Lederle Consumer Health
A Division of Whitehall-Robins
     Healthcare
Five Giralda Farms
Madison, NJ 07940
800-282-8805

3M Personal Health Care
Building 515-3N-02
St. Paul, MN 55144-1000
800-537-2191

Marlyn Nutraceuticals
14851 N. Scottsdale Road
Scottsdale, AZ 85254
800-462-7596

McNeil Consumer Products
Camp Hill Road
Fort Washington, PA 19034
800-523-6225

Muro Pharmaceutical
890 East Street
Tewksbury, MA 01876-1496
800-225-0974

Ohm Laboratories
P.O. Box 7397
North Brunswick, NJ 08902
800-527-6481

Pfizer
Consumer Health Care Group
235 E. 42nd Street
New York, NY 10017-5755
800-723-7529

Pharmaton Natural Health Products
900 Ridgebury Road
Ridgefield, CT 06877
800-243-0127

Procter & Gamble
P.O. Box 5516
Cincinnati, OH 45201
800-358-8707

Requa
Box 4008
1 Seneca Place
Greenwich, CT 06830
800-321-1085

Roberts Pharmaceutical Corporation
4 Industrial Way West
Eatontown, NJ 07724
800-828-2088

Ross Products Division
Abbott Laboratories
Columbus, OH 43215-1724
800-227-5767

Similasan Corporation
1321 S. Central Avenue
Kent, WA 98032
800-426-1644

Smithkline Beecham
Consumer Healthcare
P.O. Box 1467
Pittsburgh, PA 15230
800-245-1040

Stellar Pharmacal Corporation
1990 N.W. 44th Street
Pompano Beach, FL 33064-8712
800-845-7827

Triton Consumer Products
561 W. Golf Road
Arlington Heights, IL 60005
800-942-2009

Upjohn Company
7000 Portage Road
Kalamazoo, MI 49001
800-717-2824

Wallace Laboratories
Half Acre Road
Cranbury, NJ 08512
800-526-3840

Warner-Lambert Company
Consumer Health Products Group
201 Tabor Road
Morris Plains, NJ 07950
800-524-2854
800-223-0182

Warner Wellcome
Consumer HealthCare Products
Warner-Lambert Company
201 Tabor Road
Morris Plains, NJ 07950
800-223-0182
800-524-2624
800-562-0266
800-378-1783
800-337-7266
800-773-1554
800-547-8374

Whitehall-Robins Healthcare
American Home Products Corporation
Five Giralda Farms
Madison, NJ 07940-0871
800-322-3129
800-762-4672

J. B. Williams Company
65 Harrison Road
Glen Rock, NJ 07452
800-254-8656

Wyeth-Ayerst Laboratories
P.O. Box 8299
Philadelphia, PA 19101
800-934-5566

Note: Not all manufacturers operate toll-free phone numbers as a customer service. For product inquiries, call the number listed on the OTC product package or label.

Adapted from *PDR for Nonprescription Drugs* (Montvale, N.J.: Medical Economics Data Production Company, 1996).

Poison Control Centers

Certified Regional Poison Centers

The following poison control centers are certified by the American Association of Poison Control Centers (AAPCC), 3201 New Mexico Avenue, N.W., Suite 310, Washington, DC 20016. There may be other poison control centers in your area; however, these are the only centers that meet AAPCC standards. **In the event of an emergency,** contact the nearest hospital serving your area.

Alabama

Alabama Poison Center
408-A Paul Bryant Drive
Tuscaloosa, AL 35401
800-462-0800 (AL only)
205-345-0600

Regional Poison Center
Children's Hospital of Alabama
1600 Seventh Avenue South
Birmingham, AL 35233
800-292-6678 (AL only)
205-939-9201
205-933-4050

Arizona

Arizona Poison and Drug Information Center University of Arizona
Arizona Health Science Center,
   Room 1156
1501 N. Campbell Avenue
Tucson, AZ 85724
800-362-0101 (AZ only)
520-626-6016

Samaritan Regional Poison Center
Good Samaritan Regional Medical Center
Ancillary-1
1111 E. McDowell Road
Phoenix, AZ 85006
602-253-3334

California

Central California Regional Poison Control Center
Valley Children's Hospital
3151 N. Millbrook, IN31
Fresno, CA 93703
800-346-5922 (central CA only)
209-445-1222

San Diego Regional Poison Center
University of California–San Diego
   Medical Center
200 W. Arbor Drive
San Diego, CA 92103-8925
800-876-4766 (Accessible in
   area code 619 only.)
619-543-6000

University of California–Davis Medical Center
Regional Poison Control Center
2315 Stockton Boulevard
Sacramento, CA 95817
800-342-9293 (northern CA only)
916-734-3692

Colorado

Rocky Mountain Poison and Drug Center
8802 E. Ninth Avenue
Denver, CO 80220
800-332-3073 (CO only)
303-629-1123 (Denver metropolitan
   area)
800-860-0620 (ID only)
800-525-5042 (MT only)
800-446-6179 (Las Vegas only)

Connecticut

Connecticut Poison Control Center
University of Connecticut Health Center
263 Farmington Avenue
Farmington, CT 06030
800-343-2722 (CT only)
203-679-3056

District of Columbia

National Capitol Poison Center
3201 New Mexico Avenue, N.W.,
   Suite 310
Washington, DC 20016
202-625-3333
202-362-8563 (TTY)

Florida

Florida Poison Information Center–Miami
University of Miami,
    School of Medicine
Department of Pediatrics
P.O. Box 016960 (R-131)
Miami, FL 33101
800-282-3171 (FL only)

Florida Poison Information Center–Jacksonville
University Medical Center
University of Florida Health Science
    Center–Jacksonville
655 W. Eighth Street
Jacksonville, FL 32009
800-282-3171 (FL only)
904-549-4480

Florida Poison Information Center and Toxicology Resource Center
Tampa General Hospital
P.O. Box 1289
Tampa, FL 33601
800-282-3171 (FL only)
813-253-4444 (Tampa)

Georgia

Georgia Regional Poison Control Center
Grady Memorial Hospital
80 Butler Street S.E.
P.O. Box 26066
Atlanta, GA 30335
800-282-5846 (GA only)
404-616-9000

Indiana

Indiana Poison Control Center
Methodist Hospital of Indiana
1701 North Senate Boulevard
P.O. Box 1367
Indianapolis, IN 46206
800-382-9097 (northern IN, northern
    OH, central and southern MI)
317-929-2323

Kentucky

Kentucky Regional Poison Center
Kosair Children's Hospital
Medical Towers South, Suite 572
P.O. Box 35070
Louisville, KY 40232
800-722-5725 (KY only)
502-589-8222 (metropolitan Louisville
    and southern IN)

Louisiana

Louisiana Drug and Poison Information Center
Northeast Louisiana University
Sugar Hall
Monroe, LA 71209
800-256-9822
318-362-5393

Maryland

Maryland Poison Center
University of Maryland School of
    Pharmacy
20 N. Pine Street
Baltimore, MD 21201
800-492-2414 (MD only)
410-528-7701

National Capitol Poison Center (DC suburbs only)
3201 New Mexico Avenue, N.W.,
    Suite 310
Washington, DC 20016
202-625-3333
202-362-8563 (TTY)

Massachusetts

Massachusetts Poison Control System
300 Longwood Avenue
Boston, MA 02115
800-682-9211
617-232-2120

Michigan

Poison Control Center
Children's Hospital of Michigan
Harper Professional Building
4160 John Road, Suite 425
Detroit, MI 48201
313-745-5711

Minnesota

Hennepin Regional Poison Center
Hennepin County Medical Center
701 Park Avenue
Minneapolis, MN 55415
612-347-3141
612-337-7474 (TDD)
612-337-7387 (Petline)

Minnesota Regional Poison Center
8100 34th Avenue South
P.O. Box 1309
Minneapolis, MN 55440-1309
612-221-2113

Missouri

Regional Poison Center
Cardinal Glennon Children's Hospital
1465 S. Grand Boulevard
St. Louis, MO 63104
800-366-8888 (Also serves western IL,
    MO, and Topeka, KS.)
314-772-5200

Montana

Rocky Mountain Poison and Drug Center
8802 E. Ninth Avenue
Denver, CO 80220
800-525-5042

Nebraska

The Poison Center
Children's Memorial Hospital
8301 Dodge Street
Omaha, NE 68114
800-955-9119 (NE and WY)
402-390-5555 (Omaha)

New Jersey

New Jersey Poison Information and Education System
Newark Beth Israel Medical
    Center
201 Lyons Avenue
Newark, NJ 07112
800-962-1253

New Mexico

New Mexico Poison and Drug Information Center
University of New Mexico,
    North Campus
Health Science Library, Room 125
Albuquerque, NM 87131
800-432-6866 (NM only)
505-843-2551 (Albuquerque)

New York

Central New York Poison Control Center
SUNY Health Science Center
750 E. Adams Street
Syracuse, NY 13203
800-252-5655 (NY only)
315-476-4766

Finger Lakes Regional Poison Center
University of Rochester Medical Center
601 Elmwood Avenue
Box 321, Room G-3275
Rochester, NY 14642
800-333-0542
716-275-5151

Hudson Valley Regional Poison Center
Phelps Memorial Hospital Center
701 N. Broadway
North Tarrytown, NY 10591
800-336-6997
914-366-3030

Long Island Regional Poison Control Center
Winthrop University Hospital
259 First Street
Mineola, NY 11501
516-542-2323, -2324, -2325, -3813

New York City Poison Control Center
New York City Department of Health
455 First Avenue, Room 123
New York, NY 10016
212-340-4494
212-689-9014 (TDD)

North Carolina

Carolinas Poison Center
1012 S. Kings Drive, Suite 206
P.O. Box 32861
Charlotte, NC 28232
800-848-6946
704-355-4000

North Dakota

North Dakota Poison Information Center
MeriCare Medical Center
720 Fourth Street North
Fargo, ND 58122
800-732-2200
701-234-5575

Ohio

Central Ohio Poison Control Center
Children's Hospital
700 Children's Drive
Columbus, OH 43205
800-682-7625
614-228-2272 (TTY)
614-228-1323

Cincinnati Drug and Poison Information Center and Regional Poison Control Systems
P.O. Box 670144
Cincinnati, OH 45267
800-872-5111 (OH only)
513-558-5111

Oregon

Oregon Poison Center
Oregon Health Sciences University
3181 S.W. Sam Jackson Park Road, CB550
Portland, OR 97201
800-452-7165 (OR only)
503-494-8968

Pennsylvania

Central Pennsylvania Poison Center
University Hospital
Milton S. Hershey Medical Center
University Drive
P.O. Box 850
Hershey, PA 17033
800-521-6110
717-531-8335 (TDD)

The Poison Control Center
3600 Sciences Center, Suite 220
Philadelphia, PA 19104
800-521-6110
215-386-2100

Pittsburgh Poison Center
3705 Fifth Avenue
Pittsburgh, PA 15213
412-681-6669

Rhode Island

Rhode Island Poison Center
593 Eddy Street
Providence, RI 02903
401-444-5727

Tennessee

Middle Tennessee Poison Center
The Center for Clinical Toxicology
Vanderbilt University Medical Center
1161 21st Avenue South
501 Oxford House
Nashville, TN 37232
800-288-9999 (Accessible in area code 615)
615-936-2034

Texas

Central Texas Poison Center
Scott & White Memorial Hospital
2401 S. 31st Street
Temple, TX 76508
800-764-7661

North Texas Poison Center
Parkland Hospital
5201 Harry Hines Boulevard
P.O. Box 35926
Dallas, TX 75235
800-441-0040 (TX only)
800-764-7661

Southeast Texas Poison Center
University of Texas Medical Branch
301 University Avenue
Galveston, TX 77550
800-764-7661
409-765-1420 (Galveston)
713-654-1701 (Houston)

Utah

Utah Poison Control Center
410 Chipeta Way, Suite 230
Salt Lake City, UT 84108
800-456-7707 (UT only)
801-581-2151

Virginia

Blue Ridge Poison Center
Box 67, Blue Ridge
University of Virginia Medical Center
Charlottesville, VA 22901
800-451-1428 (central, northern, and western VA)
804-924-5543

National Capitol Poison Center (northern VA only)
3201 New Mexico Avenue, N.W., Suite 310
Washington, DC 20016
202-625-3333
202-362-8563 (TTY)

Washington

Washington Poison Center
155 N.E. 100th Street, Suite 400
Seattle, WA 98125
800-732-6985
800-572-0638 (TDD)
206-526-2121
206-517-2394

West Virginia

West Virginia Poison Center
West Virginia University
School of Pharmacy
3110 MacCorkle Avenue S.E.
Charleston, WV 25304
800-642-3625 (WV only)
304-348-4211

Wyoming

The Poison Center
Children's Memorial Hospital
8301 Dodge Street
Omaha, NE 68114
800-955-9119 (NE and WY only)
402-390-5555 (Omaha)

Source: American Association of Poison Control Centers, 3201 New Mexico Avenue, N.W., Suite 310, Washington, DC 20016.

Additional Resources

Federal Government Resources and Health Clearinghouses

Consumer Information Center
General Services Administration
P.O. Box 100
Pueblo, CO 81009
719-948-4000
     Provides a catalog of free or low-cost federal publications of consumer interest. Topics include health information.

Food and Drug Administration Center for Drug Evaluation and Research
Over-the-Counter Drug Evaluation
     Office
7520 Standish Place
Rockville, MD 20855
301-594-6740
     Provides information on the status of ingredients being evaluated for use in the manufacture of over-the-counter products.

Food and Drug Administration Center for Drug Evaluation and Research
Division of Drug Labeling Compliance
OTC Compliance Branch (HFD-312)
7520 Standish Place
Rockville, MD 20855
301-594-1065

Provides information on labeling that is required on all OTC products, including compliance with standards on quantity, dosage, main use of product, and instructions on how to use the product.

Food and Drug Administration Office of Device Evaluation (Home Medical Test Kits)
Center for Devices and Radiological
     Health
2098 Gaither Road (HFZ-440)
Rockville, MD 20857
301-443-4690
     Provides information on the types of home medical test kits that are available over the counter.

Food and Drug Administration Office of Consumer Affairs
5600 Fishers Lane (HFE-50)
Rockville, MD 20857
301-443-3170
301-443-9767 (FAX)
     Provides general information on a broad range of health-related topics and responds to consumer inquiries.

National Health Information Center
P.O. Box 1133
Washington, DC 20013-1133
800-336-4797
301-565-4167
301-984-4256 (FAX)
     Serves as a general clearinghouse on health-related topics. Also makes referrals to other groups who may provide additional information.

National Institutes of Health National Institute on Aging
9000 Rockville Pike
Bethesda, MD 20892
301-496-9265
     Provides information on all aspects of aging, including ways to improve quality of life and maintain a healthy perspective on aging.

On-Line Resources

American Medical Association
Web site: http://www.ama-assn.org
     Access articles on numerous illnesses and medical procedures.

HealthLink
Web site: http://healthlink.stanford.edu
     Published by the Stanford University Medical Center News Bureau. Call 415-723-6911 for more information.

HealthTips
Web site:
http://www.med.stanford.edu/center/
Communications/HealthTips/
     Published by the Stanford University Medical Center News Bureau. Call 415-725-6911 for more information.

Institute for Preventive Medicine and Nutrition
Web site: http://pbrewsterw@aol.com
     Access information on both homeopathic and botanical medicine.

MedicineNet
Web site: http://www.medicinenet.com
     Access user-picked ailment and disease articles written by practicing physicians. Sponsored by Information Network, a firm in San Clemente, California.

MediLife Software, Inc.
30 Monument Square
Concord, MA 01742
508-371-3170
Web site: http://www.medilife.com
     Order by mail over-the-counter products. Call 888-656-5656 to obtain software for accessing this "virtual drugstore."

National Institutes of Health
Web site: http://www.nih.gov
     Access several health databases available from the various institutes that comprise the National Institutes of Health.

U.S. Public Health Service
Web site:
http://phs.os.dhhs.gov/phs/phs.html
     Access information about public health program developed by the Public Health Service and made available to local communities through state or municipal governments or health departments.

Other Resources

Council on Family Health
225 Park Avenue South
Suite 1700
New York, NY 10003
212-598-3617
     Provides information on the proper use of medications and on other health concerns.

Health Education Foundation
600 New Hampshire Avenue, N.W.
Suite 452
Washington, DC 20037
202-338-3501
Provides information to help consumers make more informed decisions concerning health care.

National Council on Patient Information and Education
666 11th Street, N.W.
Suite 810
Washington, DC 20001
202-347-6711
Provides public education materials on the proper use of medications and encourages communication between consumers and health-care providers.

Nonprescription Drug Manufacturers Association
Publications Department
1150 Connecticut Avenue, N.W.
Washington, DC 20036
202-429-9260
Provides information on the safe way to use OTC products in a program of self-care. Publications list available upon request.

Suggested Reading

Books

Beckham, Nancy. *Family Guide to Natural Therapies: Easy-to-Prepare Remedies for More Than 120 Everyday Health Problems, from Arthritis to Warts.* New Canaan, Conn.: Keats Publishing, 1996.

Clinebell, Howard. *Well-Being: A Personal Plan for Exploring and Enriching the Seven Dimensions of Life: Mind, Body, Spirit, Love, Work, Play, the World.* San Francisco: Harper, 1992.

Consumer Reports Books and U.S. Pharmacopeial Convention. *The Complete Drug Reference.* Mount Vernon, N.Y.: Consumer Reports Books, 1997.

Covington, Timothy R., ed. *Handbook of Nonprescription Drugs.* 10th ed. Washington, D.C.: American Pharmaceutical Association, 1993.

Dacher, Elliot S. *Whole Healing: A Step-by-Step Program to Reclaim Your Power to Heal.* New York: NAL-Dutton, 1996.

Gottlied, Bill. *New Choices in Natural Healing: Over 1,800 of the Best Self-Help Remedies from the World of Alternative Medicine.* New York: St. Martin's Press, 1996.

Graedon, Joe and Teresa. *Graedons' Best Medicine: From Herbal Remedies to High-Tech Rx Breakthroughs.* New York: Bantam, 1991.

Medical Economics Data Production Company. *PDR for Nonprescription Drugs.* Montvale, N.J.: 1996.

Pizzorno, Joseph E. *Total Wellness: Improve Your Health by Understanding the Body's Healing Systems.* Rocklin, Calif.: Prima, 1996.

Powell, Don R. *Self-Care: Your Family Guide to Symptoms and How to Treat Them.* Allentown, Pa.: People's Medical Society, 1996.

Prevention Magazine Health Books, editors of. *Doctors Book of Home Remedies.* Emmaus, Pa.: Rodale, 1990.

Schneider, Meir and Maureen Larkin. *Handbook for Self-Healing: Your Personal Program for Better Health & Increased Vitality.* New York: Viking-Penguin, 1994.

Simon, Anne. *Before You Call the Doctor: Safe, Effective Self-Care for Over 300 Common Medical Problems.* New York: Fawcett, 1993.

Vickery, M.D, Donald M. and James F. Fries, M.D. *Take Care of Yourself: A Consumer's Guide to Medical Care.* 5th ed. Reading, Mass.: Addison-Wesley, 1993.

Periodicals

Alternatives: For the Health-Conscious Individual
Mountain Home Publishing
P.O. Box 829
Ingram, TX 78025
$69, monthly

American Health
American Health
28 W. 23rd Street, 8th Floor
New York, NY 10010
$17.97, bimonthly

Consumer Reports on Health
Consumer Reports
Subscription Department
P.O. Box 52148
Boulder, CO 80322
$24, monthly

FDA Consumer
Superintendent of Documents
U.S. Government Printing Office
Washington, DC 20402
$12.10/year

Harvard Health Letter
Harvard Health Letter
P.O. Box 420300
Palm Coast, FL 34142-0300
$24, monthly

Harvard Women's Health Watch
Harvard Women's Health Watch
P.O. Box 420234
Palm Coast, FL 32142-0234
$24, monthly

Health Letter
Public Citizen Health Research Group
2000 P Street, N.W.
Washington, DC 20036
$18, monthly

Healthline
Healthline Publishing
830 Menlo Avenue, Suite 100
Menlo Park, CA 94025
$24, monthly

Johns Hopkins Medical Letter: Health After 50
Johns Hopkins Medical Letter
P.O. Box 359179
Palm Coast, FL 32035
$24, monthly

Mayo Clinic Health Letter
Mayo Clinic
200 First Street, S.W.
Rochester, MN 55905
$24, monthly

National Headache Foundation
Quarterly
National Headache Foundation
5232 N. Western Avenue
Chicago, IL 60625
$15, quarterly

Network News
National Women's Health Network
514 Tenth Street, N.W.
Washington, DC 20004
$25, bimonthly

Nutritional Action Health Letter
Center for Science in the
    Public Interest
1875 Connecticut Avenue, N.W.
Suite 300
Washington, DC 20009-5728
$19.95, 10 issues a year

Women's Health Advocate
Newsletter
Aurora Publications
P.O. Box 420089
Palm Coast, FL 32142
$24, monthly

Pamphlets and Brochures

Dietary Supplements: More Is Not
Always Better
National Institutes of Health
National Institute on Aging
9000 Rockville Pike
Bethesda, MD 20892

Medicine: Before You Take It,
Talk About It
The National Council on Patient
    Information and Education
666 11th Street, N.W.
Suite 810
Washington, DC 20001

Medicines and You: A Guide for
Older Americans and How to Avoid
Drug Interactions

Council on Family Health
225 Park Avenue South
Suite 1700
New York, NY 10003

Nonprescription Drugs: Modern
Medicines for Mature Americans
Nonprescription Drug Manufacturers
    Association
Publications Department
1150 Connecticut Avenue, N.W.
Washington, DC 20036

Nonprescription Medicines:
What's Right for You?
Nonprescription Drug Manufacturers
    Association
Publications Department
1150 Connecticut Avenue, N.W.
Washington, DC 20036

Safe Use of Medicine by
Older People
National Institutes of Health
National Institute on Aging
9000 Rockville Pike
Bethesda, MD 20892

Pharmaceutical and Medical Terms

Absorption

The process by which substances are absorbed through the intestinal tract into the bloodstream to be used by the body.

Active ingredients

The ingredients in the medicine that produce the therapeutic effect. Labels on over-the-counter products are required by law to identify all active ingredients and to identify and list quantities of certain ingredients, such as alcohol, whether active or not.

Acute

Refers to a condition with symptoms that are severe, develop quickly, and do not last a long time, as opposed to a chronic condition.

Adverse effect or reaction

Any reaction to a drug that becomes a serious condition, or even a hazard in and of itself, and occurs at normal doses.

Allergen

A foreign substance that can cause an allergic response in the body but is only harmful to some people. Some common allergens (also called antigens) are pollen, mold, animal dander, house dust, and various foods.

Allergy

Hypersensitivity, or overreaction, to substances such as drugs, food, and pollen.

Bioequivalence

Since the mid-1970s, the Food and Drug Administration has required that generic drugs have the same therapeutic effects as brand-name drugs when administered to people under the conditions spelled out in the labeling. When this is the case, the drug products are said to be bioequivalent.

Brand name

The registered trade name given to a drug product by its manufacturer. A brand name designates a proprietary drug and, as such, one that is protected by patent or copyright. In general, brand names are shorter, easier to pronounce, and thus more readily remembered than their generic counterparts.

Caplet

A small tablet that is shaped like a capsule.

Capsule

A small, dissolvable container, usually made of gelatin, that contains a dose of medication for swallowing. Some capsules have special coatings to prevent the release into the stomach of drugs that may be irritating; other capsules are designed to release their contents into the small intestine slowly and steadily so that a drug need not be taken as frequently.

Cardiovascular system

The system that allows circulation of oxygen and blood. It consists of the heart and blood vessels.

Central nervous system (CNS)

One of the two main divisions of the nervous system of the body. The central nervous system is made up of the brain and the spinal cord and deals with information to and from the peripheral nervous system (the motor and sense nerves outside the CNS). The CNS is the main network of coordination and control for the entire body.

Chronic

Refers to a condition with symptoms that last a long time—weeks, months, or years—as opposed to an acute condition.

Complication

A secondary reaction, infection, or other negative event that makes recovery from illness more difficult and/or longer.

Congenital

Present from birth, but not necessarily inherited.

Constrict

To close or reduce in size an opening or passage of the body.

Contraindication

Any condition or disease that renders some particular line of treatment improper or undesirable. Some contraindications are *absolute,* in that the use of the drug would expose the person to extreme hazard; other contraindications are *relative,* in that the condition or the disease does not entirely preclude the use of the drug.

Cream

Any fluid mix that is very thick. Creams are often used to apply medicine to the surface of the skin.

Dilate

To widen the opening or increase the size (as of a body opening, blood vessel, or tube).

Disorientation

A state of mental confusion regarding place, time, or personal identity.

Dosage

The therapeutic regimen governing the size, frequency, and number of doses, or amounts, of a medicine to be administered.

Drug-condition interactions

May take place when an existing medical condition makes certain medicines potentially harmful. If a person has diabetes or asthma, for example, unwanted reactions may occur with nasal decongestants.

Drug-drug interactions

Occur when two or more medicines react with one another, causing unexpected side effects in the user. The activity of one medicine may be decreased or increased when a second drug is taken, or the combination of two drugs may cause an entirely different effect than is intended.

Drug-food interactions

Result from medicines reacting with foods or beverages. Foods can interact with drugs in a variety of ways: by either slowing down or speeding up the time the medication takes to travel to the part of the body where it's needed, or by preventing a drug from being absorbed properly. In addition, the natural and artificial chemicals in foods can render drugs useless or even dangerous.

Drug tolerance

A condition in which greater and greater amounts of a drug are needed to be effective.

Emulsion

A combination of two liquids that do not mix with each other, such as water and oil.

Expiration date

The date beyond which the product should not be used.

Flare-up

A period of time when symptoms of a condition worsen.

Food and Drug Administration (FDA)

The Food and Drug Administration is the federal agency responsible for approving all prescription and nonprescription med-icines on the basis of safety, effectiveness, and proper labeling.

Gargle

A liquid preparation that is used to wash and freshen the mouth and is usually not meant to be swallowed.

Gastrointestinal system

The system that consists of the organs of the gastrointestinal tract, from the mouth to the anus.

Gel

A substance that is firm even though it contains a lot of liquid. Gels are often used to soothe irritated skin, to stop oozing or bleeding, and to apply other drugs to an area to be treated.

Gelcap

Any capsule or tablet coated with gelatin.

Generic drugs

Every drug has a generic name, usually a condensed version of the original chemical name, which is suggested and filed for by the pharmaceutical company that invented the drug. The manufacturer also registers the drug under the company's own promotional name, and that name is the brand name. For example, acetaminophen is the generic name for the brand-name remedies Tylenol, Anacin-3, and Panadol. A generic drug, which does not have to be the same size, shape, or color of the brand-name product, duplicates the active ingredients of the brand-name drug.

Genetic

Inherited.

Half-life

The time required for one-half of a given drug to be eliminated from the body.

Hypersensitivity

An exaggerated bodily response to a foreign stimulus.

Hypoallergenic

Having little likelihood of causing an allergic reaction.

Idiopathic

Term referring to a disease or condition of unknown cause.

Inactive ingredients

The ingredients in a medicine that provide the "delivery system," as opposed to the ones that produce the therapeutic effect. Among other necessary functions, inactive ingredients serve as flavors, colors, binders, lubricants, and preservatives.

Indications

What the medicine is for.

Inflammation

The body's protective response to irritation, injury, or infection. Its definitive signs are redness, heat, swelling, and pain. Inflammation is usually accompanied by an accumulation of white blood cells, which help destroy invading microorganisms and are involved in the repair of damaged tissue. Thus, inflammation is an essential part of the body's response to infection or injury.

Ingestion

The act of taking any substance, such as medications and food, into the body through the mouth.

Local

Pertaining to a small, defined circumscribed area of the body; not general or systemic.

Lotion

A liquid preparation applied to protect the skin or to treat a skin disorder.

Measurements and Equivalents

Weights, Metric System

1 kilogram (kg)	= 1,000 grams
1 gram (g, gm)	= 1,000 milligrams
1 milligram (mg)	= 1,000 micrograms

Weight Equivalents (approximate)

65 milligrams	= 1 grain (gr.)
28.35 grams	= 1 ounce (oz.)
0.454 kilograms	= 16 ounces (1 pound or 1 lb.)
(454 grams)	= (1 pound)
1 kilogram	= 2.2 pounds (lb.)

Linear Measurement Equivalents (approximate)

1 millimeter (mm)	= 0.04 inch (in.)
1 centimeter (cm)	= 0.4 inch (in.)
2.5 centimeters	= 1 inch (in.)
30.5 centimeters	= 1 foot (ft.)
1 meter	= 39.37 inches (in.)

Metric Liquid Measurements

1 liter (l)	= 1,000 milliliters (ml) or 100 centiliters (cl) or 10 deciliters (dl)
1 deciliter (dl)	= 100 milliliters (ml) or 10 centiliters (cl)
1 centiliter (cl)	= 10 milliliters (ml)

Liquid Measurement Equivalents (approximate)

4.7 milliliters	= 1 household teaspoonful
5 milliliters	= 1 medical teaspoonful
8 milliliters	= 1 dessert spoonful
15 milliliters	= 1 tablespoon (Tb.), ½ fluid ounce
30 milliliters	= 1 fluid ounce
60 milliliters	= 1 wineglassful
120 milliliters	= 1 teacupful
240 milliliters	= 8 fluid ounces, 1 cup
500 milliliters	= 1+ pint
1,000 milliliters	= 1+ quart

Medication errors

Mistakes, negligence, or miscalculations committed in the process of prescribing and administering a drug to a patient or in monitoring the effects of a drug. Medication errors can involve the type of drug or its dosage, the prescription, the method of dispensing, or the lack of communication between health professionals.

Narcotic

A drug—made from opium or made artificially—that is used to relieve pain. It changes one's sense of pain and may cause a heightened sense of well-being, mental confusion, mood changes, and deep sleep. Repeated and long-term use of a narcotic may result in physical and psychological addiction or may simply result in a tolerance for the drug that makes it less effective unless dosage is increased.

Nervous system

The brain, spinal cord, and nerves throughout the body.

Nonprescription medicine

Any medicine that can be bought without a doctor's prescription. Distribution of nonprescription medicines is unrestricted, and the medicines may be sold, for example, in grocery stores as well as pharmacies.

Ointment

A semisolid preparation that is applied externally. Also called salve.

Overdosage

Too great a dose of a therapeutic agent such as a medication; a lethal or toxic amount of a therapeutic agent such as a medication.

Over-the-counter (OTC) medicine

The same as nonprescription medicine.

pH

A scale showing the levels of acid or alkaline in a solution.

Photosensitivity

A drug-induced change in the skin resulting in a rash or exaggerated sunburn upon exposure to the sun or ultraviolet lamps.

Placebo

A pharmacologically inactive substance, given as if it were a real dose of a needed drug.

Placebo effect

Occurring after a substance is taken, a physical or emotional change that is not the result of any special effect of the substance.

Prescription drugs

Medicines prescribed by a doctor or dentist and dispensed only by them or by a registered pharmacist.

Prognosis

A medical forecast about the likely course and/or outcome of a condition or disease.

Renal

Pertaining to the kidneys.

Secondary effects

Complications of drug use that do not occur as part of the medicine's primary pharmacological activity. These are usually unwanted and undesirable consequences and, as such, may be classified as adverse effects.

Seizure

A sudden, brief episode characterized by changes in consciousness, perception, uncontrollable behavior, and/or muscular motion.

Side effects

Effects on the body apart from the principal action of the medicine. Side effects are usually undesirable, but some cause only minor inconvenience. For example, drowsiness is a side effect of certain antihistamines.

Solution

A mixture of one or more substances dissolved in another substance.

Suppository

An easily melted cone or cylinder of material mixed with a drug. It is designed to be placed in the rectum, urethra, or vagina.

Symptom

An alteration in normal feeling or functioning noticed by a patient that can help to detect a condition or disease.

Syndrome

A group of signs or symptoms that together comprise or characterize a disorder.

Systemic

Pertaining to the whole body rather than to a single area or part of the body.

Tablet

A small, solid dosage form of medication. Most tablets are intended to be swallowed whole, but some may be chewed, dissolved in liquid before being swallowed, or dissolved in the mouth before being swallowed. Some tablets have special coatings to prevent the release into the stomach of drugs that may be irritating; other tablets are designed to release their contents into the small intestine slowly and steadily so that a drug need not be taken as frequently.

Teratogen

An agent that causes malformation of a developing embryo or fetus.

Topical

Pertaining to the surface of the body.

Toxic

Poisonous.

Toxicity

The capacity of a drug to dangerously impair body function or to damage body tissues.

Tremor

Involuntary trembling.

Urgent

Refers to a condition that must be addressed immediately.

Vascular

Pertaining to the circulatory system.

Vital signs

Basic indicators of a person's health status, including breathing, blood pressure, body temperature, and pulse.

Withdrawal

The process of adjustment that occurs when the use of a habit-forming substance to which the body has become habituated is discontinued, or withdrawn.

Appendix

Potential Candidates for Rx-to-OTC Switch

Ingredient	Adult Dosage (if listed)	Product Category
acyclovir	200 mg	antiviral
albuterol sulfate	2 mg	bronchodilator
astemizole	–	antihistamine
azithromycin	–	antibiotic
beclomethasone dipropionate	nasal spray 0.042%	allergy treatment
cholestyramine	–	cholesterol-lowering agent
colestipol hydrochloride	–	cholesterol-lowering agent
cyclobenzaprine Hcl	–	muscle spasm treatment
diflunisal	–	nonsteroidal anti-inflammatory
econazole nitrate	1%	antifungal
erythromycin	–	antibiotic
etodolac	200 mg	nonsteroidal anti-inflammatory
fluconazole	–	antifungal
ibuprofen extended release	–	nonsteroidal anti-inflammatory
ketoconazole	1% shampoo	dandruff shampoo
loratadine	–	antihistamine
methacarbamol	–	muscle relaxant
mupirocin	–	topical antiviral
nabumetone	–	nonsteroidal anti-inflammatory
nitrofurantoin monohydrate	–	urinary tract antibiotic
nystatin	–	antifungal
penciclovir	–	topical antiviral
piroxicam	–	nonsteroidal anti-inflammatory
sucralfate	–	antiulcer
sulindac	300 mg/day	analgesic
theophylline	–	bronchodilator

Source: Nonprescription Drug Manufacturers Association.

Index

A

Abrasion, 24
Acetaminophen, 53, 54, 55, 56, 58
  fever reducer, 65
  menstrual pain, 66–67
Acne, 24, 111–113
Activated charcoal, 19, 86–87
Additives (in vitamin supplements), 206, 208
Advertising (OTC products), 2, 5
Alcohol
  in ear medications, 178
  in mouthwashes, 143
  in oral medications, 68
  in teething preparations, 146
  in topical medications, 111–112, 116
Alcohol, rubbing, 18
Allergy, 24, 68–77
  dermatitis, 30
  eczema, 31
  hay fever, 34
  hives, 35
Alpha-galactosidase enzyme, 90
Alpha-hydroxy acids, 104–105
Aluminum, 82, 83, 165
Aluminum acetate, 103, 114, 118, 119, 178
Aluminum chlorohydrate, 166
Aluminum salts, 82, 166
Aluminum zirconium, 166
American Dental Association (ADA), 138, 139, 141, 142, 143, 144
Aminobenzoic acid (ABA), 128
Ammonia, 18, 108
Ammonium chloride, 171
Ammonium salts, 173
Analgesics, 56–58
Anaphylaxis, 25
Anesthetics, local, 97–99
  burns, 101–102

canker and cold sore, 148
  hemorrhoid, 106, 107, 108
  insect bite, 108
  poison ivy, 110
Ankle sprain, 45
Antacids, 55, 81–84
Anthelmintics, 165
Anthranilates, 128
Antibiotics, 103, 113–114
Anticoagulants
  and aspirin, 55
  and salicylates, 59
Antidiarrheal treatments, 88–90
Antidote, universal, 19
Antiemetics, 84–85
Antiflatulents, 90
Antifungals, 114–116, 179
Antihistamines, oral, 66, 72–74
  antiemetics, 84–85
  chicken pox, 121
  menstrual pain, 66
  poison ivy, 111
  sleep aids, 175–176
Antihistamines, topical
  insect bite, 108–109
  poison ivy, 111
  skin irritations, 96, 99–100, 101
Antiperspirants, 165–166
Antipruritics, 110, 180
Antipyretics, 64–65
Antiseptics, 111, 116–117
Antitussives. See Cough suppressants
Appetite suppressants, 167
Aromatic oils, 144
Arthritis, 24, 62–64, 100
Artificial saliva, 142
Artificial tears, 152
Aspirin, 53, 54, 55, 56
  arthritis, 63
  canker sore, 147
  fever reducer, 65
  inflammation, 57–58

prevention of stroke and heart attack, 58
  toothache, 145
Asthma, 24–25, 55, 168–169
Astringents, 118–119
  burns, 102
  douches, 173
  hemorrhoid, 107, 108
  poison ivy, 111
Athlete's foot, 25, 36, 114–115, 116
Athletic bandages, 185
Attapulgite, 89, 90
Avobenzone, 129

B

Bacitracin, 113, 114
Backache, 25
Bad breath. See Halitosis
Baking soda, 18
Baldness. See Hair loss
Bath oils, 119, 120
Bath products, 119–120
Bath soaps, 120
Bed-wetting, 189
Bedpan, 185
Bee sting, 25, 45
Benzalkonium chloride (BAK), 151, 156
Benzocaine, 97, 98
  appetite suppressants, 167
  burns, 102
  insect bite, 108, 109
  lozenges, 78
  poison ivy, 110
  teething preparations, 146
  vaginal antipruritics, 180
Benzophenones, 128
Benzoyl peroxide, 112, 113
Beriberi, 213
Beta-carotene, 208, 210–211
Biotin, 213
Bisacodyl, 92

Bismuth subsalicylate, 81, 88, 89–90
Bite, insect, 18, 25–26, 45, 108–109
Bleaching kits (teeth), 140
Blepharitis, 26, 154
Blood glucose monitoring, 195–196
Blood pressure, high, 194–195
  and appetite suppressants, 167
  and magnesium, 218
  and oral decongestants, 69
Blood pressure monitoring, 194–195
Blood sugar. See Blood glucose monitoring
Body odor, 26, 165–166, 170
Body temperature, 32, 64–65, 202–203
Boric acid, 103, 178
Botulism, 33
Bowel cancer test, 196–197
Braces, 185
Breast feeding. See Nipples, cracked
Breast pumps, 186
Brompheniramine maleate, 74
Bronchitis, 26
Bronchodilators, 168–169
Bruise, 26
Brush burn. See Abrasion
Bunion, 27, 120
Burns, 27, 59, 101–103
Burow's solution, 102, 103, 114, 118, 119, 178
Butamben, 99
Butoconazole nitrate, 179

C
Caffeine, 56, 171, 177
Calamine, 96, 118–119, 122
Calcium, 216
Calcium carbonate, 82
Calcium polycarbophil, 91
Calluses, 27, 120–121
Camphor, 60, 109, 117, 147, 148
Cancer
  colorectal, 196–197
  and selenium, 218

skin (and benzoyl per-oxide), 112
  and vitamin A, 210–211
  and vitamin C, 210
Candidiasis. See Yeast infection
Canes, 186–187
Canker sore, 44, 147
Capsaicin, 61, 62, 63
Capsicum preparations, 61
Carbamide peroxide, 145, 173, 174
Carpal tunnel syndrome, 27, 43, 185
Cellulose derivatives, 91
Cervical collar, 187
Cervical pillow, 187
Cetylpyridinium chloride, 144
Chain stores (OTC products), 7–8
Chicken pox, 27–28, 121–122
Chlorhexidine, 151, 157
Chlorpheniramine maleate, 74, 77
Cholesterol, 177, 197
Cholesterol test, 197–198
Chromium, 216
Cimetidine, 83
Cinnamates, 128
Clemastine fumarate, 73
Clioquinol, 116
Clotrimazole, 115, 179
Coal tar, 125–126, 133–134
Codeine, 76
Coffee, 18
Cold packs, 187
Cold sore, 45, 147–148
Colds, 28, 68–77, 210
Collodion solution, 121, 130
Colloidal oatmeal, 122
Commodes, 188
Compression shorts, 188
Condoms, 162
Conjunctivitis, 28
Constipation, 19, 28, 91–94, 106
Contact lens products, 150–151, 155–160
  handling safely, 155, 158
  hard contact lenses, 155–156
  rigid gas permeable contact lenses, 156–157, 159
  soft contact lenses, 157–160

Contraceptives, 161–163
Contusion. See Bruise
Copper, 216–217
Corn removers, 120–121
Corns, 28
Cough, 28–29
Cough suppressants, 75–77
Counterirritants, 58–62, 100
  arthritis, 63–64
  douches, 173
  insect bite, 109
Cradle cap, 29, 132
Cramps, menstrual. See Dysmenorrhea
Creams, skin, 96
Creams and gels, contraceptive, 163
Crutches, 188
Cut, 29
Cyclizine, 85
Cystitis, 29
Cytostatic agents, 133, 134

D
Dandruff, 29, 132–134
Dandruff shampoos, 132–134
Danthron, 2
Decongestants
  oral, 69–70
  topical, 70–71
Demulcents, 18, 19, 152
Denture adhesives, 141
Denture cleansers, 141
Dentures, 29–30
Deodorants, 165, 170
Dermatitis, 98, 103–105
  allergic contact, 30
Dermatitis, atopic. See Eczema
Dextromethorphan, 75–76, 77
Diabetes, 90, 195–196
Diaper rash. See Rashes, diaper
Diarrhea, 30, 88–90
Dibucaine, 99, 102, 108
Dimenhydrinate, 84–85
Dimethicone, 105
Diphenhydramine, 77, 85, 100, 108, 175, 176
Diphenhydramine hydrochlo-ride, 73
Diuretics, 171–172

Docusate, 93, 174
Douches, 172–173
Doxylamine, 176
Dyclonine, 78, 79
Dysmenorrhea, 30, 66–67

E

Ear drops, 15
Ear examination, 198–199
Ear infection. See Otitis media
Ear, swimmer's, 31, 178
Ear syringes, 188
Ear wax, 31, 173–174
Earache, 30
Eczema, 31, 96, 104
EDTA, 151, 160
Egg white, 18
Elbow, tennis, 31, 43
Emetics, 19, 86–87
Emollients, 96, 104–105
Enemas, 188–189
Enuresis. See Bed-wetting
Ephedrine, 168, 169
Ephedrine sulfate, 106–107
Epinephrine, 106, 107, 168–169
Epinephrine hydrochloride,
    106, 107
Epsom salts, 18
Eucalyptus oil, 62
Eugenol, 146
Expectorants, 76–77
Expiration dates, 4, 10, 13
    vitamin supplements, 207–
    208
Eyedrops, 14
Eye ointments, 14
Eyeglasses, 189
Eyelid scrubs, 154–155
Eyes. See also Blepharitis;
    Scleritis
    bloodshot, 31
    dry, 31–32, 150–152
    irritated, 32, 150–151, 153–
    154
Eyestrain, 32
Eyewashes, 154

F

Fainting, 18
Famotidine, 84
Fatigue, 32
Fever, 32
Fever blister, 45, 147–148
Fever reducers, 64–65
First-aid supplies, 17
Flatulence, 32–33, 90
Flu. See Influenza
Fluoride, 138
Fluoride mouthwashes, 143
Foams, contraceptive, 162–163
Folic acid (folate), 212
Food and Drug Administration
    (FDA), 1, 2, 5, 8–9, 11,
    193
Food poisoning, 33
Foot odor, 33, 170
Fracture, 33
Fungal nail infection, 36, 124
Fungal skin infection, 36

G

Gastroenteritis, 33
Gingivitis, 34, 138, 139, 142,
    143–144. See also
    Periodontitis
Glaucoma, 14, 73, 153
Glycerin, 94, 104, 181
Gout. See Arthritis
Grippers, 191
Guaifenesin, 76, 77
Guanethidine, 136
Gums. See Gingivitis;
    Periodontitis

H

Hair loss, 34, 135–136
Halitosis, 34, 143
Hamamelis water. See Witch
    hazel
Hand braces, 185
Hay fever, 34
Headache, 34–35

Heart disease
    and aspirin, 58
    and caffeine, 177
    and magnesium, 218
    and vitamin A, 210
Heartburn, 35, 81
Heat packs, 187
Heating pads, 187
    and counterirritants, 60
Hemorrhoid, 35, 106–108, 191
Hexachlorophene, 2
HIV/AIDS test, 199–200
Hives, 35
Home remedies, 18–19
Homeopathic remedies, 20–21
Humidifiers, 189–190
Hydrocortisone
    burns, 103
    dandruff, 132
    diaper rash, 122
    insect bite, 109
    nonprescription, switch to, 3
    psoriasis, 126
    seborrhea, 134
    skin irritations, 96–97, 101
    vaginitis, 180
Hydrogen peroxide, 18, 116,
    145, 158, 159
Hyperhidrosis, 166
Hypertension. See Blood
    pressure, high
Hypoglycemia, 216

I

Ibuprofen, 54, 57, 58, 63
    fever reducer, 65
    menstrual pain, 66, 67
Impetigo, 35
Indigestion, 35–36, 81
Infection, 36, 113
Inflammation, 36
Influenza, 36–37
Inhalers, 14
Insect bite. See Bite, insect
Insomnia, 37, 175–176
Iodine, 117, 217
Iron, 217
Isopropyl alcohol, 117, 158,
    174, 178

J

Jellyfish sting, 19
Jock itch, 36, 37, 114–115, 116

K

Keratin, 104
Keratolytic agents, 111,
    112–113, 115, 126, 129,
    134
Ketoprofen, 53, 54, 57, 58
Kidney
    and acetaminophen, 56
    and phenazopyridine
        hydrochloride, 178
    and salicylic acid, 112
Knee
    injuries, 37
    jumper's, 37
    runner's, 37–38
    sprain, 45
Knee braces, 185

L

Labeling (OTC products), 2, 4,
    8–11
    vitamin supplements, 207
Laceration. See Cut
Lanolin, 104, 105
Laryngitis, 38
Laxatives, 91–94, 106
Leukocytes, 204
Lice, 38, 135
Lidocaine, 97, 98, 102
Lips, chapped, 38
Liver
    and acetaminophen, 56
    and salicylic acid, 112
Loperamide, 88–89, 90
Lozenges, 77–79
Lung function test, 200

M

Magnesium, 218
Magnesium chloride, 19
Magnesium salts, 83
Magnifiers, 190

Measurement standards
    (supplements), 209
Meclizine, 85
Medicare, 183–184
Medicine cabinet supplies, 16
Menopause, 25
Menorrhagia treatments, 54, 66
Menstrual pain, 30, 66–67
Menthol, 60, 64, 78, 109, 147,
    148
Merbromin, 117
Mercurochrome, 117
Methapyrilene, 2
Methyl cellulose, 150, 152
Methyl salicylate, 59–60, 62,
    109
Miconazole, 115, 116, 180
Miliaria. See Rashes, prickly
    heat
Milk, 18–19
Milk of magnesia, 19
Mineral oil, 19, 93, 105
Minerals, 208–210, 216–219
    chelation, 206
    toxicity, 216, 217, 218, 219
Minoxidil, 135–136
Motion sickness, 38, 84
Mouth, dry, 38, 142
Mouthwashes, 77–79, 142–144
Muscle cramp, 39
Muscle soreness, 39
Mustard, dry, 19
Mustard oil, 61

N

Nail area infection, fungal, 36,
    124
Naphazoline, 71, 153, 154
Naproxen, 53, 54, 55, 57, 58,
    63
Nasal aspirator, 190
Nasal dilators, 184
Nasal drainage, 39
Nasal moisturizers, 72
Nasal passages, 39
Nausea, 39–40, 84
Neomycin, 114
Niacin, 212
Nicotine addiction, 40. See also
    Smoking cessation aids

Night blindness, 210
Nipples, cracked, 40
Nitrites, 204
Nizatidine, 84
Nonprescription Drug
    Manufacturers of America
    (NDMA), 8, 10, 11
Nonsteroidal anti-inflammatory
    drugs (NSAIDs), 53–57,
    64, 66
Nose drops, 14
Nose spray, 14

O

Oatmeal bath products, 119,
    120
Obesity, 40
Oil of cloves, 19
Oil of wintergreen, 59–60
Ointments, skin, 96
Olive oil, 19
Ophthalmic decongestants,
    153–154
Oral debriding rinses, 144–145
Oral infection, 36
Oral medicine, taking, 13
Oral rehydration therapy, 87–88
Osteomalacia, 215
Osteoporosis, 207, 216
Otitis media, 40, 199
Otoscope, 190–191
Ovulation prediction test,
    200–201
Oxymetazoline, 71, 154

P

Pacifier, fever, 203
Package inserts, 11
Packaging, 4–5, 13, 208
Pain, chronic, 41
Pain relievers, 53–64
Pamabrom, 66, 171
Pantothenic acid, 213
Para-aminobenzoic acid
    (PABA), 128, 129
Paregoric, 88
Pelvic inflammatory disease,
    172

Perineal cushion, 191
Periodontal disease. *See* Gingivitis; Periodontitis
Periodontitis, 41, 142. *See also* Gingivitis
Permethrin, 135
Petroleum jelly, 19, 93, 105, 127
Pharmacies, independent, 7–8
Pharmacist, choosing, 5–8
Phenazopyridine hydrochloride, 178–179
Phenol, 79, 99, 117
Phenolphthalein, 92
Phenylephrine, 70, 71, 107, 153
Phenylephrine hydrochloride, 106, 107
Phenylpropanolamine (PPA), 69–70, 167
Pimples. *See* Acne
Pinkeye. *See* Conjunctivitis
Pinworms, 41, 165
Plaque, dental, 34, 41, 138, 139, 142, 143–144
  test, 198
  toothbrush, 192
Poison ivy, 41–42, 110–111
Poison oak, 41–42, 110–111
Poison sumac, 41–42, 110–111
Poisoning, 18, 19, 42, 86–87
Polymyxin B sulfate, 113, 114
Polyvinyl alcohol (PVA), 150, 152, 154
Potassium, 218
Potassium sorbate, 151
Povidone-iodine, 79, 117, 173
Povidone (PVP), 150
Powders, medicated, 123, 124–125
Pramoxine, 99, 108, 110
Pregnancy. *See also* Contraceptives
  and acetaminophen, 58
  and aspirin, 58
  and douches, 172
  and ibuprofen, 65
  and NSAIDs, 55
  and vaginal antifungals, 179
  and vitamin supplements, 205
Pregnancy test, 201–202

Premenstrual syndrome (PMS), 42, 66, 177
Preservatives (eye products), 151
Prickly heat. *See* Rashes, prickly heat
Product tampering, 11–12
Propylene glycol, 104
Pseudoephedrine, 69
Psoriasis, 42, 125–126, 133
Psyllium, 92
Pyrantel pamoate, 165
Pyrethrum extract, 135
Pyridoxine, 211
Pyrilamine, 100
Pyrithione zinc, 132, 133, 134

R

Ranitidine, 84
Rashes. *See also* Dermatitis; Eczema
  diaper, 42, 122–123
  prickly heat, 43, 124–125
Reachers, 191
Rectal cream and ointment, 15
Rectal suppositories, 15
Repetitive motion injuries, 43. *See also* Carpal tunnel syndrome
Resorcinol, 113
Reye's syndrome, 55, 60, 122
Riboflavin, 214
Rickets, 215
Ringworm, 36, 43
Runny nose, 39

S

Safety and effectiveness cate gories (FDA), 2
Sales (OTC products), 2, 205
Salicylates, 59–60, 62, 89, 109, 128
Salicylic acid, 112–113, 121, 126, 129, 134
Saliva, artificial, 142
Salt (emetic), 19
Salt substitutes, 218
Sanguinarine, 144

Scabies, 97, 109
Scar, 43
Scleritis, 43
Seborrhea, 26, 43–44, 126, 132–134. *See also* Dandruff
Selenium, 218–219
Selenium sulfide, 133, 134
Sexually transmitted diseases (STDs), 161–163
Shampoos, medicated, 132–134
Shingles, 44
Shower stools, 191
Simethicone, 81, 90
Sinusitis, 44
Sitz bath, 191
Skin. *See also* Acne; Fungal skin infection; Rashes
  dry, 44, 103–105
Skin patches, 14
Skin protectants, 126–127
  burns, 102–103
  cold sore, 148
  hemorrhoid, 107–108
Sleep aids, 175–176
Slings, 185
Smoking cessation aids, 176–177. *See also* Nicotine addiction
Snoring, 184–185
Soaps
  bath, 120
  medicated, 112
Soapsuds (emetic), 19
Sodium benzoate, 144
Sodium bicarbonate, 81, 145, 173
Sodium borate, 152, 154
Sodium lauryl sulfate, 144
Sodium perborate, 173
Sodium peroxyborate monohy drate, 145
Sorbic acid, 151
Sores. *See* Canker sore; Cold sore
Spermicides, 162–163
SPF ratings, 128
Splints, 185
Sprain, 45, 100
Sprays, skin, 96
Staphylococcic infection, 113

Starch (demulcent), 19
Steroids, 97, 122
Stimulants, 18, 19, 177
Sting, bee, 25, 45
Stool softeners, 93, 106
Storage (OTC products), 12–13
 vitamin supplements, 208
Store brands, 4
Streptococcic infection, 113
Sty, 154–155
Sulfur, 111, 112, 113
Sunburn, 18, 19, 45, 101–103
Sunscreens, 127–129
Suppositories, contraceptive,
 163
Swimmer's ear, 31, 178
Syrup of ipecac, 86

T

Tampering, product, 11–12
Tannic acid, 19, 174
Tartar, 46, 138
Tea, 19
Tears, artificial, 152
Teething, 46, 145–146
Temperature, body, 32, 64-65,
 203
Tendinitis, 37, 43, 46
Tendons, inflammation, 31
Tenosynovitis, 43, 46
Tetrahydrozoline, 153-154
Theophylline, 168
Thermometers, 202–203
Thiamin, 212–213
Thimerosal, 151
Throat, sore, 46, 77–79
Thyroid (and iodine), 117
Toenail, ingrown, 46, 174
Tolnaftate, 115, 116, 124
Tooth, discoloration, 47
Tooth, sensitivity, 47, 139
Tooth whiteners, 138–139, 140
Toothache, 19, 47, 145–146
Toothbrushes, 191–192
Toothpastes, 138–139

Trichomoniasis, 48
Tripelennamine, 100, 108
Triprolidine hydrochloride, 74
Trolamine salicylate, 59, 62
Turpentine oil, 61

U

Ulcer
 duodenal, 47
 gastric, 47–48
 peptic, 48
Undecylenate acid, 116, 124
Urethritis, 48
Urinals, 192
Urinary pain relievers, 178–179
Urinary tract infection, 48, 178,
 203. See also Cystitis
Urine test, 203–204
Urushiol, 110

V

Vaginal antifungals, 179
Vaginal antipruritics, 180
Vaginal atrophy, 25
Vaginal lubricants, 181
Vaginal medicines, 15
Vaginal pouches, 162
Vaginitis, 48, 180
Vaginosis, bacterial, 48
Vaporizers, 189–190
Vasoconstrictors, 106–107, 108
Vegetable oils, 105
Vertigo, 49
Vinegar, 19
Vitamin A, 210–211
Vitamin B1, 212–213
Vitamin B2, 214
Vitamin B3, 212
Vitamin B6, 211
Vitamin B12, 211
Vitamin C, 210, 214
Vitamin D, 214–215
Vitamin E, 206, 215

Vitamin K, 215
Vitamins, 205–215
 absorption, 207
 cost, 207
 expiration dates, 207–208
 fat-soluble, 205, 208
 labels, 207
 natural versus synthetic, 206
 Recommended Dietary
  Allowances (RDAs), 209
 special formulations, 205–
  207
 toxicity, 208, 211, 212, 213,
  214, 215
 water-soluble, 205, 207, 208
Vomiting. See Nausea
Vulvitis, 49

W

Walkers, 192
Wart removers, 129–130
Warts, 49
Water retention, 49, 171–172
Whitening polishes (teeth), 140
Witch hazel, 103, 118, 119
Wound infection, 49
Wrinkles, 50, 105
Wrist braces, 185

X

Xylometazoline, 71

Y

Yeast infection, 19, 48, 50, 179

Z

Zinc, 210, 219
Zinc oxide, 118–119, 123, 127
Zinc undecylenate, 116